"This magisterial and constructive critique of C. S. Lewis reveals him as a sensitive commentator on some centrally important areas of human interaction. Lewis came to embody and think through multiple perspectives on human beings of all ages in their extraordinary complexity. The very social sciences of which he was so suspicious may both confirm his intuitions whilst correcting his mistakes. This valuable book breaks out of some of the Lewis-reading straightjackets and encourages us to see why he is still well worth our careful attention."

—**Ann Loades**, St. Chad's College and University of Durham

"In a fascinating chapter about her own relationship to C. S. Lewis, Mary Stewart Van Leeuwen lays all her cards on the table. Then she traces Lewis's changing views of gender step by step through his prodigious output of books and letters until the end of his life, considering not only his work, but the man himself, and the way he has been viewed by others. Van Leeuwen's spirit is generous; her prose, wonderfully clear; her arguments, powerful; and her insight, remarkable. Whether you're a scholar, a Lewis fan, or a general reader, you will find yourself turning pages with pleasure."

—**Jeanne Murray Walker**, University of Delaware

"Van Leeuwen's work is a valuable addition to the various books on C. S. Lewis. Respecting but not romanticizing him, Van Leeuwen explores Lewis's strengths, influences, and weaknesses, particularly as his writing deals with the relationships between women and men. This adds another excellent volume to Van Leeuwen's own work, taking Scripture seriously in conjunction with her own academic discipline, pressing us to affirm the love of God, and rejecting distorted views of gender."

—**Debra K. Block Clark**, InterVarsity Christian Fellowship

A Sword
between the Sexes?

C. S. Lewis and the Gender Debates

Mary Stewart Van Leeuwen

Brazos Press

a division of Baker Publishing Group
Grand Rapids, Michigan

Published by Brazos Press
a division of Baker Publishing Group
P.O. Box 6287, Grand Rapids, MI 49516-6287
www.brazospress.com

Printed in the United States of America

Library of Congress Cataloging-in-Publication Data
Van Leeuwen, Mary Stewart, 1943–
    A sword between the sexes? : C. S. Lewis and the gender debates / Mary Stewart Van
Leeuwen.
        p.   cm.
    Includes bibliographical references and index.
    ISBN 978-1-58743-208-8 (pbk.)
    1. Lewis, C. S. (Clive Staples), 1898–1963. 2. Sex role—Religious aspects—Christianity. I.
Title.
BX4827.L44V36 2010
305.3092—dc22   2009032091

10   11   12   13   14   15   16   7   6   5   4   3   2   1

For Ken and Susan Stewart:
family by formation, family by faith

Contents

Introduction

C. S. Lewis has been alternately lionized and demonized for a view of men and women that was both essentialist and hierarchical. "Gender is a reality, and a more fundamental reality than sex," he wrote in 1943, in defense of gender essentialism. "Masculine and feminine meet us on a plane of reality where male and female would be simply meaningless. Masculine is not attenuated male, nor feminine attenuated female. On the contrary, the male and female of organic creatures are rather faint and blurred reflections of masculine and feminine."[1] Two years later he wrote, in defense of gender hierarchy: "I do not believe God created an egalitarian world. I believe the authority of parent over child, husband over wife, learned over simple, to have been as much a part of the original plan as the authority of man over beast. I believe that if we had not fallen, patriarchal monarchy would be the sole lawful form of government."[2]

But by 1960 Lewis had begun to equivocate, and to acknowledge that gendered behavior is in many ways a social construction. "In most societies at most periods," he wrote in *The Four Loves*, "Friendships will be between men and men and women and women . . . Where men are educated and women are not . . . or where they do totally different work, they will usually have nothing to be friends about. But we can easily see that it is this lack, rather than anything in their natures, which excludes Friendship: for where they can be companions they can also become Friends . . . The necessary common ground exists between the sexes is some groups but not in others. It is notably lacking

1. C. S. Lewis, *Perelandra* (London: the Bodley Head, 1943; repr., New York: MacMillan, 1965), 200.
2. C. S. Lewis, "Membership," reprinted in *The Weight of Glory and Other Essays* (Grand Rapids: Eerdmans, 1965), 30–42 (quotation from p. 36).

in many residential suburbs."[3] And in one of his last but least-read books, *A Grief Observed*, he concluded that "there is, hidden or flaunted, a sword between the sexes till an entire marriage reconciles them." As he reflected on his own short, late-life marriage to a woman who had recently died of cancer, he described the relationship in ways that show a pointed rejection of *both* gender essentialism and gender hierarchy. "A good wife contains so many persons in herself," he wrote. "What was [Joy] not to me? She was my daughter and my mother, my pupil and my teacher, my subject and my sovereign, and always, holding all these in solution, my trusty comrade, friend, shipmate, fellow soldier. My mistress, but at the same time all that any man friend (and I have had good ones) has ever been to me. Solomon calls his bride Sister. Could a woman be a complete wife unless, for a moment, in one particular mood, a man felt almost inclined to call her Brother?"[4]

The purpose of this book is to trace the route by which Lewis moved slowly from the former to the latter position—from an often-polemical defense of gender essentialism and gender hierarchy to a much more gender-egalitarian view. In the process, I have neither lionized nor demonized him, so those who are hoping for one or the other stance (and there are legions of both hero-worshipers and scoffers among readers of Lewis's work) will certainly be disappointed. On the other hand, I hope that readers will not be disappointed if they are interested in learning more about Lewis's ambiguous relationship with his historical era, and his work's continuing relevance—both negative *and* positive—for the psychology of gender. Lewis the Belfast-born Edwardian, Lewis the prodigal who re-embraced Christianity as a young adult, Lewis the Oxbridge rationalist-cum-romantic writer of stories, essays, and literary criticism—all these aspects of his person help us to understand better Lewis's theory and practice (often inconsistent with each other) with regard to gender. Delving into them has taken me on a very stimulating journey.

As always happens in the course of writing a book, I have incurred many debts along the way. To begin with, I join (I'm sure) many other C. S. Lewis scholars in expressing gratitude to Walter Hooper, Lewis's literary executor, for the massive work he has done to bring virtually all of Lewis's correspondence into published form in three thick volumes. Lewis was one of the last of the great (and graceful) English letter-writers, and his lifelong stream of correspondence helps to show how he developed, defended, qualified, and revised his views on gender in ways that may surprise those who have read only his formally published works. I am particularly grateful to the staff of the Marion Wade Center at Wheaton College for access to copies of Lewis's letters that had not yet been published as I began writing, and to Michael

3. C. S. Lewis, *The Four Loves* (London: Geoffrey Bles, 1960; repr., London: Collins, 1963), 68–69.
4. C. S. Lewis, *A Grief Observed* (London: Faber and Faber, 1964), 39–40.

Maudlin of HarperSanFrancisco for a prepublication peek at the third volume of the letters at a later stage. In London I profited from staff help at the Victoria and Albert Museum and the Marylebone Library. Much of my travel research, and most of my writing, was made possible by sabbatical and faculty development funding from my home institution, Eastern University in St. Davids, Pennsylvania. I am also grateful to Grace Tazelaar for hosting me during a week of research at the Wade Center in Wheaton, Illinois. And Terry Morrison, of the Graduate Christian Fellowship, is to be thanked (or chided) for launching the entire project with his invitation to me to give the 2004 C. S. Lewis lecture at the University of Tennessee.

I had the opportunity to present various chapters to a range of other audiences as well, and received much valuable feedback as a result. I would like to thank Valparaiso University (Indiana), the Institute for Christian Studies (Toronto), Westmont College (California), the Illinois Cornerstone Festival, Christians for Biblical Equality, and the British Association of Christians in Psychology (BACIP) for invitations to share parts of this work. Special thanks go to two BACIP officers—Martin Baker of the University of East London, and Sara Savage of Cambridge University—for stimulating conversations in the context of that organization's 2008 conference, and to several of my own students at Eastern University who were eager to read and evaluate parts of the manuscript.

Many colleagues made helpful comments on the manuscript as it took shape. At Eastern University, my erstwhile dean and English literature colleague Betsy Morgan did a detailed evaluation of every chapter draft, and Raymond Van Leeuwen, Phillip Cary, and Julie Elliott were frequent conversation partners. Colleagues at other places in disciplines as varied as communications (Laura Simmons), mathematics (John Roe), theology (Kevin Giles and Joel Kok), church history (Ruth Tucker), counseling psychology (Judith Kolman and Diane Marshall) and sociology (David Lyon) weighed in on specific chapters in a consistently helpful way, as did Lee Bryant, John Hodges, Andrew Lazo, Ian MacDonald, and Jon Trott.

Any errors that remain are, of course, my own. Readers will learn from the first chapter that my own history of interaction with C. S. Lewis is an ambivalent one. Coming of age in the 1960s, I drew from Lewis equal parts of inspiration (as a much-needed role model for the Christian intellectual life) and exasperation (for his *ex cathedra* pronouncements about gender roles and relations). Yet I resolved not to be seduced back into either uncritical admiration or reflex resentment as I worked on this volume. That turned out to be easier than I thought, because digging deeply into all of Lewis's writings, and into the substantial secondary literature that has accumulated on him, reveals a much more complex picture than either his hero-worshipers or scoffers have tried to paint of him. Like all of us, Lewis was a work in progress, and his letters especially bear witness to this. As early as 1955 he confided to Dorothy L.

Sayers that he didn't like "either the ultra masculine or the ultra feminine . . . I prefer *people*."[5] How he journeyed to his "preference for people" from his earlier endorsement of gender essentialism and gender hierarchy turns out to be a complex and fascinating tale, with ongoing significance for the psychology of gender.

Ardmore, Pennsylvania
Pentecost 2009

5. C. S. Lewis to Dorothy L. Sayers, August 5, 1955, in Walter L. Hooper, ed., *The Collected Letters of C. S Lewis*, vol. 3 *1950–1963* (San Francisco: HarperSanFrancisco, 2007), 639 (emphasis original).

1

Surprised by Jack

An Ambivalent Journey

Academics usually choose what to write about according to fairly rational criteria. They write for love of a topic, sometimes for money, to strengthen their chances for promotion or tenure, or because colleagues have asked them to join a project for which they seem qualified. But occasionally a topic comes along and seems to choose *them*, insisting, as it were, that it be pursued, though if it had been suggested ten or twenty years earlier it would have been dismissed with a laugh or a shrug as being too far from their interests or expertise to take on. That is what happened to me with this book.

It began—at least officially—with an invitation to give the annual C. S. Lewis lecture at the University of Tennessee in March of 2004. My first impulse was to decline with polite regrets. My formal training is in academic psychology, and most treatments of Lewis have been by scholars from his own field of literary criticism, or by others analyzing his Christian apologetics, ethics, or use of Scripture. Moreover, though I had taught for almost a quarter century in Christian liberal arts settings, where many students have absorbed Lewis's *Chronicles of Narnia* as children and sampled his other writings as young adults, my own background was quite different. However, it shared some odd similarities with Lewis's, even though I was born more than a generation later and an ocean away from his Belfast birthplace. And as a scholar I had occasionally crossed paths with Lewis via his pronouncements about science, social science, and relations between the sexes.

In the end I cautiously agreed to give a lecture embracing aspects of the above three topics.[1] But having discharged that obligation, I found myself wanting to dig further into the rich trove of primary and secondary sources I had sampled in its preparation. I was first of all intrigued by aspects of Lewis's thought that had received less attention than his work as a literary critic, Christian apologist, and writer of latter-day fairy tales. But to my surprise I also found myself existentially engaged in a way that recalled my first exposure to him as an undergraduate in the early 1960s. This was partly because in preparing the lecture I consulted some of the very copies of his books (*Mere Christianity*, *Surprised by Joy*, *The Four Loves*) that I had read back then: fragile, yellow-paged paperbacks whose covers announced that they had cost three English shillings, or fifty cents Canadian. It is a bit like getting into a time machine to reread annotations made in books some forty years ago—but in my case all the more so, as it would be almost another decade before I finally responded to the claims of God on my life while doing doctoral research in Africa. Because my interest in Lewis is such a complex mix of the intellectual and the existential, the affirmative and the questioning, it may help readers to know something of its history before I begin my more formal analysis.

Parallel Lives

I grew up in the 1950s in a mainline Canadian church whose chief virtue for my development was that its pastors and teachers never used the Bible to limit me as a female. But lest you be tempted to give them too much credit, this was probably because they didn't seem to treat the Bible as authoritative for much of anything. Although evangelical renewal movements have sprung up in most North American mainline denominations in the past few decades, they certainly weren't common in the 1950s. The emerging norm back then was pretty much a blend of two tendencies that Lewis bluntly deplored: "Christianity-and-water, the view which simply says there is a good God in Heaven and everything is all right—leaving out all the difficult and terrible doctrines about sin and hell and the devil, and the redemption,"[2] and a kind of Christ-of-culture syncretism. "You know," Lewis's senior devil Screwtape reminded his junior apprentice Wormwood, "Christianity and the Crisis, Christianity and the New Psychology, Christianity and the New Order . . . If they must

---

1. Parts of this were published in "A Sword between the Sexes: C. S. Lewis's Long Journey to Gender Equality," *Christian Scholars Review* 36, no. 4 (Summer 2007): 391–414, some of which is included in this volume.

2. C. S. Lewis, *Mere Christianity* (London: Collins, 1952), 42.

be Christians, let them at least be Christians with a difference. Substitute for the faith itself some Fashion with a Christian coloring. Work on their horror of the Same Old Thing."[3]

However, church was still a vehicle of respectability and upward mobility— perhaps especially for my parents, who were schoolteachers and first-generation urban transplants from modest rural backgrounds. Their own roots were in Canadian Methodist and Presbyterian churches, but in 1925 most of these had merged, along with Congregationalist churches, to become the United Church of Canada. My impression, as a child growing up, was that my parents struggled with some puzzlement to assimilate the watered-down theology emerging from this church union. But I think that their residual sense of rural inferiority, and an ambivalent urge to be more urbane, led them to go along with most of what was handed down by the "progressive" leaders of their new denomination. In such an atmosphere it was expected that teenagers would be confirmed in the church, but never made very clear how seriously—other than as a rite of social passage—they should take the professions of faith they were urged to make before the congregation. Predictably, this led to resistance and accusations of hypocrisy from some adolescents, including myself, as I vacillated between thinking that church membership would demand too much of me and suspecting that it would demand too little. But in the end, like the adolescent C. S. Lewis (better known to his friends and family as "Jack"), "I allowed myself to be prepared for confirmation, and confirmed, and to make my first Communion . . . eating and drinking to my own condemnation."[4]

Strangely enough (or perhaps not, given the universality of parent-child tensions) I was confirmed in the church for much the same reason that Lewis was, though neither of us would say this relieved us of responsibility for our actions. His mother having died when he was nine, the adolescent Jack Lewis had a turbulent relationship with his father, who in today's psychological parlance would be said to have serious boundary problems. "His nerves had never been of the steadiest and his emotions had always been uncontrolled. Under the pressure of anxiety his temper became incalculable; he spoke wildly and acted unjustly." This is how Lewis remembered his father's behavior in the months surrounding his mother's death, with the result that "the unfortunate man, had he but known it, was really losing his sons as well as his wife."[5]

Albert Lewis, the son of Welsh shipbuilders transplanted to Belfast, was a police court solicitor whose legal training came via an apprenticeship after his formal secondary education was finished. An intense lover of the law, but also of Anglican liturgy and English literature, he had both the desire and the means to educate his two sons in English public schools. But he could not always keep

---

3. C. S. Lewis, *The Screwtape Letters* (London: Geoffrey Bles, 1942), 135.

4. C. S. Lewis, *Surprised by Joy: The Shape of My Early Life* (London: Collins, 1955), 130.

5. Ibid., 21. Lewis's only sibling, Warren (nicknamed "Warnie") was three years older than Jack.

up with their fast-developing minds, particularly Jack's. In the wake of his
wife's death (he never remarried) and given his "sentimental, passionate and
rhetorical nature,"[6] he was intensely dependent on them emotionally, never
seeming to understand that good fences not only make good neighbors, but
good family relations as well. "There were so many unbridgeable misunderstandings," the midlife C. S. Lewis wrote of his father:

> Once I received a letter from my brother in my father's presence, which he
> immediately demanded to see. He objected to some expressions in it about a
> third person. In defence of them I pleaded that they had not been addressed
> to him. "What nonsense!" answered my father. "He knew you would show me
> the letter, and intended you to show me the letter." In reality, as I well knew,
> my brother had foolishly gambled on the chance that it would arrive when my
> father was out. But this my father could not conceive. He was not overriding by
> authority a claim to privacy which he disallowed; he could not imagine anyone
> making such a claim.[7]

So intrusive was his father that, from a very early age, Jack learned never
to come home "without first going through my own pockets and removing
anything that I wished to keep private."[8] To make matters worse, although
he had a reputation for considerable skill as a lawyer, Albert Lewis could be
maddeningly opaque in ordinary conversation, asking questions whose answers
he ignored or misunderstood, veering off into *non sequiturs*, and clinging to
emotional rhetoric in situations where reasoned exchange was more fitting.
In such a situation, his atheist-leaning son concluded, it would be impossible
to explain his reasons for not wanting to join the church. His father, Jack
predicted, would invoke "the beauty of the Authorized Version, the Christian
tradition and sentiment and character. And later, when this failed, there would
have been anger between us, thunder from him and a thin, peevish rattle from
me. Nor could the subject, once raised, ever have been dropped again."[9] In
the end, the young Lewis decided, it was easier simply to go along with the
confirmation process, metaphorically crossing his fingers behind his back as
he made profession of faith.

It was a Scots-Canadian mother, rather than an Ulster-Presbyterian descended father, who was the irrational and emotionally intrusive parent in
my case, though like Jack's father she performed well in her professional
setting, which was the elementary school classroom. Otherwise, what Lewis
writes about domestic tensions in his family of origin is very familiar. It

6. Entry on Lewis, Albert James, in Walter Hooper, ed., *The Collected Letters of C. S.
Lewis*, vol. 1, *1905–1931* (San Francisco: HarperSanFrancisco, 2004), 1006–8 (quotation from
pp. 1006–7).

7. Lewis, *Surprised by Joy*, 130.

8. Ibid., 98.

9. Ibid., 130–31.

was mainly to avoid similar confrontations with my mother that I resigned my agnostic adolescent self to going through the motions of confirmation. To be fair, I need to note that my mother was probably suffering even then from the beginnings of a brain tumor that would go undiagnosed (in an era before brain scan technology) for some fifteen years, and eventually lead to her death. To what extent this accounted for her erratic mood swings we simply don't know. One silver lining in this rather dark domestic cloud was the fact that I and my brother (who was a year and a half older) set aside an earlier rivalry and started supporting each other in both emotional and practical ways. The lifelong bond between C. S. Lewis and his brother Warren—forged in somewhat similar circumstances—is something I understand quite well.[10]

We did grow up with two parents, unlike the Lewis siblings. But my father, though by reputation a good teacher in the structured setting of the high school classroom, was mostly an absent presence at home. He had his own childhood demons to deal with, one of which was the fact that he was conceived out of wedlock, and was thus the occasion for his own parents' shotgun wedding. Taciturn to the point of being almost inaccessible, he was a workaholic whose default setting was to ignore emotional confrontations among other family members until he decided that a certain threshold of chaos or disrespect by his children had been reached. Then he would intervene like a roaring lion to impose order, though he very rarely resorted to physical punishment. Afterward he would retreat into his seemingly endless rounds of preparing painstakingly detailed geography lessons, grading papers, and, in the summer, maintaining (mostly by himself) the large Victorian yellow brick house where we lived.

The chief exception to this pattern occurred during weekend and holiday visits to my father's rural relatives, who lived about an hour's drive away, near the shores of Lake Huron. As descendants of Ulster-Presbyterian farmers who had immigrated to Upper Canada in the 1830s, my Stewart relatives specialized in deadpan humor. Some were great storytellers, regularly exchanging what Lewis called "wheezes"—that is, good-natured anecdotes about the foibles of their fellow human beings, accompanied by deft imitations of their subjects' vocal and bodily eccentricities.[11] In this familiar atmosphere both my parents would unbend somewhat, aided I suspect by the fact that they had acquired a certain amount of status as educated folk who had moved to the city. When, at the urging of a friend, I first read Lewis's *Surprised by Joy* as a university sophomore, I immediately resonated with the Ulster wit that peppered his writing. Much later when my brother and I, along with

10. See, for example, Lewis, *Surprised by Joy*, chaps. 1 and 8; Clyde S. Kilby and Marjorie Lamp Mead, eds., *Brothers and Friends: The Diaries of Major Warren Hamilton Lewis* (San Francisco: HarperSanFranciso, 1982).

11. Lewis, *Surprised by Joy*, 10.

our respective spouses, visited Belfast and County Down to do genealogical research on the Stewarts, we were surprised and amused by how familiar the patterns of social interaction were. We had long ago been exposed to them in Huron County, Ontario.

We had also been exposed to the legacy of Protestant-Catholic hostility that surrounded Lewis before and after the official creation of Northern Ireland in 1921. "I do not like church here at all," the nine-year-old Jack wrote to his father after arriving at his first English school, full of Ulster Protestant rectitude: "It is so frightfully high church that it might as well be Roman Catholic."[12] Later, as a young Oxford don and an even younger Christian, Lewis recognized the cost of such self-righteous dualism. "I had quite forgotten the most unpleasant feature of an Irish [church] service," he wrote to his brother in 1934 during a visit to County Down: "the large number of people present who have obviously no interest in the thing, who are merely 'good prodestants' [sic] . . . I am sure the English practice of not going unless you believe is a much better one."[13]

Among my own Ulster-Canadian ancestors, a number belonged to the Grand Orange Lodge, the Canadian incarnation of the Loyal Orange Lodge, formed after 1688 when Dutch Prince William of Orange came to the British Isles to dislodge Catholic King James II and restore "the liberties of Englishmen and the Protestant Religion."[14] One great-great uncle was instrumental in bringing the first Orange Lodge charter to the small Ontario town of Blyth. Its anti-Catholic sentiments—though somewhat diluted by the 1950s—were a pervasive feature of my childhood. Like the "good prodestants" of Lewis's Northern Ireland, some of my forebears seem to have had a better idea of what they were against than what they were for, religiously speaking. As a younger child, for instance, I sometimes asked my mother if we were Christians; she would reply, evasively, "Well, we're churchgoers." And one of the less benign "wheezes" circulating during my childhood was a piece of anti-Catholic doggerel, sung to the jig-tune *Cock of the North*:

> Dickle, dockle, holy water,
> Sprinkle the Catholics, every one!
> Dickle, dockle, holy water,
> Make way for the boys with the drum!

The "boys with the drum" were the Orangemen whose in-your-face parades are a feature of Northern Ireland to this day. As an Oxford undergraduate, Lewis expressed "a natural repulsion to the noisy, drum-beating, bullying

---

12. C. S. Lewis to Albert Lewis, October 3, 1908, Hooper, ed., *Collected Letters*, vol. 1, 7.

13. Walter Hooper, ed., *The Collected Letters of C. S. Lewis*, vol. 2, *1931–1949* (San Francisco: HarperSanFrancisco, 2004), 132–33.

14. http://www.grandorangelodge.ca/history.html (August 29, 2006).

Orange-men."[15] In 1920 he penned a cynical letter to his father about the Belfast rioting that preceded the separation of Northern Ireland from the Republic of Ireland. "I am glad to note that so far it has been confined to its traditional grounds at the other end of town," he wrote. "A wise man these days will do well to survey the situation chiefly from the study. When I come home . . . I shall buy [a badge] with green on one side and orange on the other, turning the appropriate color outwards according to circumstances."[16] Though not yet a confessing Christian, Lewis recognized that whatever Christianity meant, it couldn't be reduced to anti-Catholic—or, for that matter anti-Protestant—sloganeering. Indeed, when he later published *Mere Christianity*, he observed that hostility to its contents came "more from borderline people whether within the Church of England or without: men not exactly obedient to any communion . . . And this suggests that at the centre of each there is a something, or a Someone, who against all divergences of belief, all differences of temperament, all memories of mutual persecution, speaks with the same voice."[17]

Undergraduate Unease

Clearly I had a number of reasons from my Ulster-Scots Canadian childhood to identify with C. S. Lewis when I started reading some of his books in university. But as the years went by, at least two more were added. You might think, for example, that my family's connections to farming would have facilitated open and realistic conversations about sex. This in fact was somewhat true when it came to cats: my childhood household included a female cat that delivered herself of nineteen litters of kittens before reaching the feline equivalent of menopause. But prior to the social upheavals of the 1960s, human sexuality was a topic rarely discussed in polite society, except in single-sex health education classes where self-conscious teachers used ponderous scientific language to describe the processes that were roiling our adolescent bodies.

These were of course discussed in more graphic terms among friends when we felt we could risk it, or furtively read about in second-rate novels; but there was virtually nothing to turn to in between these two extremes. It was as if when Christian faith became more nominal in middle-class Canadian society, a kind of gnostic fear of the body gradually replaced the biblical notion that physical urges, though subject to distortion, are part of God's creation and eminently redeemable. Writer Margaret Atwood wryly captured the nature of the times in an essay on the classic twentieth century Canadian novel *Anne of*

15. C. S. Lewis to Arthur Greeves, July 24, 1917, Hooper, ed., *Collected Letters*, vol. 1, 330.

16. C. S. Lewis to Albert Lewis, July 25, 1920, Hooper, ed., *Collected Letters*, vol. 1, 500.

17. Lewis, *Mere Christianity*, 9.

Green Gables, which she, like me, had read several times as a youth and adult. Affirming it as a well-crafted tale that deserves its enduring place in children's literature, Atwood nevertheless noted that its author, Lucy Maud Montgomery, "carefully stay[ed] within the conventions available to her: nobody goes to the bathroom in this book."[18]

Of course the flip side of gnostic disdain for the body is unchecked hedonism, since it hardly matters what you do with your body if your aspirations are to a higher intellectual plane. The sexual revolution was rumbling to the surface of campus life in the early 1960s, and it was as I joined many others vacillating between prudery and license that I read Lewis's autobiography of his early life, *Surprised by Joy*. I was, to put it mildly, astonished by this bachelor Oxford don's frank yet compassionate treatment of sex, and by the way he defended the ideal of chastity while not treating sexual lapses as the worst of sins. For example, that he would even—in a totally nonprurient manner—discuss adolescent homosexuality was a source of amazement to me, living in an era when such attraction was for the most part what Oscar Wilde called "the love that dares not speak its name." When discussing the consensual homosexual acts that occurred among some of his boys' school classmates, Lewis relativized the seriousness of such practices even as he held fast to the norm of heterosexual monogamy:

> There is much hypocrisy on this theme. People commonly talk as if every other evil were more tolerable than [homosexual acts]. But why? . . . Cruelty is surely more evil than lust, and the World [of power-hungry self-promotion] at least as dangerous as the Flesh. The real reason for all the pother is, in my opinion, neither Christian nor ethical. We attack this vice not because it is the worst but because it is, by adult standards, the most disreputable . . . The World will lead you only to Hell; but sodomy may lead you to jail and create a scandal, and lose you your job . . . If those of us who have known a school [like Malvern] dared to speak the truth, we should have to say that pederasty, however great an evil in itself, was, in that time and place, the only foothold or cranny left for certain good things. It was the only counterpoise to the social struggle; the one oasis . . . in the burning desert of competitive ambition . . . [It] was the only chink left through which something spontaneous and uncalculating could creep in.[19]

18. Margaret Atwood, "Afterword: Anne of Green Gables," in *Writing with Intent: Essays, Reviews, Personal Prose, 1983–2005* (New York: Carroll and Graf, 2005), 115–20 (quotation from p. 117).

19. Lewis, *Surprised by Joy*, 89–90. The reference to "jail" refers to the fact that sodomy was still a crime under English law when Lewis was writing in the 1950s. Consensual, private homosexual acts were decriminalized in the UK only in 1967. It should be noted that some of Lewis's Malvern contemporaries, including his brother, maintained that he overestimated the extent of homosexual preoccupation and behavior among Malvern students of his era. Be that as it may, his balanced treatment of the issue was still quite unusual for his time. For more on this period in Lewis's life, see, for example, George Sayer, *Jack: C. S. Lewis and His Times* (San Francisco: Harper and Row, 1988), chap. 4.

As an all-wise university sophomore, I did not agree with many of Lewis's assertions on human psychology—nor do I now, for reasons that will become clear. Nor was I ready to throw my lot in with the God of Christianity whose ways he described in such a learned yet accessible fashion. But there were things Lewis wrote that simply cut a swath through the confusion of sexual messages emerging in the 1960s, things that rang true even if I was unwilling to act on them. The same wisdom he showed about adolescent homosexuality in *Surprised by Joy* was evident, for example, in his treatment of heterosexual romantic feeling as something neither to be trivialized nor used to trump all other demands. "The event of falling in love," he wrote, "is of such a nature that we are right to reject as intolerable the idea that it should be transitory. In one high bound it has overleaped the massive wall of our selfhood . . . Spontaneously and without effort we have fulfilled the law (towards one person) by loving our neighbor as ourselves." But in the same breath he insisted that Eros, unchecked by any other considerations, becomes an idol that cannot bear the weight of the promises with which it began:

> It seems to sanction all sorts of actions [that couples] would not otherwise have dared. I do not mean solely, or chiefly, acts that violate chastity. They are just as likely to be acts of injustice or uncharity against the outer world. The pair can say to one another in an almost sacrificial spirit, "It is for love's sake that I have neglected my parents—cheated my partner—failed my friend at his greatest need." These reasons in love's law have passed for good. The votaries may even come to feel a particular merit in such sacrifices; what costlier offering can be laid on love's altar than one's conscience? And all the time the grim joke is that this Eros whose voice seems to speak from the eternal realm is not necessarily even permanent. He is notoriously the most mortal of all our loves.[20]

The fickleness of romantic attraction is of course well known to young adults, who expend much emotional energy dealing with its fallout. Lewis was saying, in effect, that no human longings—what he elsewhere called "second things"—can deliver even their valid creational goods until they find their place in relation to "first things"—certain moral and spiritual realities that require our primary loyalty.[21] "Treat 'Love' as a god and you in fact make it a fiend," is how he put it in a 1942 letter to one of his friends.[22] And his use of words like *injustice* and *uncharity* struck me at a particularly deep level. It was to be several years before the second wave of feminism emerged and claimed my allegiance

20. C. S. Lewis, *The Four Loves* (London: Geoffrey Bles, 1960; London: Collins, 1963), 104–5. Citations are from the Collins edition.

21. C. S. Lewis, "First and Second Things," originally published as "Notes On the Way," in *Time and Tide*, June 27, 1942, 519–20. Reprinted in Walter Hooper, ed., *God in the Dock: Essays On Theology and Ethics* (Grand Rapids: Eerdmans, 1970), 278–81.

22. C. S. Lewis to Daphne Harwood, March 6, 1942, Hooper, ed., *Collected Letters*, vol. 2, 510.

in its challenge to the injustices borne by my own sex. But Lewis's examples of uncharity in the name of Eros were particularly attention-grabbing in the elite Canadian university setting in which I first read them, and they pointed to yet another reason for me to listen to him. Why was this so?

I had wanted to study psychology ever since my middle-school days, when I had started reading the textbooks my older sister brought home from university. But by the time I entered university in the early 1960s, academic psychology was suffering from what might be called a bad case of physics envy. In its eagerness to be accepted as a legitimate "science" it had embraced what philosophers call the Unity of Science thesis—namely, that there is only one method that all genuine sciences employ, and this method consists of giving deterministic, causal explanations that are empirically testable.[23] By this standard, if psychology aspired to be a "real" science it would have to become as much like physics as possible. Now, as a methodological corrective to certain past, ill-supported pronouncements about human behavior and mental life (including many from psychoanalysis) this was not an entirely bad move. Indeed, I will argue later that it was partly Lewis's reluctance to affirm the relative but real value of empirically-based social science that led him, for much of his life, to embrace some very questionable views about women, men, and their relationships. But methodological correctives seldom stay within their original limits. They more often become full-blown—and usually unacknowledged—metaphysical worldviews, especially in times of great social change when older belief systems are being unreflectively marginalized in the name of progress.

This is in fact what was happening during my undergraduate days. We were being taught as apprentice logical positivists to regard "facts" and "values" as quite distinct. Facts—based on input to the senses or instrumental extensions of them—were in principle totally objective, whereas values, including those arising from religious or aesthetic sources, were completely subjective. Facts were said to be intersubjectively verifiable (they could be agreed upon by impartial observers), whereas values were completely idiosyncratic. Facts could be verified or falsified by observation, whereas values were arbitrary and thus not empirically testable: they were literally *non*sense. And finally, beliefs about facts could be judged logical or illogical, but values, being merely faith- or feeling-based, were simply nonrational.

On this account of reality, as philosopher Stephen Evans has described it, "the world consists of brute facts, and values are only introduced when a subject turns up who has a personal preference."[24] Hand in hand with this

23. For accessible introductions to this debate, see, for example, Alexander Rosenberg, *Philosophy of Social Science* (Boulder, CO: Westview, 1995); C. Stephen Evans, *Preserving the Person: A Look at the Human Sciences* (Downers Grove, IL: InterVarsity, 1977).

24. C. Stephen Evans, *Wisdom and Humanness in Psychology: Prospects for a Christian Approach* (Grand Rapids: Baker Books, 1989), 107.

epistemology went an increasingly physicalist (what Lewis would call "naturalist" or "realist") anthropology: the view that the human mind was reducible to the brain, which in turn was reducible to the sum of its physical-chemical parts and processes, as these had evolved over time following the blind forces of natural selection. You can perhaps guess where all this was leading: if moral principles, along with everything else, are merely the result of random processes and purely impersonal forces—mechanical, biological, psychological, or social—then humans are no more morally accountable for their behaviors than a car is morally accountable for having a flat tire. Individuals have no reason to observe any moral strictures, if they can get away with doing otherwise and prefer to do so.

This is not to say that complete moral anarchy had descended on the North American university scene by the early 1960s. In practice people are often better than their theories, especially when from a degree of inertia they are living off the moral capital of their past. And there was still a sense that universities should somehow act *in loco parentis*, so students were not completely abandoned to the sexual meat market, or to the binge-drinking and self-promoting ethos that pervades some campuses at the start of the twenty-first century. [25] But things were certainly heading in that direction. I can recall, for example, a roommate who lent her car to a male friend to run a sudden (but, as it turned out, fictitious) errand. He—and the car—did not reappear for several days. When he did, rather than apologizing for his deceit (and for the empty gas tank) he sat her down and explained that this was really what human beings were like: totally calculating and self-serving, so she might as well just get used to it. It was almost as if he expected her to thank *him* for the lesson in interpersonal *realpolitik* he had bestowed on her. Like Dostoevsky's Ivan Karamazov, he seems to have concluded that if there is no God, everything is permitted.

I will defer till later a discussion of developments in philosophy of science showing that the line between facts and values is fuzzier than early twentieth-century logical positivists believed. My point here is that as an undergraduate, I read Lewis's account in *Surprised by Joy* of his own seduction by logical positivism a generation earlier as an Oxford student. Lewis described how he and many of his unbelieving classmates had taken on an antiromantic "New Look" and become physicalists, and how his friend Owen Barfield finally forced him to recognize the inconsistencies of such a stance:

> We accepted as rock-bottom reality the universe as revealed by the senses. But at the same time we continued to make for certain phenomena of consciousness all the claims that really went with a theistic or idealistic view. We maintained

25. See, for example, William H. Willimon and Thomas H. Naylor, *The Abandoned Generation: Rethinking Higher Education* (Grand Rapids: Eerdmans, 1995), but also the novel by Tom Wolfe, *I Am Charlotte Simmons* (New York: Farrar, Straus and Giroux, 2004).

that abstract thought (if obedient to logical rules) gave indisputable truth, that our moral judgment was "valid" and our aesthetic experience not merely pleasing but "valuable" . . . Barfield convinced me that [this] was inconsistent. If thought were a purely subjective event, these claims for it would have to be abandoned. If one kept (as rock-bottom reality) the universe of the senses, aided by instruments and coordinated so as to form "science," then one would have to go much further—as many have gone since—and adopt a Behavioristic theory of logic, ethics, and aesthetics . . . I was therefore compelled to give up realism. I had been trying to defend it ever since I began reading philosophy . . . [Now I had to] admit that mind was no late-coming epiphenomenon, that the whole universe was, in the last resort mental; that our logic was participation in a cosmic *Logos*.[26]

This still sounds more like Platonic idealism than Christian theism, as Lewis might be the first to acknowledge: his fuller embrace of the latter would not occur until about a decade later. Furthermore, he did not know that his undergraduate confidence in the power of logic to produce indisputable truth was soon to be challenged. In later writings Lewis would often cite arithmetical calculation as an example of the inexorable power of logic, bowing to the work of the famous Cambridge mathematicians Bertrand Russell and Alfred North Whitehead.[27] But in 1931 Czech mathematician Kurt Gödel showed that even within rigidly logical mathematical systems there are propositions or questions that cannot be proved or disproved on the basis of the axioms within that system. So, Gödel concluded, it is undecidable whether the basic axioms of arithmetic won't give rise to contradictions. If human reason participates in a cosmic *Logos*, it apparently does so with less certainty than rationalists of earlier eras believed. We see through a glass, but darkly: whatever our epistemological tools, we know only in part.[28]

Nonetheless, in *Surprised by Joy* Lewis did expose a central inconsistency of logical positivism and its physicalist cousin, and his argument was to stay with me on some subliminal level for years to come, helping eventually to prod me into the embrace of Lewis's God. If, as doctrinaire positivists claimed, "The only meaningful statements are those that are empirically or analytically [i.e., logically by definition] true," then this central claim of positivism

26. Lewis, *Surprised by Joy*, 166–67. As an Oxford undergraduate in the early 1920s Owen Barfield was in the process of becoming an anthroposophist, following the romantic-idealist teachings of Rudolf Steiner, though he was eventually received into the Anglican church in 1949. An account of his continuing debate with Lewis on anthroposophical ideas can be found in Lionel Adey, *C. S. Lewis's "Great War" With Owen Barfield* (Victoria, BC: University of Victoria Press, 1978).

27. Russell's and Whitehead's *Principia Mathematica* (1910–1913) was a much-lauded attempt to establish axioms that would provide a rigorous basis for all types of mathematics.

28. 1 Cor. 13:12. For accessible discussions of Gödel's theorem see, for example, Stuart Shanker, *Gödel's Theorem in Focus* (London: Routledge, 1989); Torkel Franzen, *Gödel's Theorem* (Wellesley, MA: A.K. Peters, 2005).

(which is neither empirical nor analytic) is self-refuting: its adherents cut off the very epistemological limb on which they sit. Furthermore, if all thought is merely the mechanical result of the thinker's biological state and learning history, then the very enterprise of science—which assumes that its conclusions are *not* arbitrary, but supported by valid rules of inference—is meaningless. How, for example, could B. F. Skinner, to whose work I was even then being introduced, claim anything about the actual truth of behaviorist claims if all thoughts—including his own about behaviorism in particular and science in general—are merely the inevitable result of genetics and learning history, both of which could (quite randomly) have been otherwise?

Finally, as the undergraduate Lewis also had to concede, a consistent logical positivism renders all moral prescriptions (such as "Work for the betterment of humankind") subjective and meaningless, since such statements are neither empirically nor analytically grounded. During his adult life most of Lewis's Oxbridge logical positivist colleagues were not, in practice, moral nihilists. Indeed some, like Bertrand Russell when he joined the anti–nuclear bomb campaign, were concerned social and political activists, ready even to go to jail for their moral convictions. For Lewis, this did not rescue them from intellectual inconsistency: it simply meant that as people they were, by God's grace, better than their theories. This was a theme he would take up in more detail in later writings, including *The Abolition of Man* and *Miracles*.[29]

Challenging the Schizophrenic Student Mind

A major effect of my limited exposure to Lewis as an undergraduate was to make me admit (however grudgingly) that it was possible to embrace a robust Christian orthodoxy without putting my mind into cold storage. That was no mean feat, given the intellectually schizophrenic mind-set common in almost all Protestant churches as I was growing up. Most churchgoers of that era had assimilated one of two responses to the claim that facts are quite distinct from values.[30] At one extreme, fundamentalists (some of whom studied at a small Bible college in the very neighborhood of my childhood home) were understandably suspicious of the logical positivists' effort to sideline religious authority as a source of truth. But rather than argue that truth comes in forms other that what can be supported by scientific rationality, many of them chose

29. C. S. Lewis, *The Abolition of Man* (Oxford: Oxford University Press, 1943); *Miracles* (London: Geoffrey Bles, 1947; rev. ed., London: Collins, 1960). See also Victor Reppert, *C. S. Lewis's Dangerous Idea: In Defense of the Argument from Reason* (Downers Grove, IL: InterVarsity, 2003).

30. See also Mary Stewart Van Leeuwen, "Scuttling the Schizophrenic Student Mind: On Teaching the Unity of Faith and Learning in Psychology," in Arlin C. Migliazzo, ed., *Teaching As an Act of Faith: Theory and Practice in Church-Related Higher Education* (New York: Fordham University Press, 2002), 21–40.

to rationalize and scientize the Bible, reducing it to little more than a list of historically and scientifically literal propositions.

Thus (ironically) while claiming to fight "godless science," fundamentalists let this same scientific mind-set dictate a limited definition of truth that they then proceeded to impose on Scripture.[31] Many young people raised in this tradition did not find their way into universities or liberal arts colleges at all. Instead, they gathered in separatist Bible college enclaves, where Scripture was effectively treated as the only needed textbook for understanding history, psychology, geology, and so on. And for those who did enroll in Christian liberal arts colleges, this "biblical positivist" mind-set continued to be influential. For example, the late Clyde Kilby, a Wheaton College English professor and pioneering Lewis scholar, recalled in the 1960s being asked by a pious college board member why he taught courses on novels, since "novels are all lies."[32] As a child, I did find something very winsome in the piety and zeal of my fundamentalist neighbors. By attending their Bible Clubs over a couple of years, and one of their summer camps for a couple of weeks, I got a better introduction to the Bible than I would ever get in school or church. But the pervasive indifference—often hostility—of the subculture toward other kinds of learning was increasingly off-putting as I got older.[33]

In my own mainline church setting, young people were exposed to an opposite but equally dualistic strategy: they were taught largely to accept the modern distinction between facts and values. On this account, the college classroom was the place to learn the reputedly neutral facts and techniques of physics, biology, psychology, and so on. Outside the classroom, if they wished (and not many did), they could develop the "spiritual" side of their faith and learn how this could inspire personal character development and public service. From this perspective, a "Christian" psychologist was simply a "good" psychologist—a well-trained professional who did not mistreat or overcharge clients, or fabricate data when doing research, and who also might tithe professional and personal resources for the sake of the church and social progress more generally. Call this, if you will, the "add God and stir" approach to relating faith and learning, since it accepts without question the reigning theories and methods of any given discipline. Lewis would no doubt see it as an example of Christianity-and-water. So did I, though at the time I lacked the conceptual vocabulary to put my discomfort into words.

31. For a discussion of the historical roots of this mind-set, see, for example, George Marsden, *Fundamentalism and American Culture* (New York: Oxford University Press, 1980).

32. I have been unable to track down the origin of this quotation, which I believe was in a 1970s article in (the now defunct) *Eternity* magazine.

33. Lewis's own approach to Scripture is analyzed in Michael J. Christensen, *C. S. Lewis on Scripture: His Thoughts on the Nature of Biblical Revelation, Inspiration, the Role of Revelation and the Question of Inerrancy* (Waco: Word, 1979). See also C. S. Lewis, *Reflections on the Psalms* (London: Collins, 1961), especially chap. 11.

What Lewis kept alive in my subconscious, even as I went on to pursue a thoroughly secular graduate school education, was the possibility of a "third way," one which was articulated in more detail by scholars of the Calvinist tradition in which I eventually found an intellectual and ecclesial home. Christians in this tradition have been among the strongest critics of logical positivism, even though they have always affirmed science as a valid way of exploring God's creation. Well before the advent of postmodernism, scholars working in the Reformational tradition of Dutch politician and theologian Abraham Kuyper resisted the creeping dichotomy between facts and values. They insisted that all living and learning is filtered through a prior set of faith-based convictions, if not to Christian theism then to naturalism, Marxism, pantheism, or some other worldview in the marketplace of ideas. Against modernism and with the postmodern critique, these Kuyperian Calvinists asserted that there is no such thing as "immaculate perception" or a "view from nowhere" in *any* sort of academic work. All scholarship proceeds from the faith-based foundation of the scholar's worldview, whether recognized or not.[34]

None of these scholars have denied the presence of propositional truths in Scripture. But they have viewed these truths through a wider, redemptive-historical lens. Seen through this lens, the Bible is not primarily a "flat book" of doctrines and rules but a cumulative, God-directed narrative whose successive acts (creation, fall, redemption, and future hope) comprise a continuing, cosmic drama in which all persons are players. Moreover, within each of those players the impulse to worship is a primary aspect of created personhood. Hence all human thought patterns will be guided by a worldview that reflects allegiance to the one true God or else (inevitably) to some substitute idol.

So it was naive of positivist thinkers to assert that religious convictions were purely subjective and emotional, and could be relegated to private life, neatly isolated from public and supposedly neutral rationality. On the contrary, all of life is religiously motivated, and all human beings are characters in search of an author. If they do not yield to the true Author of the cosmic drama, they will certainly succumb, in varying degrees, to worship of one or more aspects of creation—such as science, politics, art, or sex—things that are God's good gifts in their rightful place but that when substituted for God get turned into idols. "It is simple to make an idol," wrote the Reformed theologian Lewis Smedes. "Just slice one piece of created reality off from the whole and expect

34. The following are recommended for a further introduction to this tradition: Abraham Kuyper, *Lectures on Calvinism: The Stone Foundations Lectures of 1898* (Grand Rapids: Eerdmans, 1970); Albert Wolters, *Creation Regained: Biblical Basics for a Reformational World View* (Grand Rapids: Eerdmans, 1985); Luis Lugo, ed., *Religion, Pluralism and Public Life: Abraham Kuyper's Legacy for the Twenty-First Century* (Grand Rapids: Eerdmans, 2000); David K. Naugle, *Worldview: The History of a Concept* (Grand Rapids: Eerdmans, 2002); and David T. Koyzis, *Political Visions and Illusions: A Survey and Christian Critique of Contemporary Ideologies* (Downers Grove, IL: InterVarsity, 2003).

miracles from it."[35] The parallel with C. S. Lewis's analysis of Eros, and his distinction between "first things" and "second things," is obvious.

Mixed Messages

So far, you can see that as a young person I had many reasons—both intellectual and personal—to regard Lewis as a positive model, an advocate for a robust Christianity whose scope included the life of the mind as well as piety and personal morality. It is important for readers to know this—to understand that my debt to him is very great and a major motivation for writing this book. But now I need to point out that Lewis was at the same time a major stumbling block to my acceptance of Christianity. This was due to the mixed messages he sent about the nature (both actual and ideal) of women, men, and their relationships in books that I read as an undergraduate, such as *Mere Christianity*, *The Four Loves*, and *Surprised by Joy*.[36] Moreover, much of what he said about these topics he claimed as part of "mere" Christianity ("the belief that has been common to nearly all Christians at all times")[37] and thus presumably not open to dispute by any who would call themselves orthodox believers, in contrast to Christianity-and-water adherents. In the following chapters I will do a more systematic analysis of Lewis's pronouncements on gender and male-female relations. For now I will share a few examples that brought me up short when I first read them, as a young woman who had been valedictorian of her high school class and went on to win the medal in psychology upon finishing university.

One piece that struck me very early on was Lewis's description of his friendship with Owen Barfield, whom I have already mentioned as one of Lewis's early intellectual and religious influences. He contrasted Barfield with Arthur Greeves, his "first friend" from Belfast, who was so much like Lewis in his tastes as to be something of an alter ego. Barfield, however, was the essence "of every man's Second Friend":

> The Second Friend is the man who disagrees with you about everything. He is not so much the *alter ego* as the anti-self. Of course he shares your interests;

35. Lewis Smedes, *Sex for Christians* (Grand Rapids: Eerdmans, 1976), 26.

36. It should be noted that these three works remain among Lewis's most-read books, in contrast to later and less-read works in which his view of gender and gender relations was changing to a more egalitarian and less-essentialist stance. These (to be discussed in a later chapter) include his last novel, *Till We Have Faces* (London: Geoffrey Bles, 1956), *A Grief Observed* (London: Faber and Faber, 1961), and *The Discarded Image* (Cambridge: Cambridge University Press, 1964). A recent biography of Lewis also presents evidence for this shift in Lewis's children's books, the *Chronicles of Narnia*, namely Alan Jacobs's *The Narnian: The Life and Imagination of C. S. Lewis* (San Francisco: HarperSanFrancisco: 2005).

37. Lewis, *Mere Christianity*, 6.

otherwise he would not become your friend at all. But he has approached them all at a different angle. He has read all the right books but has got the wrong thing out of every one. It is as if he spoke your language but mispronounced it. How can he be so nearly right and yet, invariably, just not right? He is as fascinating (and infuriating) as a woman.[38]

What, I wondered, did Barfield think of such a description? Was it a compliment or an insult in this context to be labeled "as fascinating and infuriating as a woman"? I was reminded of my own confusion when I was occasionally told by male professors, after turning in a particularly good paper, that I was to be congratulated because I had shown I could "think like a man." Were women and men really such different species that Owen Barfield and I, in transgressing the "known" boundaries of masculinity and femininity, were each to be considered a sport of nature?

Lewis goes on to say about this friendship: "Actually (though it never seems so at the time) you modify one another's thought; out of this perpetual dog-fight a community of mind and a deep affection emerge. But I think he changed me a good deal more than I him." This was prescient in ways that Lewis perhaps did not realize when *Surprised by Joy* was published in 1955, a year before his marriage to the American writer and poet Joy Davidman. As we will see later, in his notebook written after her death from cancer in 1960, *A Grief Observed*, Lewis effectively retracted many of his earlier views on the essence of masculinity and femininity. That volume was not even available in North America until after I had finished university.[39] In the meantime, I continued to be puzzled by Lewis's pronouncements about women and men.

For example, in *Mere Christianity*, a 1952 compendium of World War II–era essays and broadcast talks, Lewis included both an Aristotelian and a Freudian argument for male headship in marriage. He noted the need for a tiebreaker when domestic disagreements arise, then explained why that tiebreaker should always be the husband:

> The relations of the family to the outer world—what might be called its foreign policy—must depend, in the last resort, upon the man because he always ought to be, and usually is, much more just to outsiders. A woman is primarily fighting for her own children against the rest of the world . . . She is the special trustee of their interests. The function of the husband is to see that this natural preference is not given its head. He has the last word in order to protect other people from the intense family patriotism of the wife.[40]

38. Lewis, *Surprised by Joy*, 160–61.

39. *A Grief Observed* was first published under the pseudonym N. W. Clerk, which Lewis had also previously used for some of his published poetry. It was reprinted by Faber in 1964 under Lewis's real name.

40. Lewis, *Mere Christianity*, 100.

Both Aristotle and Freud held that women were driven more by emotion and less by reason than men. For Aristotle (and his Thomistic followers in medieval Christendom) all things exist in a hierarchical *scala naturae*, or "ladder of nature," beginning with inanimate matter and proceeding to plants, animals, humans, and ultimately the "unmoved mover" that gives all natural objects their purposes. But on the human part of the ladder women occupy a lower rung: in relation to men they are less rational (given to opinions more than true knowledge), unequal (fit for obedience rather than rule), and passive (even in pregnancy providing only the "matter" in which the man's reproductively complete seed or "form" grows).[41] For Freud also, "anatomy is destiny": he saw women even in adulthood as having less-developed superegos than men and hence less capacity for disinterested justice. For Freud, as for Aristotle, this was rooted in biology, but mediated by women's less-successful resolution of the Oedipal problem in early childhood.[42]

Lewis did not directly refer to the Aristotelian and psychoanalytic assumptions behind this argument for husbandly headship. He simply wrote that he spoke "quite frankly as a bachelor, because it is a reason you can see from the outside better than the inside"—thus implicitly universalizing his own limited observations.[43] However, in *The Four Loves* he was more explicit, blending Aristotelian and Pagan/Jungian terms in his analysis of sexuality. "In the act of love," he wrote, "we are not merely ourselves . . . In us all the masculinity and femininity of the world, all that is assailant and responsive, are momentarily focused. The man does play the Sky-Father and the woman the Earth-Mother; he does play Form and she Matter."[44] This so-called reality—Lewis called it the "Pagan sacrament" of the sex act—led (he believed) to somewhat sadomasochistic games in "most pairs of lovers," a practice he regarded as "harmless and wholesome" provided the participants did not forget their first loyalty to God:

> A woman who accepted as literally her own this extreme self-surrender would be an idolatress offering to a man what belongs only to God. And a man would have to be the coxcomb of all coxcombs, and indeed a blasphemer, if he arrogated to himself, as the mere person he is, the sort of sovereignty to which Venus for a moment exalts him. But what cannot be lawfully yielded or claimed can be lawfully enacted. Outside this ritual or drama he and she are two immortal

---

41. Aristotle's views on gender relations are variously described in his *Politics*, his *Ethics*, and his *Nicomachean Ethics*. Analyses of their impact on later Western thought can be found in Arthur O. Lovejoy, *The Great Chain of Being: A Study of the History of an Idea* (Cambridge, MA: Harvard University Press, 1936); Prudence Allen, *The Concept of Woman: The Aristotelian Revolution, 750 B.C–A.D. 1250* (Grand Rapids: Eerdmans, 1997).

42. James Strachey, ed., *The Standard Edition of the Complete Works of Sigmund Freud*, vol. 19 (London: Hogarth Press and Institute of Psychoanalysis, 1974), 241–60.

43. Lewis, *Mere Christianity*, 100.

44. Lewis, *Four Loves*, 95.

souls, two free-born adults, two citizens . . . But within this rite or drama they become a god and goddess between whom there is no equality—whose relations are asymmetrical.[45]

For Lewis, at this point in *The Four Loves*, this inequality meant that men and women could come together in affection and erotic love, but not—or at least not at the same time—in friendship. The rightness of separate spheres (public and domestic) for men and women, once they are husbands and wives, he seemed to take for granted. It is bad enough, he wrote, when a leisured, culturally aspiring wife tries to make a down-to-earth, businesslike husband share her artistic and literary tastes. It is even worse when a less-educated wife tries to horn in on the intellectual conversations her husband has with his male peers. "What might have been a real discussion is deliberately diluted and peters out in gossip, anecdotes and jokes."

Her presence has thus destroyed the very thing she was brought to share. She can never really enter the circle because the circle ceases to be itself when she enters it . . . She may be quite as clever as the men whose evening she has spoiled, or cleverer. But she is not really interested in the same things, nor mistress of the same methods . . . She does not realize that the husband she has succeeded in isolating from his own kind will not be very worth having; she has emasculated him . . . The sensible women who, if they wanted, would certainly be able to qualify themselves for the world of discussion and ideas, are precisely those who, if they are not qualified, never try to enter it or destroy it. They have other fish to fry. At a mixed party they gravitate to one end of the room and talk women's talk to each other . . . It is only the riff-raff of each sex that wants to be incessantly hanging on to the other.[46]

What is one to make of such statements in what continue to be among C. S. Lewis's best-selling works?[47] It would be too strong to call his pronouncements on women in these books "Texts of Terror"—the title of biblical scholar Phyllis Trible's volume that grapples with grim accounts of women's abuse in the Old Testament.[48] And literature scholar Lionel Adey was certainly less

45. Ibid., 95–96.
46. Ibid., 70–72. In other parts of *The Four Loves*, as we will see later, Lewis defends the possibility of male-female friendship and attributes its current rarity to social forces, rather than differing gender essences.
47. English-language editions of Lewis's books in 2006 sold at the rate of about two million copies per year. In Amazon.com and Amazon.uk sales, approximately half are of his seven-volume *Chronicles of Narnia* (written between 1950 and 1955). The next four rankings are *Mere Christianity* (1952), *The Screwtape Letters* (1942), *The Great Divorce* (1945), and *The Four Loves* (1960).
48. These include the rejection of Hagar by Abraham (Gen. 16:1–16 and 21:9–21), the rape of David's daughter Tamar by her brother Amnon (2 Sam. 13:1–22), the rape and death of a Levite's concubine (Judg. 19:1–30), and the sacrifice of Jephthah's daughter (Judg. 11:29–40). Phyllis

than prescient about recent world events when he wrote in 1998 that "only an Islamic conquest of the Western world can restore women to what [Lewis] saw as their role."[49] But whether the Lewis of these writings (and others) should be labeled a misogynist, or woman-hater, is something about which even his more sympathetic biographers disagree.

Roger Lancelyn Green and Walter Hooper, both of whom knew Lewis personally, agree that for much of his life, "it is probably true . . . that Lewis could properly be called a misogynist on at least the 'theoretical level,' though decidedly not so in his personal relations with individual women."[50] By contrast, Humphrey Carpenter wrote that "it would be wrong to say that [Lewis] despised women. He was no misogynist. But he did regard the female mind as inferior to the male . . . 'not really meant for logic or great art.'"[51] Wheaton College's Alan Jacobs believes that conclusions about Lewis's misogyny "largely [rest] on misunderstandings, but there is no question that Lewis shared the attitudes toward women common to men, and especially Christian men, of his time (and, we should add in fairness, of many other times)."[52] And A. N. Wilson, regarded by many as a less sympathetic biographer, described Lewis for most of his life as being prone to "spells of club-room misogyny," and when writing about women as "sometimes falling into appalling sentimentality, sometimes writing ridiculous masculine-minded nonsense about 'a woman's place.'"[53]

My own reaction as a young woman to the examples of Lewis's writing I have just discussed was to feel trapped in a version of what one of my colleagues (a scholar of rhetoric) later called "the 3:16 bait-and-switch." What she meant by this was that some evangelical preachers expend much effort first addressing their audiences in a disarmingly generic fashion, proclaiming the universal good news of John 3:16 (NIV): "For God so loved the world that he gave his one and only Son, that whoever believes in him shall not perish but have eternal life." Then, having successfully drawn women as well as men to Christian commitment by stressing how level the ground is before Christ's cross, they proceed to emphasize another 3:16, this time Genesis 3:16 (NIV): "To the woman [God] said, I will greatly increase your pains in childbearing; with pain you will give birth to children. Your desire will be for your husband, and he will rule over you."[54]

Trible, *Texts of Terror: Literary-Feminist Readings of Biblical Narratives* (Philadelphia: Fortress, 1984).

49. Lionel Adey, *C. S. Lewis: Writer, Dreamer and Mentor* (Grand Rapids: Eerdmans, 1998), 279.

50. Roger Lancelyn Green and Walter Hooper, *C. S. Lewis: A Biography* (London: Collins, 1974), 213–14.

51. Humphrey Carpenter, *The Inklings* (New York: Ballentine, 1981), 180.

52. Jacobs, *The Narnian*, 253.

53. A. N. Wilson, *C. S. Lewis: A Biography* (London: Norton, 1990), 292 and 183.

54. Helen M. Sterk, "Gender Relations and Narrative in a Reformed Church Setting," in Mary Stewart Van Leeuwen, Annelies Knoppers, Margaret L. Koch, Douglas J. Schuurman, and

Though Lewis was less inclined to such crude proof-texting, it still seemed
that what he gave with one hand—the possibility of a Christian intellectual
life with like-minded believers—he took away with the other. My mind was
almost certainly unfitted for such fellowship by virtue of my sex, according
to Lewis, and even if it wasn't, marriage would probably soon put an end
to any intellectual pretensions I might have acquired as one of the fortunate
females to have gone on to higher education. Small wonder, perhaps, that I set
Lewis aside for another ten years in spite of my covert admiration for some of
his observations about sexuality and his critique of logical positivism. Small
wonder too that after finishing my first degree and before going on to doctoral
studies, I joined the Canadian equivalent of the Peace Corps and spent two
years teaching high school in Africa, in a setting where people were much less
inclined than in the Anglo-American world to use a person's sex as a criterion
for giving or withholding responsibility.

In retrospect, I was perhaps fortunate *not* to have been raised in the North
American evangelical subculture, where Lewis after his death in 1963 was increasingly turned into a plaster saint and his every pronouncement (though often
ignoring its context) treated by some almost as Holy Writ.[55] Otherwise, I might
have felt profoundly conflicted about both my pursuit of graduate training and
my embrace of feminism in the late 1960s. One of Lewis's literary biographers,
Margaret Hannay, has pointed out that his depictions of gender do matter, in
that they push intelligent women seekers away from the rest of his work.[56] So
it was perhaps providential that I did not start reading Lewis again until after
my teaching stint in Africa where, as it turned out, I was posted to a secondary
school run by the Salvation Army. Though not always consistent in practice, the
thoroughly evangelical "Sally Anns" had been in principle committed to gender
equality since their mid-nineteenth century beginnings. Within its ranks, officers
marry other officers, are promoted together as they gain experience, and run
Army Corps (the equivalent of churches) as copastors. Much the same spirit
pervaded their educational and evangelistic work in central Africa, where I also
met a fellow teacher, Major Eva Burrows of Australia, who was to become the
General of the Salvation Army two decades later.

All of this made me better prepared—and certainly more inclined—to
read Lewis with a critical as well as an appreciative eye, once I became a seri-

Helen M. Sterk, *After Eden: Facing the Challenge of Gender Reconciliation* (Grand Rapids:
Eerdmans, 1993), 184–221.

55. Even Lewis admirers have expressed concern about the possibilities for distortion in
the "cult of C. S. Lewis." See, for example, Chad Walsh, "C. S. Lewis: Critic, Creator and
Cult Figure," *Seven: An Anglo-American Literary Review* 2 (1981): 60–79; James Como, ed.,
Remembering C. S. Lewis: Recollections of Those Who Knew Him (San Francisco: Ignatius,
2005), 235; Jacobs, *The Narnian*, x; and Candice Fredrick and Sam McBride, *Women Among
the Inklings: Gender, C. S. Lewis, J. R. R.. Tolkien and Charles Williams* (Westport, CN: Greenwood, 2001), xi–xvi.

56. Margaret P. Hannay, *C. S. Lewis* (New York: Frederick Ungar, 1981).

ous rather than a nominal Christian. I was ready to begin separating what might rightly be called "mere" Christianity in his writings, especially about gender, from conclusions rooted in other influences. For example, how much of Lewis's stance reflected the Edwardian era into which he was born and the largely male culture of Oxford and Cambridge where he spent most of his life? Was Lewis, like his logical positivist adversaries, a better man than his theories—that is, were his relationships with actual women more mutually respectful and egalitarian than his published writings? To what extent did his pronouncements about women and men change throughout his life, and why? And just how much did Lewis—or anyone else of his era—really know about the psychology of gender? Teasing apart the threads represented by these questions is my task in the rest of this book.

2

A More Fundamental Reality than Sex?

C. S. Lewis's Views on Gender

One of the first scholars to analyze C. S. Lewis as a Christian writer was the American poet and Episcopal priest Chad Walsh.[1] A friend of Lewis from the late 1940s on, and of his American wife even before she met him, Walsh had this to say about Lewis two decades after his death:

C. S. Lewis was a man who lived alienated from the twentieth century and its dominant philosophic and religious assumptions. The only part of a newspaper he valued was the crossword puzzle. He knew so little about science that he thought a slug was a reptile . . . Though he lectured on the Italian Renaissance with great wealth of learning, he had not the faintest longing to buy a ticket to Florence and see its works of art. Indeed, he found the world of the British Isles more than adequate for his exploration, and never set foot on foreign soil except during World War I, and after his marriage when he humored his dying wife by venturing to Greece. Most of his adult life was spent in the company of men, and women were shadowy figures on the fringes of his consciousness . . . He had no faith at all in the common assumptions of progressive [social] evolution. Indeed, he believed that no more than a century or two ago the

1. Chad Walsh, *C. S. Lewis: Apostle to the Skeptics* (New York: MacMillan, 1949).

35

western world had taken a decisive turn in the wrong direction, losing the proper vision of man in relation to God and His universe . . . It is difficult to think of many twentieth-century writers who so cheerfully flayed the century in which they lived.[2]

Walsh's agenda in this particular essay was basically positive: to affirm Lewis's continuing appeal as a writer despite his very human and historical limits. And as Walsh notes, women were rather less salient for him during most of his lifetime than were men. But as the previous chapter has already noted, Lewis had much to say in both his scholarly and imaginative writings about women, men, and their actual and supposedly ideal relationships. Appealing to Scripture and Christian tradition (though not always consistently), as well as his knowledge of philosophy and literature, he defended for much of his life a view of male-female relations that was both essentialist and hierarchical. In his earlier works gender essentialism is seen in his conviction that masculinity and femininity are deep spiritual "essences"—quasi-Platonic forms, ideals, or archetypes—to which we are called by both God and nature to conform in order to ensure our welfare as persons and society. His belief in gender hierarchy is seen in his defense of male headship in marriage and an exclusively male priesthood in the Anglican church.

These views, at least in theory, did not extend to a belief in universal male headship—the notion that women must be under the authority of men not just in church and family, but all other spheres of life, such as the academy, the marketplace, and the political forum. But given his oft-stated convictions about the inferior nature of women's minds (though on this, as we will see, his writings are inconsistent), Lewis, particularly as a young don, did not support much academic mingling of the sexes. He did have students—both in classes and tutorials—from Oxford's women's colleges throughout his career, and to at least one of these he was an active and encouraging mentor.[3] For more than a decade he was also an active faculty mentor and "bonny fighter" in Oxford's Socratic Club, working with its founder and coordinator Stella Aldwinckle, pastoral advisor to the women students at Oxford.[4] But unlike male students, women were never invited to gatherings to share "beer and Beowulf" and other topics both lighthearted

2. Chad Walsh, "C. S. Lewis: Critic, Creator and Cult Figure," *Seven: An Anglo-American Literary Review* 2 (1981): 60–79 (quotation from p. 60).

3. See, for example, Lewis's correspondence with Mary (Shelley) Neylan in Walter Hooper, ed., *The Collected Letters of C. S. Lewis*, vol. 1, *1905–1931* (San Francisco: HarperSanFrancisco, 2004). During Lewis's time at Oxford there were five women's colleges, in contrast to nearly thirty for men.

4. For a history of the Oxford Socratic Club (including a record of its invited speakers during its existence from 1942 to 1954), see Walter Hooper, "Oxford's Bonny Fighter," in James T. Como, ed., *Remembering C. S. Lewis: Recollections of Those Who Knew Him* (San Francisco: Ignatius, 2005), 241–308.

and profound.[5] Nor were women invited to meetings of the Inklings, Lewis's literary discussion group that met twice weekly from 1933 to 1949. That group included academics like Charles Williams, Owen Barfield, and J. R. R. Tolkien, visiting scholars and regular nonscholars (such as his brother Warren and his personal physician, R. E. Havard), but never women.[6]

Prior to taking up teaching duties at Oxford in 1924, Lewis expressed a fear that the limited capacities of women students would make his work more difficult.[7] In 1927 he supported a proposal imposing a quota on women admitted to Oxford, siding with the majority of dons who were, as he put it, "anti-feminists," and expressing his relief in a letter to his brother that "the appalling danger of our degenerating into a women's university . . . has thus been staved off."[8] Indeed, when Lewis himself first entered Oxford as an undergraduate, women could not receive Oxford degrees, even after completing the same academic requirements as male students. It was not until 1920 that they were allowed to write BA or MA (Oxon.) after their names, and not until 1947 that Cambridge University, where Lewis spent his final years as an academic, followed suit by granting degrees to its women students.[9]

The Man Who Stuck His Neck Out

In a later chapter I will undertake a more detailed analysis of the social and historical setting in which Lewis came of age, and in which he became a serious Christian during his early thirties. In this chapter I will mainly survey Lewis's stated beliefs about gender, as seen in a representative sample of his fiction, apologetic works and essays, letters, and literary criticism. I will note how his views were somewhat changeable even in his earlier writings, and how they shifted much more in his final works. In the next chapter I will argue that if "mere Christianity" is, as Lewis defined it, "the belief that has been common

5. See his letter to his father, C. S. Lewis to Albert Lewis, November 29, 1927, and note 84, Hooper, ed., *Collected Letters*, vol. 1, 732.

6. Humphrey Carpenter, *The Inklings* (New York: Ballentine, 1981); Candice Fredrick and Sam McBride, *Women Among the Inklings: Gender, C. S. Lewis, J. R. R.. Tolkien and Charles Williams* (Westport, CN: Greenwood, 2001).

7. C. S. Lewis to Albert Lewis, July 26, 1922, Hooper, ed., *Collected Letters*, vol. 1, 598.

8. C. S. Lewis to Warren Lewis, July 9, 1927, ibid., 703.

9. Oxford and Cambridge opened their first colleges for women only in the 1870s, while denying women formal degrees. However, as women regularly came at or near the top in examinations, it became more and more difficult to withhold from them the credentials they had earned. For a discussion of these academic changes and the parallel movement for women's suffrage in early twentieth-century England, see Roy Hattersley, *The Edwardians* (New York: St. Martin's Press, 2004), chap. 10. See also Vera Brittain, *The Women at Oxford: A Fragment of History* (New York: MacMillan, 1960).

to nearly all Christians at all times,"[10] then many of his early and midlife pronouncements about gender fall short of this standard.

However, before embarking on this task, I need to make a crucial historical qualifier on Lewis's behalf. He was born in 1898, less than thirty years after the British parliament had passed the Married Women's Property Act, which permitted wives to have independent control of their personal property and income. Prior to this legislation, a married woman's entire material welfare depended on her husband's assets and his willingness to share them. She could not count on her own income as a waged worker or property holder, because all property brought by a wife into marriage, and all income she earned thereafter, legally belonged to her husband.[11] Moreover, middle- and upper-class wives (and all who aspired to be like them) were not even supposed to earn income. Stanford University historian Marilyn Yalom summarizes this Victorian ethos:

> Gone were the premodern days when the labor of wives and children entered into the middle-class family economy and a respectable wife could work alongside her husband in his shop. The hallmark of the lady was that she did not have to work for pay. Only members of the working class and small farmers continued to depend on their wives for joint production and supplemental income. [Middle- and upper-class wives' main responsibilities were] 1) obeying and satisfying their husbands, 2) keeping one's children physically and morally clean, and 3) maintaining the household . . . Much of the third category was performed by paid domestics, which meant that the privileged matron had to be commander of an army of servants. Aristocratic families in their country estates might have as many as twenty or twenty-five, while a middle-class urban wife would make do with one, two or five, depending on her circumstances.[12]

Gender and class norms thus interacted in complex ways in Victorian Britain. Nondomestic activity for higher-class wives was limited mainly to attending church, visiting friends, enjoying the arts and "suitable" reading material, or engaging in charitable work. In what came to be known as the "cult of true womanhood" or "doctrine of separate spheres," only men were suited for competitive activity in the public spheres of scholarship, trade, military service, and politics. By contrast women, previously regarded as not just ra-

10. C. S. Lewis, *Mere Christianity* (London: Collins, 1952), 6.

11. The basis for common law in nineteenth century England and America was Sir William Blackstone's 1753 *Commentaries on the Laws of England*, which stated that by marriage "the husband and wife are one person in law: that is, the very being, or legal existence of the woman is suspended during the marriage, or at least incorporated and consolidated into that of the husband, under whose wing, protection and cover, she performs everything." A popular summary of this principle of "couverture" (or husbandly "covering") was "Husband and wife are one person, and that person is the husband." See Marilyn Yalom, *A History of the Wife* (New York: HarperCollins, 2001), especially chap. 5.

12. Ibid., 180–81.

tionally inferior, but morally less developed and sexually more volatile than men, were in the Victorian era elevated to the status of "angels of the home." In this role—provided they did stay mainly in the private realm—they were seen as men's moral and sexual superiors, able to model for their husbands and children the biblical and decidedly noncompetitive virtues of self-control, love, gentleness, and self-sacrifice.

In the Edwardian era in which C. S. Lewis grew up, the doctrine of separate spheres for men and women continued to be seen as "natural" and "biblical." Although set aside to some extent during both world wars (when women were recruited to fill jobs left vacant by men drafted into the armed services) it remained generally unquestioned until the second wave of feminism began on both sides of the Atlantic in the mid-1960s. One result of this dichotomy was that gender relations in general—and women in particular—were largely dismissed as serious scholarly topics. Indeed, as recently as 1990 British social theorist Elaine Storkey, while doing research on Scottish church history, expressed her amazement on discovering that, aside from Mary Queen of Scots, there were no women living in Scotland between the years of 1170 and 1928! Of course what she really discovered, and was reporting with mock seriousness, was that none of her historical sources *made reference* to any women other than Mary Queen of Scots.[13]

"Invisible Woman" historiography is what feminist scholars were later to call such writing, which focuses almost totally on the public institutional activities of powerful males. And it is not just women that are thus rendered invisible, but all persons not part of the intellectual, political, economic, or religious elites. So for Lewis to treat gender as a serious topic, alongside his attempts to make philosophy and theology accessible to the general public, was to take a risky step away from the reigning norms of intellectual discourse.[14] In this respect he was like the Dutch theologian Abraham Kuyper—another Christian thinker of wide scope with whom he overlapped in lifespan. Both men were articulate Christian writers who wrote not infrequently about gender roles and relations. By taking on this rarely discussed and intellectually-denigrated topic, both risked getting a lot of things only half-right and others simply wrong.[15]

13. Elaine Storkey, "The Hidden History of Women in the Church" (lecture, Calvin College, Grand Rapids, MI, March 12, 1991).

14. Lewis's violation of academic discourse norms drew less criticism (during his lifetime) with regard to his views on gender than with regard to his boldly Christian apologetics. One biographer has noted that "Oxford never forgave him for violating the code of detached irony, for crusading instead of keeping his conversion private. His theological writings caused virtual social ostracism at Oxford . . . [and] one colleague admitted to voting against him [for an Oxford professorship] as the author of *Screwtape*." Margaret P. Hannay, *C. S. Lewis* (New York: Frederick Ungar, 1981), 15, 20. See also Carpenter, *The Inklings*, 229.

15. Kuyper lived from 1837 to 1920. For an analysis of his writings on gender and family, see Mary Stewart Van Leeuwen, "Abraham Kuyper and the Cult of True Womanhood," *Calvin Theological Journal* 31, no. 1 (April 1996): 97–124; and "The Carrot and the Stick: Kuyper on

Like well-known Christians of many eras, they were prophetically astute in some areas, and liable (like all human beings) to blind spots in others.

For example, Australian literary critic Kath Filmer has argued that women in Lewis's writings are portrayed as chaste goddesses at one extreme, and as sexual temptresses or jealously possessive maternal figures at the other, with further possibilities largely ignored or invalidated.[16] But Kuyper was equally dualistic when writing about properly "Christian" gender roles only a few decades earlier. "Man and woman are fundamentally different in kind," he asserted, "and whoever has man take his place at the cradle and woman at the lectern makes life *unnatural*."[17] Indeed, he continued,

> The woman's position of honor is most effectively maintained if she can sparkle in private life, and in the public domain, for which the man is the appointed worker, she will never be able to fulfill anything but a subordinate role, in which her inferiority would soon come to light anyway. The woman who, in order to cover this up, wants to imitate the man, does not elevate herself, but descends on the social ladder . . . Whoever is ashamed of [her] own kind damages [her] own honor.[18]

In sum, like most influential men—and indeed many women—of his time, Lewis took for granted the doctrine of separate spheres, at least in many of his published writings. And when he took satirical aim at self-martyring wives and mothers in *The Four Loves*[19] and *The Great Divorce*[20] he seems not to have sufficiently recognized that when a society confines any group of people to a reduced sphere of influence, it runs the risk that they will become jealously possessive of the limited prerogatives it affords them.

Nevertheless, by even attempting to write seriously about gender and family issues he may have helped women who read his works to feel less invisible than other writers of his time.[21] So perhaps it is not surprising that Lewis's correspondents, once he became famous, were mostly female and that a couple of them,

Gender, Family, and Class," in Luis Lugo, ed., *Religion, Pluralism and Public Life: Abraham Kuyper's Legacy for the Twenty-First Century* (Grand Rapids: Eerdmans, 2000), 59–84.

16. Kath Filmer, *The Fiction of C. S. Lewis: Mask and Mirror* (New York: St. Martin's Press, 1993), chap. 6.

17. Abraham Kuyper, *De Eerepositie der Vrouw* (Kampen, Netherlands: Kok, 1932), 13 (emphasis original). This volume is based on a series of newspaper articles originally published in 1914. Page references are to the unpublished English translation by Irene Brouwer Konyndyk, Calvin College, Grand Rapids, MI, 1990.

18. Ibid., 28.

19. C. S. Lewis, *The Four Loves* (London: Collins, 1963), chap. 3.

20. C. S. Lewis, *The Great Divorce* (London: Geoffrey Bles, 1946), chap. 11.

21. Except perhaps for the emerging psychoanalytic theorists, whose influence on Lewis I will consider in a later chapter. An equally prolific writer about relations between the sexes was Lewis's friend and fellow Inkling Charles Williams, whose "theology of romantic love" was to attract so many young female acolytes that at times it threatened his marriage. See Alice Mary

prior to his own marriage at age fifty-six, convinced themselves (and others) that they were engaged or married to him. One, who ended up in London's Holloway Prison for running up hotel bills in Lewis's name, told the prison chaplain she was dying and had to see Lewis one last time. That he actually paid her a visit (only to find her perfectly healthy in body, if not in mind) says much for his thoughtfulness toward actual women, even as his would-be bride's behavior illustrates how desperately some may act when their worlds are as limited as they were under the doctrine of separate spheres.[22] This paradoxical mix—Lewis as a person who limited women in theory but took them more seriously in practice—will be dealt with in more detail in later chapters but should be kept in mind as I survey his views about gender in this one.

Lewis's "Modern Fairy-Tale for Grown-Ups"

C. S. Lewis was a medieval and Renaissance literature scholar with no formal training in the natural or social sciences and little aptitude for mathematics.[23] But as a historian of ideas he had a keen sense of the dangers of scientism— that is, the assumption that the methods of science can in principle yield exhaustive and ultimate knowledge about all of reality. In 1945 he published a dystopian novel titled *That Hideous Strength*. Subtitled "A Modern Fairy-Tale for Grown-Ups," it was a futuristic fantasy about what might happen in a small university setting when science becomes the only source of authority and the language of value and meaning is replaced by the supposedly neutral currency of empirical reference and efficient causality. The third in Lewis's popular trilogy of science fiction novels, its title was drawn from a sixteenth-century poetic reference to the Tower of Babel.[24] It is a commentary on the place of science in a society coping with the aftermath of World War II, but also a forum for displaying Lewis's views on gender.

Hadfield, *Charles Williams: An Exploration of His Life and Work* (Oxford: Oxford University Press, 1983).

22. See Alan Jacobs, *The Narnian: The Life and Imagination of C. S. Lewis* (San Francisco: HarperSanFrancisco: 2005), 252–53.

23. That Lewis was even able to take advantage of his undergraduate classics scholarship at Oxford's University College was something of a historical fluke. Prior to doing so, he was required to pass university-wide entrance exams (known as responsions) showing that he was competent in various academic areas, including elementary algebra. His pre-university tutor, William Kirkpatrick, was so concerned that Lewis would fail responsions that he had him learn several modern languages in order to quality for the Foreign Service, should he fail to get into Oxford. Lewis failed his mathematics responsions twice, but having then delayed his university career to serve in World War I, he was exempted from retaking them because he was an ex-serviceman. See his own letters about this on pp. 316 and 428, and Walter Hooper's editorial comments on pp. 194, 264, and 336 of *Collected Letters*, vol. 1.

24. Gen. 11:1–9. The first two novels in the trilogy are *Out of the Silent Planet* (London: Bodley Head, 1938) and *Perelandra* (London: Bodley Head, 1943).

At a crucial point in its plot Lewis records the following exchange between Elwin Ransom, the novel's hero, who directs a small commune of beleaguered Christian followers, and Jane Studdock, a young academic woman estranged from her husband:

"Your trouble," said the Director [to Jane], "has been what the old poets called *Daungier*. We call it pride. You are offended by the masculine itself: the loud, irruptive, possessive thing. The male you could have escaped, for it exists only on the biological level. But the masculine none of us can escape. What is above and beyond all things is so masculine that we are all feminine in relation to it."
"You mean I shall have to become a Christian?" said Jane.
"It looks like it," said the Director.[25]

Throughout this novel Lewis defends both an essentialist and a hierarchical view of gender. Stereotypical masculinity and femininity are portrayed as timeless archetypes, deeper even than biological sex, and apparently more significant for the organization of social life than the common humanity of women and men. Indeed, in the above dialogue Lewis portrays God as representing the highest ideal, or form, of masculinity. In his fictitious university town of Edgestow, academically trained males have frequent debates about ethics, epistemology, and human nature, reflecting the elite "world without women" that was still the dominant university culture in the 1940s.[26] Its women characters are either contentedly ensconced in domesticity or hovering around the fringes of male academic and professional life in a state of relative obscurity.

In his writings of the 1940s and '50s, Lewis often warned that scientific hubris—especially when its techniques are applied to people—would not lead to "the relief of man's estate"[27] but to political totalitarianism and a view of humans (except for those of an elite "Inner Ring") as eminently expendable.[28]

25. C. S. Lewis, *That Hideous Strength: A Modern Fairy-Tale for Grown-Ups* (London: John Lane the Bodley Head, 1945), 315–16. See also David C. Downing, *Planets in Peril: A Critical Study of C. S. Lewis's Ransom Trilogy* (Amherst, MA: University of Massachusetts Press, 1992).

26. For a historical analysis of the male Oxbridge culture and its ecclesiastical roots, see David F. Noble, *A World Without Women: The Christian Clerical Culture of Western Science* (New York: Oxford University Press, 1992).

27. This phrase comes from Francis Bacon's (1620) *Novum Organum*, an early English treatise on the inductive method in science, which challenged Aristotle's long-accepted *Organon* and its postulation of "final causes" or purposes in nature, in addition to material, efficient, and "formal" causes.

28. See especially C. S. Lewis, *The Abolition of Man* (Oxford: Oxford University Press, 1943), chap. 3; *Miracles* (London: Geoffrey Bles, 1947; rev. ed., London: Collins, 1960), chaps. 3–5; his 1944 essay, "The Inner Ring," reprinted in C. S. Lewis, *The Weight of Glory and Other Addresses* (Grand Rapids: Eerdmans, 1965), 55–66; and his 1954 essay on "The Humanitarian Theory of Punishment," reprinted in Walter Hooper, ed., *God in the Dock: Essays On Theology and Ethics* (Grand Rapids: Eerdmans, 1970), 287–300.

As the power-hungry Lord Feverstone explains to Mark, the gullible young sociologist newly recruited to Belbury, the scientific think-tank, "Man has got to take charge of Man. That means, remember, that some men have got to take charge of the rest . . . You and I want to be the people who do the taking charge, not the ones who are taken charge of."[29] Indeed, William Hingest, the one truly conscientious scientist at Belbury, is eventually murdered by his corrupt colleagues, the end result of a process in which truth, beauty, and goodness have been reduced to products of chance and impersonal causes:

> Despair of objective truth had been increasingly insinuated into the scientists . . . Indifference to [truth] and a concentration upon mere power had been the result . . . Dreams of the far future destiny of man were dragging up from its shallow and unquiet grave the old dream of Man as God.[30]

Lewis in the 1940s thus saw a great threat in the misuse of natural science, with its triumphalist appeal to mathematics and experimentation, one in which human freedom and accountability might be cast aside as outdated illusions. His Cambridge University contemporary, C. P. Snow, hoped that the social sciences would emerge as a mediating voice between the increasingly polarized worldviews of the humanities and the natural sciences,[31] but Lewis was skeptical. Aside from a qualified respect for Freudian psychoanalysis, and a much greater admiration of "the other great psychologist, Jung,"[32] he saw practitioners of the social sciences mainly as shallow thinkers and the lackeys of technologically minded natural scientists.

So it is no accident that the young college don Lewis places on the path of spiritual reeducation in *That Hideous Strength* is a sociologist, Mark Studdock—Jane's husband—whose petulant response to the dilemma he creates by joining Belbury is to assume no responsibility at all. Mark does finally realize that, in embracing Feverstone's might-makes-right philosophy, he has not only set aside moral standards regarding the treatment of others, but also any grounds for moral indignation over his own later mistreatment at Belbury. Yet his response is still to pass the buck. "Damn the whole thing . . . Why had he such a rotten heredity? Why had his education been so ineffective? Why was the system of society so irrational? Why was his luck so bad?"[33] Lewis comments:

> It must be remembered that in Mark's mind hardly one rag of noble thought, either Christian or Pagan, had a secure lodging. His education had been neither

29. Lewis, *That Hideous Strength*, 42.
30. Ibid., 203.
31. C. P. Snow, *The Two Cultures and the Scientific Revolution* (Cambridge: Cambridge University Press, 1959).
32. Lewis, *Mere Christianity*, 79.
33. Lewis, *That Hideous Strength*, 224.

scientific nor classical—merely "Modern." The severities both of abstraction and of high human tradition had passed him by, and he had neither peasant shrewdness nor aristocratic honour to help him. He was a man of straw, a glib examinee in subjects that require no exact knowledge.[34]

The Universality of Gender Archetypes and Gender Hierarchy

Mark Studdock has embraced naturalism—which Lewis elsewhere called "a philosophy for boys" because of its logical and moral incoherence[35]—and has been hoisted by his own petard as a result. His redemption requires him to become an adult and take responsibility for his own choices and for the welfare of others, including his estranged wife. This at first blush seems to reflect the generic repentance and sanctification required of all persons who would become Christians. But on closer analysis, it turns out not to be so. For Lewis writing in the 1940s, humans are so inescapably gendered—in their creation, in their fallenness, in the implications of their redemption—that they are considered almost different species. They are metaphysically opposite sexes, not the "neighboring sexes" that his colleague Dorothy Sayers proposed in one of her own essays of the 1940s.[36] And in Lewis's "Modern Fairy-Tale for Grown-Ups" it is not just Mark Studdock, the shallow, positivist sociologist, who needs a spiritual rebirth. It is also his new wife Jane, an English literature student trying to finish her thesis on John Donne.

As opposing sides gather in the story—Belbury representing science gone wrong, and the community of St. Anne's representing Christians who, however fumblingly, at least want to be on the side of right—Lewis paints a rather limited picture of what Christian females should aspire to. As chaste single women, they can become learned professionals like Grace Ironwood, the doctor who treats Jane for the strange dreams she is having, and who interacts on a somewhat collegial level with director Ransom. As married women, they can become like Mrs. Dimble, the wife of one of Jane's professors, who, though childless herself, channels her maternal instincts into taking care of her husband's students. But they should not, like Jane, try to combine both in pursuit of a third possibility. God, it appears, can only count to two.[37]

---

34. Ibid., 185. Note in this passage that Lewis also takes for granted certain class stereotypes, such as "peasant shrewdness" and "aristocratic honour."

35. C. S. Lewis, *"De Futilitate"* (an address given at Magdalen College during World War II). Reprinted in Hooper, ed., *God in the Dock*, 57–71 (quotation from p. 71).

36. Dorothy L. Sayers, "The Human-Not-Quite-Human," in *Unpopular Opinions: Twenty-One Essays* (London: Gollancz, 1946). Reprinted in *Are Women Human?* (Downers Grove, IL: InterVarsity, 1975), 37–47 (quotation from p. 37).

37. Several analysts of Lewis's writings have noted that he overused the strategy of disjunction—that is, an "either/or" rhetorical technique that sets up two polarized alternatives and assumes these are the only possibilities. This led Chad Walsh, in *C. S. Lewis: Apostle to the Skeptics*, to

Ransom has come to his conclusions about the gendered nature of all reality as a result of prior trips to Malacandra (Mars) and Perelandra (Venus), which he eventually discovers are governed by "masculine" and "feminine" intelligences respectively.[38] It is during his sojourn on Perelandra that Ransom acquires his status as a kind of Christ figure, for this planet is an unfallen Eden, with its own version of the primordial Adam and Eve: Tor and Tinidril. These two are temporarily separated at the time of Ransom's arrival, he to be instructed by Maleldil, the high God of the universe, in all that he will need to know in order to rule over the planet, and she to be tested to see if she will stay obedient to Maleldil and to her husband. In her unfallen state, Lewis explained to one correspondent while writing the novel, Tinidril was meant "to combine characteristics which the Fall has pulled poles apart—she's got to be in some ways like a Pagan goddess and in other ways like the Blessed Virgin."[39]

Why the asymmetry between Tor and Tinidril? Is the elegant "Green Lady," as Ransom calls her, not created to be coruler of Perelandra with her husband in a way that parallels God's creation mandate to humans of both sexes?[40] Yes and no, the story's narrator (Lewis, thinly disguised) tells us. The Lady must stoop to conquer in a way not demanded of her husband. Her greatest happiness really lies in accepting her secondary station as woman and wife, but she is vulnerable to the temptation to try to rise above it, and in doing so becoming the cause of her planet's corruption. She is in danger of acting like Eve, her earthly counterpart—or at least Eve as her story is retold in Milton's *Paradise Lost*, which was in many ways Lewis's literary model for *Perelandra*.[41]

Admittedly, Lewis writes, "It must be part of the Divine plan that this happy creature should mature, should become more and more a creature of free choice, should become, in a sense, more distinct from God and from her husband in order thereby to be at one with them in a richer fashion." But, he adds, this can only happen rightly under her husband's guidance: "This present temptation, if conquered, would itself be the next, and greatest step

---

comment wryly: "It is always possible that God can count beyond two" (207). See also Hannay, *C. S. Lewis*, chaps. 5 and 7; Jacobs, *The Narnian*, chap. 10; and Michael J. Christensen, *C. S. Lewis On Scripture: His Thoughts on the Nature of Biblical Revelation, Inspiration, the Role of Revelation and the Question of Inerrancy* (Waco: Word, 1979), chap. 3.

38. There is no evidence that Lewis inspired the title of John Gray's best-selling self-help book, *Men Are from Mars, Women Are from Venus* (New York: HarperCollins, 1992), but it is noteworthy how many internet-based booksellers and Christian websites promote this book and Lewis's novels on the same page.

39. C. S. Lewis to Sister Penelope Lawson CSMV, November 9, 1941, in Walter Hooper, ed., *The Collected Letters of C. S. Lewis*, vol. 2, *1931–1949* (San Francisco: HarperSanFrancisco, 2004), 496.

40. Gen. 1:27–28: "Male and female [God] created them. God blessed them, and God said to them, 'Be fruitful and multiply, and fill the earth and subdue it, and have dominion over the fish of the sea and over the birds of the air and over every living thing that moves upon the earth.'"

41. C. S. Lewis, *A Preface to Paradise Lost* (Oxford: Oxford University Press, 1942), especially chaps. 11 and 16–18.

in the same direction: an obedience freer, more reasoned, more conscious than any she had known before. But . . . the fatal false step . . . once taken, would thrust her down into the terrible slavery of appetite and hate and economics and government which our race knows so well."[42] These remarks are significant not just for Lewis's view of gender but for his view of societal activities, including "economics and government." Unlike some British Anglicans, who viewed these arenas of human activity as rooted in creation, and no more or less fallen than any other, Lewis saw them largely as results of the fall.[43]

Ransom's calling, he realizes, is to protect the Lady from taking this "fatal false step." If necessary, he must fight to death with Edward Weston, the corrupt scientist from Earth who has become the mouthpiece of a bent angel, or "eldil," who aims to establish control over the planet through the Green Lady's disobedience. Under Lewis's pen, Weston's attempts to lead her from the path of obedience alternate between antifeminist satire and feminine stereotypes. In his role as tempter, Weston tries to make the Lady see herself as courageous and noble in taking action independently of her husband. He casts her as a pioneer of risk and originality. He suggests that she is made for greater creativity than simply bearing offspring, even though Ransom tries "to convince her that children [are] fruit enough."[44] Weston appeals alternately to her sense of self-sacrifice and her embryonic "touch of theatricality."[45] He tries to unleash her vanity by showing her (even while still unfallen) how to dress up in clothes. He easily exploits her emotions, while Ransom grows increasingly frustrated by her "progressive disregard of the plain intellectual bones of the problem" and his own struggle "to recall to her mind the *data*."[46]

Ransom, at great cost, finally succeeds in killing Weston, after which the Lady sees the folly of her desire for independence and thanks Ransom, her interplanetary knight errant, for saving her from giving in to it. By now her husband, King Tor, has returned (having conveniently missed the entire temptation process) to share with her the many things about art, architecture, and so on that he has learned in his absence.[47] This knowledge has been given to him by Maleldil, the High God, and she will be his inspiration as he develops

42. C. S. Lewis, *Perelandra* (New York: MacMillan, 1965), 133.

43. One important British social thinker who rooted government in creation was the moral theologian Frederick Denison Maurice (1805–72). For an introduction to his thought, see, for example, Ellen K. Wondra, ed., *Reconstructing Christian Ethics: Selected Writings of F. D. Maurice* (Louisville: Westminster John Knox, 1995).

44. Lewis, *Perelandra*, 131.

45. Ibid., 133.

46. Ibid.

47. Lewis's stated reason for separating the primal pair in *Perelandra* was to avoid Milton's mistake in attempting to portray unfallen sexuality, and as a result confusing Eros with the real reason for the fall—Eve's pride and (according to both Milton and Lewis) Adam's too-great love for his wife, which led him to join her in eating the forbidden fruit. Unfortunately, he only succeeds in seeming to let Adam off the hook—and in portraying Eve as responsible for

it further. To Ransom's cautious inquiry as to why he was spared the rigors of his wife's temptation, the King replies with a hearty laugh that earthly ideas of justice simply don't apply on this unfallen planet: "All is gift . . . Through many hands, enriched with many different kinds of love and labor, the gift comes to me. It is the Law. The best fruits are plucked for each by some hand that is not his own."[48]

As a result of his experience on Perelandra, Ransom comes to realize that gender is "not just an imaginative extension of sex." Lewis explains:

> Our ancestors did not make mountains masculine because they projected male characteristics onto them. The process is the reverse. Gender is a reality, and a more fundamental reality, than sex. Sex is, in fact, merely the adaptation to organic life of a fundamental polarity which divides all created beings. Female sex is simply one of the things that have feminine gender; there are many others. Masculine and feminine meet us on planes of reality where male and female would be simply meaningless. Masculine is not attenuated male, nor feminine attenuated female. On the contrary, the male and female of organic creatures are rather faint and blurred reflections of masculine and feminine.[49]

Thus in *That Hideous Strength* Ransom (now back on earth) says to Jane, just prior to her conversion: "A virginal rejection of the male, He would allow. Such [feminine] souls can bypass the male and go on to meet something far more masculine higher up, to which they must make an even greater surrender." But, he adds, "Mother Dimble . . . is a Christian wife. And you, you know, are not. Neither are you a virgin . . . I'm afraid there's no niche in the world for people who won't be either Pagan or Christian."[50]

In this sequel to *Perelandra*, Lewis strongly hints at what can happen to women who do not embrace either neutral celibacy or wifely submission. They will become like Fairy Hardcastle, the head of the private police force at Belbury, who acts like "one of the boys": dressing in corsetless uniforms, smoking cigars, walking and sitting with legs apart, and surrounded by vacuous and sycophantic young girls. There is no third way. Jane must choose, and if she is to be Christian, she will choose for archetypal femininity and wifely obedience in a universe that, at its core, is one continuous hierarchy:

> "Religion" [Jane thought] ought to mean a realm in which her haunting female fear of being treated as a thing, an object of barter and desire and possession, would be set permanently at rest and what she called her "true self" would soar upward and expand in some freer, purer world . . . But supposing one were a

humanity's fall—to an even greater extent than Milton did. See Lewis, *A Preface to Paradise Lost*, chap. 18.

48. Lewis, *Perelandra*, 209–10.

49. Ibid., 200.

50. Lewis, *That Hideous Strength*, 314–15.

48 A Sword between the Sexes?

thing after all—a thing designed by Someone Else and valued for qualities quite different from what one had decided to regard as one's true self? Supposing all those people who, from bachelor uncles down to Mark and Mother Dimble, had infuriatingly found her sweet and fresh when she also wanted them to find her interesting and important, had all along been simply right and perceived the sort of thing she was?[51]

A moment later, Jane has her conversion experience: she is thrust "into a world, or into a Person, or into the presence of a Person . . . with no veil or protection in between." She then sees that she is indeed "a person (not the person she thought) yet also a thing, a made thing, made to please Another and in Him to please all others, a being made this very moment, without its choice, in a shape it had never dreamed of."[52] By the novel's end, she is ready to return to her changed (but still less-than-perfect) husband, and to put her marriage ahead of her academic aspirations. "Go in obedience and you will find love," Ransom urges her; and he adds (recalling his words to the Green Lady during her temptation), "You will have no more dreams. Have children instead."[53]

As in Marriage, So in the Church

I noted earlier that in *The Four Loves*, Lewis likened the sex act to a "Pagan sacrament" shared by "a god and goddess between whom there is no equality," even though "outside this ritual or drama he and she are two immortal souls, two free-born adults, two citizens."[54] No one can compel the Jane Studdocks of this world to embrace wifely submission. But truly Christian women will not sidestep feminine submission to the masculine—either as celibate singles "married" to God, or as married women obedient both to husbands and to a masculine God. They will also accept their subordination to a male priesthood. As in marriage, so in the church.

In his 1948 essay arguing against opening up the Anglican priesthood to women, Lewis (revising his view of women's mental limitations expressed elsewhere) declared that women are "no less capable than men of piety, zeal, learning and whatever else seems necessary for the pastoral office." A woman can be a competent pastoral visitor, church administrator, or even a preacher. It is not the case that she is "necessarily or even probably less holy or less charitable or stupider than a man."[55] What she cannot do, wearing the "femi-

51. Ibid., 318.
52. Ibid, 318–19.
53. Ibid., 379–80.
54. Lewis, *Four Loves*, 95–96.
55. C. S. Lewis, "Priestesses in the Church?" reprinted in Hooper, ed., *God in the Dock*, 234–39 (quotation from p. 235). This essay, written well before the debate about women's or-

nine uniform," is sacramentally represent the people of God at the altar. This, Lewis wrote, is because God represents ultimate masculinity, beside whom everything and everyone else is less masculine and more feminine by contrast:

> The innovators are really implying that sex is something superficial, irrelevant to the spiritual life. To say that men and women are equally eligible for a certain profession is to say that for the purposes of that profession their sex is irrelevant . . . This may be inevitable for our secular life. But in our Christian life we must return to reality . . . the kind of equality which implies that equals are interchangeable (like counters or identical machines) is, among humans, a legal fiction. It may be a useful legal fiction. But in the church we turn our back on fictions. One of the ends for which sex was created was to symbolize for us the hidden things of God . . . [Thus] only one wearing the masculine uniform can (provisionally, and till the *Parousia*) represent the Lord to the Church: for we are all, corporately and individually, feminine to Him.[56]

At the same time, Lewis drew boundaries around male headship: it will disappear at the Lord's return (the *Parousia*), and even before then it is limited to certain aspects of marital and ecclesiastical life. Moreover, in his wartime essay "Membership" he affirmed women's political and legal equality and wrote that he would "view with the strongest disapproval any proposal to abolish [universal] suffrage, or the Married Women's Property Act."[57] But even so, he wrote, such equality "is medicine, not food":

> I do not believe God created an egalitarian world. I believe the authority of parent over child, husband over wife, learned over simple, to have been as much a part of the original plan as the authority of man over beast. I believe that if we had not fallen . . . patriarchal monarchy would be the sole lawful form of government. But since we have learned sin . . . the only remedy has been to take away the powers and substitute a legal fiction of equality . . . Equality is for me in the same position as clothes. It is a result of the Fall and the remedy for it . . . But it is the hierarchical world, still alive and (very properly) hidden behind a façade of equal citizenship, which is our real concern . . . As democracy becomes more complete in the outer world and opportunities for reverence are successively removed, the refreshment, the cleansing, and invigorating returns to inequality, which the Church offers us, become more and more necessary.[58]

---

dination in the Anglican Church in Britain, was occasioned by a suggestion that the Anglican Church in Hong Kong should open up the priesthood to women, in part because of the needs brought on by the recent chaos of World War II. It is the only writing in which Lewis dealt specifically with this issue.

56. Ibid., 237–39.
57. C. S. Lewis, "Membership," reprinted in *Weight of Glory*, 30–42 (quotation from p. 37).
58. Ibid., 36–38.

Here we also see Lewis's conviction that the activities of civil society, largely including those of governance, are results of the fall, rather than being positive possibilities built into creation. It is a conviction that helps explain Lewis's lifelong public indifference to Christian involvement in social reform.

So far we have seen Lewis defending women's political and legal equality, only to add that if they aspire to be faithful *Christian* women, they will embrace symbolic and actual inequality in church and marriage. Lest his readers assume that this sanctions heavy-handed male tyranny, Lewis qualified his stance further in *The Four Loves*. But he suggested instead that wives are often like hapless children who will require constant tutoring from sanctified husbands. Though he explicitly discouraged his male readers from seeking such asymmetry in marriage, he nonetheless pictured manly endurance of it—if it occurs—as the most complete reflection of Christ's relationship to the church. He did not condone heavy-handedness toward wives; but he did patronize them, even as he romanticized the possibilities for husbandly chivalry:

> The husband is the head of the wife just in so far as he is to her what Christ is to the church. He is to love her as Christ loved the church—read on—*and gave his life for her* (Eph. 5:25). This headship, then, is most fully embodied . . . in him whose marriage is most like a crucifixion . . . in the sicknesses and suffering of a good wife or the faults of a bad one . . . in his unwearying (never paraded) care or inexhaustible forgiveness: forgiveness, not acquiescence. As Christ sees in the flawed, proud, fanatical or lukewarm church on earth the Bride who will one day be without spot or wrinkle, and labors to produce the latter, so the husband whose headship is Christlike (and he is allowed no other) never despairs. He is a King Cophetua who after twenty years still hopes that the beggar-girl will one day learn to speak the truth and wash behind her ears.[59]

A Late Life Transformation

In light of all this, as Alan Jacobs notes, "it would be easy enough to say that Lewis can represent women only as virtuous little girls, inaccessible saints, or domestic tyrants."[60] But it is important to note that Lewis's writings on gender began to change toward the time of his death in 1963. More than one biographer argues that this began even as he was writing *The Chronicles of Narnia*, between 1949 and 1956. Margaret Hannay, for example, notes that Lewis himself was aware of his "expository demon"—that is, a tendency to make characters in his adult fiction sound like C. S. Lewis giving a sermon— and recognized that writing children's fiction would discipline him against this

---

59. Lewis, *Four Loves*, 97–98 (emphasis original). The reference to King Cophetua refers to an 1842 poem by Tennyson ("The Beggar Maid"), which retells the legend of an African king who found that his love for a young beggar woman was greater than all his wealth and power.

60. Jacobs, *The Narnian*, 261.

temptation.[61] Jacobs goes further: it is not just that Lewis avoids parading his essentialist and hierarchical views of gender in the seven *Narnia* stories; he crafts his characters and plots like an author who, to an increasing extent, no longer believes in them. In these tales Lewis tends to pair boy and girl characters "of roughly equal narrative interest and with a general moral equality as well . . . None of these characters is perfect: all are flawed, but flawed in very familiar ways, and all are capable of virtue when the going gets rough."[62]

Indeed, the two main "problem children" of the series (Edmund and Eustace) are boys, though they too make progress in virtue. By contrast, the character granted special moral or spiritual insight (in finding the wardrobe, in having a unique vision of Aslan) is Lucy, a girl and the youngest of the four Pevensie children. Some critics are troubled by the fact that in the final volume of the series Susan, the eldest, does not return with her siblings to Narnia. In fact, we are told, she is "no longer a friend of Narnia . . . she's interested in nothing now-a-days except nylons and lipstick and invitations."[63] But her absence, Jacobs plausibly argues, is not because Lewis is demonizing Susan's emerging female sexuality but because, like Mark Studdock in *That Hideous Strength*, she has become so eager for social acceptance, for becoming part of an exclusive Inner Ring, that she ignores her siblings and her earlier friends. Like the willing inhabitants of hell in Lewis's *The Great Divorce*, she has—at least for now—locked herself out of heaven.[64]

More recently, Michael Ward—who was for several years curator of The Kilns, Lewis's house in Oxford—has argued that Lewis used the seven planets of medieval cosmology (Earth, Moon, Sun, Venus, Mars, Jupiter, and Saturn) as the imaginative grid for the seven *Narnia* chronicles.[65] This seems plausible when we recall how important some of these "planetary intelligences" (Mars, Venus, Earth) were in Lewis's earlier space trilogy. But in the space trilogy, they

61. Hannay, *C. S. Lewis*, 207. Lewis himself admits to his "expository demon" in a 1952 essay, "On Three Ways of Writing for Children," reprinted in Walter Hooper, ed., *Of Other Worlds: Essays and Stories* (New York: Harcourt Brace Jovanovich, 1975), 22–34 (quotation from p. 28).

62. Jacobs, *The Narnian*, 259.

63. C. S. Lewis, *The Last Battle* (London: Bodley Head, 1956), 154.

64. Jacobs, *The Narnian*, 260. For a further analysis of "the problem of Susan" see Greg Easterbrook, "In Defense of C. S. Lewis," *The Atlantic Monthly* 288, no. 3 (October 2001): 46–49. In 1957 Lewis wrote to a boy reader concerned about Susan's fate: "The books don't tell us what happened to Susan. She is left alive in this world at the end, having turned into a rather silly, conceited young woman. But there's plenty of time for her to mend, and perhaps she will get to Aslan's country in the end—in her own way." But he also adds, "I think that whatever she had seen in Narnia she *could* (if she was the sort who wanted to) persuade herself, as she grew up, that it was 'all nonsense.'" C. S. Lewis to Martin Kilmer, January 22, 1957, in Walter Hooper, ed., *The Collected Letters of C. S. Lewis*, vol. 3, *1950–1963* (San Francisco: HarperSanFrancisco: 2007), 826 (emphasis original).

65. Michael Ward, *Planet Narnia: The Seven Heavens in the Imagination of C. S. Lewis* (New York: Oxford University Press, 2008).

are used very explicitly to defend gender archetypes—that is, the association of Mars with masculinity and Venus with femininity. In the *Narnia* chronicles this connection has ceased to be significant.

A Strong but Flawed Woman Ruler

Undoubtedly the least-read of Lewis's novels—but his own favorite among all of them—is *Till We Have Faces*, published in 1956.[66] This, writes literature scholar Margaret Hannay, is a book "in which the reader can forget Lewis speaking and enter fully into the mind of a character. The 'expository demon' in him seems under control as never before; it is the most imaginative of all his works." Even more, "The misogyny of some of Lewis's earlier works seems to be reversed in this novel told from a woman's perspective."[67] Its story is a recasting of the classical myth of Cupid and Psyche. In the original version of the myth, Psyche, envied for her beauty, is abandoned on a mountain as sacrifice to a monster, but is rescued by Cupid one night and carried away to a palace as his bride. She is, however, forbidden to look upon Cupid's face. Psyche's sisters, envious of her happiness, nag her into lighting a lamp one night in order to see her husband's features. He awakens in the process, re-proaches her for her lack of faith, and vanishes along with his palace, leaving Psyche alone on the mountainside. Eventually, after a number of trials, she is reunited with Cupid who, impressed by her fidelity, has asked Zeus to bring her back and immortalize her in marriage to him.

Lewis's adaptation of this myth features the strong woman ruler of a small nation on the fringes of the classical Greek world, a person struggling against pride and idolatry and toward belief in a way that parallels Lewis's own faith journey as recorded in *Surprised by Joy*. In Queen Orual of Glome we see a physically ugly woman, but one so strong and gifted that people repeatedly say it is a pity she wasn't born a male. As Lewis often did, Orual—trained in philosophy by an educated Greek slave captured in one of her father's wars—struggles to discern when rationality must give way to faith and the acceptance of mystery. Her beloved, beautiful younger sister Istra, like Psyche in the original myth, has been chosen by the temple priests to be left as a sacrifice in a secret mountain valley, in order to placate the gods and end a nationwide drought. Unlike Psyche, however, Istra has always longed to live on the mountain, sensing that it will give her a joy deeper and greater than she could ever experience in Glome.

66. C. S. Lewis, *Till We Have Faces* (London: Geoffrey Bles, 1956). In a 1960 letter to an appreciative reader of this novel, Lewis wrote: "That book, which I consider far and away the best I have written, has been my one big failure both with the critics and with the public." C. S. Lewis to Anne Scott, August 26, 1960, Hooper, ed., *Collected Letters*, vol. 3, 1181.

67. Hannay, *C. S. Lewis*, 126.

When Orual undertakes a quest to find her sister after her abandonment on the mountain, she is shocked to find Istra radiantly happy, claiming to be married to a god whose face she cannot gaze upon and living in a palace that only she can see. Enraged at the prospect of losing someone who has been so central to her own happiness, and ambivalent about believing in the god to whom Istra is united, Orual blackmails her sister into lighting a lamp to see his face one night—with tragic consequences. The valley is destroyed, Istra is banished weeping, and Orual gets a glimpse of the god, who reproaches her for her unbelief, but also prophesies that she too "shall be Psyche [i.e., Istra]."[68] Indeed, Orual does become a person of faith and beauty—but not until she sees herself face to face: not until she confronts both the limits of her intelligence and the reality of her jealous possessiveness. When this finally happens, Orual receives not justice, but mercy, from the gods who assemble to judge her. The story ends as Orual, gazing into a pool, sees both her own image and that of her sister—distinct from each other, but both beautiful.

Lewis himself explained that he consciously crafted this story on a number of levels. The first is simply that of historical imagination: Lewis's background in classical and medieval mythology, and his skill as a literary craftsman, make it easy for readers to believe "what it might have been like in a little barbarous state on the borders of the Hellenistic world of Greek culture, just beginning to affect it."[69] The second level reflects Lewis's belief in the existence of "anonymous Christians"[70]—people making the best of the pagan religion in which they have been raised, and in the process being guided, however cloudily, toward the one true God. The final level hearkens back to Lewis's distinction between "first" and "second" things: human love is a good and natural quality, but when elevated to the status of an idol, it becomes "tyrannically possessive and ready to hate when the beloved ceases to be its possession. What such love particularly cannot stand is to see the beloved passing into a sphere where it cannot follow." Writing about his last novel to Wheaton College English professor Clyde Kilby in 1957, Lewis added that

this is what is probably happening in at least five families in your home town. Someone becomes a Christian, or in a family nominally Christian already, does

68. Lewis, *Till We Have Faces*, 174.
69. C. S. Lewis to Clyde S. Kilby, February 10, 1957, in W. H. Lewis, ed., *Letters of C. S. Lewis*, rev. and enl. ed, ed. Walter Hooper (San Diego: Harcourt, 1988), 462.
70. The phrase "anonymous Christians" was actually coined later, by Catholic theologian Karl Rahner in his *Theological Investigations*, vol. 6 (London: Darnton, Longman and Todd, 1969). Lewis acknowledges a similar view when he writes, for example, that, "the world does not consist of 100 per cent. Christians and 100 per cent. non-Christians. There are people (a great many of them) who are slowly ceasing to be Christians but who still call themselves by that name . . . There are people in other religions who are being led by God's secret influence to concentrate on those parts of their religion which are in agreement with Christianity, and who thus belong to Christ without knowing it" (*Mere Christianity*, 173).

something like becoming a missionary or entering a religious order. The others suffer a sense of outrage. What they love is being taken away from them! . . . Oh, come back come back, be sensible, be the dear son we used to know . . . And is the reply easy for a loving heart to bear?[71]

Some biographers think the character of Orual was partly based on Lewis's wife of later years, Joy Davidman, a brilliant woman who was physically very plain. Others, like Margaret Hannay, believe "there is more of Lewis than of Joy in Orual. Under his hearty exterior, he was a sensitive and gentle person, one who believed he had an ugly soul."[72] Still others, like Alan Jacobs, think that if any character reflects Lewis in the story, "it is not Orual, but rather Psyche [or Istra], whose love for the God of the Grey Mountain enrages Orual, even though, in Psyche's understanding, her love for her new husband will only strengthen and deepen her love for her family. Psyche is in a sense the church, but also every believer insofar as every believer is a member of the church."[73] In any event, the story is both very complex and very generically human in the struggles it depicts. The "expository demon" of Lewis's earlier fiction, which neatly lined up characters in terms of masculine and feminine stereotypes, has largely disappeared.

Moving Beyond Gender Stereotypes

In his 1960 book *The Four Loves*, Lewis at many points appears to accept the doctrine of separate spheres as a creational given. Yet at other points he freely acknowledges that it is a historical construction:

> In most societies at most periods Friendships will be between men and men or between women and women. The sexes will have met one another in Affection and in Eros but not in this love. For they will seldom have had with each other the companionship in common activities which is the matrix of Friendship. Where men are educated and women not, where one sex works and the other is idle, or where they do totally different work, they will usually have nothing to be friends about. But we can easily see that it is this lack, rather than anything in their natures, which excludes Friendship: for where they can be companions they can also become Friends. Hence in a profession (like my own) where men and women work side by side, or in the mission field, or among authors and artists, such Friendship is common . . . In one respect our own society is unfortunate . . . The necessary common ground, the matrix, exists

71. C. S. Lewis to Clyde S. Kilby, October 2, 1957, Hooper, ed., *Collected Letters*, vol. 3, 830–31.
72. Hannay, *C. S. Lewis*, 125.
73. Jacobs, *The Narnian*, 262.

between the sexes in some groups but not in others. It is notably lacking in many residential suburbs.[74]

It may be discomfiting to read Lewis's assertion that the defining feature of friendship is simply shared activity: it is just as likely to be about emotional support and self-disclosure, and this not exclusively among women.[75] And we may understandably wince at his suggestion that women who don't work for wages are necessarily "idle." In addition, Lewis seems happily to have endorsed the *status quo* of the English class system of his time, which allowed some women to develop alongside men and others not. Far from being uncomfortable with such class disparity, he stated that "the peculiar trouble of our own age is that men and women, haunted by rumors and glimpses of happier groups where no such chasm between the sexes exists, and bedeviled by the egalitarian idea that what is possible for some ought to be (and therefore is) possible to all, refuse to acquiesce in it."[76]

Nevertheless, Alan Jacobs points out, in *The Four Loves* Lewis takes a position "that many of his fellow dons and fellow traditional Christians would have strenuously objected to: he affirms the existence of real friendship between men and women . . . [He admits that] erotic complications can arise, of course, but they need not do so. And though Lewis does not say so in this context, he knew perfectly well that the same problems can arise in same-sex relationships."[77] The earlier C. S. Lewis, so often bound to notions of polarized gender stereotypes, has begun to equivocate.

This period also coincides with Lewis's work on *The Discarded Image*, an introduction to medieval and Renaissance literature based on a course he regularly gave at Oxford.[78] It is an engaging, detailed portrait of the medieval worldview, and one that clearly illustrates its hierarchical cosmology—but with one significant difference. In a book where one would expect Lewis, given his earlier writings, to include an exposition on gender hierarchy in the Aristotelian ladder of nature and in its descendant, the medieval "great chain of being," there is not a word on this topic. Indeed, his only explicit mention of gender relations is a leveling one, when he challenges the modern illusion that medieval persons of both sexes lived static lives. On the contrary, he

74. Lewis, *Four Loves*, 68–69.

75. For a review of the relevant empirical literature on men's and women's friendships, see, for example, Hilary M. Lips, *Sex and Gender: An Introduction*, 5th ed. (New York: McGraw Hill, 2005), chap. 11.

76. Lewis, *Four Loves*, 69. In the decade when Lewis began teaching at Oxford, only about 2 percent of young adults in the UK went to university. By contrast, 43 percent of UK secondary school graduates were going on to some form of tertiary education in 2003 (with a greater proportion of it state subsidized than in the US).

77. Jacobs, *The Narnian*, 256–57.

78. C. S. Lewis, *The Discarded Image: An Introduction to Medieval and Renaissance Literature* (Cambridge: Cambridge University Press, 1964).

writes, "Kings, armies, prelates, diplomats, merchants and wandering scholars were continually on the move. Thanks to the popularity of pilgrimages, even women, and women of the middle class, went far afield; witness [Chaucer's] Wife of Bath and Margery Kempe."[79] (Kempe was a fifteenth-century religious mystic who was also married and the mother of fourteen children.)

In writing *The Discarded Image* was Lewis simply compartmentalizing, as he was often said to do in both lectures and tutorials—that is, avoiding controversial views with his mostly secular students, views that he would continue to defend in writings for a more Christian audience? Or were his views on the immutability of gender hierarchy and gender essentialism undergoing a decisive shift? Since *The Discarded Image* was published only after his death (and he mentions it only in passing in his last letters), we may never know for sure. What is indisputable is that his indifference to the details of gender hierarchy in this analysis of the medieval worldview correlates with the softening of views on gender stereotypes in Lewis's other late writings.

Finally, there is Lewis's painful reflection on his wife's death, *A Grief Observed*, written when she died of cancer in 1960 after just four years of marriage, leaving Lewis the widowed stepfather of her two young sons. Like *Till We Have Faces* and *The Discarded Image*, it is one of his least-read books.[80] "There is," he wrote in that volume, "hidden or flaunted, a sword between the sexes till an entire marriage reconciles them."[81] The extent to which that reconciliation took place is so vividly recalled in this memoir that it is hard not to see Lewis's previous tendencies toward misogyny as a crude cover for the scars of an early-wounded, and in some ways insecure, man. In the first, most agonizing stage of his grief he writes:

79. Ibid., 143. On p. 59 Lewis also refers to Chalcidius's medieval exposition of Aristotle, "arguing that matter, though not inherently evil, being the potentiality of all particular bodies is doomed to . . . the privation of form. That is why matter craves her perfecting or embellishment as the female desires the male." However, it is not clear whether the last phrase of this sentence is simply part of Chalcidius's view or is endorsed by Lewis's own editorial comment.

80. As late as 1991 Lewis's biographer and literary executor, Walter Hooper, claimed that *A Grief Observed* was simply carefully constructed fiction, made to seem autobiographical in order to help the average man or woman who had lost a spouse. See Hooper's essay, "C. S. Lewis: The Man and His Thought," in Cynthia Marshall, ed., *Essays on C. S. Lewis and George MacDonald: Truth, Fiction and the Power of the Imagination* (Lewistown, NY: Edwin Mellen, 1991), 9–30. It is difficult to know how Hooper came to this conclusion since, a mere two months after Joy Davidman's death, Lewis was describing his grief process in letters in terms that are closely reflected in *A Grief Observed*. See, for example, his letter to Mary Willis Shelburne, September 24, 1960, in Hooper, ed., *Collected Letters*, vol. 3, and compare to *A Grief Observed* (London: Faber and Faber, 1961), 38, 41–42, and 47. Hooper reversed his claim in a 1996 book, *C. S. Lewis: A Companion and Guide* (London: HarperCollins, 1996), 194–201, apparently in part due to the protests of Douglas Gresham, Joy Davidman's son and Lewis's stepson. See also Douglas Gresham, *Lenten Lands* (New York: MacMillan, 1988), 130–31.

81. Lewis, *A Grief Observed*, 40.

The most precious gift that marriage gave me was this constant impact of something very close and intimate yet at the same time unmistakably other, resistant—in a word, real. Is all that work to be undone? Is what I shall still call [Joy] to sink back horribly into being not much more than one of my old bachelor pipe-dreams? Oh my dear, my dear, come back for a moment and drive that miserable phantom away. Oh God, God, why did you take such trouble to force this creature out of its shell if it is now doomed to crawl back—to be sucked back in?[82]

A few days later, he pictures his marriage in a pointedly nonhierarchical fashion, noting in the process that both his wife and his mother fell victim to deaths by cancer:

One flesh. Or, if you prefer, one ship. The starboard engine is gone. I, the port engine, must chug along somehow till we make harbor. Or rather, till the journey ends. How can I assume a harbor? A lee shore, more likely, a black night, a deafening gale, breakers ahead—and any lights shown from the land probably being waved by wreckers. Such was [Joy's] landfall. Such was my mother's. I say their landfalls, not their arrivals.[83]

As he struggles through his own grief and reflects further on what he has learned from his marriage, Lewis again reverses his earlier assumptions about gender hierarchy, as well as his view that women and men cannot normally be both friends and lovers:

A good wife contains so many persons in herself. What was [Joy] not to me? She was my daughter and my mother, my pupil and my teacher, my subject and my sovereign; and always, holding these all in solution, my trusty comrade, friend, shipmate, fellow soldier. My mistress, but at the same time all that any man friend (and I have had good ones) has ever been to me . . . Solomon calls his bride Sister. Could a woman be a complete wife unless, for a moment, in one particular mood, a man felt almost inclined to call her Brother?[84]

And finally in a pointed rejection of his earlier insistence that gender, as a spiritual ideal, is a more fundamental reality than biological sex, Lewis asserts:

82. Ibid., 18. Lewis originally published *A Grief Observed* under a pseudonym, and in it referred to his wife Joy simply as "H."—the initial of her first name, Helen. His publishers quickly recognized the book's actual authorship and after his death persuaded his literary trustees to have it reissued under his real name.

83. Ibid., 29. It is of interest that Lewis first considered publishing the book using the pen name *Dimidius*, which means "Halved"—a significant commentary on the meaning of "one flesh" (Gen. 2:24) in marriage.

84. Ibid., 39–40.

It is arrogance in us [men] to call frankness, fairness, and chivalry "masculine" when we see them in a woman; it is arrogance in them [women] to describe a man's sensitiveness or tact or tenderness as "feminine." But also what poor, warped fragments of humanity most mere men and mere women must be to make the implications of that arrogance plausible. Marriage heals this. Jointly the two become fully human. "In the image of God created He *them*." Thus, by a paradox, this carnival of sexuality leads us out beyond our sexes.[85]

Looking Ahead

In later chapters I will argue that Lewis was moving toward this late-life embrace of gender equality and gender role flexibility on largely experiential grounds, influenced by women colleagues and friends, by his interaction with female pupils and children, and by his marriage to Joy Davidman. In the meantime, how are we to account for his earlier views on gender, so strongly defended in most of his adult fiction, essays, and writings on Christian apologetics? What assumptions about Scripture and Christian tradition inform these writings, and especially what assumptions about creation, sin, and redemption, as these apply both to individual persons and to societal structures? I believe that as we explore the answers to such questions in the following chapters, we can continue to appreciate both the contributions and the limitations of Lewis's thinking.

85. Ibid., 40–41 (emphasis original).

3

"Mere" Christianity?

Sources and Results of Lewis's Views on Gender

In 1939, just after Germany invaded Poland and England was drawn into World War II, C. S. Lewis wrote the following to his Belfast friend Arthur Greeves:

> The next few years will be ghastly, but though my *nerves* are often staggered, my faith and reason are alright. I have no doubt that all this suffering will be for our ultimate good if we use it rightly . . . but I can't help wishing one could *hibernate* till it's all over! . . . As [Warnie] said in his last letter what makes it worse is the ghostly feeling that it has all happened before—that one fell asleep during the last war and had a delightful dream and has now waked up again.[1]

The "next few years" produced one of the most destructive conflicts in human history: over forty-six million soldiers and civilians died, many suffering prolonged agony in prisoner-of-war camps, jails, or concentration camps. Lewis's brother Warren ("Warnie"), a Sandhurst-trained army officer, was pulled out of retirement and sent to France, returning only after the evacuation of Dunkirk. Lewis himself, though exempted from active duty as a university

---

1. C. S. Lewis to Arthur Greeves, September 15, 1939, in Walter Hooper, ed., *The Collected Letters of C. S. Lewis*, vol. 2, *1931–1949* (San Francisco: HarperSanFrancisco, 2004), 274 (emphasis original).

don, joined the Home Guard and spent "one night in nine mooching about the most depressing and malodorous parts of Oxford with a rifle."[2]

The conflict continued to cast a long shadow over England in the form of post-war food rationing. Warren Lewis, faced with yet another reduction in the weekly potato ration a full two years after the war's end, wrote in his diary that "now the last 'filler' food disappears from the diet, and the days of real hunger come upon us. It's extraordinary how one is conditioned by a secure past: even now I can't grasp the fact that I, WHL, will go to bed hungry and get up hungry; these, I say, are things that happen to nations one reads about in the papers, not to me."[3]

C. S. Lewis was not a pacifist, and he explained why in a World War II lecture to an Oxford pacifist group. If one nation aggressively invades another, it may be the lesser of two evils to resist: in a still-fallen world we must sometimes make such tragic and difficult choices. Christ's injunction to "turn the other cheek,"[4] he believed, applied to individuals handling the frictions of daily life, not to the issue of government-led war, which is sanctioned, at least implicitly, in both the Gospels and the New Testament epistles. Moreover, while liberal-democratic nations commendably tolerate pacifists and craft legislation to protect them in living out their worldview (as, for example, the Amish are protected in America) this very protection is underwritten by the willingness of the majority to take up arms. Lewis argued that a huge increase in the number of pacifists, far from making war less likely, would risk crippling a nation by putting it at the mercy of a more aggressive neighbor.[5]

Be Careful What You Wish For

Even so, Lewis knew better than to romanticize conflict or to treat it ultimately as anything but a tragic consequence of human sin. As a young recruit in the trenches of World War I, he wrote to his friend Arthur Greeves that he had only his love of beauty to set against "the dominion of matter over us . . . out here, where I see spirit continually dodging matter (shells, bullets, animal

2. C. S. Lewis to Arthur Greeves, December 27, 1940, in the Supplement to Walter Hooper, ed., *The Collected Letters of C. S. Lewis*, vol. 3, *1950–1963* (San Francisco: HarperSanFranciso: 2007), 1538.

3. Clyde S. Kilby and Marjorie Lamp Mead, eds., *Brothers and Friends: The Diaries of Major Warren Hamilton Lewis* (San Francisco: HarperSanFranciso: 1982), 322 (diary entry from November 1947).

4. Matt. 5:39.

5. C. S. Lewis, "Why I Am Not a Pacifist," in Walter Hooper, ed., *The Weight of Glory and Other Essays*, expanded ed. (New York: HarperCollins: 2001), 64–90. The Amish example is my addition. On Lewis's respect for truly conscientious (as opposed to opportunistic) objectors to war, see his letter to his brother of February 11, 1940, Hooper, ed., *Collected Letters*, vol. 2, 343–47.

fears, animal pains)."[6] This turn to aesthetic idealism in the face of war's horrors was to become one step in Lewis's journey back to Christian faith.[7] Later, recovering from his own war wounds, he wrote to his father about the recurring battlefield nightmares he experienced.[8] "I could sit down and cry over the whole business," he confessed, when recalling that nearly all the friends in his battalion had perished.[9] Even as a mature Christian almost thirty years later, he would write to a Catholic Benedictine friend that, among other things, "the shadow of the last war and [the experience of the present one] have given me a very pessimistic view of existence."[10]

What, then, would Lewis have thought of a best-selling book, written some forty years after his death, claiming that Adam, the primal male, was essentially created for war and wild adventure outside of Eden, but had to suppress these traits when God put him in the garden to live with Eve? A book that defined male sin as a passive willingness to be domesticated—for example, as a husband, a tame priest, or (like Lewis) a tenured academic? That defined men's salvation in terms of recovering and acting on their God-ordained desire for "a battle to fight"—along with equally essential desires for "an adventure to live" and "a beauty to rescue"? A book, moreover, that frequently invoked C. S. Lewis's writings in support of its "biblical" vision of masculinity?

John Eldredge, in his 2001 book *Wild at Heart: Discovering the Secret of a Man's Soul*,[11] claimed, as Lewis did in his space trilogy, that gender is a more fundamental reality than sex.[12] Moreover, he asserted, our very souls are gendered: we do not image God as generic human beings, but only as metaphysically gendered men and women. For this reason, Eldredge added—with a distinct nod toward gnosticism—we need not look to science or social science for any clues about gender: the nature-nurture debate about the origins of behavioral sex differences is largely irrelevant if the answers are fundamentally

6. C. S. Lewis to Arthur Greeves, May 23, 1918, Walter Hooper, ed., *The Collected Letters of C. S. Lewis*, vol. 1, *1905–1931* (San Francisco: HarperSanFrancisco, 2004), 370–73.

7. Thus, in his preface to the third edition of *Pilgrim's Regress*, Lewis wrote that his own spiritual journey was "from 'popular realism' to Philosophical Idealism; from Idealism to Pantheism; from Pantheism to Theism; and from Theism to Christianity." C. S. Lewis, *The Pilgrim's Regress: An Allegorical Apology for Christianity, Reason and Romanticism* (London: Geoffrey Bles, 1933), 5.

8. C. S. Lewis to Albert Lewis, November 17, 1918, Hooper, ed., *Collected Letters*, vol. 1, 416–18.

9. C. S. Lewis to Albert Lewis, June 29, 1918, ibid., 387–89.

10. C. S. Lewis to Dom Bede Griffiths, OSB, December 20, 1946, Hooper, ed., *Collected Letters*, vol. 2, 746–48.

11. John Eldredge, *Wild at Heart: Discovering the Secret of a Man's Soul* (Nashville: Nelson, 2001). Despite (or perhaps because of) its theology, this book sold two million copies in the first few years after its release and received the Gold Medallion Award of the Evangelical Christian Publishers Association in 2002.

12. Ibid., 35. Other invocations of Lewis occur on pp. 19, 32, 37, 121, 128, 139, 159, and 216.

spiritual.[13] These ideas were developed further in the 2005 book *Captivating*, coauthored by Eldredge and his wife, and devoted, as the subtitle puts it, to "unveiling the mystery of a woman's soul."[14]

For the Eldredges, who are Christian counselors, there is an archetypal fit between men's and women's souls. Just as all men crave (or should crave) a battle to fight, an adventure to win, and a beauty to rescue, so all women long (or should long) to be swept up in a romance, to play an irreplaceable—though secondary—role in an adventure, and to be the beauty in a particular story. And just as man's sin can be understood as a failure to act in accordance with his wild soul, so woman's sin is a failure to recognize that she is the crown of God's creation, created to use her beauty to arouse and inspire others.[15] Indeed, in the Eldredges' exegesis of Genesis 3, Satan chose to tempt Eve rather than Adam because, as the formerly splendid Lucifer, he hated Eve's beauty with a special intensity. Adam's primal sin was that, unlike Ransom in Lewis's *Perelandra*, he failed to rescue Eve before she gave in.[16]

Regardless of their stand on the question of male headship in church and/or family, reviewers from a wide range of Christian traditions routinely panned these books. Because the authors support their case by appealing to adventure and romance stories and films more than anything else—including the Bible—several reviewers pointed out that popular culture does not provide an unambiguous portrait of our ideal selves.[17] Some criticized the way the Eldredges chose to do theology from the bottom up: using women's and men's experiences in order to evaluate God's purposes, rather than the reverse.[18] (Ironically, while disparaging systematic empirical research, they are quite happy to exploit the

13. Ibid., 8. Gnosticism, a movement with partially Platonic roots, was an early competitor with Christianity. It held that humans are essentially divine souls trapped in a material world created by an inferior deity, the "demiurge," alongside whom there was a superior supreme being who represents pure spiritual good. To free oneself from inferior, material embodiment, gnostics claimed, one must acquire a certain kind of esoteric or secret "wisdom"—sometimes identified with Jesus Christ, but available only to a select, "enlightened" few.

14. John and Stasi Eldredge, *Captivating: Unveiling the Mystery of a Woman's Soul* (Nashville: Nelson, 2005). This book ranked first on the Christian Booksellers Association website for several months after its publication and received that association's Book of the Year Award in 2006.

15. Ibid., chap. 10. Chapter 9 explains how literal sexual arousal helps wives to draw out their husbands' "masculine" souls. Chapters 7 and 8 explain, among other things, how to have a "spiritual" romance with God, meant to be especially comforting to women who have no husbands or have to put up with nasty ones. Indeed, the authors write, "the root of all holiness is Romance" (113).

16. Ibid., chaps. 3 and 5. Invocations of Lewis occur on pp. 20, 39, 53, 178, and 202.

17. For example, Jason Byassee, "Licensed to Thrill: Three Pop Theology Books to Leave Behind," *Sojourners Magazine*, December 2004, 32–33.

18. Donna Thoennes (2005), "Who's Captivating Whom?" https://www.cbmw.org/Journal/Vol-11-No-2/Who-s-Captivating-Whom-A-Review-of-John-and-Stasi-Eldredge-s-Captivating.

power of anecdote.) Others took issue with John Eldredge's watered-down view of sin—that for men, it amounts to the substitution of a false, timid self for the one meant for battle, adventure, and beauty[19]—and with his suggestion that aggressive conflict is built into creation, rather than being a tragic result of the fall.[20] And still other reviewers noted that single people of both sexes are left in a kind of limbo by the suggestion that humans are not whole until they have found their archetypal opposite.[21]

C. S. Lewis fervently wished that other Christians would try, as he did, to translate "theological college English" into the vernacular.[22] But with his robust view of God's holiness and humans' capacity for self-deception, he would not have welcomed a popular theology that accepts subjective experience as a starting point for understanding sin and redemption. Yet these books, and others like them that have become best sellers, have regularly invoked Lewis's writings to support their arguments.[23] To what extent is Lewis himself responsible for such slippage? What sources did he appeal to or ignore as he wrote about gender throughout his life? In the rest of this chapter I will address these questions by examining Lewis's use of Scripture, the Christian creeds, and theological tradition. We will see that the younger Lewis, eager to synthesize his beloved medieval "discarded image" with Christianity, flirted with the fourth-century Arian heresy—that is, the extension of a supposedly hierarchical "chain of being" to the Father, Son, and Spirit of the Trinity. In later years, Lewis rejected this position, even as he became progressively less concerned to defend his earlier vision of gender archetypes and gender hierarchy. But to set the stage for this discussion, readers first need to understand Lewis's view of revelation.

19. Brynn Camery-Hoggat and Nealson Munn, "*Wild at Heart*: Essential Reading or 'Junk Food of the Soul'?" *Priscilla Papers* 19, no. 4 (Autumn 2005): 24–26.

20. Mark Mulder and James K. Smith, "Are Men Really Wild at Heart?" *Perspectives: A Journal of Reformed Thought* 19, no. 8 (2004): 18–22.

21. Byron Borger, "John Eldredge's *Wild at Heart*: A Critique" (Pittsburgh: Coalition for Christian Outreach, June 2002), http://www.heartsandmindsbooks.com/reviews/john_eldredges_wild_at_heart_a/.

22. Letter to John Beddow of the Christian Workers' Union, October 7, 1945, Hooper, ed., *Collected Letters*, vol. 2, 673–75. Here Lewis declined a request to write a book for factory workers: "I know nothing at all of the realities of factory life . . . It is inconceivable that there is no one among you who can do this quite as well as I could . . . So my advice is that you get on with it at once . . . People praise me as a 'translator', but what I want is to be the founder of a school of 'translation'. I am nearly forty-seven. Where are my successors?"

23. For example, Elisabeth Elliott, *Let Me Be A Woman* (Wheaton: Tyndale, 1982), and also "The Essence of Femininity" in John Piper and Wayne Grudem, eds., *Recovering Biblical Manhood and Womanhood: A Response to Evangelical Feminism* (Wheaton: Crossway, 1991), 394–99; Leanne Payne, *Crisis in Masculinity* (Westchester, IL: Crossway, 1985); Stu Webber, *Tender Warrior: Every Man's Purpose, Every Woman's Dream, Every Child's Hope* (Sisters, OR: Multnomah, 1993).

C. S. Lewis's View of Revelation

Lewis's understanding of revelation in general, and of God's revelation in Scripture, was complex and cannot be simply understood in either conservative or liberal theological terms. On the one hand, he clearly believed not only that all the writers of the Bible (which he repeatedly calls "Holy Scripture") were inspired by God, but that God's inspiration extended to the editing, preservation, and canonical organization of both testaments.[24] On the other hand, his training as a classics scholar and literary critic led him to propose that there were greater and lesser degrees of inspiration both in Scripture and outside it. Indeed, toward the end of his life he wrote that "if every good and perfect gift comes from the Father of lights, then all true and edifying writings, whether in Scripture or not, must be in some sense inspired."[25]

Lewis's conviction that all truth is God's truth, even when those uncovering it fail to acknowledge the God to whom they are beholden, is widely shared by Christian scholars. But in the wake of human finitude and fallenness, how do we know when truth is being uncovered? How, for example, are we to separate wheat from chaff in the history of religion? For Lewis, as for many Anglican scholars of his time, God's revelation was historically progressive. Even primitive humans' vague sense of the numinous, or awe-inspiring, contained at least a faint apprehension of the one true God, Lewis thought.[26] Then, as various religions developed a common sense that there was some kind of universal moral law that humans routinely break, God was revealed further.[27] God was understood even more when the Jews discerned that the source of this moral law was the numinous and infinite, yet personal, Creator of the universe. However, Lewis wrote in his earliest apologetic work, "even on Paganism and Pantheism morality is always breaking in, and even Stoicism finds itself willy-nilly bowing the knee to God":

> It may be madness—a madness congenital to man, and oddly fortunate in its results—or it may be revelation. And if revelation, then it is most really and truly in Abraham that all peoples shall be blessed, for it was the Jews who fully and unambiguously identified the awful Presence haunting black mountaintops and thunderclouds with "the *righteous* Lord" who "loveth righteousness" [Ps. 11:8].[28]

24. C. S. Lewis, *Reflections on the Psalms* (London: Geoffrey Bles, 1958), chap. 11.

25. C. S. Lewis to Clyde S. Kilby, May 7, 1959, Hooper, ed., *Collected Letters*, vol. 3, 1045.

26. Here Lewis draws explicitly on Rudolf Otto's well-known work, *The Idea of the Holy* (London: Oxford University Press, 1923).

27. Lewis was firmly convinced that there are fewer differences among the major religions in their understanding of the moral law than might at first seem to be the case. See, for example, *Mere Christianity*, book I, and *The Abolition of Man*, chaps. 1 and 2.

28. C. S. Lewis, *The Problem of Pain* (London: Geoffrey Bles, 1940; London: Collins, 1972), 11 (emphasis original). Page references are to the Collins edition.

The final stage of revelation occurred when God took on human flesh, when the Law and the Prophets and the Jewish system of sacrifice for sin culminated in the life, death, and resurrection of Jesus Christ. "Only a bad person needs to repent: only a good person can repent perfectly," Lewis wrote in *Mere Christianity*. "But . . . suppose our human nature which can suffer and die was amalgamated with God's nature in one person—then that person could help us. He could surrender His will, and suffer and die, because He was man; and He could do it perfectly because He was God."[29] Thereafter, Christ's body on earth, in the form of the church, spreads by what Lewis likened to a kind of "good infection."[30] Those united to him "catch" his living Spirit, which works steadily with whatever raw material they have brought to him, until they are fully transformed into Christ's image after death or (in another Lewisian metaphor) until history ends, "the author walks onto the stage, [and] the play is over."[31]

If one accepts this theory of progressive revelation, it follows that even within the biblical texts, there are different degrees and types of inspiration. For Lewis, Christ's teachings held the most authority, followed by those of his apostles and the earlier prophets whose writings point to him.[32] Other Hebrew Scriptures — chronicles, poetry, stories, wisdom literature—carry God's word in different ways, and need not always be literally (i.e., historically or "scientifically") true to convey what God wanted them to. Thus, for Lewis, the book of Job conveys truths about God's sovereignty whether or not Job actually existed; the book of Jonah conveys truth about God's desire to save all people even if its eponymous antihero never actually spent three days in a whale's belly.

Furthermore, if mythic stories can function this way in the Hebrew Scriptures, they can function in similar if less focused ways in other mythic traditions: as ways that bits of God's truth "gets through." The last chapter noted how Lewis developed this idea when he adapted the Cupid and Psyche myth in *Till We Have Faces*. He also did so earlier, in *The Pilgrim's Regress*, an allegorical tale written shortly after he became a Christian.[33] In addition,

29. C. S. Lewis, *Mere Christianity* (London: Collins, 1952), 56–57.

30. Ibid., book IV, chap. 4.

31. Ibid., 63.

32. C. S. Lewis, *Miracles* (New York: MacMillan, 1960), 133–34. In his 1959 essay, "Modern Theology and Biblical Criticism," Lewis concluded that the gospel accounts of Jesus (not excluding the recorded miracles) are basically historical, and that the Bultmannian attempt to eliminate mythical, unhistorical elements is misguided, as it has no criteria for separating the historical from the unhistorical: the Gospel texts we have are the texts we have. But he accepted much critical scholarship of the Bible as being valuable and, speaking for his original audience of Anglican theological students, he asserted "We are not fundamentalists." Reprinted in Walter Hooper, ed., *Christian Reflections* (Grand Rapids: Eerdmans, 1967), 152–66 (quotation from p. 163).

33. Lewis, *Pilgrim's Regress*. See also his 1944 essay "Myth Became Fact," reprinted in Walter Hooper, ed., *God in the Dock: Essays On Theology and Ethics* (Grand Rapids: Eerdmans, 1970), 63–67.

Lewis's conversion owed much to a midnight conversation in 1931 with two Christian colleagues, Hugo Dyson and J. R. R. Tolkien, who explained to the skeptical young don that Christ should be thought of in terms of a unique "myth became fact." In a letter written shortly after this conversation, Lewis expressed it as follows:

> Now what Dyson and Tolkien showed me was this . . . The story of Christ is simply a true myth: a myth working on us in the same way as the others, but with this tremendous difference that *it really happened*: and one must be content to accept it in the same way, remembering that it is God's myth where the others are men's myths: i.e., the Pagan stories are God expressing Himself through the minds of poets, using such images as He found there, while Christianity is God expressing Himself through what we call "real things."[34]

Lewis's Use of Scripture

How then did Lewis appeal to various levels of inspiration in Scripture to advance his ideas about gender? In the last chapter we saw how he adapted the biblical account of humankind's creation and fall to paint an archetypal and hierarchical view of gender, especially in *Perelandra* and *That Hideous Strength*, the second and third volumes of his romantic space trilogy. Yet in 1949, just after completing that trilogy, he warned an American correspondent "not [to] confuse my romances with my theses. In the latter I state and argue a creed. In the former much is merely supposed for the sake of the story."[35] And to the same correspondent, in response to a question posed a few months later, he asserted that "there's no question of 'seeking a positive gospel' for modern man: only of seeking how to make him understand the existing and immutable gospel."[36]

In these letters Lewis was being consistent with his view of revelation as progressive: myths and stories (including his own) may contain glimmers of God's truth, but Scripture clearly points toward and is fulfilled in Christ, whose teachings reveal God's purposes most authoritatively. For Lewis all this is summarized, again under God's guidance, in the creeds of the early church. Thus, if immutable gender archetypes and gender hierarchy are part of "mere" Christianity, we would expect Lewis to make his case for them first and foremost from the Gospels, then from other Christian Scriptures, then from the creeds and church tradition and—finally and least certainly—from other sources.

34. C. S. Lewis to Arthur Greeves, October 18, 1931, Hooper, ed., *Collected Letters*, vol. 1, 976–77 (emphasis original).

35. C. S. Lewis to Edward T. Dell, April 2, 1959, Hooper, ed., *Collected Letters*, vol. 2, 914.

36. C. S. Lewis to Edward T. Dell, October 25, 1949, ibid., 989.

The Gospels: However, Lewis made no appeal to the Gospels to defend his theory of gender archetypes and gender hierarchy, for the simple reason that there is nothing clearly there to draw on. He did have something to say about Christ's affirmation of the "one flesh" permanence of marriage, and his rejection of easy divorce.[37] But an analysis of his other writings seems to yield only one other citation of a gospel text in relation to gender—one that, if anything, undermines traditional stereotypes. In a 1945 letter to an American who was considering becoming a Roman Catholic, Lewis wrote that, while he endorsed the Catholic church's suspicion of modernism, he rejected its theology of the Blessed Virgin Mary: "I reject it because it seems utterly foreign to the New Testament: where indeed the words 'Blessed is the womb that bore thee' receive a rejoinder pointing in exactly the opposite direction."[38] The reference here is to Luke 11:27–28, where an anonymous woman in an adoring crowd cries out to Jesus "Blessed is the womb that bore you, and the breasts that nursed you!" Jesus' sharp rejoinder to the woman is: "Blessed rather are those who hear the word of God and obey it."

Of course there is no evidence in the Gospels that Jesus disparaged family relations, especially given his stance on the permanence of marriage. He affirmed the created sociability of humans in the illustrations from family and village life that appear in his parables. He also affirmed parenthood as an important calling for both men and women. But he did not permit such roles to become "first things"—that is, to take idolatrous precedence over the wider goals of God's kingdom. Nor did he ever suggest, as Lewis did in *Mere Christianity*, that wives and mothers are more irrationally protective of their family and thus will not show as much justice to outsiders as husbands and fathers.[39] We must therefore descend further on Lewis's hierarchy of inspiration to understand how he supported the view of gender relations he held for much of his life.

The Book of Acts: For Lewis, the acts and teachings of Christ's apostles ranked a close second to the authority of Jesus himself. And indeed, he made at least two appeals to the New Testament book of Acts in his defense of gender archetypes and gender hierarchy. The first affirms Lewis's view that some social arrangements may be tolerated as a result of the fall, but are not thereby to be considered normative. In his 1954 volume on *English Literature in the Sixteenth Century*, Lewis devoted a chapter to Reformation-era Bible translation and the controversies amid which it took place. In it he noted that Protestant Reformers like John Knox believed "that the rule of women 'was a deviation from the original and proper order of nature' and 'to be

37. Matt. 19:3–9; Mark 10:2–9 (cf. Gen. 2:24), discussed in *Mere Christianity*, book III, chaps. 5–6.
38. C. S. Lewis to H. Lyman Stebbins, May 8, 1945, in Hooper, ed., *Collected Letters*, vol. 2, 646.
39. Lewis, *Mere Christianity*, book II, chap. 6.

ranked, no less than slavery, among the punishments of the fall of man.'"[40] Nevertheless, Knox conceded that history and custom have combined to set occasional female monarchs on thrones, and in the interests of public tranquility this should not be challenged. Knox pointed out that when the apostle Philip converted the Ethiopian eunuch to Christianity, he did not then tell him to try to depose Candace, the Ethiopian queen in whose household he served.[41] Lewis remarked that England's Queen Elizabeth I would have regarded Knox's argument as a case of damning her with faint praise, since "no woman likes to have her social position defended as one of the inevitable results of the fall."[42]

There is nothing in Scripture that points to such a conclusion, but it appears to have been one that Lewis favored, at least through the mid-1950s. For example, in the first chapter of his autobiography *Surprised by Joy* (published a year after *English Literature in the Sixteenth Century*) Lewis referred to his childhood fear of insects. Then he remarked: "You may add that in the hive and the ant-hill we see fully realized the two things that some of us most dread for our own species—the dominance of the female and the dominance of the collective."[43] This comment is important for two reasons, the first rhetorical and the second substantive. First, by placing it in the first few pages of a book meant to portray the call to Christian life as a "joyful" one, Lewis in a single phrase has risked alienating at least half his readership, and that with a comment quite irrelevant to the autobiographical point he was sharing.

Second, as I noted in the previous chapter, Lewis was strongly inclined to view almost all human institutions, or "collectives," as rooted not in creation, but in the fall: they are "medicine, not food," as he put it in his 1940s essay "Membership."[44] And with admirable—or questionable—consistency, he even included his own life's work as a university scholar in this judgment. Thus, in his 1939 essay "Christianity and Literature" he wrote that the Christian "has no objection to comedies that merely amuse and tales that merely refresh . . . We can play, as we can eat, to the glory of God . . . But the Christian knows from the outset that the salvation of a single soul is more important than the production or preservation of all the epics and tragedies in the world."[45]

40. C. S. Lewis, *English Literature in the Sixteenth Century, Excluding Drama* (Oxford: Clarendon Press, 1954), 199. The internal quotation is from John Knox's 1558 treatise, *The First Blast of the Trumpet against the Monstrous Regiment of Women*.

41. Acts 8:26–40.

42. Lewis, *English Literature*, 199–200.

43. C. S. Lewis, *Surprised by Joy: The Shape of My Early Life* (London: Collins, 1959), 13.

44. C. S. Lewis, "Membership," reprinted in *The Weight of Glory and Other Addresses* (Grand Rapids: Eerdmans, 1965), 37.

45. "Christianity and Literature" originally appeared in Lewis's volume *Rehabilitations and Other Essays* (London: Oxford University Press, 1939), and is reprinted in Walter Hooper, ed., *Christian Reflections* (Grand Rapids: Eerdmans, 1967), 1–11 (quotation from p. 10).

I have already noted my adherence to a theological tradition that takes issue with Lewis's view, more Platonic than biblical, that the activities and things of this life are at most shadows or siren calls meant to beckon us toward the more "solid" and eternal realities of heaven. But even if one agreed with Lewis on this point, why single out "the dominance of the female" as an especially offensive feature of the "collectives" of a fallen world?[46] It is a bit like acknowledging that Adam's toil in cultivation and Eve's in childbirth are both consequences of the fall, then adding that Eve's burden means childbearing women should do without anesthetics and forceps, while Adam's struggle with thorns and thistles in no way forbids the use of fertilizers and pesticides.

Lewis's other appeal to the book of Acts was more direct, but unfortunately less accurate. In his 1948 essay arguing against the ordination of women in the Anglican church, he stated that Jesus' mother "was absent from the descent of the Spirit at Pentecost."[47] He took this as evidence (along with Jesus' embodiment as a male) that the feminine cannot operate on the same plane as the masculine, either on earth or in heaven. But in fact, Acts 1:14 speaks of all Jesus' disciples, "together with . . . Mary the mother of Jesus," devoting themselves to prayer in an upper room in Jerusalem just prior to Pentecost. Moreover, when the Holy Spirit descended at Pentecost, the apostle Peter is recorded as affirming that this was a fulfillment of Joel's prophecy, in which God promised to pour out his spirit on "sons and daughters . . . menservants and maidservants."[48] It is hard to conclude that Peter would have invoked this very specific comparison if there had not been women (including Christ's mother) at Pentecost along with men. And the account of Pentecost, far from being a text that excludes women from leadership, is one of several that has been taken as pointing toward their inclusion.

The Pauline Epistles: In the last chapter I cited Lewis's use of Paul's words in Ephesians 5 to support his view that while husbandly headship is God's intention, it should be characterized not by heavy-handedness, but by self-sacrifice. That brief bit of exegesis occurred in his 1960 volume, *The Four Loves.*[49] But a more detailed appeal to the Pauline epistles appeared in the 1939 essay, "Christianity and Literature," originally presented to an Oxford student Christian group just a few years after Lewis's own conversion. His chief point in that essay was that while Christians must aspire to high literary

---

46. Elsewhere Lewis did use the very same insect analogy to show that he regarded government as being a necessary result of the fall, but less "real" than the life of the church. Thus in 1948 he wrote: "As the State grows more like a hive or an ant-hill it needs an increasing number of workers who can be treated as neuters. This may be inevitable for our secular life. But in our Christian life we must return to reality. There we are not homogeneous units, but different and complementary organs of a mystical body." C. S. Lewis, "Priestesses in the Church?" reprinted in Hooper, ed., *God in the Dock*, 238.

47. Ibid., 236.

48. Joel 2:28–29; cf. Acts 2:14–20 (RSV).

49. C. S. Lewis, *The Four Loves* (London: Collins, 1963), 97–98.

standards, they should not fall into the idolatrous trap of valuing originality for its own sake or seeing themselves as creating (like God) "out of nothing." Instead they should simply try to express what is true and beautiful as humble stewards of God's gifts. But in the process of making that very good point, Lewis advanced some significant suggestions (and he was careful to say they were only that) not only about hierarchy between men and women, but also within the Trinity. He began with this qualifier:

> As a layman and a comparatively recently reclaimed apostate I have, of course, no intention of building a theological system—still less of setting up a [string] of New Testament metaphors as a criticism on the Nicene or the Athanasian creed, documents which I wholly accept. But it is legitimate to notice what kinds of metaphor the New Testament uses; more especially when what we are in search of is not dogma but a kind of flavor or atmosphere.[50]

The kind of biblical metaphor that interested Lewis here is what he called a "proportion sum," formally expressed as "A is to B as B is to C." Thus, in 1 Corinthians 11:3 the apostle Paul writes that the head of a woman is her husband, just as the head of every man is Christ and the head of Christ is God; a few verses later he writes that man is the image and glory of God, just as woman is man's glory. That this suggests some kind of hierarchy, not just in gender relations but even among the members of the Trinity, Lewis believed, was shown by Jesus' proclamation that "the Son can do nothing on his own but only what he sees the Father doing."[51] Thus, Lewis suggested, there is

> a fairly Pauline picture of [a] whole series of Head relations running from God to woman . . . And I suppose that of which one is the image and glory is that which one glorifies by copying or imitating . . . And it seems to me a quite clear picture; we are to think of some original divine virtue passing downwards from rung to rung of a hierarchical ladder, and the mode in which each lower rung receives it is, quite frankly, imitation. What is perhaps most startling in this picture is the apparent equivalence of the woman-man and man-God relations with the relation between Christ and God, or, in Trinitarian language, with the relation between the First and Second Persons of the Trinity.[52]

Over a decade later, in *Mere Christianity*, he used similar language in his description of Trinitarian relations. The relation between human fathers and sons, he wrote, "is more like the relation between the First and Second Persons [of the Trinity] than anything else we can think of . . . The Father delights in His Son; the Son looks up to His Father."[53]

50. Lewis, "Christianity and Literature," 5.
51. John 5:19.
52. Lewis, "Christianity and Literature," 4, 5.
53. C. S. Lewis, *Mere Christianity*, rev. ed. (London: Collins, 1955), 147.

Lewis's Use of the Church Creeds and Christian Tradition

Lewis's inclination, as a young Christian, was thus to infer from Paul's letters a hierarchical relationship between men and women, then to extend the "ladder" metaphor to relations between God and Christ. This points to the continuing influence of Aristotle, whose "ladder of nature" portrayed all of organic life as imbued with "soul" (*psyche* or *anima*) but in ascending degrees of complexity: plants having the least, animals somewhat more, humans (especially freeborn males) even more with the addition of rationality, and the supremely rational, heavenly "unmoved Mover" having the highest soul of all. In his 1942 treatise on Milton's *Paradise Lost*, Lewis noted that this conception of the universe dominated Western thought from Aristotle's to Milton's time.[54] With God at the top of a great ladder or chain of being, and unformed matter at the bottom, every entity had a natural station that entailed obeying those above and ruling over those below. And Milton pictures God the Father and God the Son in the same hierarchical relationship that Lewis later suggested in his lecture on Christianity and literature.[55]

According to this worldview, much harm results from not embracing one's appointed station. Thus, in Lewis's analysis of Milton's epic poem, Lucifer sinned by rebelling against his natural superiors, God and the higher heavenly hosts. Conversely, Adam sinned by being too accommodating of his wife and failing to rule over her as her natural (male) superior. In three famous lines about the primal couple before their fall, Milton summarizes both his archetypal and hierarchical view of gender relations:

> For contemplation he and valor formed,
> For softness she and sweet attractive grace;
> He for God only, she for God in him [56]

We saw in our earlier consideration of *Perelandra* and *That Hideous Strength* that Lewis, through midlife, was very much attracted to this worldview.[57] But he professed an even higher allegiance to the confessions of the church, formulated in the first few centuries of its existence: the Apostles', Nicene, and Athanasian Creeds.[58] And these documents, like the Gospels, have nothing to say about hierarchy in gender relations. The first two are concerned to

54. C. S. Lewis, *A Preface to Paradise Lost* (London: Oxford University Press, 1942), chap. 11.

55. Ibid., 79. See also Milton, *Paradise Lost*, VI (New York: The Heritage Press, 1940), 719 and 746.

56. Milton, *Paradise Lost*, IV, 296–98.

57. See also his 1940 essay, "The Necessity of Chivalry," reprinted in C. S. Lewis, *Present Concerns*, edited by Walter Hooper (San Diego: Harvest, 1987), 13–16.

58. Although the early church father Athanasius lived between AD 296 and 373, the so-called Athanasian Creed was composed sometime after AD 450. It might better be called the

summarize doctrinal "first things": the Bible's overall teachings on creation, sin, and redemption, and their significance for all of humankind and human history. All three, in progressively more detail, develop the doctrine of the Trinity: God the Father, Son, and Holy Spirit. Indeed, the second and third of these documents were both specifically aimed at combating the Arian heresy. Arius, an early fourth century theologian in Alexandria, taught that Christ was not eternal, and that he was subordinate to God the Father not only functionally, when he became human (this was already accepted as clear teaching of Scripture) but in his very being or substance.[59]

Abstract philosophizing about God's being was of less interest to the writers of the Bible than understanding what God was like and what God did in terms of mighty acts in the cosmic drama of creation and redemption. But it was of great concern to the followers of Arius who, like Lewis, were much influenced by Greek philosophy. As Anglican New Testament scholar Kevin Giles explains, "Beginning with a Greek understanding of God as pure spirit [the Arians] concluded that God could not enter this material world and take on human flesh. The Son must be therefore a subordinate god, of *different being or substance* from the Father."[60] Athanasius, the fourth-century theologian after whom the Athanasian Creed was named, realized that the issue couldn't be decided merely by lining up proof-texts (plenty of that had already been done by both sides in the debate). To answer any question not dealt with in detail by the Bible, one had to determine what was primary or foundational in Scripture concerning that question, then work out the implications in dialogue with other theologians—that is, try to discern where Scripture was *pointing*. And there is little doubt that Lewis largely agreed with this method of linking Scripture to doctrine. In one of his last popular theological books, he rejected (not for the first time) simple proof-texting as a way of understanding Scriptural teaching. Concerning the Bible's "raw materials" he wrote that

> the total result is not "the Word of God" in the sense that every passage, in itself, gives impeccable science or history. It carries the Word of God; and we (under grace, with attention to tradition and to interpreters wiser than ourselves, and with the use of such intelligence and learning as we may have) receive that word from it not by using it as an encyclopedia or an encyclical but by steeping ourselves in its tone or temper and so learning its over-all message.[61]

"Augustinian Creed," because it reflects St. Augustine's teaching on the Trinity (Kevin Giles, Personal Communication, December 2007).

59. For a detailed discussion of these debates in the context of contemporary theology, see Kevin Giles, *The Trinity and Subordinationism: The Doctrine of God and the Contemporary Gender Debate* (Downers Grove, IL: InterVarsity, 2002); and *Jesus and the Father: Modern Evangelicals Reinvent the Doctrine of the Trinity* (Grand Rapids: Zondervan, 2006).

60. Giles, *The Trinity and Subordinationism*, 4 (emphasis original).

61. Lewis, *Reflections*, 94.

Using this same method to clarify the nature and status of the persons within the Trinity, the early church took a clear, anti-Arian stand. Thus the Athanasian Creed states: "We worship one God in Trinity and Trinity in Unity; neither confounding the persons nor dividing their substance . . . the Godhead of the Father, of the Son, and of the Holy Spirit is all one; the glory equal, the majesty coeternal . . . the Father is almighty, the Son almighty, and the Holy Spirit almighty . . . none is greater or less than another." Regarding the humanity and deity of Christ, the creed is equally explicit: Jesus is "perfect God and perfect man . . . equal to the Father as touching His Godhead, and inferior to the Father as touching his manhood . . . He is God and man . . . one, not by conversion of the Godhead into flesh, but by taking of that manhood into God." In other words, in his essential *being* Jesus is to be seen as equal to God in eternity; only in his incarnate *function* or role as Savior was he temporarily—and voluntarily—less than God. As Paul summarized it in the great hymn of Philippians 2,

> Have this mind among yourselves, which is yours in Christ Jesus, who, though he was in the form of God, did not count equality with God a thing to be grasped, but emptied himself, taking the form of a servant, being born in the likeness of men. And being found in human form he humbled himself and became obedient unto death, even death on a cross. Therefore God has highly exalted him and bestowed on him the name which is above every name, that at the name of Jesus every knee should bow, in heaven and on earth and under the earth, and every tongue confess that Jesus Christ is Lord, to the glory of God the Father.[62]

Eastern and Western Christian Creeds, from the Council of Nicaea to the Protestant Reformation and beyond, have concluded that the Bible's basic message is that the Father, Son, and Holy Spirit are one in being and power.[63] Lewis was certainly familiar with these historical documents. Yet at least through midlife, he apparently preferred to understand the relationship between God and Christ as *essentially*—not just functionally—hierarchical. In 1941 he wrote frankly about this to his Benedictine friend and former student, Dom Bede Griffiths, while preparing the radio talks that were the basis of his book *Mere Christianity*: "About the Son being subject to the Father (as God—of course [He is] obviously subject as Man in the Incarnation)—yes, that's what I think: but was recently contradicted by a theologian. Can you back me up? What is

62. Phil. 2:5–11 (RSV).
63. This stance is also reflected in the Thirty-Nine Articles of the Anglican Church, to which Lewis also professed adherence. Milton's own Arian leanings can be seen not only in *Paradise Lost*, but in his *De Doctrina Christiana*, both of which were written shortly after the mid-seventeenth century.

the correct interpretation of 'equal to His Father as touching His Godhead' in the Athanasian Creed?"[64]

We do not know how Griffiths replied, but it is safe to guess that, as a Roman Catholic, he did not support Lewis. As Kevin Giles notes in *The Trinity and Subordinationism*, Catholics have consistently held that the theological tradition supports a nonhierarchical understanding of the Father, Son, and Holy Spirit.[65] Indeed, it is hard to see how the younger Lewis could have read the entire Athanasian Creed and thought he could conclude otherwise; yet apparently he did just that.[66] And his linking of hierarchy between God and Christ to hierarchy between men and women has continuing results that we need to explore further.

Some Continuing Consequences

In the late 1980s in America, two evangelical organizations were formed with quite different agendas, captured in quite different names: "The Council on Biblical Manhood and Womanhood" (CBMW) and "Christians for Biblical Equality" (CBE). Each group issued statements about gender relations that it claimed were based on a high view and a close reading of the Bible, but the two groups came to very different conclusions. CBMW deplored "the increasing promotion given to feminist egalitarianism" and asserted that "Adam's headship in marriage was established by God before the fall, and was not a result of sin." Although affirming that "both Adam and Eve were created in God's image, equal before God as persons," and that "in the church, redemption in Christ gives men and women an equal share in the blessings of salvation," the Council's founders went on to say that "nevertheless, some governing and teaching roles within the church are restricted to men."[67]

The founding statement of CBE was very different. In its reading of the Bible, men and women were created for full and equal partnership. Further, Adam's rule over Eve occurred only as a result of the fall, and "through faith in Jesus Christ we all become children of God . . . heirs to the blessings of salvation without reference to race, social or gender distinctives." Thus in

64. C. S. Lewis to Dom Bede Griffiths, December 11, 1941, Hooper, ed., *Collected Letters*, vol. 2, 503.

65. Giles, *Trinity and Subordinationism*, chaps. 1 and 4.

66. In fact, in "Christianity and Literature" (p. 6) he wrote that his "picture" of hierarchy between God the Father and God the Son "does not seem to me to conflict with anything I have learned from the Creeds, but greatly to enrich my conception of Divine sonship." Yet on p. 5, Lewis pulls his punches somewhat, stating that it is "only from certain points of view, and in certain respects" that "we are encouraged . . . to regard the Second Person Himself as a step, or stage, or degree." But he does not explain this qualifier at all.

67. "The Danvers Statement" (1989), www.cbmw.org. See also Piper and Grudem, eds., *Recovering Biblical Manhood and Womanhood*.

marriage "neither spouse is to seek to dominate the other, but each is to act as servant of the other . . . [sharing] responsibilities of leadership on the basis of gifts, expertise and availability." And in the church, "spiritual gifts of women and men are to be recognized, developed and used . . . at all levels of involvement."[68]

In line with Christians from Athanasius to C. S. Lewis, each group acknowledges that both Scripture and Christian tradition must be studied to shed light on contemporary ethical questions. The gender hierarchicalists of CBMW claim that both Scripture *and* tradition support a hierarchical view of both trinitarian *and* gender relations: they argue that women are subordinate to men in the same way that Christ is subordinate to God. Unlike the younger Lewis, however, they are less apt to appeal to Aristotle and Milton and more likely to borrow the language of sociology to make their point.

Their argument goes as follows: it is possible for two people to be "equal" while at the same time differing in functional roles and authority. For example, a police constable and a police sergeant are personal equals—indeed, they have equal power to make arrests. Still (the argument goes) the sergeant has more authority than the constable, whose role is more restricted. So too with the relation of God to Christ, the argument continues: they are equal as divine *persons*, but Christ is submissive to God in terms of his *role*—not just historically during his incarnation, but eternally. And, the argument concludes, the same is true of men and women in marriage and the church. The "blessings of salvation" are equally available to both as *persons* equally made in God's image and redeemed by Christ. But their *roles* in marriage and church necessarily and permanently differ: women are to submit to men in a way that is not reciprocated. Women are "equal in essence but eternally subordinate in role."[69]

68. "Men, Women and Biblical Equality" (1989), www.cbeinternational.org. See also Ronald W. Pierce, Rebecca Merrill Groothuis, and Gordon D. Fee, eds, *Discovering Biblical Equality: Complementarity Without Hierarchy* (Downers Grove, IL: InterVarsity, 2004). For an account of similar disputes between Evangelical gender hierarchicalists and gender egalitarians in Australia, see Giles, *Trinity and Subordinationism*, chap. 3 and Appendix A. See also David Blankenhorn, Don Browning, and Mary Stewart Van Leeuwen, eds., *Does Christianity Teach Male Headship? The Equal-Regard Family and Its Critics* (Grand Rapids: Eerdmans, 2004).

69. Wayne Grudem, *Systematic Theology: An Introduction to Biblical Doctrine* (Grand Rapids: Zondervan, 1994), 251; see also 455–68. Kevin Giles rightly notes that it is impossible to declare women both "equal in essence" and "eternally subordinate in role," since if someone can never be equal in function, then it must be because they lack some essential quality. Analogies like that of the police constable in relation to the police sergeant are thus inappropriate, since any given constable may in principle become a sergeant, given the requisite talents and experience; and any given sergeant can be demoted to the status of constable, given the requisite incompetence. For contemporary gender hierarchicalists, however, there are no conditions under which women's and men's authority functions could be equal or interchangeable, either in marriage or in the church. The language of being "equal in essence but subordinate in roles"

Those advancing this argument know, as Lewis did, that this is not a confessional issue—that is, one that can be used as a litmus test for deciding who is or is not a Christian. They recognize the absence of any explicit statements about gender in any of the historic church confessions, Catholic or Protestant. Indeed, the Council on Biblical Manhood and Womanhood labeled its founding statement a list of "affirmations"—not "confessions"—and was careful to recognize "the genuine evangelical standing of many who do not agree with all our convictions."[70] Still, its architects insist, both types of hierarchy (divine and human) represent not only the trajectory of Scriptural teaching, but also what mainstream Christian tradition has always taught. To believe otherwise, as Lewis wrote when he argued in 1948 against the ordination of women, would be, if not quite heretical, at least "to cut ourselves off from the Christian past . . . [and show] an almost wanton degree of impudence."[71] Moreover, a visit to the CBMW website shows that Lewis's writings are not infrequently quoted in support of this position.

But is this chain of command from God to Christ to man to woman the consistent, historical teaching of the church, either in the Aristotelian way that Lewis envisaged, or in the contemporary version that borrows the sociological languages of permanently "different roles" while claiming to endorse "equality of personhood"? We have already seen that, beginning with the Nicaean and Athanasian Creeds, Roman Catholic and Protestant theologians alike have consistently rejected the idea of Jesus' essential subordination to God the Father.[72] To what extent do these same traditions support Lewis's arguments for the subordination of women in marriage and the church?

Kevin Giles has shown in *The Trinity and Subordinationism* that there certainly is a long tradition of Christian (and, indeed, non-Christian) thought which assumes hierarchy in gender relations. Indeed if, like Lewis, we are to define "mere" Christianity as "the belief that has been common to nearly all Christians at all times"[73] then that set of beliefs, from the church fathers through the Protestant reformers to the Puritan divines, has at various times included the following:

- Women are a subordinate class or race who are intrinsically inferior to men.

---

is thus an attempt to co-opt sociological language to make gender subordination seem more palatable to twenty-first-century sensibilities. Moreover, it makes incorrect use of the sociological term "role" which refers by definition to behaviors that are *assigned* and potentially *changeable*, and not to something which (like eye color) is immutable. See Giles, *Trinity and Subordinationism*, chap. 8.

70. "The Danvers Statement," www.cbmw.org/Danvers.

71. Lewis, "Priestesses in the Church?" 235.

72. Giles, *Trinity and Subordinationism*, chaps. 1–5.

73. Lewis, *Mere Christianity*, 6.

- Women are not fully made in the image of God, since they were created second.
- Women are to accept their subordinate lot in life because they are more prone to sin and are more easily deceived than men.
- Women are to remain silent not just in church, but in every public gathering. (At some points in history, women were not even allowed to sing in church.)
- Women as a "class" or "race" are under men's protection and authority in all spheres of life, not just church and family. The subordination of women to male clergy, and to husbands, are just two applications of the norm that women are under the authority of men in all times and places.[74]

Such beliefs have been common throughout church history, some more at some times than others. Yet these same assumptions have *never* been part of official church creeds and confessions. Philosopher Philip Cary points out that, given their classical education and leanings, "the ancient church fathers were hierarchicalists to a man." And yet they could not and did not affirm hierarchy in the Trinity:

> One of the striking things about the original Nicene theologians . . . is that by being faithful to the purpose of clarifying the divinity of Christ, they ended up undermining the ancient commitment to a metaphysical hierarchy of being . . . They believed in hierarchical subordination throughout the universe: women subordinate to men, servants to masters, subjects to rulers, inanimate to animate, animals to humans. But despite themselves, what they found at the utmost height of the chain of being was equality in the very essence of God. And the reason was Christ: the biblical witness did not allow them to make Jesus Christ less deserving of worship and adoration than God the Father.[75]

The conclusions of the Nicene and Athanasian theologians were thus profoundly countercultural and, Cary adds, contemporary Christians can also expect countercultural results when they recognize these conclusions about the doctrine of the Trinity. Did this happen to C. S. Lewis as he matured in the faith? There is evidence to suggest that it did.

Less than Merely Christian?

To begin with, the traditional assumptions about women's inferiority listed above clearly demand too much, both from Lewis and from other defenders of

---

74. Giles, *Trinity and Subordinationism*, chap. 6.
75. Philip Cary, "The New Evangelical Subordinationism: Reading Inequality into the Trinity," *Priscilla Papers* 20, no. 4 (Autumn 2006): 42–45 (quotation from p. 45).

gender hierarchy in marriage and the church. For if they are all part of "mere" Christianity, then it is clear that even in his earliest years as a Christian writer, Lewis was something less than merely Christian. To begin with, Lewis did not endorse men's authority over women in spheres other than church and family. Though he regarded government and economic institutions as temporary expedients to regulate fallen people, he nonetheless applauded women's suffrage and the Married Women's Property Act. Outside of marriage and church settings, he regarded men and women as "two immortal souls, two free-born adults, two citizens."[76] In some of his earlier writings he did espouse the Aristotelian notion of women's inferior rational and moral capacity. But later he began explicitly rejecting such a stance, for example when he stated that if friendship between women and men is rare, this is largely because of the asymmetry in their educational opportunities, "rather than anything in their natures."[77] And as early as 1948, even when arguing against women's ordination, Lewis stated clearly that he did not regard a woman as "necessarily, or even probably, less holy or less charitable or stupider than a man."[78]

In the long sweep of Christian tradition, *none* of these gender egalitarian assumptions would have been acceptable. Indeed, as late as the nineteenth century many Christians would not have accepted the political equality of *males* of all classes and races. Church leaders from John Chrysostom through Martin Luther to John Wesley would have seen Lewis's endorsement of civic gender equality as placing him among those who, in his own words, "cut [themselves] off from the Christian past [and show] an almost wanton degree of impudence."[79] Yet, as we have seen, though Lewis nostalgically endorsed the "great chain of being" in his novels and literary criticism of the 1940s, by the time he wrote *The Discarded Image* (his introduction to medieval and Renaissance literature) in the 1960s, his concern to defend gender hierarchy had disappeared completely.

In that same volume Lewis also reversed his earlier views about hierarchy within the Trinity. He acknowledged the influence of neo-Platonism on medieval thought, with its notion that God "emanates" mind, which in turn emanates souls, then bodies and other matter in a series of ever-less pure debasements from the realm of pure spirit. But, he added, the hierarchical neo-Platonic "trinity" of God, mind, and soul is very different from the Christian Trinity: "The Second Person of the Christian Trinity is the Creator, the provident wisdom and creative will of the Father in action. The idea that He became less one with, or turned away from the Father by creating would be repugnant to Christian theology."[80]

76. Lewis, *Four Loves*, 96.
77. Ibid., 68.
78. Lewis, "Priestesses in the Church?" 236.
79. Ibid., 235.
80. C. S. Lewis, *The Discarded Image: An Introduction to Medieval and Renaissance Literature* (Cambridge: Cambridge University Press, 1964), 67.

It is clear from this brief excursion into church history that belief in male headship has come in varying degrees. For most of Western (not just church) history that headship was claimed to be universal. It was applied not only to gender relations in marriage and the church, but in every other sphere of life as well—although this was complicated by class considerations, so that upper-class women were clearly in authority over lower- or slave-class men, just as Aristotle had deemed "natural."[81] In the version Lewis defended until at least his midlife, male headship was limited to the priestly, sacramental function in the church, and to a largely symbolic—but ideally Christlike and sacrificial—role in marriage. As Alan Jacobs has noted,[82] the first of these already puts Lewis at odds with most (especially evangelical) Protestants, who do not share his high view of the priestly role and who, if they endorse male headship in church, are more concerned to keep women from the teaching or preaching roles for which Lewis proclaimed they were just as fit as men. And with regard to his view of male headship in marriage, it is clear that "the belief that has been common to nearly all Christians at all times" has been much more misogynist than even the younger Lewis would have dreamt of endorsing.

Nevertheless, no version of male headship has ever come close to attaining doctrinal status in the church. For example, despite Roman Catholicism's consistent reservation of priestly status to men, its doctrinal teaching throughout history on marriage has stressed its sacramental nature, its indissolubility, and the bonding and procreative dimensions of marital sexuality. Catholic historical theologian Daniel Cere summarizes this tradition:

> There has never been a tradition of formal doctrinal teaching endorsing [marital] subordination within the Catholic tradition. For much of that tradition the question of household order was treated as an issue of political ethics, and theologians were content to follow the Pauline tradition of dependence on Aristotle's treatment of household order. In the modern period the issue was quietly shelved as church teaching focused on the covenantal nature of marital love. In the face of new moral perspectives on conjugal relations, John Paul II tells us that continued affirmation of one-sided subordination in marriage would be morally equivalent to employing Ephesians 5 as a Christian justification for

81. In his *Politics* and his *Nicomachean Ethics* Aristotle theorized that some people (notably those deficient in rationality) were naturally fitted to be the slaves of those whose minds were superior. The early influence on Lewis of Aristotle's theory of permanent class differences can be seen in his 1943 essay on "Equality," where he states: "A great deal of democratic enthusiasm descends from the ideas of people like Rousseau, who believed in democracy because they thought mankind so wise and good that everyone deserved a share in the government. . . . The real reason for democracy is just the reverse. Mankind is so fallen that no man can be entrusted with unchecked power over his fellows. Aristotle said that some people were only fit to be slaves. I do not contradict him. But I reject slavery because I see no men fit to be masters." Reprinted in Lewis, *Present Concerns*, 17–20 (quotation from p. 17).

82. Jacobs, *The Narnian*, 254.

the institution of slavery . . . Christianity may in some historical circumstances permit, but certainly does not teach male headship in marriage.[83]

Lewis's defense of a male priesthood was largely motivated by a concern not to widen the breach between Anglican and Roman Catholic Christians. To that end he wrote in 1948 to Dorothy L. Sayers, his fellow novelist, literary critic, and Christian apologist:

> I am guessing that, like me, you disapprove of something [women's ordination] which would cut us off so sharply from all the rest of Christendom, and which would be the very triumph of what they call "practical" and "enlightened" principles over the far deeper need that the Priest at the Altar must represent the Bridegroom to whom we are all, in a sense feminine. Well, if you do, really I think you will have to give tongue. The defence against the innovation must if possible be done by a woman.[84]

But though Sayers was, if anything, even more Anglo-Catholic in her leanings than Lewis, she politely declined to "give tongue" in the debate over women's ordination. She agreed that it would "erect a new and totally unnecessary barrier between [Anglicans] and the rest of Catholic Christendom," but she pointed out that it would also *decrease* differences with those Protestant free churches that emphasized preaching more than the sacrament of communion. In the end, she wrote to Lewis,

> I fear you would find me rather an uneasy ally. I can never find any logical or strictly theological reason against [women's ordination]. In so far as the Priest represents Christ, it is obviously more dramatically appropriate that a man should be, so to speak, cast for the part. But if I were cornered and asked point-blank whether Christ Himself is the representative of male humanity or of all humanity, I should be obliged to answer "of all humanity"; and to cite the authority of St. Augustine for saying that woman is also made in the image of God.[85]

Ironically, in his crusade against women priests, Lewis's attempt to co-opt this famous Anglo-Catholic woman scholar backfired. But there is a further and more serious irony that Lewis, in the end, did not get drawn into. In their refusal to read hierarchy back into Trinity, today's gender egalitarians are in fact *closer* to the Catholic and Orthodox Christians whose unity with Anglicans

83. Daniel Mark Cere, "Marriage, Subordination and the Development of Christian Doctrine," in Blankenhorn et al., *Does Christianity Teach Male Headship?* 92–110 (quotation from p. 110). The internal reference is to Pope John Paul II's 1988 Apostolic Letter, *Mulieris Dignitatem* ("On the Dignity of Women"), section 24.

84. C. S. Lewis to Dorothy Sayers, July 13, 1948, quoted in Barbara Reynolds, *Dorothy L. Sayers: Her Life and Soul* (New York: St. Martin's Press, 1993), 358.

85. Dorothy Sayers to C. S. Lewis, July 1948, ibid., 359.

Lewis was so concerned to advance. Today, as Philip Cary has noted, gender egalitarians' "disagreements with the Eastern Orthodox and Roman Catholic Tradition about such matters as the ordination of women are minor . . . compared to conservative evangelicals' abandonment of the Great Tradition of the Trinity."[86] And in the end, Lewis did not abandon the Great Tradition. Instead, despite his attachment to classical and medieval cosmology, Lewis abandoned his earlier flirtation with the Arian heresy.[87] And in the process he became progressively less strident in his defense of gender archetypes and gender hierarchy.

Overall, Lewis's defense of male headship in church and marriage seems to die the death of many qualifiers—from Scripture, from the church creeds, from accumulated church tradition, and from changes in Lewis's own views over time. It was also challenged by Dorothy L. Sayers, a Christian intellectual whose rise to fame preceded Lewis's, and for whom Lewis had a great deal of admiration. In the chapter that follows, we will return to the social setting of the Edwardian age in which Lewis and Sayers were born and consider some significant historical events of that era. This will add to our understanding of the themes and variations that appear in Lewis's writings about gender.

86. Cary, "The New Evangelical Subordinationism," 42.

87. Lewis scholar Michael Ward, in his *Planet Narnia*, has written that "Christ's submission to the Father . . . was one of [Lewis's] favourite Christological themes. Lewis accepted the Nicene and Athanasian Creeds with their insistence on the co-eternity of the Son with the Father, but believed that the essential equality of divine being among the Persons of the Trinity was not incompatible with an ordering, even a kind of hierarchy, therein" ([Oxford: Oxford University Press, 2008], 135). In Ward's view, Lewis never abandoned this position. However, his analysis does not take account of Lewis's rather clear rejection of the neo-Platonic hierarchicalization of the Trinity in Lewis, *Discarded Image,* 67. (See note 80 above.)

4

"Not the Only Fundamental Difference"

The Edwardian World of C. S. Lewis and Dorothy L. Sayers

According to one of his former students "C. S. Lewis grew up in the Edwardian age, and his chief allegiances were to that age. He became a Fellow of Magdalen College in 1925, and from then on it was easy for him to ignore the modern world . . . Even before he got his fellowship, he had noticed the 1920s only to draw away from them in hostile dissent . . . He was an Old Western man, his attitudes dating from before Freud, before modern art or poetry, before the machine even."[1]

As we have already seen, such an assessment of Lewis is at best incomplete, especially in light of his lifetime output. Nevertheless, to grow up in the era of England's Edward VII (1901–14) was indeed to be poised on the brink of major social change. In some ways the Edwardian era represented a continuation of Victorian piety and a stable, duty-based social order, in contrast to the later rise in secularism and individualism that Lewis regularly deplored. On the other

1. John Wain, "A Great Clerke," in James T. Como, ed., *Remembering C. S. Lewis: Recollections of Those Who Knew Him* (San Francisco: Ignatius, 2005), 152–63 (quotation from p. 157).

hand, it was an age in which English hereditary privilege was rapidly giving way to tax-funded universal education and social security, resulting (as even Lewis occasionally acknowledged) in greater economic justice across classes and a better quality of students at ancient universities like Oxford. And it was arguably the last era in which the middle class could assume that the doctrine of separate spheres for women and men was completely "natural." For one thing, there were almost two million "surplus women" in Britain after the loss of so many men in World War I, and it was clear that not all of them could be supported by extended families or an uncertain patchwork of charities. In addition, it became harder to deny women the right to vote and compete with men in universities and the professions after the dangerous and mind-stretching jobs many of them had assumed during the Great War.[2]

There were other ways in which continuity battled with change in the Edwardian era. For example, when C. S. Lewis was a ten-year-old schoolboy in Hertfordshire, England entered what one social historian called "that strange territory of eugenics, the notion that by breeding, and limitation of birth, the social problems caused by poverty and over-population could be eliminated."[3] We have already seen the complex way in which class and gender interacted in Victorian and Edwardian England. With the advent of eugenics, conservatives on both these issues found an ambiguous ally—one which, even though it drew on the secular materialism of Darwin's theory of evolution, might still be used to keep various groups in their appointed places. As an adult, Lewis was acutely attuned to the dangers of eugenics, especially in his World War II writings, which reflect his concern about its horrific misuse in Germany and elsewhere.

The Eugenics Society, founded in 1908, had as its first president Francis Galton, a pioneer developer of statistical analyses and intelligence tests. A Cambridge-educated mathematician of middle-class Quaker background, Galton was a first cousin to Charles Darwin, whose work had already shaken the Victorian world with its theory of evolution by natural selection. Building on the work of economist Thomas Malthus, who asserted that animal populations always grew faster than their supplies of food, Darwin concluded that competition for scarce resources resulted in the survival of the fittest members of a species. These were individuals who, by the luck of random natural variation, had the optimal qualities for getting the food they needed and so were able to survive, reproduce abundantly, and pass their biological advantages on to their offspring.

2. See, for example, Vera Brittain, *Testament of Youth: An Autobiographical Study of the Years 1900–1925* (London: Victor Gollancz, 1933); and Roy Hattersley, *The Edwardians* (New York: St. Martin's Press, 2004), chap. 10.

3. A. N. Wilson, *After the Victorians: The Decline of Britain in the World* (New York: Farrar, Straus and Giroux, 2005), 267. Francis Galton himself coined the term "eugenics," to mean "good birth."

English country gentleman had, of course, been practicing *artificial* selection for generations, patiently breeding desired characteristics into their horses, dogs, and racing pigeons. Now, in wake of Darwin and Malthus, eugenicists claimed not only that human overpopulation was an imminent disaster, but that the wrong kinds of people were having too many children, and the right kinds of people too few. Should it not be possible to breed desirable qualities—mental as well as physical—into the human race, just as pigeon-fanciers selectively mated their stock to get faster, sleeker birds? Galton and his fellow eugenicists thought this could be done by encouraging marriages between healthy and intelligent people while discouraging them among the less well-endowed.[4] They were convinced that traits such as scientific, artistic, or legal ability were as biologically determined (and thus as amenable to selective breeding) as height, nose shape, and eye color. A decade after the appearance of Darwin's *The Origin of Species*, Galton wrote *Hereditary Genius*, the result of his attempt to see whether "eminence" or high reputation—which he took as an accurate indicator of "genius"—ran in families. He assessed the frequency of such eminence among the offspring of eminent parents (e.g., judges, statesmen, scientists, poets, musicians, high-level clergy) and compared it to that among offspring of the population at large. The results seemed clear: the children of illustrious individuals were much more likely to be illustrious themselves than were the children of ordinary people.[5]

The Continuing Relevance of Class and Gender

It is ironic that the man who first developed the idea of statistical correlation could so quickly forget what novice social science students routinely learn today—namely, that correlation does not necessarily indicate causation. Since children inherit their parents' environments along with their genes, there is no way Galton could have known whether nature, nurture, or some combination of both caused the class differences in "eminence" that he found. Yet

4. In Britain, adherents of "positive eugenics" proposed financial incentives or social honors to get intelligent people to marry each other, and celibate monastic-style communities for the less intelligent. In the early twentieth century America, proponents of "negative eugenics" were more dominant: thirty-three states passed compulsory sterilization laws for persons deemed feeble-minded, insane, criminalistic, alcoholic, diseased, deformed, or chronically impoverished. Sterilization of the mentally deficient was still being practiced by some states as late as the 1970s. It was only after its even greater misuse by Nazi Germany that eugenics began to fall out of favor among "progressive" thinkers (including many liberal religious leaders) on both sides of the Atlantic. See, for example, Daniel Kevles, *In the Name of Eugenics: Genetics and the Uses of Human Heredity* (Cambridge, MA: Harvard University Press, 1998); and Christine Rosen, *Preaching Eugenics: Religious Leaders and the American Eugenics Movement* (New York: Oxford University Press, 2004).

5. Francis Galton, *Hereditary Genius: An Inquiry Into Its Laws and Consequences* (London: MacMillan, 1869).

his automatic presumption that such differences in achievement were due to innate biological factors should not surprise us. Victorian intellectuals moved in a milieu where Aristotle's ladder of nature and its medieval descendant, the great chain of being, were for many still an accepted picture of reality. Darwin's theory, in suggesting that the rungs on the ladder were not as fixed as Aristotle believed, simply provided a scientific gloss for the eugenic notion that some classes should propagate more freely than others, in the interests of improving the human species.

Galton wrote in an era when Gregor Mendel's pioneering genetic work had yet to be widely read, so he did not recognize genes as a mechanism for biological heredity. He assumed that, however it happened, mothers and fathers contributed equally to their children's traits. Even so, the residue of Aristotelian thinking—as well as his adherence to the doctrine of separate spheres—can be seen in his belief that women only needed traits such as physical beauty, nurturance, and verbal skill to be eugenically fit, whereas men carried the "rational" traits that enabled their sons to become lawyers, judges, poets, scientists, etc. To complicate matters further, the emerging nineteenth-century feminist movement was not above placing class concerns before those of female solidarity. For example, some Victorian feminists argued that middle-class women were naturally more moral because of their superior nurturing capacities, and that through "rational reproduction" they could steadily improve the British imperial race.[6]

C. S. Lewis was one Edwardian who emphatically rejected eugenics. He was agnostic about evolution as a theory of natural species change, and even speculated freely about the possibility of God-directed evolution.[7] But he had too robust a belief in human depravity to trust in any schemes for helping human evolution along, and issued prophetic warnings about the misuse of eugenics in his World War II-era writings.[8] However, with rare exceptions he also wrote as if the only alternative was to cling to the earlier ideal of a fixed social order, in which everyone would happily assume their places in terms of class and gender, the lower deferring to the higher and the higher exercising *noblesse oblige* toward the lower.

In a 1943 article challenging modern ideas of equality, Lewis showed the ambiguous hold this model still had on him with regard to class: "Aristotle said that some people were only fit to be slaves. I do not contradict him. But I

6. See Angelique Richardson, *Love and Eugenics in the Late Nineteenth Century: Rational Reproduction and the New Woman* (Oxford: Oxford University Press, 2003).

7. See especially, C. S. Lewis, *The Problem of Pain* (London: Geoffrey Bles, 1940; reprinted, London: Collin, 1957), chap. 5.

8. See, for example, *The Abolition of Man* (chap. 3); *That Hideous Strength* (chap. 2); and his 1944 Socratic Club address, "Is Theology Poetry?" reprinted in C. S. Lewis, *Screwtape Proposes a Toast and Other Pieces* (London: Collins Fontana, 1965), 41–58.

reject slavery because I see no men fit to be masters."[9] Commenting a few years earlier on the newly-revised Oxford English syllabus, he endorsed the classical Greek view that lower orders of people should provide material support for the select few capable of serious thinking. "Education," he wrote, should be "a preparation for leisure, which according to [Aristotle] is the end of all human activity . . . Human life means to me the life of beings for whom the leisured activities of thought, art, literature, conversation are the end, and the preservation and propagation of life merely the means."[10] In Lewis's context, this clearly referred to a system in which aristocrats and Oxbridgean scholars were to be served by the lower classes.

As with Galton a generation earlier, it was all too easy for Edwardians to conflate class membership with innate limitations. In the England that existed just prior to C. S. Lewis's childhood, the vast majority of children simply didn't attend school in any regular way. They labored in factories, farms, or trade from a very young age, and only about half were even able to attend "Sunday schools" where they might acquire the minimal literacy needed to read the Bible. The Sunday school movement was promoted by evangelical Anglicans in the face of resistance from the church's Anglo-Catholic wing, but even so, it shared the latter's assumptions about the naturalness of class hierarchy. Many of its stalwarts—women as well as men—wanted to alleviate the physical and spiritual poverty of the cities in part to prevent the excesses of the French revolution from taking hold in England. Thus Hannah More, a member of the wealthy evangelical Clapham Sect, placed strict limits on what was taught in her own Sunday school: "I allow of no writing for the poor," she warned. "My object is not to teach dogmas and opinions, but to form the lower classes to habits of industry and virtue."[11] And in an even clearer nod to Greek and medieval cosmology, she wrote:

> Beautiful is the order of society, when each according to his place, pays willing honor to his superiors—when servants are prompt to obey their masters, and masters deal kindly with their servants; when high, low, rich and poor—when landlord and tenant, master and workmen, minister and people . . . sit down satisfied, each with his own place.[12]

9. C. S. Lewis, "Equality," reprinted in C. S. Lewis, *Present Concerns*, ed. Walter Hooper (San Diego: Harvest, 1987), 17–20 (quotation from p. 17).

10. C. S. Lewis, "Our English Syllabus," in *Rehabilitations and Other Essays* (London: Oxford University Press, 1939), 81–82.

11. Martha More, *Mendip Annals* (London: Nisbet, 1859), 6. In More's day, the English poor could rarely even enter the large cathedrals, which—rather like present-day elite country clubs—required families to pay an annual fee for pew occupancy. Their worship was thus effectively restricted to the smaller churches.

12. Quoted in Brian Simon, *The Two Nations and the Educational Structure, 1708–1870* (London: Lawrence and Wisehart, 1964), 133. See also Margaret L. Koch, "Feminism and Chris-

Only in 1880 did primary education in England become compulsory for every child up to age ten, and only in 1891 did parents cease having to pay fees at local schools. By the year of Lewis's birth (1898) only 7 percent of English working class children were going on to academic secondary education. Not until 1918, when Lewis was preparing to return to Oxford after World War I, did secondary schooling became state-supported and compulsory for all children, and even then only up to age fourteen.

In Scotland, by contrast, every parish had supported a coeducational primary school since the seventeenth century, thanks to John Knox's conviction that universal literacy was vital to the formation of a God-fearing nation. By the time England moved to provide state funds for secondary schools in 1902, there were already four hundred tax-supported secondary and technical schools in Scotland, in a country with only a tenth the population of England and Wales combined.[13] Even Francis Galton had been forced to temper his theory about the biological basis for "eminence" after surveying almost two hundred male scientists—both English and Scottish—who were members of the Royal Society in the 1870s. Asked what had contributed to their interest and expertise in science, most Scottish respondents praised the school system in which they had been educated, whereas most English respondents said that, if anything, their own (supposedly elite) schooling had retarded their development as scientists. Galton adjusted his earlier position, now writing that only the *potential* for high achievement was inherited, and that it had to be nurtured by the right environment. He even went so far as to suggest, a generation before it actually occurred, that England should adopt features of the Scottish approach to education.[14] Regrettably, none of this tempered his enthusiasm for the eugenics movement, which quickly spread from England to both America and Europe with tragic results, notably—but not exclusively—in Nazi Germany.[15]

This brief excursion into the history of British education reminds us, as Dorothy L. Sayers noted in 1938, that while "there is a fundamental difference between men and women . . . it is not the only fundamental difference." With an ironic humor for which she was already famous, she pointed out that

---

tian Vision: Lessons from the Past," in Mary Stewart Van Leeuwen et al., *After Eden: Facing the Challenge of Gender Reconciliation* (Grand Rapids: Eerdmans, 1993), 19–43.

13. Hattersley, *The Edwardians*, chap. 12.

14. Francis Galton, *English Men of Science: Their Nature and Nurture* (London: MacMillan, 1874). Galton is credited with introducing the now-famous phrase "nature versus nurture" into the debate about the origins of intelligence, and with conducting the first survey ever in his study of Royal Society fellows.

15. See Nicholas Wright Gillham, *A Life of Sir Francis Galton: From African Exploration to the Birth of Eugenics* (New York: Oxford University Press, 2001); Kevles, *In the Name of Eugenics*; and Rosen, *Preaching Eugenics*.

there is a sense in which my charwoman [i.e., house cleaner] and I have more in common than either of us has with say, Mr. Bernard Shaw . . . [but] in a discussion about art and literature, Mr. Shaw and I should probably find we had more fundamental interests in common than either of us had with my charwoman. I grant that, even so, he and I should disagree ferociously about the eating of meat—but that is not a difference between the sexes . . . Then there are points on which I, and many of my generation of both sexes, should find ourselves heartily in agreement, but on which the rising generation of young men and women would find us too incomprehensibly stupid for words. A difference in age is as fundamental as a difference of sex, and so is a difference of nationality. *All* categories, if they are insisted upon beyond the immediate purpose they serve, breed class antagonisms and disruption in the state, and that is why they are dangerous.[16]

It would be another generation before social scientists caught up with Sayers and began showing the extent to which gender, class, and national "categories" are socially constructed, and critical theorists began showing how such groups interact in shifting relations of dominance and submission.[17] Given such complications, we may better understand the development of Lewis's views on gender if we compare him in more detail to a woman contemporary of similar background, education, intellectual interests, and Christian conviction. At the end of the last chapter we met Dorothy L. Sayers when she declined Lewis's 1948 request to speak out against women's ordination in the Anglican Church. By that time Sayers, like Lewis, was an Oxford MA, a published poet, author of several novels in a popular new genre (detective novels in her case, science fiction in Lewis's), and a BBC broadcaster who had helped strengthen Christian faith during the dark days of World War II (doing radio drama in her case, popular theological talks in Lewis's).[18] She had also written and directed two plays for the Canterbury Arts Festival,[19] published books on Christian doctrine and creativity, and was on her way to becoming a

16. Dorothy Sayers, "Are Women Human?" in *Unpopular Opinions* (London: Victor Gollancz, 1946), reprinted in *Are Women Human?* (Grand Rapids: Eerdmans, 1971), 17–36 (quotation from p. 33). Sayers was rather insistent about wanting to be publicly cited as "Dorothy L. Sayers," so I have adhered to that convention as far as stylistically possible.

17. An accessible introduction to critical theory can be found in Annelies Knoppers, "A Critical Theory of Gender Relations, " in Van Leeuwen et al., *After Eden*, 225–67.

18. Sayers, like Lewis, completed her first volume of poetry while still a student at Oxford, under the title *Opus I* (Oxford: Basil Blackwell, 1916). Her detective novels, featuring the aristocratic sleuth, Lord Peter Wimsey, include *Whose Body?* (London: Fisher Unwin, 1923) and *Clouds of Witness* (London: Fisher Unwin, 1926); *Unnatural Death* (London: Ernest Benn, 1927) and *The Unpleasantness at the Bellona Club* (London: Ernest Benn, 1928); *Strong Poison* (1930), *Five Red Herrings* (1931), *Have His Carcass* (1932), *Murder Must Advertise* (1933), *The Nine Tailors* (1934), *Gaudy Night* (1936), and *Busman's Honeymoon* (all published in London by Victor Gollancz). Her wartime broadcast play was *The Man Born to Be King* (London: Victor Gollancz, 1943).

19. The same setting for which T. S. Eliot had written *Murder in the Cathedral* in 1935.

distinguished translator of Dante's *Divine Comedy* from Italian into English verse.[20] Toward the end of their careers, both she and Lewis would be offered honorary doctorates.[21]

By what similar and different paths did these two precocious Edwardian children—one male and one female—develop their talents and come to a place of adult fame? As Anglicans who shared some of the same High Church leanings as they grew older, how did they agree or differ in their understanding and application of the Christian story? Were they united by a common class background, or divided by the gender norms of their era? What follows is a comparison of the lives of Lewis and Sayers in terms of family background, education, primary relationships, and some of their intellectual projects. From it we will see that Lewis's ideas about class and gender, forged in the Edwardian era, in some ways reinforced each other and sometimes diverged.

Two Edwardian Middle-Class Children

C. S. Lewis and Dorothy L. Sayers both grew up in the shadow of Anglican church rectories. Lewis's maternal grandfather, the Rev. Thomas Hamilton, baptized him as an infant in 1898 and continued to be the family's rector at St. Mark's Dundela, in the Belfast suburb of Strandtown, until his death in 1905. Dorothy Leigh Sayers, born in 1893, was a grandchild of one Anglican clergyman, and the only child of another. Her father, the Rev. Henry Sayers, was head of Oxford's Christ Church Choir School until she was four years old, then rector of a church in rural East Anglia. At the end of the nineteenth century, the Church of England was still a powerful force religiously and politically. But there was another way in which its national influence was felt. A. N. Wilson notes that

> the clergy were seldom rich, but they were treated as if they were gentlemen: very often they were. Nearly all of them had degrees. High Church, Low Church, Broad Church, they were disseminated throughout the land. If they were even half good at their jobs, they and their wives and families mixed with everyone in their parish. They were extraordinary agents of social communication. It meant that almost everyone . . . was within five miles of a man who could read

20. Sayers's Canterbury Festival play was *The Zeal of Thy House* (London: Gollancz, 1938). Her theological works include *The Mind of the Maker* (London: Methuen, 1941) and *Creed or Chaos?* (London: Methuen, 1947). Her translations of Dante Alighieri's *Divine Comedy* include *Vol. 1: Hell* (1949), *Vol. 2: Purgatory* (1955), and *Vol. 3: Paradise* (1962; completed by Barbara Reynolds), all published in London by Penguin.

21. Sayers was so honored by Lambeth and Durham, Lewis by Manchester and St. Andrews. Sayers refused the Lambeth honorary Doctor of Divinity degree on the grounds that she wasn't a professional theologian. Lewis received a third honorary doctorate from Laval University in Quebec, but was unable to travel to do the convocation address there.

ancient Greek. Their families, often impoverished but growing up with a certain set of shared values which could loosely be defined as decency, were notably more bookish, more self-reliant than other middle-class families who had more servants or who moved in narrower social fields. It is no wonder that such a very high proportion of writers, creative men and women of other talent, teachers, civil servants, and of course clergy, came from "clergy families."[22]

In such families, schooling began at home, began early, and proceeded more seamlessly than in a formal classroom. Both Lewis and Sayers were avid readers at an early age, and both were encouraged to engage in arts, crafts, amateur dramatics, and country hikes with friends and relatives in an era when extended family members still lived close to each other. Jack began studying French and Latin at age seven with his mother, who had honors degrees in mathematics and logic from Queen's University in Belfast.[23] Dorothy began Latin and violin at age six with her father in his country church rectory, and thanks to a French-born governess was soon almost as fluent in French as in English.

For middle-class Edwardians, private schools—routinely for boys, but sometimes also for girls—were the next step. Legislative reforms leading to tax-supported universal primary education were under way in both England and Ireland by this time, but social norms still dictated that higher-class children should go to the "best" schools. Ironically, since money and social rank, more than competitively established ability, were the criteria for entering such schools, they weren't always as good as they claimed to be. C. S. Lewis wrote with some bitterness in *Surprised by Joy* about his first boarding school in England, whose sadistic headmaster was later certified insane. And despite the presence of better teachers at Malvern, his elite public school in early adolescence, he remembered student life there as "almost wholly dominated by the social struggle; to get on, to arrive, or having reached the top, to remain there . . . In some boys' lives everything was calculated to the great end of advancement. For this games were played; for this clothes, friends, amusements and vices were chosen."[24]

Edwardian girls' boarding schools may not have been as much like a chapter out of *Lord of the Flies*, but they were even less apt to stress intellectual development than their male counterparts. Because they had been groomed for adornment and domesticity, rather than economic self-sufficiency, Victorian girls of an earlier generation were less likely to study Latin and Greek,

22. Wilson, *After the Victorians*, 314.

23. From its inception in 1878, Queen's University Belfast had taught women students on exactly the same terms as men, something which would not be the case until 1920 at Oxford and 1948 at Cambridge.

24. C. S. Lewis, *Surprised by Joy: The Shape of My Early Life* (London: Collins, 1955), 89.

and more likely to spend time learning how to knit, sing, sketch, and speak French. This ethos persisted into the Edwardian era, despite the passage of the Married Women's Property Act in 1870 and the recommendations of the 1869 Taunton Commission on Education.[25] However, Dorothy L. Sayers's parents were exceptional: having had their only child when they were almost forty, they doted on her, recognized her precocity, and gave her all the intellectual advantages of the rectory. She was also surrounded by strong women: in addition to her mother, there was a grandmother, a maiden aunt, and from time to time her older cousin Ivy in the household. She did indeed learn to sew and knit, but in the context of making theatrical costumes and relishing the challenge of going from two to four needles when her aunt taught her how to make socks.

Not until she was fifteen was she sent to Godolphin, a girls' boarding school in Salisbury. It was a superior school whose curriculum might give her a chance at a scholarship to Somerville, one of the Oxford women's colleges, established in 1878. At school she added German to her linguistic repertoire, played first violin in the orchestra (even performing once in London's Albert Hall), took piano lessons, and energetically produced and acted in an assortment of plays in various languages. "It is true," writes Sayers's biographer Barbara Reynolds, "that she was not the conventional type of school girl, good at games and experienced in communal living."

> Nevertheless, she had a great deal to offer. Her command of French was exceptional (this may have aroused resentment at first), she played the piano and the violin, she could sing, act and produce plays, she could write, she was lively and exuberant, above all, she enjoyed *sharing* her enthusiasms with her friends—the very reverse of a loner.[26]

During her time at Godolphin she was confirmed in Salisbury Cathedral, and though like Jack Lewis she may have harbored private doubts about tak-

---

25. One historian notes that "in its evaluation of the education of girls, the Taunton Commission found grossly untrained teachers, subjects pursued unsystematically, too little discipline, poor French instruction, [and] defective math instruction. It found that girls were usually ahead of boys until the age of 12, when their learning stalled and made little further progress. In its final report, the Commission declared that the main obstacle to change was the unwillingness of parents to take trouble over the education of their daughters, and their apathy, or even opposition towards measures for improvement. [One commissioner] had this to say: 'We find as a rule . . . an inferior set of school-books, a vast deal of dry, uninteresting task-work, rules put into the memory with no explanation of their principles, no system of examination worthy of the name . . . [and] a tendency to fill and adorn rather than to strengthen the mind.'" Deborah Taft, "Victorian Education," www.gober.net/victorian/reports/schools.html (accessed November 2006).

26. Barbara Reynolds, *Dorothy L. Sayers: Her Life and Soul* (New York: St. Martin's Press, 1993), 29. See also Barbara Reynolds, ed., *The Letters of Dorothy L. Sayers*, vol. 1, *1899 to 1936* (New York: St. Martin's Press, 1995), 1–64.

ing this step, her teenage letters home show only distaste for Edwardian-style religious emotionalism and an enthusiasm for the beauty and rigor of Christian doctrine.[27] Just before her eighteenth birthday, she took the Cambridge Higher Local Examinations and came first in all of England, with distinctions in French and spoken German.[28] A year later she had captured the Gilchrist Scholarship to Somerville College. Nineteen-year-old Dorothy L. Sayers was Oxford bound.

Class Similarities, Gender Differences

Apparently without ever comparing notes on the matter, C. S. Lewis and Dorothy L. Sayers both looked back on their childhoods and concluded that they had been insufferable prigs. They were budding snobs with high-powered intellects who often talked down to people of supposedly lesser minds, rather like Hermione Granger before she started socializing with some of her more relaxed classmates in today's *Harry Potter* stories. In an unpublished autobiographical account written at age forty, Sayers "looked back at the childish figure that had been herself . . . so lacking in those common virtues which were to be attained in after years at so much cost and with such desperate difficulty . . . She must, she knew, have been a disagreeable child. Strangers rightly considered her a prig."[29] And in 1931, when his brother was beginning to compile several generations of family papers, Lewis thanked his friend Arthur Greeves for lending him the letters he had received from Jack during their youth, but added:

> To me, as I re-read them, the most striking thing is their egotism: sometimes in the form of priggery, intellectual and even social: often in the form of downright affectation (I seem to be posturing and showing off in every letter) . . . I can now honestly say that I envy you the much more artless letters you were writing me in those days: they all had at least the grace of humility and of affection. How ironical that the very things wh[ich] I was proud of in my letters should make the reading of them a humiliation to me now![30]

27. For example, Sayers read and admired G. K. Chesterton's *Orthodoxy* as a teenager, and enthusiastically listened to him lecture while a student at Oxford (Reynolds, *Dorothy L. Sayers*, 38, 52). Her insistence on the importance of clear belief over transient religious feelings was later reflected in her volume *Creed or Chaos?* (London: Methuen, 1947).

28. These national examinations, established in 1857 as a way of standardizing school curricula and levels of academic achievement, had been opened to girls' school students in 1867.

29. Quoted in Reynolds, *Dorothy L. Sayers*, 250.

30. C. S. Lewis to Arthur Greeves, October 1, 1931, in Walter Hooper, ed., *The Collected Letters of C. S. Lewis*, vol. 1, *1905–1931* (San Francisco: HarperSanFrancisco, 2004), 973.

It is surely significant that Lewis's assessment of his younger self appears in a letter where he also says that he has "just passed on from believing in God to definitely believing in Christ—in Christianity."[31] Likewise, Sayers's self-critical reflections occurred when she was turning from the lucrative field of detective fiction to the challenge of making the Christian story come alive in plays and essays. Clearly, these two late-developing Christians shared a common background: one that was middle-class, bookish, and inclined to train its children for intellectual over material achievement. At the cost of some sacrifice by their parents, both got the best English schooling possible, Sayers at Godolphin, and Lewis at Malvern, then as the pupil of an eccentric but brilliant tutor with whom he boarded in Surrey for almost three years. Both won scholarships to Oxford, Dorothy to Somerville in 1912, and Jack to University College in 1916.

It is at this point that gender would begin to make a significant difference in their lives. It was only two years before Dorothy L. Sayers went to Oxford that the university had officially recognized the presence of women in its midst. From the opening of their first residence hall in 1879, women had by turns been seen as tourists, paying guests, and infiltrators.[32] Their lecturers and tutors were mainly male dons working overtime to teach them—some out of conviction, most just to earn extra income—and until 1893, no woman student could attend lectures or tutorials (or even walk into town) without a chaperone. Oxford dons were not allowed to marry until the 1870s, and in the early decades of the twentieth century both town and the university were still overwhelmingly male bastions. One contemporary of Lewis's noted that, even after World War I, Oxford "was still a semi-monastic institution; some of the dons clearly detested women; and the only moral offences they condoned were discreetly managed homosexual passions."[33]

Women had to petition to attend lectures at the men's colleges, and some (including Lewis's later home, Magdalen) simply refused point blank to allow women on their premises until as late as 1906. Edward Pusey, a late nineteenth-century theologian at Christ Church and a leader of the Anglo-Catholic Oxford Movement, had deplored the opening of women's residence halls as "one of the greatest misfortunes that have happened in our own time at Oxford." His

31. Ibid., 974.

32. Vera Brittain, *The Women at Oxford: A Fragment of History* (New York: MacMillan, 1960), chaps. 3–5.

33. Poet Peter Quennell, as quoted in A. N. Wilson, *C. S. Lewis: A Biography* (London: Norton, 1990), 65. As late as the 1940s, most Oxford dons were unmarried, "their lives centered, professionally and personally, around the university and relationships with male counterparts . . . [and] even in the 1950s marriage was considered as failing at one's profession" (Candice Fredrick and Sam McBride, *Women Among the Inklings: Gender, C. S. Lewis, J. R. R. Tolkien and Charles Williams* [Westport, CN: Greenwood, 2001], 4). Indeed, both as an undergraduate and after his appointment as a don in 1925, Lewis was unusual in having off-campus lodgings with his fictive "family," Janie Moore and her daughter Maureen.

Oriel College divinity colleague, John Burgon, preached a sermon in which he reminded the female "interlopers" in the congregation that "inferior to us God made you, and inferior you will remain till the end of time. But you are not the worse off for that."[34] Though the principals and tutors at the women's colleges (of which there were four by Sayers's time) were not without strong male advocates in the other colleges, in general they were treated as being in Oxford on sufferance, with the possibility of being expelled at any time.

Until close to the turn of the century, women could not even write the same examinations as men, for entrance to Oxford or for graduation.[35] By the time Dorothy L. Sayers arrived in 1912, this prohibition had been lifted, but women still could not receive Oxford degrees, even after meeting all the qualifications and not infrequently outperforming men in the same programs of study. Even after women had been taking regular examinations for over twenty years, writer Vera Brittain (who came to Somerville two years after Sayers) dryly recalled that "the [University] Statutes continued unblushingly to publish the remarkable information that no one could be admitted to these examinations who was not a member of the university. Presumably the women donned a magic cloak of invisibility as soon as they entered the Examination Schools."[36]

By Sayers's time, older women chaperones at lectures and tutorials were a thing of the past, though they were still required at social functions,[37] and all student societies—dramatic, debating, political—were separated by sex.[38] Perhaps the biggest problem was that without official degrees it was unclear what women were qualified to do after leaving Oxford. Many who did not marry immediately—including Sayers—managed to get teaching jobs in the rapidly expanding state school system. The few who stayed at Oxford as tutors in the women's colleges continued to have an ambiguous status, and when Oxford degrees were retrospectively opened up to women in 1920, some gray-haired lady dons who were acknowledged experts in their fields found themselves

34. Both quoted in Brittain, *Women at Oxford*, 69.

35. Not all of the early women's college administrators opposed this double standard. Elizabeth Wordsworth, the first principal of Lady Margaret Hall (opened in 1878), "had no great sympathy with the aspirations of modern women scholars, and was more interested in a girl's religious outlook than in any claim to her 'rights.' The ideal [woman] student, in her own words, was 'better with the hands than the head, and best of all with the heart'" (Brittain, *Women at Oxford*, 56).

36. Ibid., 132.

37. Social chaperonage ended only in 1926. Sayers wrote of an occasion when female students were taken to the theater, and she by chance found herself sitting next to a male student who was an old family friend. She anxiously clambered over several rows of seats to explain to the chaperone that this arrangement was not preplanned, and was allowed to retain her seat (Reynolds, *Dorothy L. Sayers*, 63–64).

38. One exception was the Oxford Bach Choir, for which Sayers successfully auditioned as a contralto, and for whose director—New College organist Hugh Percy Allen—she confessed to having romantic feelings during her student days (Reynolds, *Dorothy L. Sayers*, chap. 3).

having to write examinations they had not previously taken because in their own student days they had been prohibited from doing so.[39]

Dangerous Liaisons

But if separation and relegation to second-class status were meant to keep Oxford women in their place, by the time Dorothy L. Sayers arrived in 1912 the strategy was beginning to backfire. Their restricted mobility may have been a source of irritation, but it also created time and space for women students to study hard, with increasingly impressive exam results on the part of those whom Pusey's God had supposedly made "inferior till the end of time." Because they could not join the Oxford Union (the men's debating society) the women of Somerville developed their own model parliament, which became a famous training ground for the expanding women's suffrage movement in the first two decades of the twentieth century.[40] Segregation by sex also meant that gifted women became close friends and often remained supportive of each other well beyond their Oxford days. C. S. Lewis's literary discussion group, the Inklings, did not start until several years after his appointment as a fellow of Magdalen College. By contrast, Dorothy L. Sayers and some women friends formed what they called the Mutual Admiration Society while they were students at Somerville, and continued to share ideas, essays, and manuscripts-in-progress for the rest of their lives.[41]

In the decade following the trauma of World War I, and with the equivalent of a first-class degree in Medieval and Modern Languages, Sayers took a series of jobs teaching high school French and German. She eventually settled in London in 1922, in a job writing copy for an advertising agency. This was a well-paid position, though one whose manipulative tactics she increasingly disliked as time went on. But it left her time to write the detective novels whose profits would eventually free her to return to more serious scholarship. Regrettably, as one of the "surplus women" of marriageable age in the post-war era, she had few educated male peers with whom to form serious romantic bonds. On the rebound from one such relationship at age thirty, she became pregnant during a fleeting liaison with an unemployed car mechanic.

To her credit, she decided to have the child. She managed to conceal the pregnancy from family and colleagues, and after giving birth to a son in a

39. Brittain, *Women at Oxford*, chap. 7. Dorothy Sayers was among the several hundred women who returned to Oxford in October of 1920 to receive their long-denied MA and/or BA degrees.

40. In 1918 women were finally able to vote, but only if they were over thirty (to assuage fears that their votes might overwhelm those of adult males). Only in 1928 was the voting age for women lowered to twenty-one, the same age as for males.

41. Brittain, *Women at Oxford*, chap. 6; Reynolds, *Dorothy L. Sayers*, chap. 3.

secluded maternity hospital, asked her cousin Ivy—in strictest confidence—to raise the child in her home near Oxford.[42] Supporting young John Anthony from infancy on (he eventually won a scholarship to Oxford and did a degree in "Modern Greats"—that is, philosophy, politics, and economics), she told no one else about his existence except the man she eventually married at age thirty-three: Atherton ("Mac") Fleming, a World War I veteran and a journalist, who co-adopted the boy with Dorothy. This marriage, between two professional writers who both loved the London literary scene, was by most accounts a good one until physical and mental problems from the war began to catch up with Fleming. By the late 1940s Sayers was supporting both a husband and a child, and despite her now-considerable success as a fiction writer, she struggled to cope with Mac's medical bills and the support of her son. As it turned out, her husband died suddenly of a stroke in 1950, but amazingly, it was not until Sayers's own death in 1957 that any of her friends knew about her son, who revealed his parentage at that time.[43]

During almost this entire time, having moved relatively seamlessly from undergraduate days to a fellowship at Magdalen College, C. S. Lewis was teaching just a few miles from where Sayers's child was being raised.[44] Lewis and Sayers eventually met by correspondence in 1942, and in person some time thereafter. The 1920s was a decade of backlash against women's presence at Oxford, in spite—or perhaps because—of the fact that they had qualified for degrees since 1920. In 1927 the Congregation (i.e., faculty and administrators) of Oxford voted to limit indefinitely the number of women students who could be admitted, and to prohibit the establishment of any more women's colleges.[45] Lewis, a fellow of the college that had been the last to open its lectures to women, was among those who supported this proposal, writing to his brother that

the Term . . . produced one public event of good omen—the carrying in Congregation of a Statute limiting the number of wimmen [sic] at Oxford. The ap-

42. Ivy Shrimpton and her widowed mother were already supporting themselves by doing foster care for other young children. The father of the child, Bill White, disappeared soon after his birth.

43. Reynolds, *Dorothy L. Sayers*, chaps. 5–11.

44. Lewis did spend an extra year at Oxford (supported by his father), adding a first in English to his previous firsts in classics and ancient philosophy, in order to improve his chances of a fellowship, which, as it turned out, was to be in English language and literature. He also had a one-year replacement appointment teaching philosophy at his own undergraduate college before being appointed to Magdalen.

45. The quota for women students was capped at about six hundred, which was then approximately one-sixth the number of male undergraduates. That this was not a dramatic or permanent backlash can be seen in the fact that the vote in favor of this policy (229 to 164) was far from overwhelming. The policy was eased in 1948, and completely eliminated in 1953 (Brittain, *Women at Oxford*, chap. 8).

palling danger of our degenerating into a woman's university . . . has thus been
staved off. There was fierce opposition, of course, our female antagonists being
much more expert than we in the practice of "whipping" in the parliamentary
sense[46] . . . The queer thing was that one solitary woman voted against her sex.
She has since married and given up her job. *Una de multis face nuptial digna*
["One of the many worthy of the bridal torch."][47]

Though Lewis and Sayers did not know each other at this time, her opinion
of Oxford's retrograde move was pretty clear. Her most complex detective
novel (and her own personal favorite) was *Gaudy Night*, which is set in a fictitious Oxford women's college in the mid-1930s. The plot of the novel turns
on the resentment that tradition-bound male academics—and their female
supporters—harbor toward women scholars whose commitment to intellectual integrity will not be compromised by submission to social norms about
women's "proper place." Interestingly, in one of the novel's minor themes
Sayers, like Lewis, warned about the totalitarian tendencies of the eugenics
movement. But unlike Lewis (who was to write in *Perelandra* that for women,
"children are fruit enough"[48]) she also made a point of criticizing the movement's enthusiasm for treating intelligent women mainly as incubators for
superior children.[49]

It should be clear by now that Lewis was hardly unique in his attitudes
about women. Still, one might be excused for expecting a somewhat different
posture from a man whose mother was an honors graduate from a university
(Queen's Belfast) that had accepted women on exactly the same terms as men
since its founding in 1878. What personal demons may have contributed to
this disjunction? Early in his career Lewis had argued against what he called
"the personal heresy"—that is, trying to understand writing in terms of the
author's own psychology, instead of in terms of its (supposedly) objective
form and content.[50] But more than one of Lewis's biographers has noted
that it is neither excessively Freudian nor taking refuge in the personal heresy

46. That is, "whipping up support" for their side.
47. C. S. Lewis to his brother, Warren Lewis, July 9, 1927, Hooper, ed., *Collected Letters*,
vol. 1, 702–3.
48. C. S. Lewis, *Perelandra* (New York: MacMillan, 1965), 131.
49. Dorothy L. Sayers, *Gaudy Night*. A "Gaudy" (in Oxford-speak) is a gala celebration for
which graduates of a given college reassemble (from the Latin verb *gaudere*, to rejoice). For a
more detailed analysis of feminist themes in this novel, see Chris Willis, "'Suspicion in the SCR':
Gaudy Night, Feminism and Higher Education for Women," *Sidelights on Sayers: The Journal
of the Dorothy L. Sayers Society* 47 (1998); and Susan Haack, "After My Own Heart: Dorothy
L. Sayers's Feminism," *The New Criterion* 19, no. 9 (May 2001): 10–18.
50. C. S. Lewis and E. M. W. Tillyard, *The Personal Heresy: A Controversy* (London: Oxford
University Press, 1929). Fredrick and McBride note that many Lewis hagiographers "have come
to use the term *personal heresy* for any reading of an author's personal life into his or her work.
Yet [they] turn a blind eye toward 'the personal heresy' when personal data support their own
point of view [about Lewis]" (*Women Among the Inklings*, xvi).

to observe that after losing his own mother at age nine, he was vulnerable as a young adult to forming a long-term attachment with a substitute.[51] When he did so, it turned out to be with a woman whose influence on his life was highly ambiguous, by turns warmly supportive and—especially as she grew older—possessive and tyrannical.

As an undergraduate, Lewis had arrived at Oxford just after being called up for service in World War I, and as Oxford was being transformed into a gigantic army training facility. When he met Janie Moore, the mother of a fellow-soldier, she was twenty-six years his senior. She was also Irish, the daughter of a clergyman, genteel (though with less formal education than his mother), mysteriously separated from her husband, and generous and hospitable to a fault.[52] Lewis, it appears, was ripe for infatuation. When Mrs. Moore's own son died during the war, Lewis became her lifelong fictive son, and she his mother.[53] She moved to Oxford to be near him, occupying over several years a variety of rented quarters with her younger child, Maureen. As an undergraduate, Lewis risked spending as much of his time (and his living allowance) with her as he could, to the increasing bewilderment and alarm of his father and brother.[54] Early in his academic career, he copurchased a house near Oxford—The Kilns—with her and with his brother, who, with some ambivalence, seems to have joined "the family" (as Lewis called it) on retiring from the army in order to have a continuing relationship with his sibling. This domestic arrangement lasted until Janie Moore's death in 1951.

51. Roger Lancelyn Green and Walter Hooper, C. S. Lewis: A Biography (London: Collins, 1974), chaps. 2–5; George Sayer, Jack: C. S. Lewis and His Times (San Francisco: Harper and Row, 1988), chaps. 6–9; Wilson, C. S. Lewis, chaps. 7–9.

52. Warren Lewis wrote that Janie Moore was a woman "of very limited mind . . . In twenty years I never saw a book in her hands" (See Walter Hooper, ed., Letters of C. S. Lewis [New York: Harcourt Brace Jovanovich, 1993], 32–33). However, C. S. Lewis described her as reading works by Charlotte Bronte, E. M. Forster, and Leo Tolstoy, and himself as reading aloud to her a book on World War I, some of these occasions occurring while Warren Lewis was living with them. See, for example, Walter Hooper, ed., The Collected Letters of C. S. Lewis, vol. 2, 1931–1949 (San Francisco: HarperSanFrancisco, 2004), 694, 706.

53. Though they did not know each other very well before being deployed, Lewis and Mrs. Moore's son Paddy had actually agreed that, if either were killed during the war, the other would take responsibility for the deceased's mother or father. However, it seems unlikely that Lewis would have fulfilled this promise at such close quarters had he not already developed an even closer relationship with Paddy's mother than he had with Paddy himself.

54. A. N. Wilson also points out how risky it was for Lewis, as an undergraduate, to behave this way: "To have slept out of college was a very serious offense. To be shown to have associated with a member of the opposite sex was yet more serious . . . Mrs. Moore was neither Lewis's wife nor his mother, and though she may have been something just as innocent, it would have put his career in jeopardy had the authorities known about her. He would certainly never have had any hope of a college fellowship; even in the 1950s, Oxford dons who were deemed to have led irregular lives with the opposite sex found themselves 'resigning' their fellowships" (C. S. Lewis, 65, 66).

Wounded Healers

In recent years the consensus among Lewis's biographers has been that his relationship with Janie Moore was probably also a sexual relationship, at least until Lewis became a Christian at age thirty-two.[55] In later life Janie Moore destroyed Lewis's accumulated letters to her, and Arthur Greeves was asked to hold in confidence (and later destroyed) almost all letters from Jack that made any reference to sex. But the remaining correspondence shows the convoluted arrangements Lewis undertook to keep the details of his domestic life hidden from his father right up to the latter's death in 1929. In addition, Janie Moore's daughter Maureen, who was twelve when Jack met her mother, has recalled the efforts made to send her to church every Sunday so that the two adults could be alone together.[56] But his biographers also agree that after his conversion, Lewis must have begun (however slowly) to embrace the life of celibacy that he now saw as the only Christian alternative to actual marriage.[57] "When I first came to the University," Lewis later wrote, "I was as nearly without a moral conscience as a boy could be. Some faint distaste for cruelty and for meanness about money was my utmost reach—of chastity, truthfulness and self-sacrifice I thought as a baboon thinks of classical music."[58] But he also recalled the effect on him of friends who were committed to keeping the moral law, and whose standards he came to admire: "The recognition of new standards is accompanied with the sense of shame and guilt; one is conscious of having blundered into society that one is unfit for. It is in light of such experiences that we must consider the goodness of God."[59]

So Lewis and Sayers—two brilliant, educated, and increasingly famous defenders of the Christian faith—each harbored a secret from their sexually active, young-adult past. What is striking is the extent to which each took lifelong responsibility for the results. Late in life Sayers—whose appropriation of her faith tended to be very cerebral—was to write to a colleague that "of all the presuppositions of Christianity,"

> the only one I really . . . can swear to from personal inward conviction is sin. About that I have no doubt whatever and never have had. Neither does any doctrine of determinism or psychological maladjustment convince me in the

55. See, for example, Alan Jacobs, *The Narnian: The Life and Imagination of C. S. Lewis* (San Francisco: HarperSanFrancisco: 2005), chap. 5; Wilson, *C. S. Lewis*, chaps. 6 and 7; and Walter Hooper, *C. S. Lewis: Companion and Guide* (San Francisco: HarperSanFrancisco: 1996), 712–14.

56. Wilson, *C. S. Lewis*, 66–67.

57. Ibid., 127–29; Jacobs, *The Narnian*, 151–53.

58. Lewis, *The Problem of Pain*, 26..

59. Ibid.

very least that when I do wrong it is not I who do it and that I could not, by some other means, have done better.[60]

By the 1930s, Sayers was "doing better": supporting her growing son both financially and with visits and letters as she wrote fiction, essays, Christian drama, and apologetics. And Lewis, having forged a relationship with another of the war's "surplus women" before his conversion, had to decide what his Christian responsibilities were to this genteelly-impoverished female who was almost sixty years old.

His conclusion seems clear from a letter sent to his brother in 1930. About sharing a household with Janie Moore and her daughter he wrote: "Whether I was wise or foolish, to have done so originally, is now only a historical question: once having created expectations, one naturally fulfills them." Discussing the possibility of sharing that home with his brother Warnie, he added: "I am sure you did not entertain the idea that you and I could set up a purely [Lewis-centered] household with the others simply as 'staff' or 'chorus.' One hopes of course that we should live in a 'blend.'"[61] And "live in a blend" is evidently what they did: Jack more and more treating (and referring to) Janie Moore as "my mother," Warnie joining the household but also sharing Jack's work space at Magdalen College. They were bachelor brothers who shared a home with an older lady and her growing daughter—an entirely respectable arrangement for two Oxford men who had both returned to the church of their childhood as thirty something adults.

Lewis's biographers differ as to whether his early years with Janie Moore brought a needed balance to his highly cognitive Oxford life, or kept him from doing more scholarship by turning him into a meek and dutiful householder.[62] Lewis's undergraduate diaries show him enjoying routine domestic tasks and also enjoying most of the guests who passed through, freely helping Maureen Moore with her studies and hobbies, and only occasionally feeling burdened if there was a passing household crisis. Janie Moore "was generous and taught me to be generous too," he later told his former student and biographer, George Sayer. "If it were not for her, I should know little or nothing about ordinary domestic life as lived by most people."[63] On the other hand, having begun her relationship with Jack as a fellow-apostate from the Anglican church, Moore permanently resented his return to Christianity, and even spoke sarcastically of

60. Dorothy L. Sayers to John Wren-Lewis, April 1954, as quoted in Reynolds, *Dorothy L. Sayers*, 68.

61. C. S. Lewis to Warren Lewis, January 12, 1930, Hooper, ed., *Collected Letters*, vol. 1, 871.

62. Sayer argues for the first; Warren Lewis, as well as Green and Hooper, argue for the second; Wilson concludes that there is evidence for both.

63. Sayer, *Jack*, 89–90. Sayer adds, from his personal acquaintance with Lewis, that "if he had lived the cloistered existence of a bachelor don, his writing would have suffered from a loss of warmth, humanity, and the understanding of human pain and suffering" (203).

"blood feasts" when he and his brother went to take communion at the local parish church.[64] Lewis's biographers regularly infer that when writing (as he often did) about the resentment families can display when one member gets more serious about religion, he was thinking at least partly of Janie Moore.

By 1941 Lewis would ask his friend and colleague, the Anglican nun Penelope Lawson:

> Have you room for an extra prayer? Pray for *Jane* if you have. She is the old lady I call my mother and live with (she is really the mother of a friend)—an unbeliever, ill, old, frightened, full of charity in the sense of alms, but full of uncharity in several other senses. And I can do so little for her.[65]

Moore was by all accounts chronically incapable of relating amicably to the various women hired to help out at The Kilns. As a result, few lasted there for long, and Lewis often found himself forced into the role of mediator in domestic disputes. And after the stresses of World War II (including hosting a string of young evacuees who would provide inspiration for the children in Lewis's *Narnia* chronicles), Moore's bodily and mental health deteriorated rapidly, putting Lewis under increasing physical, temporal, and financial burdens until her 1951 death in a nursing home. By this time, Lewis was almost fifty-three years old, having never married. A few months later, he wrote to one of his American correspondents about his life with Janie Moore:

> Strictly between ourselves, I have lived most of it (that is now over) in a house wh[ich] was hardly ever at peace for 24 hours, amidst senseless wranglings, lyings, backbitings, follies and *scares*. I never went home without a feeling of terror as to what might have developed in my absence. Only now that it is over . . . do I begin to realize quite how bad it was.[66]

A Cautious Conversation

Thus despite a competent and accomplished mother, whom he lost at a young age, Lewis's affiliation with conservative Magdalen College—added to his domestic life with the increasingly unpredictable Janie Moore—may have retarded his acceptance of women as equals. In a 1969 letter to Walter Hooper (Lewis's literary executor), poet Ruth Pitter—who was in a mutually mentoring

---

64. Green and Hooper, *C. S. Lewis*, 197. Janie Moore claimed that the loss of her own son Paddy in World War I had put her off God permanently.

65. C. S. Lewis to Sister Penelope, BVM, November 9, 1941, Hooper, ed., *Collected Letters*, vol. 2, 496.

66. C. S. Lewis to Mary Van Deusen, April 18, 1951, Walter Hooper, ed., *The Collected Letters of C. S. Lewis*, vol. 3, *1950–1963* (San Francisco: HarperSanFranciso: 2007), 108 (emphasis original).

relationship with Lewis from 1946 on—speculated about the effects of such factors on his attitude toward women:

> An interesting subject, Jack's views on women . . . I have thought that losing his mother (cruel loss at age 8, and horribly emphasized by the circumstances) must have seemed a black betrayal. If he was mistrustful of women, it was not hatred, but a burnt child's dread of fire . . . It is a pity that he made his first (and perhaps biggest) impact with [*The Screwtape Letters*], in which some women are only too well portrayed in their horrors, rather like Milton's Satan—is it this perhaps that has made people think he hated [women]? . . . I have wondered whether his experience with the "mother" he adopted did not find a steam-vent [in *Screwtape*].[67]

After his embrace of Christianity in 1931, this prejudice was less evident on the actual than on the theoretical level, as we will see when we consider his relations with some other women in the next chapter. But in the meantime, as Sayers's *Gaudy Night* was going to press in the mid-1930s, Lewis was beginning to write *Out of the Silent Planet*, the first volume of his space trilogy. We saw earlier that in its sequels—*Perelandra* and *That Hideous Strength*—Lewis regularly read classical and medieval notions about gender archetypes and gender hierarchy back into his understanding of Christianity. Since most of these assumptions went well beyond the biblical record and the Christian creeds, how did he justify this stance? And how, after they became colleagues, did Dorothy L. Sayers respond?

We have seen that, as a young don, Lewis's attraction to Christianity was heightened when two of his colleagues assured him that becoming a Christian did not mean having to renounce his love of classical mythology. Indeed, as they explained it, a major function of mythology was to anticipate the coming of Christ, and to build up a store of imagery through which pagans could understand the significance of the incarnation when they finally heard about it. As Lewis later put it in his post-conversion allegory, *The Pilgrim's Regress*, mythic stories throughout history have been one way that "the Landlord succeeded in getting a lot of messages through."[68] Indeed, the wise hermit in this story tells Pilgrim John (Lewis's alter ego) "the definition of a Pagan—a man so traveling that, if all goes well, he arrives at Mother Kirk's [i.e., Mother Church's] chair." Pagan myths, the hermit asserts, are "a starting point from which *one* road leads home and a thousand roads lead into the wilderness."[69] And when John is tempted to conclude that his strange pilgrimage experiences

67. As quoted in Don W. King, "The Anatomy of a Friendship: The Correspondence of Ruth Pitter and C. S. Lewis, 1946–1962," *Mythlore* 91 (Summer 2003): 2–24 (quotation from pp. 13–14).

68. C. S. Lewis, *The Pilgrim's Regress: An Allegorical Apology for Christianity, Reason and Romanticism* (London: Geoffrey Bles, 1933), 153.

69. Ibid., 155 (emphasis original).

are only "mythic" (in the sense of being "untrue fantasies") a voice from behind him assures him that it is otherwise:

> Child if you will, it *is* mythology . . . but then it is My mythology . . . This is My inventing. This is the veil under which I have chosen to appear even from the first until now. For this end I made your senses and for this end your imagination, that you might see My face and live . . . Have you not heard among the Pagans the story of Semele? Or was there any age in any land when men did not know that corn and wine were the blood and body of a dying yet living God?[70]

Lewis thus seems to have concluded that if more clearly biblical themes such as the "dying yet living God" are foreshadowed in ancient myths, then other mythic themes that he found personally attractive—such as the ultimate masculinity of God and the archetypal gendering of all creation—could also come along for the ride. This, of course, does not follow, since Lewis himself warned that from Pagan myths "*one* road leads home and a thousand roads lead into the wilderness."[71] But until somewhat later in his life, he wrote as if whatever he selected to put on that "one road" regarding gender relations was indeed part of "mere" Christianity.

How did Sayers react to such claims? In 1948, when Lewis asked her to speak out against the movement for women's ordination, he invoked "the far deeper need that the Priest at the Altar must represent the Bridegroom [i.e., Christ] to whom we are all, in a sense feminine."[72] Sayers's response to this was fairly brusque:

> One has to be very careful with that "Bridegroom" imagery. It is so very apt to land one in Male and Female Principles, Eleusis, and the womb of the Great Mother. And that sort of thing doesn't make much appeal to well-balanced women, who look on it as just another example of men's hopeless romanticism about sex, and who are apt either to burst out laughing or sniff a faint smell of drains.[73]

Eleusis was the place where ancient Greeks could be inducted into a mystery cult, which revered the cycle of the seasons by honoring Demeter, the goddess of agriculture. And Sayers's reference to the "faint smell of drains"

---

70. Ibid., 171.

71. Even pagan myths of the dying and rising god are to be taken as pointers to Christ only with some qualification, since in most versions the "dying and rising," rather than being unique historical events, continue in endless repetition, reflecting the annual agricultural cycle of dormancy and fruitfulness.

72. C. S. Lewis to Dorothy Sayers, July 13, 1948, Hooper, ed., *Collected Letters*, vol. 1, 860.

73. Dorothy L. Sayers to C. S. Lewis, July 19, 1948, in Barbara Reynolds, ed., *The Letters of Dorothy L. Sayers*, vol. 3, *1944–1950* (Cambridge: The Dorothy L. Sayers Society & Carole Green, 1998), 387.

suggests the sulfurous odor associated with evil—or at least with rotten eggs! Sayers was warning Lewis not to fall into a Pagan mind-set by treating sex as an essential feature of God, rather than an aspect of God's creation that, like humans' other bodily needs, is "very good"[74] but not what makes either men or women image God. A few years earlier she had alerted the Anglican Bishop of Coventry to the same danger:

> All other religions and gods and ethical systems have been preoccupied with sex one way or the other, whether the upshot of the thing is a ferocious asceticism or "nameless orgies." But when you get hold of [the Son of] God personally, you come up against a blank wall. He just doesn't bother about it. He doesn't seem to notice it. If you force the subject on His attention he merely observes that a dirty look is as bad as [adultery] and that men are in no position to cast stones at women . . . You don't realize, perhaps, how extraordinary that is. It's unparalleled. There has been nothing like it before or since.[75]

The normally combative Lewis, who had already submitted his article arguing against priestesses in the church, replied briefly to Sayers's concern, and acknowledged its validity: "I see your point: but have been goaded into [an editorial] which I hope is not too Eleusian or too drainy."[76] Even more tellingly, he did not challenge Sayers's skepticism about "Male and Female Principles," or archetypes—the very ideas he had labored so hard to include in the theological subtext of his space novels. In some ways it would be too simple to call Sayers a feminist: like Lewis, she had too robust a view of human depravity to romanticize any class of people just because it had suffered injustice. But unlike Lewis she believed that gender was an incidental, not an essential trait, and that the common humanity of men and women was more fundamental than any differences between them. Women, she wrote, should be accepted as human beings, "not as an inferior class and not, I beg and pray all feminists, as a superior class—not, in fact, as a class at all . . . We [forget] that a category only exists for its special purpose and must be forgotten as soon as that purpose is served."[77] To Sayers, the mind was androgynous, and to assume otherwise—as a misogynist *or* a romantic feminist—was dangerous:

> I have a foolish complex against allying myself publicly with anything labeled feminist. You will say that this is kicking down the ladder I climbed up by; and

74. Gen. 1:31.

75. Dorothy L. Sayers to the Bishop of Coventry, June 26, 1944, in Reynolds, ed., *Letters of Dorothy L. Sayers*, vol. 3, 28. See also Laura K. Simmons, *Creed Without Chaos: Exploring Theology in the Writings of Dorothy L. Sayers* (Grand Rapids: Baker Academic, 2005), especially chap. 10.

76. C. S. Lewis to Dorothy Sayers, July 20, 1948, Hooper, ed., *Collected Letters*, vol. 2, 863.

77. Sayers, "Are Women Human?" 33.

so it is. All the same, I feel that at this time of the day one can probably do more by taking the feminist position for granted. I mean that the more clamor we make about "the women's point of view," the more we rub it into people that the women's point of view is different, and frankly I do not think it is—at least in my job. The line I always want to take is, that there is the "point of view" of the reasonably enlightened human brain, and that this is the aspect of the matter which I am best fitted to uphold.[78]

In the 1950s, as Sayers turned her energies toward making lively translations of medieval Italian and French poetry, she and Lewis corresponded more and more as fellow scholars. He wrote detailed letters praising her translations of Dante's *Inferno* and *Purgatorio* and of *Le Chanson de Roland*,[79] and Sayers replied in kind as he issued successive volumes of *The Chronicles of Narnia*. Their common passion for medieval and Renaissance literature may be one reason why Lewis once jokingly referred to Sayers as "Sister Dinosaur."[80] But on the issue of generic humanity superseding the secondary qualities of gender, she was anything but a dinosaur in her views. "I do not know what women *as women* want," she wrote in 1938,

but as human beings they want, my good men, exactly what you want yourselves: interesting occupation, reasonable freedom for their pleasures, and a sufficient emotional outlet. What form the occupations, the pleasures, and the emotion may take depends entirely on the individual. You know that this is so with yourselves—why will you not believe that it is so with us?[81]

Fundamental Differences Revisited

We have seen in this chapter that as a child of the Edwardian era, C. S. Lewis grappled with significant social changes in England regarding both class and gender. His views were not static on either of these issues. With regard to class, this privileged scholar, who in 1939 had agreed with Aristotle on the

78. Dorothy L. Sayers to Nancy Pearn, May 29, 1936, Reynolds, ed., *Letters of Dorothy Sayers*, vol. 1, 391–92.

79. *The Song of Roland*, trans. Dorothy L. Sayers (Harmondsworth, UK: Penguin, 1957).

80. C. S. Lewis to Dorothy Sayers, July 1, 1957, Hooper, ed., *Collected Letters*, vol. 3, 863. See also his letter to Sayers of April 6, 1955, where Lewis jokingly asks: "Sh[oul]d we someday form a Dinosaurs' Club (with an annual dinner in the Victoria and Albert [Museum]?" Ibid., 596. In his 1954 inaugural address on assuming the Chair of Medieval and Renaissance Literature at Cambridge, Lewis famously referred to himself as a "dinosaur" in the context of defending the study of old texts: "Speaking not only for myself, but for all other Old Western men whom you may meet, I would say, use your specimens while you can. There are not going to be many more dinosaurs." C. S. Lewis, *They Asked for a Paper* (London: Geoffrey Bles, 1962), 9–25 (quotation from p. 25).

81. Sayers, "Are Women Human?" 32.

necessity of well-supported leisure for intellectuals, admitted a year later to a Christian monastic friend who questioned this view: "I think your criticisms on my Aristotelian idea of leisure are largely right. I wouldn't write that essay now. In fact, I have recently come to the conclusion that a besetting sin of mine all my life has been one I never suspected—laziness—and that a good deal of the high sounding doctrine of leisure is only a defense of *that*. The Greeks [sinned] in owning slaves and [in] their consequent contempt for labor."[82]

And with regard to gender, it is likely that Lewis's slowly changing views owed much to the intellectual and Christian ties he forged with Dorothy L. Sayers, a woman of his own class and educational background. In 1955 he confessed to her that he had only "dimly realized that the old-fashioned way (my Father did it exquisitely) of talking to all young women was v[ery] like an adult way of talking to young boys." With his improved understanding of the origin and effects of such condescension, he added: "It explains not only why some women grew up vapid but also why others grew up (if we may coin the word) *viricidal*."[83] In another letter that year he mentioned to Sayers his concern that some of the illustrations for the *Narnia* stories were a bit too effeminate, and added: "I don't like either the ultra feminine or the ultra masculine myself. I prefer *people*."[84]

Sayers must surely have rejoiced to read this. In her 1947 essay, "The Human-Not-Quite-Human," she had mocked the received view that women are not "people"—and, obliquely, Lewis's earlier view that they are mostly either saints or temptresses:

> [People believe women] lie when they say they have human needs: warm and decent clothing; comfort in the bus; interests directed immediately to God and His universe, not intermediately through any child of man. They are far above man to inspire him, far beneath him to corrupt him; they have feminine minds and feminine natures, but their mind is not one with their nature like the minds of men; they have no human mind and no human nature.[85]

Her response to these assumptions came from her reading of the Gospels:

> Perhaps it is no wonder that women were first at the Cradle and last at the Cross. They had never known a man like this Man—there never has been such

82. C. S. Lewis to Dom Bede Griffiths, July 16, 1940, Hooper, ed., *Collected Letters*, vol. 2, 422.

83. *Viricidal* roughly means, "wanting to kill men." C. S. Lewis to Dorothy Sayers, November 27, 1955, Hooper, ed., *Collected Letters*, vol. 3, 676 (emphasis original).

84. C. S. Lewis to Dorothy Sayers, August 5, 1955, Hooper, ed., *Collected Letters*, vol. 3, 639 (emphasis original).

85. Dorothy L. Sayers, "The Human-Not-Quite-Human," in *Unpopular Opinions: Twenty-One Essays* (London: Gollancz, 1946), 46.

another. A prophet and teacher who never nagged at them, never flattered or coaxed or patronized; who never made arch jokes about them, never treated them either as "the women, God help us!" or "The ladies, God bless them!"; who rebuked without querulousness and praised without condescension; who took their questions and arguments seriously; who never mapped out their sphere for them, never urged them to be feminine or jeered at them for being female; who had no axe to grind and no uneasy male dignity to defend; who took them as he found them and was completely unself-conscious. There is no act, no sermon, no parable in the whole Gospel that borrows its pungency from female perversity; nobody could possibly guess from the words and deeds of Jesus that there was anything "funny" about women's nature.[86]

But Dorothy L. Sayers was not the only woman whose interaction with Lewis helped to change his views on the psychology of gender. In the following chapter, we will meet some others.

86. Ibid., 47.

5

A Better Man than His Theories

C. S. Lewis as a Mentor and Colleague to Women

We have seen that C. S. Lewis and Dorothy L. Sayers—two brilliant Edwardians who shared an Oxford heritage—developed a mutually mentoring and mutually respectful relationship in spite of their initial differences on the topic of gender archetypes, roles, and relationships. One reason for this was that Sayers, like many others, admired Lewis's ability to make Christian themes come alive to his readers through the writing of satire (such as *The Screwtape Letters*), children's stories (such as the *Chronicles of Narnia*), and apologetics (such as *Mere Christianity*). Over the course of her life Sayers, like Lewis, had correspondents who asked her to recommend thoughtful Christian works, and she routinely pointed them to Lewis's books—although sometimes with caveats about his blind spots regarding women. "I do admit," she wrote to one correspondent just after World War II, "that he is apt to write shocking nonsense about women and marriage. (That, however, is not because he is a bad theologian but because he is a rather frightened bachelor)."[1] And to Barbara Reynolds—the Dante

---

1. Barbara Reynolds, ed., *The Letters of Dorothy L. Sayers*, vol. 3, *1944–1950* (Cambridge: The Dorothy L. Sayers Society & Carole Green, 1998), 375. Sayers is of course using the term "theologian" very loosely here, probably as a synonym for "Christian apologist," as Lewis himself never claimed to be a professional theologian. Margaret Hannay was later to summarize the mixed character of Lewis's "theological" writing by noting that "*Mere Christianity* [is] the

scholar who would later become her official biographer—she wrote a few years later that she liked Lewis "very much, and always find him stimulating and amusing. One just has to accept the fact that there is a complete blank in his mind where women are concerned."[2]

But Sayers already knew that C. S. Lewis was a better man than his theories when it came to women. He had a thoroughly collegial relationship with her based on their mutual interest in literature and Christian apologetics. During his one and only foray into the question of women's ordination, Sayers, as we saw, effectively rapped his knuckles regarding his tendency to read pagan gender archetypes back into church order. And she was far from being the only female with whom Lewis had an intellectual relationship of mutual respect. For much of his life Lewis may have *believed* that the mind was far from androgynous, but he was more than capable of *behaving* otherwise, even before his late marriage to Joy Davidman, even before he met Dorothy Sayers, and despite his ambivalent, three-decade relationship with Janie Moore.

In this chapter I will examine some of the relationships Lewis had with women students, friends, and colleagues during his thirty-year tenure at Oxford's Magdalen College and his remaining years at Cambridge's Magdalene College.[3] I will look at his interactions with students, then at some of his relations with women inside and outside of the academy, using as primary sources Lewis's early diaries and lifelong letters, and as secondary sources accounts by selected persons who were his students, colleagues, and friends. Because of its importance for understanding the psychology of gender as part of the social sciences, I will also pay particular attention to the much-discussed Socratic Club debate Lewis had in 1948 with his Oxford colleague, philosopher Elizabeth Anscombe.

---

most popular and the most disparaged of his works, probably because its fans have spoken of it as a profound piece of theology, while it is, and was designed to be, only a primer . . . Anyone ignorant of Christian doctrine can learn much from it, but anyone seriously interested in theology must go beyond it, reading both Lewis's sources, the patristic writers like St. Augustine and St. Athanasius, and more contemporary theologians. But the very simplicity of *Mere Christianity* makes it likely to endure." Margaret P. Hannay, *C. S. Lewis* (New York: Frederick Ungar, 1981), 265–66.

2. Barbara Reynolds, ed., *The Letters of Dorothy L. Sayers*, vol. 4, *1951–1957* (Cambridge: The Dorothy L. Sayers Society & Carole Green, 2000), 144.

3. Lewis considered it both ironic and amusing that in moving from Oxford to Cambridge in 1955, he ended up in a second college named for St. Mary Magdalene, the spelling of the name differing only by one vowel at the end. In his letter of acceptance he wrote: "A professorial fellowship at Magdalene [College Cambridge] is exactly what I would like best. I should like (among other things) to remain under the same patroness. Why should one trouble the celestial civil service with unnecessary change?" C. S. Lewis to Sir Henry Willink, June 10, 1954, in Walter Hooper, ed., *The Collected Letters of C. S. Lewis*, vol. 3, *1950–1963* (San Francisco: HarperSanFranciso: 2007), 488.

A Reluctant but Rigorous Tutor

Oxford University is today so widely associated with academic excellence that it is difficult to imagine a time when this was not the case. But in the words of George Sayer, a former student and later biographer of C. S. Lewis, "For a long time—indeed until the beginning of the Second World war—admission to Oxford depended far more on being able to pay the fees or on having been to the right schools than on possession of academic ability."[4] Indeed, from its founding in the thirteenth century until the early 1800s Oxford could hardly even be called a university, in the sense of having a set of courses and standards that embraced all of its constituent colleges. Each of Oxford's original, medieval colleges was independently chartered by the Crown, sometimes to cater to the church-scholarly needs of a particular diocese, from which it drew both its students and its endowments. By the end of the eighteenth century, the number of colleges had multiplied, but teaching standards varied greatly. Only about a third of the fellows even gave lectures, and those that did often cancelled them if too few students showed up. In fact, Sayer notes, "It was possible for undergraduates to choose, not only the books on which they would be examined, but also, by paying a modest fee [they could even choose] their examiners. The exams would be mainly or entirely oral reviews, and the questions, if the student knew his examiner, quite predictable."[5]

In the nineteenth century, a series of Royal Commissions was appointed to strengthen Oxford's university structure and its standards for evaluating undergraduates, or "commoners" as they were originally called. The ancient parochialism of its colleges was abolished, and professors had to open their courses to men (though not, as we have seen, to women) of other Oxford colleges. Since colleges now had to compete with each other for students, teaching standards began to rise. But they remained uneven through the rest of the nineteenth century, and Oxford degrees were actually considered inferior to those granted by the newer metropolitan universities in cities like London, Manchester, and Birmingham. It was in this situation that the famous tutorial system was born, with university fellowships now awarded to people who were likely not just to be good scholars, but reliable mentors of students assigned to them for one-on-one tutoring.

George Sayer notes that when C. S. Lewis began his career as a fellow and tutor in 1925, there were still notoriously lazy Oxford tutors who did not always bother to show up for appointed meetings with students. "But for a conscientious man like Jack, tutoring was hard work, especially if one considers that he had lectures to give, classes to take, college business to attend to, and his

4. George Sayer, *Jack: C. S. Lewis and His Times* (San Francisco: Harper and Row, 1988), 117.
5. Ibid., 116.

own academic writing to get on with."[6] And Lewis had no illusions about the academic quality and motivation of most of his students. Early in his career he issued some scathing remarks about Oxford students who came from the elite public schools such as Malvern, his own school in early adolescence:

> When I came I found that any Magdalen undergraduate who had interests beyond rowing, drinking, motoring and fornication, sought his friends outside the college, and indeed kept out of the place as much as he could . . . I sometimes wonder if this country will kill the public schools before they kill it. My experience goes on confirming the ideas about them which were first suggested to me by Malvern long ago. The best scholars, the best men and (properly understood) the best gentlemen seem now to come from places like Dulwich [in London] or to be wafted up on county scholarships from [state] secondary schools. Except for pure classics (and that only at Winchester, and only a few boys even there) I really don't know what gifts the public schools bestow upon their nurslings, beyond the mere surface of good manners: unless contempt of the things of the intellect, extravagance, insolence, self-sufficiency and sexual perversion are to be called gifts.[7]

Even the biographers who have been most inclined to idealize him admit that for Lewis, tutoring was the price to be paid for the more attractive life of scholarship.[8] It was a disappointment to him in 1947 when he was voted down for the professorial Chair of English Literature at Merton College, and again in 1951 for a Professorship of Poetry—posts that would have relieved him of all tutoring obligations and given him more time for writing.[9] Nonetheless, for thirty-five years at Oxford he was a demanding yet fair tutor who, in the words of a former student, seemed to accept his pupils "with ironic resignation."[10] Although he admitted to being irritated by certain clever pupils who were conceited or lazy, he seems to have been scrupulously neutral in his

6. Ibid., 117.

7. C. S. Lewis to his father, Albert Lewis, November 3, 1928, in Walter Hooper, ed., *The Collected Letters of C. S. Lewis*, vol. 1, *1905–1931* (San Francisco: HarperSanFrancisco, 2004), 778–79.

8. For example, Roger Lancelyn Green and Walter Hooper, *C. S. Lewis: A Biography* (London: Collins, 1974), chaps. 3 and 6. See also Sayer, *Jack*, chap. 10; A. N. Wilson, *C. S. Lewis: A Biography* (London: Norton, 1990), chap. 10; and Alan Jacobs, *The Narnian: The Life and Imagination of C. S. Lewis* (San Francisco: HarperSanFrancisco: 2005), chap. 8.

9. A professorial chair also came with a substantially better salary. In their years as tutors and fellows, both Lewis and J. R. R. Tolkien supplemented their meager Oxford pay by grading examinations for other academic institutions, a time-consuming summer task that also reduced their hours for scholarship.

10. John Lawlor, "The Tutor and the Scholar," in Jocelyn Gibb, ed., *Light on C. S. Lewis* (London: Geoffrey Bles, 1965), as quoted in Sayer, *Jack*, 121.

actual tutoring, showing "a determined impersonality towards all except his very closest friends."[11]

On the other hand, as George Sayer notes, "he was probably at his best with shy and diffident pupils, to whom he would try to give confidence and encouragement."[12] Some of these became friends, colleagues, and even biographers of Lewis—for example, Sayer himself, who shared with Lewis a love of the fantasy novels of George MacDonald; Roger Lancelyn Green, who shared with both Lewis and Tolkien a scholarly and romantic interest in fairy tales; and Alan Griffiths (later to become the Benedictine monk Dom Bede Griffiths), who journeyed from agnosticism to Christian faith in roughly the same time period as Lewis.[13] "In every given year," Lewis observed early in his career, "the pupils I really like are in a minority, but there is hardly a year in which I do not make some real friend. I am glad to find that people become more and more the sources of pleasure as I grow older."[14] As we will see a little later, one of the pupils with whom he established a long friendship was a young woman—Mary Shelley Neylan—who became a schoolteacher and eventually a professing Christian, in part because of Lewis, and to whose first child Lewis became godfather.

Working with Women Students: "Respectful, Serious [and] a Bit Courtly"

Biographers who knew him personally concede that Lewis's "bluff manner, the lightning speed at which his mind worked . . . [were] apt to alarm or antagonize the more sensitive of his male pupils." So the same treatment, even if gender neutral, "could have seemed to show a veiled contempt to some of his female pupils who were not accustomed to anything of the kind."[15] This may have been one basis for the persistent legend that Lewis refused to teach female undergraduates. But in fact, as a twenty-seven-year-old in his very first

11. Sayer, *Jack*, 121. Lewis was, for example, privately exasperated by his notoriously lazy pupil John Betjeman, who never finished his degree but went on to become the Poet Laureate of England in 1972. Deflecting his annoyance at one point into ironic humor, Lewis wrote the following note to Betjeman in 1948 (offering him what may have been a book of bad Victorian verse): "Dear Betjeman: A student of y[ou]r works placed in my hands last night a piece of XIXth century didactic hardware so edifying in tendency & hideous in design that we all felt you were the one man in England who c[oul]d fully appreciate it. It awaits you in my rooms whenever you care to call for it." C. S. Lewis to John Betjeman, December 17, 1968, in Walter Hooper, ed., *The Collected Letters of C. S. Lewis*, vol. II, 1931–49 (San Francisco: HarperOne, 2009), 895.

12. Sayer, *Jack*, 121.

13. Griffiths was the Catholic theologian whom Lewis consulted in 1941 as to the possibility of subordinationism within the Trinity. See Walter Hooper, ed., *The Collected Letters of C. S. Lewis*, vol. 2, *1931–1949* (San Francisco: HarperSanFrancisco, 2004), 503.

14. C. S. Lewis to Arthur Greeves, December 6, 1931, Hooper, ed., *Collected Letters*, vol. 2, 24.

15. Green and Hooper, *C. S. Lewis*, 87.

year of teaching, he took on an extra philosophy class for women students at Lady Margaret Hall, and his diary entries for the spring of 1926 describe the beginning and continuation of those meetings.

On the first day, "seven girls turned up . . . As hardly any of them had read the *Dialogues* [of Plato] it was a bit difficult to get discussion going, but once they began it went fairly well." He describes them (as he does his male pupils) in terms ranging from blunt to complimentary, but at the same time shows a characteristic tendency to sympathize with the underdog. "Miss Scones and Miss Thring joined in snubbing Miss House, very acrimoniously I thought: so I did the best I could for her, but she had become sulky and frightened by them."[16] Later entries about his "L.M.H." class note such events as that "Miss Scones read a paper: really astonishingly good for an amateur. She and Miss Colborne were very good in discussion[17] . . . Home for early tea and then in to L.M.H. A good hour on Hume's theory of causation[18] . . . Had tea in the smoking room and went to L.M.H. for my class, where Miss Colborne read a paper on Skepticism and a lively discussion followed."[19] He also shows a self-conscious concern about classes that were less successful: "Out to L.M.H. Miss Colborne was away, Miss Scones surprisingly dull, and the paper read by the lumpy Miss Grant. The hour was a failure and I am rather ashamed of getting a pound for it."[20]

The Lady Margaret Hall students were taught as a group, not assigned to Lewis as individual tutorial pupils. But in later years two members of the latter category—one woman and one man—corresponded with Lewis prior to coming up to Oxford, to get his advice on what to read in preparation for joining the English school. Lewis's replies to each are notably similar. To Mary Shelley, who was transferring from the University of Reading in 1931, he writes concerning her upcoming study of medieval literature: "As regards reading for the Vac[ation], my general view is that the Vac. should be given chiefly to reading the actual literary texts, without much attention to problems, getting thoroughly familiar with stories, situation, and style, and so having all the data for *aesthetic* judgment ready: then the term can be kept for more

16. Walter Hooper, ed., *All My Road Before Me: The Diary of C. S. Lewis* (San Diego: Harcourt, 1991), 380.

17. Ibid., 387.

18. Ibid., 401.

19. Ibid., 410.

20. Ibid., 414. In his domestic life with Janie Moore prior to his Oxford donship, Lewis had been so impoverished that he often did one-on-one tutoring of Oxford students at home, about which he showed a similar pedagogical concern. For example, during one Moore household crisis in 1923 he was tutoring a student in Greek, and commented afterward in his diary: "How far it was any good I don't know, for I was very sleepy and nervy and the noise of scenes going on upstairs was worse than if I had been in them" (ibid., 210).

scholarly reading." He then gives her a detailed list of recommended editions of Chaucerian and other primary texts.[21]

A decade later, he writes in a very similar way to Derek Brewer, a prospective male pupil—albeit one who is likely to be called up as a World War II conscript in the midst of his studies.[22] Lewis suggests that before coming to Oxford he read certain relevant Latin texts, and warns him that "a fairly sound Biblical background is assumed by most of the older English writers; if you lack this, acquire it." He concludes the letter with the following advice:

> Chaucer, Shakespeare, Milton are certainties whatever shortened course or ordinary course you take. Next to these in importance come Malory, Spenser, Donne, Browne, Dryden, Pope, Swift, Johnson, Wordsworth. After that it becomes a matter of taste. The great thing is to be always reading but not getting bored—treat it not like work, more as a vice! Your book bill ought to be your biggest extravagance![23]

These are almost the only known letters Lewis wrote to students wanting a head start on their assigned texts, but it seems clear from them that he was no respecter of persons of either sex, once he had committed himself as a tutor. The next time Lewis wrote to Derek Brewer, he was welcoming him back from the war in 1945 and looking forward to tutoring him again.[24] However, the next time he corresponded with Mary Shelley it was after she had "gone down" from Oxford in 1933 with a Fourth Class degree in English. Lewis was so clearly convinced that this did not reflect her true mettle that it is worth reproducing his entire letter to her. "Dear Miss Shelley," he wrote:

> If you are not, at the moment, too sick of me and all my kind to read further, it may be worth saying that you must not run away with the idea that you are a fourth class mind. What really ruined you was a NS [not satisfactory] and a [D] on language, which would of course have spoiled even very good work elsewhere. In the Lit. your highest mark was [B+] (XIXth century).
>
> Why your literature papers were not better I do not understand. I blame myself for not having exhorted more essays from you—but I doubt if that was the whole cause. You were very *short* and *general*. But I am quite clear in my

21. C. S. Lewis to Mary Shelley, June 18, 1931, in Supplement to *Collected Letters*, vol. 3, 1524. Shelley had been a student at Reading of Lewis's colleague and fellow Inkling, Hugo Dyson, and Lewis makes clear in his letter that he had saved a place for this "Dysonian" in his roster of pupils for the upcoming term.

22. Brewer did indeed have to interrupt his education to fight in World War II, but resumed his studies with Lewis at Oxford in 1947. He eventually became a well-known Chaucer scholar who spent the later part of his academic career at Emmanuel College, Cambridge.

23. C. S. Lewis to Derek Brewer, April 18, 1941, Supplement to *Collected Letters*, vol. 3, 1540–41.

24. Ibid., 1561.

own mind that you have not done yourself justice and that your real quality is
far beyond the work you did in the Schools [examinations].

This is cold comfort to you with the world to face!—but at least it is said
quite sincerely and not merely for the sake of consoling you.

Try to forgive me both as an examiner and a tutor. If there should at any
time be any way in which I can be of use to you, let me know at once. Till then,
good-bye and good luck.[25]

We can see from this correspondence why Lewis biographer Alan Jacobs
described Lewis's relationships with women as "respectful, serious [and] a
bit courtly."[26] It is also worth noting that Mary Shelley became his pupil in
the fall of 1931, at just about the same time Lewis was becoming a more-fully
orthodox Christian.[27] But the above letter (wishing her only "good luck")
confirms what his biographers have regularly noted: Lewis did not use his
tutorial relationships as opportunities for proselytizing, or even expressing
his own personal piety. Thus when he urged Derek Brewer in 1941 to become
biblically literate prior to taking medieval and Renaissance English literature,
his advice was largely academic, since the writers of that period *did* assume
a Christian worldview and familiarity with biblical texts on the part of their
readers.

Friendship with a Former Woman Student

Mary Shelley landed on her feet in a teaching job at Dartington Hall, a coeducational progressive boarding school in Devon. The next time Lewis corresponded
with her, in 1937, it was to respond to a query about some literary-critical texts,
and also to send greetings to her husband and fellow schoolteacher, Daniel
Neylan.[28] Three years later, and then the mother of a two-year-old daughter,
she wrote to Lewis again, with some sober questions about the compatibility
of psychoanalysis and Christianity, since she had profited from the former
and was now seriously considering the latter. To this Lewis responded with
a several-page letter whose contents interestingly anticipate some of the ma-

25. C. S. Lewis to Mary Shelley, July 31, 1933, Hooper, ed., *Collected Letters*, vol. 2, 113.

26. Jacobs, *The Narnian*, 255. Indeed, all of Lewis's letters to this ex-pupil, even after he has
become a friend and spiritual adviser, are addressed to "Miss Shelley" or to "Mrs. Neylan"—
though, in keeping with the norms of his class and time, he addresses even his intimate male
correspondents by their surnames as well (e.g., "Dear Williams," "Dear Barfield").

27. It was on October 1, 1931 that Lewis wrote to Arthur Greeves that he had "just passed
from believing in God to definitely believing in Christ—in Christianity" (Hooper, ed., *Collected
Letters*, vol. 1, 974).

28. C. S. Lewis to Mary Shelley Neylan, March 8, 1937, ibid., 2ll–12. It appears from other
correspondence with Daniel Neylan (ibid., 214) that the latter was already a Christian when
he married Mary Shelley.

terial later to appear in *Mere Christianity*.[29] We can glean something about the context of this exchange from another letter Lewis wrote the same week to his brother:

> This week I received a letter from my former pupil Mrs. Neylan (the Dartington Hall mistress) who is trembling on the verge of Christianity—admits that the issue "can no longer be avoided"—and asks what to read and (more difficult still) who to see. I felt almost overwhelmed by the responsibility of my reply, and naturally the more because two other [former pupils] whose conversion had something to do with me became Papists![30] . . . The letter's gone now. I suppose if God intends to have Mrs. Neylan it won't make much difference what I've written!—yet that is a dangerous argument wh[ich] w[oul]d lead to its not mattering what you did in any circumstances.[31]

Here too Lewis was no respecter of persons. While not taking advantage of his power as a tutor to proselytize pupils while at Oxford, he clearly felt both a duty and a burden to respond to their religious questions once they had "gone down." Yet there is clear continuity with the previously-shared tutorial setting, for after recommending some contemporary Christian writers to Mary Shelley Neylan, Lewis wrote: "I think you w[oul]d also find it most illuminating to re-read now many things you once read in 'Eng. Lit.' without knowing their real importance [as Christian works]—[George] Herbert, [Thomas] Traherne, [and Thos. Browne's] *Religio Medici*."[32]

Less than a month later, Mary Neylan—still a seeker, not yet a Christian—wrote to Lewis for clarification about the meaning of the Anglican marriage service. She was concerned that its asymmetrical injunction for women to "obey" their husbands implied that the woman becomes a "slave-wife" and that it precluded her "going in for education." Lewis, while still maintaining that the male "Headship doctrine is that of Christianity" quickly added that it was inherently limited to the sphere of marriage:

> I take it to be chiefly about man *as* man and woman *as* woman, and therefore about husbands and wives, since it is only in marriage that they meet *as* epitomes of their sex. Notice that in I Cor XI just after the bit about the man being the Head, St. Paul goes on to add the baffling reservation (v. 11) that the sexes "in the Lord" don't have any separate existence. I have no idea what this means; but I take it must imply that the existence of a man or woman is not exhausted

29. C. S. Lewis to Mary Shelley Neylan, March 26, 1940, ibid., 371–76.

30. He is referring here to Alan Griffiths (who became the Benedictine monk Dom Bede Griffiths) and to George Sayer, one of his later biographers.

31. C. S. Lewis to Warren Lewis, March 29, 1940, Hooper, ed., *Collected Letters*, vol. 2, 378–79.

32. C. S. Lewis to Mary Shelley Neylan, March 26, 1940, Hooper, ed., *Collected Letters*, vol. 2, 376.

by the fact of being male or female, but that they exist in many other modes. I mean, you may be a citizen, a musician, a teacher etc as well as a woman, and you needn't transfer to all these personalities everything that is about you as a wife *qua* wife.[33]

In this and subsequent correspondence with Mary Neylan, Lewis reveals the complexity—and sometimes the inconsistency—of his views on gender relations. On the one hand, from earlier letters it is pretty clear that Neylan had continued to teach at Dartington after becoming a mother, and Lewis never suggests to her that this is an inappropriate choice, despite his stated convictions about gender archetypes. On the other hand, it eventually becomes clear that one of the things driving her into the arms of God was the realization that she was jealous of the bond her infant daughter had formed with her other caretaker.[34] By 1941 Neylan had become a Christian, and Lewis was praising her honesty about this struggle and suggesting that God had used it in a redemptive way:

> The resentment in itself is bad, but only the bad concomitant of a good thing. In your experience, I take it, the good thing was the painful realization of how far you had abdicated your maternal position—a complex privation, of joys missed and duties neglected. The bad element was the "dog in the manger" indignation at seeing that someone else had picked up what you had dropped.[35]

Clearly, for the Lewis of the 1940s there were both "wifely" and "motherly" essences, laid down by God and nature, regardless of what other roles women might take on as mere human beings. In fact, Lewis rehearsed on Mary Neylan in 1940 the "natural" argument for husbandly headship that later appeared in *Mere Christianity*:[36]

> If [marriage] is like a nation, not a club, like an organism, not a heap of stones, then, in the long run, one party or the other must have the casting vote.

33. C. S. Lewis to Mary Shelley Neylan, April 18, 1940, ibid., 392–97. As I noted in chap. 3, it was misleading for Lewis (whether deliberately or inadvertently) to call male headship a Christian "doctrine," as it has never had confessional status in the creeds of the church.

34. Presumably the child's nanny, but this is unclear.

35. C. S. Lewis to Mary Shelley Neylan, April 26, 1941, Hooper, ed., *Collected Letters*, vol. 2, 480. In a subsequent letter shortly after this Lewis writes to her, with the intent of encouraging her: "I'm sure you're doing right and that God is leading you and bringing you in pretty fast too. I shall never forget your reply, 'It looks like it,' when I suggested jealousy as one of the troubles. I never hope to see the human ship take a big wave in better style! . . . If I were to tell you as much about myself as you have told me (wh[ich] I shan't!) the record w[oul]d be much blacker than your own." C. S. Lewis to Mary Shelley Neylan, May 9, 1941, Hooper, ed., *Collected Letters*, vol. 2, 484).

36. C. S. Lewis, *Mere Christianity* (London: Collins, 1952), 99–100. Lewis began doing the BBC broadcast talks that would be the basis of *Mere Christianity* in 1941.

That being so, do you really *want* the Head to be the woman? In a particular instance, no doubt you may. But do you really want a matriarchal world? Do you really like women in authority? When you seek authority yourself, do you naturally seek it in a woman? . . . My own feeling is that the Headship of the husband is necessary to protect the outer world against the family. The female has a strong instinct to fight for its cubs. What do nine out of ten women care about justice to the outer world when the health, or career, or happiness of their own children is at stake? That is why I want a "foreign policy" of the family, so to speak, to be determined by the man: I expect more mercy from him!

Yet this fierce maternal instinct must be preserved, otherwise the enormous sacrifices involved in motherhood w[oul]d never be borne. The Christian scheme, therefore, does not suppress it but protects us defenceless bachelors from its worst ravages![37]

Mary Neylan could not be blamed if she ended up somewhat bewildered by these double messages about her essence as a woman/wife/mother. She was, after all, a trained teacher, and thus could presumably distinguish pretty well between what was just and what was merely indulgent when dealing with children, including her own. Fortunately for her (but not for the later readers of *Mere Christianity*, from which it is missing) Lewis immediately added the qualifier, "This, however is only my own idea."[38] When he was thinking most carefully and responsibly, and when actual persons—as opposed to abstract audiences—were involved, Lewis was usually aware of what he could pass off as "mere Christianity" and what he could (and should) not.

Moreover, there is little evidence from their subsequent correspondence that Lewis was engaging in a "3:16 bait-and-switch" with Mary Neylan—that is, treating her more as a generic human being when he commends the faith to her, then putting her in her (highly constrained) place as a woman once she is a committed but still relatively untutored Christian. In later letters to her, Lewis suggests some critical texts on Dante,[39] answers questions about one of his own novels (apparently her students at one point were reading the first volume of Lewis's space trilogy),[40] happily agrees to be the godfather of her first child,[41]

37. C. S. Lewis to Mary Shelley Neylan, April 18, 1940, Hooper, ed., *Collected Letters*, vol. 2, 394–95.

38. Ibid., 395.

39. Ibid., 492.

40. Ibid., 480–81, 492. See also 254–55.

41. Ibid., 517–18. Lewis was formally a godfather not only to Sarah Neylan, but also to Lucy Barfield (the adopted daughter of his friend and colleague Owen Barfield) to whom the first of the *Narnia* chronicles was dedicated; to Laurence Harwood, son of another friend and colleague, Cecil Harwood; and to Richard Francis Blake, the first son of Maureen Moore and her husband Leonard Blake. And even before becoming the legal stepfather to Joy Davidman's sons, David and Douglas, Lewis was effectively both a financial and psychological "godfather" to others as well. For example, his financial support enabled the Barfields to permanently foster another child, Jeffrey, to whom Lewis dedicated a later volume of the *Narnia* chronicles (*The*

engages in a discussion of Victorian literature,[42] and asks if he can dedicate to her his edited anthology of George MacDonald's writings.[43] In his relationship with Mary Shelley Neylan—first as a tutor, then as a Christian mentor, and friend—C. S. Lewis was indeed a better man than his theories.

Working with the Women Socratics

Ironically, even as Lewis was questioning women's rational-moral capacities to Mary Neylan, other women at Oxford were drawing up plans for an ongoing forum in which the claims for and against Christianity could be presented in a highly rational fashion. This university forum, which came to be known as the Socratic Club, was first suggested by a Somerville College student, Monica Shorten, and developed with the help of Stella Aldwinckle, an Oxford graduate in theology who had come back to serve as the Chaplain to Women Students.[44] In 1941 Shorten had complained to her newly arrived chaplain that no one seemed ready to discuss with any rigor the various questions raised about Christianity by unbelievers. As a result, Aldwinckle posted a notice inviting "all atheists, agnostics, and those who are disillusioned about religion or think they are" to meet in the Somerville Junior Common Room to help plan an "open forum for the discussion of the intellectual difficulties connected with religion and with Christianity in particular."[45]

All approved Oxford student clubs were required to have a faculty sponsor, or "president" (the term used at that time). When Aldwinckle wrote to ask Lewis if he would take on that role, he promptly replied that such a club was long overdue, and accepted the post of president, while she coordinated the club and chaired its meetings.[46] For approximately the next fifteen years (for

---

Voyage of the Dawn Treader). See also Lyle W. Dorsett and Marjorie Lamp Mead, eds., *C. S. Lewis: Letters to Children* (New York: MacMillan, 1985).

42. Hooper, ed., *Collected Letters*, vol. 2, 550.

43. C. S. Lewis to Mary Shelley Neylan, May 20, 1945, ibid., 652–53. "Bye the bye," Lewis wrote, "I've finished a selection from Geo. Macdonald [*sic*] . . . which will come out about Xmas: w[oul]d you (or not) care to have it dedicated to you? I feel it is rather yours by right as you got more out of him than anyone else to whom I introduced his books. Just let me know." The volume, with a preface written by Lewis, was indeed dedicated to Mary Neylan. See C. S. Lewis, ed., *George MacDonald: An Anthology* (London: Geoffrey Bles, 1946).

44. Aldwinckle remained in this position for twenty-five years, from 1941 to 1966. One likely reason for the Socratic Club's successful sponsoring by a women's college was that, as in World War I, Oxford's male student population was depleted by the World War II military call-up. Resources for extracurricular activities were also scarce, so the university could not afford to be picky about the origins of any clubs that were proposed.

45. *Socratic Digest*, no. 1 (1942–43), 6 (Bodleian Library, Oxford), as quoted in the Biographical Appendix entry on Stella Aldwinckle in Hooper, ed., *Collected Letters*, vol. 3, 1647.

46. A history of the Socratic Club, including a list of most of its speakers and their topics, from its opening in 1942 to its latter days in 1954, can be found in Walter Hooper, "Oxford's

twelve of which Lewis was its president) the club met weekly on Monday nights, its venue ranging from college Junior Common Rooms to the huge debating hall of the Oxford Union, with crowds ranging from several dozen to over two hundred. The usual format was to have a paper read by a Christian or an atheist, with a member of the other camp (having read the paper in advance) giving a formal reply, then to open the discussion to the entire gathering. Speakers—mostly academics, writers and artists, and other professionals—were recruited in advance for each term's program.[47] Lewis himself gave about one paper a year, and Stella Aldwinckle also delivered a few over the life of the club. The list of other speakers in the Socratic Club's minutes includes well-known scholars of various shades of belief. There are philosophers such as Anthony Flew, R. M. Hare, Elizabeth Anscombe, Iris Murdoch, Frederick Copleston, and Michael Polanyi; writers and literary critics such as Charles Williams and Dorothy L. Sayers; and theologians such as D. M. MacKinnon, Austin Farrer, and J. N. D. Kelly.

There is no doubt that, as a master of scintillating argument and quick repartee, Lewis was the major drawing card in this Christians-versus-lions forum. Stella Aldwinckle (who grew up not in England but in the more casual setting of South Africa) seems to have been a major cheerleader, jumping to her feet in her role as chair, and occasionally, after a particularly provocative paper by an atheist, urging Lewis on with phrases like "Go get 'im, Jack!"[48] It all made for splendid theater, as academic debate between articulate proponents of opposing worldviews often does, and as the club's reputation spread, copies of the annual *Socratic Digest* (containing written forms of the debates) were being requested from as far away as Canada, the US, and South Africa.[49]

Lewis himself, in his preface to the first (1943–44) *Socratic Digest* admitted that "those who founded [the club] do not for one moment pretend to be

---

Bonny Fighter," in James T. Como, ed., *Remembering C. S. Lewis: Recollections of Those Who Knew Him*, 3rd ed. (San Francisco: Ignatius, 2005), 241–308.

47. Walter Hooper comments that "a number of American students whom I've met expressed disapproval of the 'undemocratic' tradition that only once a term did an Oxford undergraduate read a paper to the [Socratic Club]. If the truth of Christianity were merely a matter of opinion, as some liberal theologians appear to think, Oxford students would have been pressed into more active service. As, however, the founders of the Socratic Club had no such fuzzy notions about the Christian revelation, but believed in a full-blooded supernatural Christianity, they were anxious . . . that both students and dons hear the best- and most-informed speakers it was possible to come up with. As a consequence, they naturally looked to those who were expert in their subject, atheists as well as Christians" (ibid., 245).

48. Ibid., 253.

49. It is an interesting irony that Valerie Pitt, the student most responsible for recording the early history of the Socratic Club, went on to become an activist for the ordination of women in the Anglican Church. As a sometime lecturer in English at Newnham College, Cambridge, she overlapped with Lewis's tenure there, and was one of the first persons to welcome him to Cambridge in 1955. In 1965 she was elected to the Assembly of the Anglican Church, and in 1967 introduced a motion to open up ordained orders to women.

neutral," but further noted that any truly Socratic unbeliever—one who, like Socrates, would "follow the argument wherever it led"—could present any complaints about that non-neutrality in a paper to be read at the club itself. "Though," Lewis added, "I doubt whether he would have the stomach if he knew with what pains the committee has scoured *Who's Who* to find intelligent atheists who had leisure or zeal to propagate their creed." Moreover, the Socratics might not be impartial, "but argument is . . . We expose ourselves, and the weakest of our party, to your fire no less than you are exposed to ours." Lewis, philosophically trained but also romantically and mystically inclined, was also aware that the kind of feisty apologetics represented by the Socratic Club format had its limits, for he immediately added: "Worse still, we expose ourselves to the recoil from our own shots; for if I may trust my personal experience, no doctrine is, for the moment, dimmer to the eye of faith than that which a man has just successfully defended."[50] Apologetic arguments might reassure young believers that Christianity was rationally defensible, and thus reduce the gap between their piety and their academic pursuits. But such arguments could not take the place of a living faith.

Two Gifted Women Intellectuals

We have already seen that Lewis did not confine his intellectual friendships to fellow academics in the university setting, but wrote regularly to Oxford graduates who worked in settings ranging from progressive boarding schools (Mary Neylan) to advertising agencies (Dorothy Sayers). Another of his correspondents was Penelope Lawson, an Anglo-Catholic nun about eight years Lewis's senior, who was a member of the Community of St. Mary the Virgin, at Wantage in Oxfordshire. Entering the community after graduating from Oxford at age twenty-two, she was sent back to Oxford to study theology, and later took the Archbishop's (Lambeth) Diploma in Theology to become a licensed Anglican theologian, after completing a thesis on the Hebrew text of the book of Psalms. By the time she died in 1977, she had published dozens of volumes—both academic and popular—on church history, doctrine, and spiritual devotion, as well as translations of the Greek and Latin church fathers.[51]

Lewis and Sister Penelope first corresponded when she wrote to compliment him on *Out of the Silent Planet*, the first volume of his space trilogy. They met in person a few years later when Lewis, on her invitation, came to Wantage to speak to members of the community. So impressed was Lewis with this band of religious women—whom he visited several times thereafter—that

50. Hooper, "Oxford's Bonny Fighter," 244.
51. Lawson's community was the first Anglican religious order to be formed since the time of the Protestant Reformation. See Walter Hooper, "Sister Penelope Lawson, CSMV," in Biographical Appendix to *Collected Letters*, vol. 2, 1055–59.

upon finishing *Perelandra* (the second volume of his space trilogy) he dedicated it to "Some Ladies at Wantage."[52] It was through them, and through Sister Penelope in particular, that Lewis began to discard some of his Belfast Protestant nervousness about high-church practices. "I am going to make my first confession [of sin] next week," he wrote to her about a year after they first began to correspond. "[That] will seem odd to you, but I wasn't brought up to that kind of thing . . . The *decision* to do so was one of the hardest I have ever made: but . . . I am committed (by dint of posting the letter before I had time to change my mind)." From then on, Lewis made regular confession to Father Walter Adams, a member of the Anglican Society of St. John the Evangelist at Cowley, a suburb of Oxford.[53]

Subsequent letters to Sister Penelope reveal a friendship developing on many levels with the person Lewis came to call his "elder sister in the Faith."[54] He repeatedly affirmed that he benefited from her training in ancient Hebrew and the Old Testament, being himself an "amateur" who knew only "a modicum of Hebrew."[55] As he was later to do with Dorothy Sayers, he read Lawson's books in manuscript and/or published form, giving substantive and stylistic suggestions along the way. When she too was asked to give broadcast talks (on Christian doctrine) during World War II, she and Lewis traded suggestions for how to approach their respective tasks. She was one of the few people with whom he shared his fears for his brother's safety when he was reactivated for front line duty in France, and his worries about Janie Moore's health—both physical and mental—as she grew older. He even appealed to Sister Penelope as a quasi-confessor for his own struggles. "I am writing, really, for company," he admitted in a 1941 letter, "for I am a sad Ass at the moment. I've been going through one of those periods when one can no longer disguise the fact that movement has been backward not forward. All the sins one thought one had escaped have been back again as strong as ever."[56] Though he never detailed what those particular "sins" might be, Lewis (taking a leaf from St. Francis of Assisi) signed many of his subsequent letters to Sister Penelope—especially when feeling vulnerable about some spiritual or other challenge—as "Brother Ass."[57]

Lewis's last known letter to her (after a long gap in correspondence following his move to Cambridge) was written in 1957, in reply to a query about

52. Hooper wryly notes that the Portuguese translation of *Perelandra* had the dedication reading "To some wanton ladies" (ibid., 1058).

53. C. S. Lewis to Sister Penelope, CSMV, October 24, 1940, Hooper, ed., *Collected Letters*, vol. 3, 452.

54. Hooper, "Sister Penelope Lawson," 1058.

55. C. S. Lewis to Sister Penelope, CSMV, August 24, 1939, Hooper, ed., *Collected Letters*, vol. 2, 264.

56. C. S. Lewis to Sister Penelope, CSMV, November 9, 1941, ibid., 495.

57. St. Francis regularly referred to his own body—with a mixture of affection and exasperation—as "Brother Ass."

rumors that he had recently married. The content of the letter reflects the mix of concerns—intellectual and personal—that Lewis had for many years shared with this scholarly Anglican nun:

> Yes, it is true. I married (knowingly) a very sick, save by near-miracle a dying, woman. She is Joy Davidman whose [book] *Smoke on the Mountain* I think you read . . . The disease is, of course, cancer: by which I lost my mother, my father and my favorite aunt. She knows her own state of course: I w[oul]d allow no lies to be told to a grown-up and a Christian. As you can imagine new beauty and new tragedy have entered my life. You w[oul]d be surprised (or perhaps you would not?) to know how much of a strange sort of happiness and even gaiety there is between us.
>
> I look forward to reading [your latest book] . . . I don't doubt that Joy and I (and David and Douglas, the two boys) will have your prayers. Douglas is an absolute charmer (11½). David, at first sight less engaging, is at any rate a comically appropriate stepson for me (13), being almost exactly what I was [at that age]—bookworm, pedant, and a bit of a prig.
>
> Yours very sincerely,
> C. S. Lewis.[58]

A final correspondent-turned-friend was the poet Ruth Pitter. Born in 1897 to two primary school teachers near London, Pitter was raised in a book loving but rather impoverished family, and so never received a university education. Another of the two million "surplus women" who came of age during World War I, she never married, but supported herself by becoming a skilled painter of folk-style furniture and other household artifacts, such as trays.[59] However, she also published eighteen volumes of poetry (her own, and anthologies of other poets' work) and won numerous prizes, including the Queen's Gold Medal for Poetry in 1955. In 1974, Britain's Royal Society of Literature gave her its highest award, the Companion of Literature, and in 1979 Queen Elizabeth made Pitter a Companion of the British Empire.[60]

58. C. S. Lewis to Sister Penelope, CSVM, March 6, 1957, Hooper, ed., *Collected Letters*, vol. 3, 837–38.

59. Lewis acknowledged the gift of one of Ruth Pitter's painted trays in a letter written to her on September 22, 1949. In the process he made oblique reference to the intellectual gulf that separated him from Janie Moore, with whom he had by then been living for some twenty years: "The Tray arrived . . . to create general delight and put up my domestic stock. No one had been the least impressed when I said I was going 'to lunch with a poet in Chelsea,' which sounded good enough to me: but now that you have risen to be 'someone who paints lovely trays,' it is a different matter" (Hooper, ed., *Collected Letters*, vol. 2, 981–82).

60. Don W. King, "The Anatomy of a Friendship: The Correspondence of Ruth Pitter and C. S. Lewis, 1946–1962," *Mythlore* 91 (Summer 2003): 2. See also Walter Hooper's brief biography of Pitter in *Collected Letters*, vol. 2, 1060–65. Pitter outlived Lewis by almost thirty years, dying in February 1992 at the age of ninety-five.

Lewis, as we have seen, had a soft spot for underdogs, including intellectually gifted people who didn't have the same social or economic advantages usually associated with the Oxford "inner ring."[61] He was introduced to Ruth Pitter's poetry at about the same time that she was reading his wartime publication, *The Screwtape Letters*. Each was monumentally impressed by the other's work. Lewis was taken by Pitter's writing because as a young man he had wanted to be a professional poet. Though he eventually realized his gifts were not adequate to such a challenge, he remained an occasional poet and an avid reader of poetry written in classical forms, to which Pitter mostly adhered.[62] Pitter came across Lewis's Christian apologetics while battling depression amid the stresses of World War II. By reading *The Screwtape Letters* and listening to the broadcast talks that would later become Lewis's *Mere Christianity*, she moved from the nominal churchianity of her childhood to a more robust faith as a member of the Anglican Church.

Ruth Pitter and C. S. Lewis finally met each other in person in 1946, and they continued a lively and erudite correspondence about poetry for the next decade. This was interspersed with visits that became more frequent after Pitter and her colleague, Kathleen O'Hara, moved their business and home from London to a rural location near Oxford. It is abundantly clear that Lewis looked up to Pitter as the more accomplished poet, and he seems to have been inspired by her to write more poetry himself. "I've just had a poem refused by the *Spectator*," he wrote to her in 1947. "But then I never was a poet like you."[63] Reacting to her successive volumes of verse, his language is full of superlatives: "I was prepared for the more definitely mystical poems, but not for this cool, classical quality. You do it time after time—create a silence and vacancy and awe all around the poem."[64] "Full of good, and studded with great work, though there are things [in them] I don't yet understand."[65] And about her first book of verse after becoming a Christian: "The new volume is an absolute Corker. I had feared that you might be one of those who, like poor

61. Lewis also mentored the novelist and literary critic Charles Williams who, like Pitter, was unable to complete university due to family poverty. As a proofreader for Oxford University Press, Williams was transferred from London to Oxford during Word War II, became a member of the Inklings, and found an enthusiastic sponsor in Lewis, who even arranged for him to give lectures on Milton at Oxford, despite his lack of formal academic credentials. In 1943 Oxford awarded Williams an honorary MA.

62. For most of his life, Lewis did not like modern poetry in the free-verse mode, and had a particular aversion to the work of T. S. Eliot until, late in life, he met Eliot after being asked to serve with him on the Anglican Commission to Revise the Psalter, at which point the two became cordial colleagues.

63. C. S. Lewis to Ruth Pitter, January 4, 1947, Hooper, ed., *Collected Letters*, vol. 2, 754.

64. C. S. Lewis to Ruth Pitter, July 19, 1946, ibid., 720. Lewis is referring to Pitter's volume *A Trophy of Arms: Poems 1926–1935* (London: Cresset, 1936).

65. C. S. Lewis to Ruth Pitter, July 12, 1946, ibid., 722. Lewis is reacting to Pitter's volumes, *The Spirit Watches* (London: Cresset, 1940) and *The Bridge: Poems 1939–1944* (London: Cresset, 1945).

Wordsworth, leave their talent behind at conversion: and now—oh, glory—you came up shining out of the [baptismal] font *far* better than you were before . . . I wonder have you yourself any notion how good some of these are?"[66]

Lewis, to be sure, also offered technical and aesthetic comments about Pitter's work. "No, no, no," he expostulated, about one of her poems in *The Bridge*. "The moderns have got at you. Don't you, of all people, be taken in by the silly idea that by simply mentioning dull or sordid facts in sub-poetical rhythms you can make a poem. The effect is certain, but it's not worth getting."[67] But overall he was more acolyte than critic in his relationship with her, frequently submitting drafts of his own poems for Pitter's scrutiny, and sometimes waiting with admitted nervousness for her response. Indeed, in a 1948 letter he expressed his fear that she might think his own effort at verse "isn't really poetry at all—a feeling repressed by your kindness and liking for my prose work."[68] Though Pitter's original reply has disappeared, she did write a comment on his query two decades later, a few years after Lewis's death:

> *Is* his poetry after all not? . . . I should like to know more about the actual process of conception in his case. Did his great learning & really staggering skill in verse inhibit the poetry? . . . He had a great stock of the makings of a poet: strong visual memory, strong recollections of childhood: desperately strong yearnings for lost Paradise & hoped Heaven . . . not least a strong primitive intuition of the diabolical . . . [But] it is almost as though the adult disciplines, notably the technique of his verse, had largely inhibited his poetry, which is perhaps, after all, most evident in his prose . . . I think he wanted to be a poet more than anything else. Time will show. But if it was *magic* he was after, he achieved this sufficiently elsewhere.[69]

Like Dorothy Sayers, Pitter knew that Lewis had blind spots when it came to women. Commenting on another 1948 letter, in which Lewis wondered if youthful exuberance was more conducive to writing short, lyrical poetry, while age confers the *gravitas* needed to write longer epics,[70] she wrote: "Beautiful letter, but he doesn't reflect that nowadays everybody has to do chores and is constantly interrupted—it is almost lyrics or nothing, especially for women

66. C. S. Lewis to Ruth Pitter, May 12, 1953, Hooper, ed., *Collected Letters*, vol. 3, 327. Lewis has just read Pitter's volume *The Ermine: Poems 1942–1952* (London: Cresset, 1953).

67. C. S. Lewis to Ruth Pitter, July 14, 1946, Hooper, ed., *Collected Letters*, vol. 2, 724.

68. C. S. Lewis to Ruth Pitter, September 29, 1948, ibid., 881.

69. Bodleian Library, *MS. Engl. lett. c. 220/3*, folios 63–64, as quoted in ibid., 882. Pitter was so impressed by the "poetic" quality of Lewis's prose (especially in his science fiction trilogy) that in 1947 she transcribed chapter seventeen of *Perelandra* (describing the coronation of planet's king and queen) into Spenserian verse. See Don W. King, "The Poetry of Prose: C. S. Lewis, Ruth Pitter and *Perelandra*," *Christianity and Literature* 49, no. 3 (Spring 2000): 331–56.

70. C. S. Lewis to Ruth Pitter, December 11, 1948, Hooper, ed., *Collected Letters*, vol. 2, 894–95.

. . . Never mind, poetry has always been done against the odds."[71] Yet before the appearance of Joy Davidman in Lewis's life, some of his friends thought that he and Ruth Pitter would have been a good match. George Sayer, who sometimes chauffeured Lewis to Pitter's cottage in the 1950s (Lewis himself never learned to drive) noted that "it was obvious that he liked her very much. He felt at ease in her presence—and he did not feel relaxed with many people. In fact, he seemed to be on intimate terms with her . . . After one visit in 1955, he remarked that, if he were not a confirmed bachelor, Ruth Pitter would be the woman he would like to marry."[72]

By this time, however, Lewis had met Joy Davidman, and after his marriage to her in 1957, his correspondence with Pitter was much less frequent. Don King, a scholar of Pitter's life and poetry, suggests that given her background and temperament, she was not the kind of woman to court Lewis aggressively, unlike the younger, more forthright, sexually experienced—and American—Joy Davidman. Lewis, in turn, was not the kind of man to take the initiative in such matters, and so it was Joy who in the end became Mrs. C. S. Lewis.[73] After Lewis's death, one of his friends mentioned to Pitter his hope that it might have been she instead, and asked her if she would have accepted a proposal of marriage from Lewis. She smiled, but refused comment.[74]

Beyond Misogyny

In its September 8, 1947, issue, *Time* magazine featured C. S. Lewis's profile on its cover, with contrasting images of Satan and a heavenly angel hovering in the background. Lewis pronounced the article about himself "ghastly—I wouldn't hang a dog on a journalist's evidence myself." His chief complaint seems to have been that he was described in the *Time* article as a misogynist. "Who said I disliked women?" he complained to one of his post-war American correspondents. "I never liked or disliked any *generalization* [i.e., entire category of people]."[75] And in this chapter we have indeed seen that, although Lewis sometimes wrote what Dorothy Sayers referred to as "shocking nonsense" about women, his actual relationships with women students and colleagues were in the main quite laudable.

In 1956, after leaving Oxford, Lewis contributed to a series in the *Cambridge Review* comparing various scholars' experiences of both Oxford and Cam-

71. Bodleian Library, *MS. Engl. Lett. c. 220/3*, folio 70, as quoted in ibid., 895.
72. Sayer, *Jack*, 211.
73. Don W. King, "Fire and Ice: The Love Poetry of Joy Davidman and Ruth Pitter," *Seven: An Anglo-American Literary Review* 22 (2005): 60–88.
74. Walter Hooper, "Ruth Pitter," Biographical Appendix to *Collected Letters*, vol. 2, 1060–64.
75. C. S. Lewis to Margaret Fuller, April 8, 1948, ibid., 849.

bridge. In that article he noted that "the Oxford don, whether in fact married or single, lives more *en garcon* [i.e., like a bachelor] than in Cambridge. You can meet him for a long time in pubs and at High Tables before you are asked to his house." He also noted that Oxford, unlike Cambridge, had no University Combination Room—a kind of faculty club where colleagues from every college could mingle. "Until quite lately," he wrote, "it was unlikely that you would meet your female [Oxford] colleagues anywhere except at the Board of Faculty or at a full dress dinner party." And, he added, "I think I may claim some tiny share in breaking down that tradition."[76] This may refer to his years of work with the all-college Socratic Club. In any case, Lewis had by this time journeyed from being a male don who supported the limiting of "wimmen" at Oxford in 1927[77] to one who was happy to take credit for opening up more opportunities to interact with them.

It is a final irony that it was one of his Oxford women colleagues who, in the end, was responsible for his being able to accept a late-life appointment to Cambridge University. In 1954, when Cambridge first approached Lewis with the offer of a fellowship, he declined the offer because, due to his family responsibilities, he felt he could not actually live in Cambridge.[78] The Cambridge search committee then offered the post to its second choice, Lewis's Oxford colleague Helen Gardner of St. Hilda's College, a fellow Anglo-Catholic with whom he sparred occasionally in faculty meetings. He later had second thoughts about the matter and wrote to Cambridge that, if their regulations permitted, he could live there during the week, and return to Oxford on weekends. By the letter of the law, the Cambridge search committee could not at that point withdraw its offer to Helen Gardner. However, within a few weeks she wrote to Cambridge to decline the chair, with no reason given.

Several years later, in a Lewis obituary prepared for the British Academy, Helen Gardner wrote: "When first approached he was unwilling to leave Oxford, and the Chair was indeed offered to someone else. Fortunately, the 'second string' declined, partly on account of having heard that Lewis was changing his mind, for it was obvious that this ought to be Lewis's chair."[79] Helen Gardner—ten years Lewis's junior—waited until 1966 to be appointed Oxford's Merton Professor of English Language and Literature. Lewis died in 1963, apparently without ever knowing what she had done for him.

---

76. C. S. Lewis, "Interim Report," reprinted in Walter Hooper, ed., *Present Concerns* (San Diego: Harvest, 1987), 92–99 (quotation from p. 97).

77. C. S. Lewis to Warren Lewis, July 9, 1927, Hooper, ed., *Collected Letters*, vol. 1, 703.

78. Those "family" responsibilities no longer included Janie Moore, who had died in 1951, but did include his brother, who by this time had become a behaviorally unpredictable binge drinker.

79. As quoted by Hooper in *Collected Letters*, vol. 3, 482.

A Socratic Debate Revisited

When considering Lewis's interactions with women, we need finally to examine his interchange with the Somerville College philosopher Elizabeth Anscombe, less because of her sex than because the content of her debate with Lewis has relevance for the chapter that follows. Anscombe was invited to address the Socratic Club in February of 1948, about half a year after the publication of Lewis's book *Miracles*.[80] Her paper was basically a critique of Lewis's own critique, in *Miracles*, of naturalism—i.e., the philosophical view that all phenomena and events can be explained in terms of natural causes, without ever appealing to supernatural interventions, which are assumed not to occur. Anscombe herself was a devout Roman Catholic, and like Lewis, an adult convert.[81] Thus her appearance at the Socratic Club was a departure from the usual Christians-versus-atheists format, and might better be described as an in-house debate between two Christians regarding the most philosophically responsible way to defend the existence of the supernatural, and hence the possibility of miracles.

Nevertheless, their interchange is important for a number of reasons. First of all, it is usually cited by Lewis biographers without a clear explanation of the philosophical issues at stake. (This is somewhat understandable, as they are not easy to grasp.) Secondly, those issues have relevance for Lewis's views about science and social science—and, by extension, for the views he held about the psychology of gender for much of his life. Thirdly, a large body of legend has accumulated in connection with this debate, ranging from the contention that Lewis was so devastated by Anscombe that he completely gave up doing rationalist apologetics (turning instead to the more romantic, narrative approach to faith that can be seen in the *Narnia* chronicles),[82] to the suggestion that his nose was put especially out of joint after being bested by a *woman* philosopher.[83] The second point (on social science and the psychology of gender) will be taken up in more detail in the next chapter, and

80. Anscombe graduated with a First in philosophy from St. Hugh's College, Oxford, in 1941. She was awarded a postgraduate fellowship at Newnham College, Cambridge, where she was a student of the famous modern philosopher Ludwig Wittgenstein, with whom she continued to work until his death, and for whose writings she was the chief interpreter and eventually the literary executor. She returned to Oxford as a Somerville College research fellow in 1946. She remained there until 1970, when she accepted a professorship in philosophy at Cambridge, where she remained until her retirement in 1986.

81. Anscombe might be described (in today's parlance) as a "completely pro-life" Catholic. She protested publicly, and in equal measure, Britain's entry into World War II, America's later use of the atomic bomb on Hiroshima and Nagasaki, and her own culture's embrace of contraception and abortion. She and her husband, philosopher Peter Geach—also a Roman Catholic convert and a student of Wittgenstein's—had seven children of their own.

82. For example, Sayer, *Jack*, chap. 16; Wilson, *C. S. Lewis*, chap. 15.

83. For example, Wilson, *C. S. Lewis*, 214; Candice Fredrick and Sam McBride, *Women Among the Inklings: Gender, C. S. Lewis, J. R. R. Tolkien and Charles Williams* (Westport,

about the third (taking offense at being bested by a female) it is sufficient to say that such conclusions are either too strong, or else highly speculative.[84] But regarding the first point—Just what *was* at issue in the Lewis-Anscombe debate?—I need to say more in preparation for the chapter to follow.[85]

We have already seen that when C. S. Lewis did philosophy as an undergraduate, Oxford was becoming an intellectual battleground between idealists and naturalists. British idealists in the late nineteenth and early twentieth centuries shared several broad convictions. They believed in a spiritual (but not necessarily personal) Absolute—that is, a single, all-encompassing reality that guaranteed some kind of coherence among all things. They held that this Absolute was pure reason, and that human reason was the faculty by which the nature of the Absolute and everything encompassed by it could be understood. They thus downplayed Kant's eighteenth-century distinction between things in themselves and our filtered apprehensions of them, insisting instead that there was, at least in principle, a coherent unity between thinking and the objects of our thought. Some were more Platonic in their idealism, assuming that the mental forms behind everything were preexistent and unchanging. Some were more Hegelian, holding that the Absolute emerged dialectically over the course of human intellectual history. But unlike their naturalist rivals, who asserted that the universe was reducible to matter and energy working according to pure chance and the laws of physics, these philosophical idealists held (in Lewis's later words) "that the whole universe was, in the last resort, mental; that our logic was participation in a cosmic *Logos*."[86]

I noted earlier that C. S. Lewis's return to Christianity began, in his undergraduate days, when he gave up his realist/naturalist "new look" and instead began cautiously to embrace the reigning form of Oxford idealism. As he put it in the preface to *Pilgrim's Regress*, "My own progress had been from 'popular realism' to Philosophical Idealism; from Idealism to Pantheism; from Pantheism to Theism; and from Theism to Christianity."[87] This does not mean that he rejected natural scientific explanations *per se*; indeed, Walter Hooper notes that "not a few of the papers read to the Socratic deal with . . . the so-called, and much exaggerated conflict between science and Christianity."

CN: Greenwood, 2001), 93–94; Michael White, *C. S. Lewis: A Life* (New York: Carroll and Graf, 2004), chap. 8.

84. See Jacobs, *The Narnian*, 231–38.

85. A detailed account of the Lewis-Anscombe debate can be found in Victor Reppert, *C. S. Lewis's Dangerous Idea: In Defense of the Argument from Reason* (Downers Grove, IL: Inter-Varsity, 2003), especially chap. 3. Reppert's volume is a shortened and more accessible version of his doctoral thesis (University of Illinois, 1989) on the same topic.

86. C. S. Lewis, *Surprised by Joy: The Shape of My Early Life* (London: Collins, 1955), 167. See also James Patrick, *The Magdalen Metaphysicals: Idealism and Orthodoxy at Oxford, 1901–1945* (Macon, GA: Mercer University Press, 1985).

87. C. S. Lewis, *The Pilgrim's Regress: An Allegorical Apology for Christianity, Reason and Romanticism* (London: Geoffrey Bles, 1933), 5.

If scientists stuck to their own territory—the purely physical—and didn't make unwarranted metaphysical or moral claims beyond their competence, Lewis conceded their worth in the academy and their usefulness outside of it. Hooper writes that "although Lewis could not be said to have been overfond of the company of scientists, he nevertheless felt a greater respect for them than for those whose education had been neither scientific nor classical and who knew only enough popularized 'science' to believe that in nature we find 'the whole show.'"[88]

In the third chapter of his original (1947) edition of *Miracles*, Lewis had challenged just this kind of "scientism"—the view that science gives us the entire truth about the whole of reality. In other words, to the naturalist "truth" comes packaged only in one form—namely, causal, deterministic explanations that are empirically testable. Lewis had originally titled this chapter "The Self-Contradiction of the Naturalist," and in it he tried to show why strict naturalists—who, if they are to be consistent, must apply their beliefs to themselves as well as everything else—actually cut off the epistemological limb on which they sit. For if human thought, like everything else, is merely the *natural* (i.e., physical-chemical) result of the thinker's biological state and learning history, then the very enterprise of science is rendered meaningless, since scientific conclusions depend on certain *logical* rules (inductive as well as deductive; empirical as well as mathematical). As Lewis put it in the 1960 edition of *Miracles*,

> All possible knowledge . . . depends on the validity of reasoning. If the feeling of certainty which we express by words like *must be* and *therefore* and *since* is a real perception of how things outside of our own minds really "must" be, well and good. But if this certainty is merely a feeling in our own minds and not a genuine insight into realities beyond them—if it merely represents the way our minds happen to work—then we can have no knowledge. Unless human reasoning is valid no science can be true.[89]

This is a defensible position, and one for which I have already expressed appreciation in the first chapter of this book. And Lewis, reflecting the Oxford idealism that was especially strong at Magdalen College, went a step further. He suggested that the human capacity for reason—our ability to discern some of the patterns of the Absolute mind behind all natural and moral laws—was itself something of a miracle which, if accepted, makes the ultimate miracle of Christ's incarnation easier to understand.[90] "Unless human reasoning is

88. Hooper, "Oxford's Bonny Fighter," 251.
89. C. S. Lewis, *Miracles* (New York: MacMillan, 1960; repr., 1978), 14. Page references are to the MacMillian edition.
90. This is what Reppert (in *C. S. Lewis's Dangerous Idea*) means by Lewis's apologetic "Argument from Reason"—that is, arguing from the existence, complexity, and necessity of

valid no science can be true," he wrote in the original edition of *Miracles*. "It follows that no account of the universe can be true unless that account leaves it possible for our thinking to be a real insight"[91]—that is, one that can be justified by an appeal to something outside itself. However, in its original version Lewis refused, unwisely, to stop there. Instead (as he not uncommonly did in the 1940s) he mounted his dualistic soapbox and concluded, by the end of this short chapter, that *only* believers in the supernatural could have any access to (or even interest in) the truth.

This, as A. N. Wilson has noted, is a flawed conclusion, for "if [Lewis's] distinction between Naturalists and Supernaturalists held good it would have to be demonstrable that the Supernaturalists had some specific means of acquiring their superior knowledge and of explaining it to the Naturalists."[92] Without such a demonstration, Lewis begins to sound more like a gnostic than a Christian. Moreover, it is not even good theological anthropology, for as we have already seen, Lewis had shown elsewhere that he understood the importance of what Reformed theologians have called "the cultural mandate" and "common grace." The former refers to the fact that God's command to unfold the potential of creation (Gen. 1:26–28) was given not just to Christians or even to generic theists, but to all of humankind, beginning with both members of the primal pair. Individuals and indeed, entire cultures, may or may not acknowledge God as the source of their intellectual and practical accomplishments, but in spite of their finitude and sinfulness, they will still pursue truth and build cultures. And they will be held accountable for the results—both good and bad—before God at the end of time, as the apostle John foresaw at the other end of the biblical drama in Revelation 21.[93]

The second (and related) concept—that of common grace—refers to the fact that God's purposes in salvation history have routinely been carried out not just by believers, but by whomever God chooses, ranging (for example) from Pharoah's daughter who rescued the infant Moses, to the pagan Magi whose astrological speculations led them to Christ's cradle.[94] So Lewis's either/or, Christians-versus-Lions stance, though sometimes rhetorically effective, was clearly overdrawn, and not just in his 1940s discussions of epistemology,

---

human reason (however incomplete and subject to distortion it may be) to the existence of a Creator who possesses (among other traits) reason in its perfect form and endows it on humans made in the Creator's image. Reppert's book defends the continuing relevance of Lewis's argument from reason.

91. As quoted in Wilson, *C. S. Lewis*, 212.

92. Ibid.

93. See, for example, Lewis's 1939 sermon "Learning in Wartime," in C. S. Lewis, *Fern-seed and Elephant and Other Essays on Christianity* (London: Collins Fontana, 1975), 26–38.

94. See, for example, Richard J. Mouw, *When the Kings Come Marching In* (Grand Rapids: Eerdmans, 1983); and *He Shines in All That's Fair: Culture and Common Grace* (Grand Rapids: Eerdmans, 2001).

but also in those on ethics.[95] In later writings, Lewis became less dualistic about the mental and moral contrast between Christians and nonbelievers.[96] Indeed, as we have seen, even his early book *Pilgrim's Regress* affirms that he believed certain pagan myths (for example, about dying and rising gods) could be "pointers" to God's ultimate revelation in Jesus Christ. So clearly (on one level) Lewis acknowledged God's use of common grace. But throughout the 1940s, his rationalist and his romantic selves often seem to have worked in parallel tracks, with little interaction between the two. Thus "Lewis the rational apologist" sometimes seemed to ignore some of the things that "Lewis the romantic myth lover" had elsewhere affirmed.

Moreover, in 1947 (when *Miracles* was first published) Lewis was two decades past his own formal work as a philosopher, and there were certain developments with which he simply had not kept up, particularly in philosophy of mind and philosophy of language. It was on some of these that Elizabeth Anscombe decided to challenge him in the forum of the Socratic Club.[97]

95. For example, in his Durham University Riddell Memorial Lectures, published in 1943 as *The Abolition of Man*, Lewis makes the same dichotomous claim about morality: "We have been trying, like Lear, to have it both ways: to lay down our human prerogative and yet at the same time to retain it. It is impossible. Either we are rational spirit obliged forever to obey the absolute values of the *Tao* [i.e., the natural moral law], or else we are mere nature to be kneaded and cut into new shapes for the pleasures of masters who must, by hypothesis, have no motive but their own 'natural' impulses . . . A dogmatic belief in objective value is necessary to the very ideal of a rule which is not tyranny or an obedience which is not slavery." C. S. Lewis, *The Abolition of Man* (Oxford: Oxford University Press, 1943), 50.

96. Thus, in *Mere Christianity* (p. 173) he acknowledges that "the world does not consist of 100 per cent. Christians and 100 per cent. non-Christians. There are people (a great many of them) who are slowly ceasing to be Christians but who still call themselves by that name: some of them are clergymen. There are other people who are slowly becoming Christians though they do not yet call themselves so . . . Consequently, it is not much use trying to make judgments about Christians and non-Christians in the mass." And in the 1960 edition of *Miracles* (pp. 36–37) he acknowledged the working of common grace without using the term. Thus, "A moment after [naturalists] have admitted that good and evil are illusions, you will find them exhorting us to work for posterity, to educate, revolutionise, liquidate, live and die for the good of the human race . . . But surely this is very odd? Just as all the books about spiral nebulae, atoms and cave men would really have led you to suppose that the Naturalists claimed to be able to know something, so all the books in which Naturalists tell us what we ought to do would really make you believe that they thought some ideas of good (their own, for example) to be somehow preferable to others . . . Do they remember while they are writing thus that when they tell us we 'ought to make a better world' the words 'ought' and 'better' must, on their own showing, refer to an irrationally conditioned impulse which cannot be true or false any more than a vomit or a yawn? My idea is that sometimes they do forget. That is their glory. Holding a philosophy that excludes humanity, they yet remain human. At the sight of injustice they throw all their Naturalism to the winds and speak like men, and like men of genius. They know far better than they think they know."

97. Her paper is included in G. E. M. Anscombe, *The Collected Papers of G. E. M Anscombe*, vol. 2, *Metaphysics and the Philosophy of Mind* (Minneapolis: University of Minnesota Press, 1981), 224–31.

A Challenge to Lewis's View of Explanation

There were three parts to Anscombe's critique of Lewis's chapter in *Miracles* on "The Self-Contradiction of the Naturalist." The third of these is the most significant for our purposes, but a passing mention should be made of the other two as well. Anscombe's first point was simply that Lewis had not sufficiently distinguished between irrational and nonrational causes in his case against naturalists.[98] Her second point was that Lewis was wrong to claim that if naturalism is true, then no human reasoning is valid.[99] But Anscombe's third—and lengthiest—point took aim at what might be called Lewis's Cartesian dualism regarding the nature of explanation.

We have already seen that Lewis showed a cautious acceptance of natural scientists, provided that they stuck to physical phenomena and didn't dabble in metaphysics (as full-blown naturalists frequently do, even though they usually deny it). In the tradition of Descartes' mind-body dualism, Lewis held that causal, deterministic explanations were perfectly fine when applied to humans' *bodies* (including their brains), but that the working of the human *mind*, as a "spiritual" entity—could only be explained in strictly nonnaturalistic terms—by an appeal to logic, for example. Anscombe, drawing on the work of her mentor Ludwig Wittgenstein, argued that this dichotomy was too simple. What counts as an explanation, she said, depends on the kind of question being asked, and questions can come from a variety of different angles, or perspectives—not just the "purely" physical or the "purely" mental/spiritual.

So, for example, if a visitor from Mars arrived at Oxford and wanted us to "explain" the lighted NO EXIT sign above one of the Somerville Junior Com-

98. A nonrational cause, Anscombe asserted, is simply a physical event, and thus cannot be labeled either "rational" or "irrational." Physical processes (those that generate everything from molecules to spiral nebulae) are neither rational nor irrational—they just are. By contrast, an irrational cause is something that produces a false belief instead of a true one—for example, the belief that all teachers are cruel because of a beating received from one teacher in childhood. Naturalists do believe that all beliefs result ultimately from nonrational causes, but irrational causes are only a small subset of these. Although the absence of these distinctions does not defeat Lewis's basic "argument from reason," Anscombe thought they made the argument less convincing to the philosophically literate, and he was sufficiently chastened that when he revised *Miracles* for its 1960 paperback edition, he wrote of naturalists' commitments to "nonrational" rather than "irrational" causality.

99. It is meaningful, Anscombe said, to argue that a *particular instance* of reasoning is valid or not, but one can't make such claims about human reasoning *in general*. This is because, on the analytic philosophical account, humans only acquire their concepts of valid and invalid reasoning by being exposed to particular examples (or "paradigm cases") of each. Thus we cannot even have the concept of invalidity without having encountered at least one case of valid reasoning as well. And so, Anscombe charged, Lewis was making an unintelligible claim when he wrote that the naturalist account excludes the possibility of valid reasoning. Lewis also took account of this criticism in the 1960 revision of *Miracles*, claiming (more cautiously) that naturalism *itself* cannot be meaningfully asserted, because if it could, it would imply that not even a single instance of our thinking is reasonable or valid.

mon Room doors,[100] we would first have to ascertain *what kind* of explanation was being sought. A physical explanation of how the lighting fixture works? A linguistic explanation of the Latin word *exit*? A philosophical explanation of Jean-Paul Sartre's use of the term *No Exit* as the title for one of his existentialist plays? A public safety explanation of the reasons why students are not allowed to go out that way? So too, Anscombe said, if someone is asked to "explain" why they believe something (for example, that miracles happen) they could respond with any one of several types of explanation: a *causal* explanation of the naturalistic kind; a *rational* explanation, showing the relationship between certain premises and the conclusion they point to; a *psychological* explanation of the person's tastes and preferences that predispose him or her to that belief; and/or a *personal history* explanation of the influences that helped lead to that belief.

Anscombe's point was that we do not need to *choose* between these explanations, because each is working on a different level, or in Wittgenstein's terms, partaking of a different "language game." And as long as someone giving a naturalistic explanation does not try to rule out of court any other type of explanation, they are entitled to give as complete an explanation as they can in causal, naturalistic terms. Moreover, she added, *how* a person comes to hold a belief—whether by socialization, mystical experience, or any combination of factors—is irrelevant to whether or not that belief can be rationally defended. "Reason" explanations work on a level quite independent of "causal" (or for that matter any other type of) explanations.

Lewis took account of this criticism in his chapter revision by not claiming (as he had earlier) that naturalism simply precludes rational thought. Instead he distinguished, as Anscombe did, between causal and logical explanations when we use the word *because*. "Grandfather is sick *because* he is allergic to the lobster he ate yesterday" is an example of the first kind. "We know grandfather is sick *because* he hasn't gotten out of bed today" is an example of the second kind.[101] However, he did take issue (I think rightly) with Anscombe's conclusion that it doesn't matter *how* we arrive at our beliefs as long as they are rationally defensible, for there is a limit to how far we can push the idea that different levels of explanation do not affect one another. So, to take a contemporary example (supplied by philosopher Victor Reppert), if a prosecutor were to say he believed in a defendant's guilt on the basis of DNA evidence (a logical explanation), we would not think much of him if we found out he hated the defendant so much that he would believe in his guilt, and push for his incarceration, regardless of any logical evidence to the contrary (an emotional explanation).[102]

100. This is my own example, not Anscombe's.
101. Lewis, *Miracles* (1960), 15.
102. Reppert, *C. S. Lewis's Dangerous Idea*, 64.

Lewis, in his revised chapter, expressed this reservation by saying that "to be caused is not to be proved. Wishful thinking, prejudices, and the delusions of madness, are all caused, but they are [logically] ungrounded. Indeed, to be caused is so different from being proved that we behave in disputation as if they were mutually exclusive. The mere existence of causes for a belief is popularly treated as raising a presumption that it is [rationally] groundless."[103] Or as philosopher Stephen Evans has expressed it,

> My belief about the causes of my beliefs is one of the factors which affects what I believe . . . Imagine a person who has been convinced that his beliefs on a certain topic are the result of physiological changes in his body. Let us imagine, for some bizarre reason, that eating cream of wheat cereal every morning produces a belief in him that Russians are planning to mount an atomic attack on his city. As soon as the person accepts the idea that there is no rational basis for the belief, but that it is in fact caused [only] by this physiological change, the belief would tend to be undermined. To recognize that a belief has *only* a causal and no rational basis tends to nullify the belief in question.[104]

On the other hand—and this is important for the chapter to follow—notice that Lewis, in his revision, still writes as if there are *only* two types of explanation, what he called "cause-effect" (or naturalistic) explanations and "ground-consequent" (or rational) explanations. Moreover—unlike both Evans and myself—he sees them as mutually exclusive: either a belief is purely caused (and thus is rationally groundless), or it is rationally defensible (and thus is not causally influenced in any way). "It looks," he wrote, "as if, in order for a train of thought to have any value, these two systems of connection [causal and logical] must apply simultaneously to the same series of mental acts. But," he continues (without any evidence to support his claim), "unfortunately the two systems are *wholly distinct*."[105] In this respect Lewis remained a stubborn Cartesian dualist: the physical aspects of human beings are amenable to cause-effect exploration, but their mental life can only be studied in terms of meaningful ideas—logical, moral, aesthetic, or religious—but not by using (even in part) the tools of the sciences. And so we need to ask: where does this leave the social sciences, those disciplines like sociology and academic psychology, which strive to come up with probabilistic, causal (or at least correlational) accounts of human behavior and mental life?

For the Lewis of the 1940s, the answer was simple: these disciplines were at best second-rate and at worst searching for inappropriate, casual generalizations to explain the uniquely free, moral, and rational capacities of persons,

103. Lewis, *Miracles* (1960), 16.
104. C. Stephen Evans, *Preserving the Person: A Look at the Human Sciences* (Downers Grove, IL: InterVarsity, 1977), 78 (emphasis original).
105. Lewis, *Miracles*, 16 (emphasis added).

thus contributing to the decline of both clear thinking and moral responsibility. As we saw in chapter 2, in his 1945 novel *That Hideous Strength*, one of Lewis's criticisms of the character Mark Studdock—a sociologist—was that his training "had been neither scientific nor classical, merely 'modern' . . . The severities both of abstraction and of high human tradition had passed him by."[106] And for Lewis, any natural scientist worth his salt would agree. Thus, in the same novel, the erudite chemist William Hingest, preparing to leave Belbury, says to Mark, "I came here because I thought it had something to do with science. Now that I find it's something more like a political conspiracy, I shall go home." When Mark protests that social policy theorizing is part and parcel of the science of sociology, Hingest curtly replies: "There *are* no sciences like sociology . . . I happen to believe that you can't study men; you can only get to know them, which is a very different thing."[107] Stephen Evans summarizes this Cartesian epistemological stance as follows:

> Applied to the social sciences, dualistic views hold some rather militant implications. Though perhaps reticent to do so because of the prestige of science, a consistent dualist, it would seem, ought to charge naturalistically inclined social scientists with trespassing on a forbidden domain. While physiology as a science of the human *body* may seem legitimate, the notion of a science of man which ignores the soul (that intellectual valuing center of activity which represents the real person or at least the center of the real person) is [seen as] a flagrant contradiction in terms.[108]

Can There Be Any Social Sciences?

Lewis's attitude was not unique: even today, many Christians continue to view humans (and the disciplines that study them) through a similar either/or, Cartesian filter. But because of his wide readership, Lewis's writings on this topic have had rather far-reaching consequences. These I will examine in more detail in the following chapter. For now we should simply note that Lewis did adjust his argument to some extent in light of Anscombe's criticisms. He also chose a less sweeping title for his revised chapter, changing it from "The Self-Contradiction of the Naturalist" to "The Cardinal Difficulty of Naturalism." All this shows that he listened to Anscombe's advice—as she

106. C. S. Lewis, *That Hideous Strength: A Modern Fairy-Tale for Grown-Ups* (London: John Lane the Bodley Head, 1945), 185.

107. Lewis, *That Hideous Strength*, 70–71. For a defense of Lewis's Cartesian dualism, based in large part on this phrase "you can only get to know them" see Paul L. Holmer, *C. S. Lewis: The Shape of His Life and Thought* (New York: Harper and Row, 1976).

108. Evans, *Preserving the Person*, 103. Here Evans is describing, not prescribing, Cartesian dualism (emphasis original).

herself later credited him with doing.[109] Indeed, Lewis was heard to say about Anscombe, shortly after the Socratic Club debate, to his fellow Inkling Robert Havard, "Of course she is far more intelligent than either of us."[110]

I have dealt with the Lewis-Anscombe debate in detail because of its implications for Lewis's views about the possibility of social science in general, and a psychology of gender in particular: one that includes empirical generalizations and strives for causal explanations, even while not excluding other types. In the following chapter we will see that, even though he was spinning a "fairy tale for grown-ups" in *That Hideous Strength*, Lewis largely believed the statement that he put into the mouth of his scientist-character Bill Hingest— namely that "there *are* no sciences like sociology"—and, by extension, like psychology, economics, or political science. Why Lewis so emphatically rejected the social sciences, and the mixed consequences that followed, is the subject of the next chapter.

109. See Anscombe, *Collected Papers*, vol. 2, ix–x. In her introduction to the volume that contains her Socratic Club paper, she maintained that her criticisms of Lewis's original chapter still held, but that his revised chapter showed a marked improvement in the overall structure of its argument.

110. Robert E. Havard, "Philia: Jack at Ease," in Como, *Remembering C. S. Lewis*, 349–67 (quotation from p. 361).

6

"You Can Only Get to Know Them"

C. S. Lewis and the Social Sciences

In the late 1940s, two well-known Harvard social theorists famously observed that each person is in some respects like all other persons, like some other persons, and like no other person.[1] This handy truism can be illustrated in many ways. For example, all human beings use language, but some speak one language and some another. Even within a single language group, there will be different dialects. And in any given language or dialect group, individuals—as early as age three—generate unique sentences that they have never heard before from anyone else. As another example, all human infants need comfort when they are tired and cranky. But some get it by being rocked in cradles, others by being carried in a mother's sling or on a father's shoulders, and others by having lullabies sung to them. And many babies get unique cradles—or slings, or lullabies—made just for them and no one else.

It has been the mandate of the social sciences, ever since they became disciplines separate from history and philosophy in the nineteenth century, to document and try to make sense of such "themes and variations" in human behavior. Cultural anthropologists do it by analyzing language patterns in premodern tribes, or by comparing the amount of time fathers and mothers spend holding their babies. Sociologists do it by looking at

1. Henry Murray and Clyde Kluckholn, eds., *Personality in Nature, Society and Culture* (New York: Knopf, 1948).

class differences in dialects or in the childrearing norms of modern society. Psychologists do it by documenting the stages children pass through as they develop language competence, and the ways in which they show attachment to their parents. And economists and political scientists explore similar (and many other) questions from their own specialized perspectives or, as Elizabeth Anscombe's mentor Ludwig Wittgenstein put it, their own disciplinary "language games."

Though they use both qualitative and quantitative methods to explore human themes and variations, social scientists always begin with theories: frameworks of ideas that suggest what to look for and make sense of what is observed. Thus sociologists of a functionalist bent tend to assume that whatever social patterns have arisen have done so for "functional"—that is, culturally survival-relevant—reasons, and so should be studied in detail, but tampered with only very cautiously. Those of a more Marxist orientation assume almost the opposite: that social institutions are mostly shaped by those in power for their own benefit and that the less-powerful are thus justified in adopting an attitude of suspicion and conflict—perhaps even a revolutionary stance—toward them.

Psychologists also have overarching theories—or models, or "paradigms," to use Thomas Kuhn's term[2]—by means of which they both explore human behavior and try to make sense of the results. Those of a psychoanalytic bent—the followers of Freud and Jung most famously—embrace a kind of conflict theory of the mind, maintaining that what we believe and want on the conscious level is often at odds (biologically or spiritually) with what we really yearn for on the unconscious level. Behaviorists, by contrast, tend to ignore the mind: they regard human actions—like those of other creatures—as being so shaped by environmental rewards and punishments that ideas, whether conscious or unconscious, have little or no significant influence on them. Humanistic psychologists have challenged both these models, insisting not only that human beings are much freer than behaviorists claim, but that if they are unconditionally valued, they will make healthy choices that benefit not just themselves but everyone else as well.

Such theoretical perspectives, or models, obviously include metaphysical commitments that go beyond the actual data that is collected. In a sense, they are (like Christianity) faith-based worldviews that presume certain answers to the most basic of human questions: *Who are we? Where are we in the universe and in history? What is the basic human problem? And what is the solution?*[3]

---

2. Thomas Kuhn, *The Structure of Scientific Revolutions* (1963; rev. ed., Chicago: University of Chicago Press, 1971).

3. For a further discussion of worldviews in general, and the Christian worldview in particular, see, for example, David K. Naugle, *Worldview: The History of a Concept* (Grand Rapids: Eerdmans, 2002); and N. T. Wright, *The New Testament and the People of God: Christian Origins and the Question of God* (Minneapolis: Fortress, 1992). For an excellent treatment of

But this does not mean social scientists only see what they want to see. Like natural scientists they have, over time, developed methods for increasing the objectivity with which they collect and interpret data—for example, the kind of double-blind experiments that are used to evaluate experimental drugs and other treatments for human problems.[4] Nevertheless, increasingly over the past half century, both natural and social scientists have recognized that there is no such thing as "immaculate perception" or a "view from nowhere" when doing research. As philosopher Ann Cudd has noted, "Science is one of our most powerful tools for understanding the world. But things in nature don't come with labels attached saying '*This is data.*' It is human beings who decide what's worth attending to, and what isn't. That is what is meant by the social construction of science."[5]

This stance is known as "critical realism," because it acknowledges both the power of science to discern deep patterns of reality, and the inability of scientists ever to do so infallibly. This was clearly expressed by C. S. Lewis in one of the last books he wrote:

> No model is a catalogue of ultimate realities, and none is a mere fantasy. Each is a serious attempt to get in all the phenomena known at a given period, and each succeeds in getting in a great many. But also, no less surely, each reflects the prevalent psychology of an age almost as much as it reflects the state of that age's knowledge. Hardly any battery of facts could have persuaded a[n Ancient] Greek that the universe had an attribute so repugnant to him as infinity, hardly any such battery could persuade a modern that it is hierarchical.[6]

Lewis wrote this at the end of *The Discarded Image*, his introduction to the medieval worldview. But Lewis's words apply equally to theories in science, social science, or any other discipline. Even though he saw it as God-given, Lewis was increasingly aware that human reasoning is fallible, in both senses of the term: it is both finite and fallen. It is finite because even when truths like the axioms of geometry appear self-evident to the mind, most of our mental life "is spent in laboriously connecting those frequent but momentary flashes [of

---

the relevance of worldviews to psychology, see Don S. Browning and Terry D. Cooper, *Religious Thought and the Modern Psychologies*, 2nd ed. (Minneapolis: Augsburg Fortress, 2004).

4. In a double-blind experiment (e.g., one testing a potential drug for depression), half the volunteer participants get the real drug, and half get a "placebo" or fake drug. Moreover, neither the persons administering each, nor the groups getting them, know which group any participant has been assigned to. This allows researchers to control for "placebo" or "expectancy" effects—i.e., improvements that occur just because they are expected by the researcher and/or the participants, and to subtract such placebo effects from those due to the actual drug being tested.

5. Quoted in Sharon Begley, "The Science Wars," *Newsweek*, April 21, 1997, 55–56.

6. C. S. Lewis, *The Discarded Image: An Introduction to Medieval and Renaissance Literature* (Cambridge: Cambridge University Press, 1964), 222.

intuition]."[7] And it is fallen because even these "unarguable intuitions on which we all depend are liable to be corrupted by passion [i.e., self-interest]."[8]

So for Lewis, the mixed character of reason—transcendent in origin, yet prone to distortion—applied, at least in theory, to all disciplines. And despite the fact that he was a humanities scholar, Lewis was not anti-empirical. "What I like about experience," he wrote in *Surprised by Joy*, "is that it is such an honest thing. You may take any number of wrong turnings; but keep your eyes open and you will not be allowed to go very far before the warning signs appear. You may have deceived yourself, but experience is not trying to deceive you. The universe rings true whenever you fairly test it."[9] This is a rather more poetic way of expressing the caveat (routinely learned by today's psychology students) that "the rat is always right." What is meant by this is that if your theory leads you to expect one thing, but your observations tell you another—then so much the worse for your theory. You may have deceived yourself, but the rat is not trying to deceive you.

Hostility to Social Science

From my summary description of the social sciences, one might think Lewis would have regarded them as he did the natural sciences: sources of partial knowledge about reality, to be respected as long as their practitioners don't claim omniscience or try to smuggle in metaphysical claims beyond their competence. Moreover, from his debate with Elizabeth Anscombe—and his willingness to revise some of his arguments against naturalism in light of her criticisms—one might expect Lewis to have expanded his view of the range of perspectives on knowledge. As Anscombe pointed out in her Socratic Club paper, one's convictions may be affected by any or all of physical, historical, psychological, and logical considerations. But except in extreme circumstances, when one of these factors seems to override all the others, the validity of our convictions is not dependent on their being *only* the result of so-called pure reason. In fact, recent work in neuroscience suggests that making valid inferences about the world around us (especially in social situations) requires the sensory, cognitive, and emotional parts of our brains to work together. Otherwise—like Dr. Spock of *Star Trek* fame—we may come to rather strange conclusions that are not nearly as accurate as we think.[10]

7. Ibid., 157. See also Stephen Thorsen, "'Knowledge' in C. S. Lewis's Post-Conversion Thought," *Seven* 9 (1988): 91–116.

8. C. S. Lewis, "The Weight of Glory," in The *Weight of Glory and Other Addresses* (Grand Rapids: Eerdmans, 1965), 36.

9. C. S. Lewis, *Surprised by Joy: The Shape of My Early Life* (London: Collins, 1955), 177.

10. See Antonio D'Amasio, *Descartes' Error: Emotion, Reason and the Human Brain* (New York: Harper Collins, 1994).

But as we have seen from his description of the young sociologist in *That Hideous Strength*, Lewis tended to regard "social science" as a suspect endeavor, perhaps even a contradiction in terms. We should not (he wrote in 1948) treat human beings as if they were interchangeable, "like counters or identical machines . . . We have no authority to take the living and sensitive figures which God has painted on the canvas of our nature and shift them about as if they were mere geometrical figures."[11] Apart from their bodily aspects, Lewis wrote, human beings should not be studied impersonally, like the rest of the natural world. "You can only get to know them," says the one uncorrupted scientist in *That Hideous Strength*—know them as actual persons, or via their uniquely human mental output: stories, art works, philosophical and religious expressions.[12] Nor can we attribute this statement simply to artistic license, as Lewis cautioned readers to treat many details of his fantasies, because soon after the novel's publication he wrote an explanation of it, affirming much the same position.[13] Indeed, in his 1942 satire *The Screwtape Letters*—the book that established his reputation as Christian apologist—Lewis had his senior devil (Screwtape) give the following advice to his young apprentice, Wormwood:

> Do not attempt to use science (I mean the real sciences) as a defense against Christianity. They will positively encourage him to think about realities he cannot see. There have been some sad cases among modern physicists. If he must dabble in science, keep him on economics and sociology.[14]

Lewis's dislike of the social sciences is evident in much that he wrote throughout the 1940s and 1950s, perhaps most famously in his 1943 Riddell Lectures, which were later published as *The Abolition of Man*. In that slim volume of about fifty pages, he refers to the activities of human "conditioners" (often with a capital "C") no fewer than twenty-four times, and in language suggesting that he feared the potential power of behavioral science was almost unlimited. Thus, "the man-molders of the new age will be armed with the

11. C. S. Lewis, "Priestesses in the Church?" reprinted in Walter Hooper, ed., *God in the Dock: Essays On Theology and Ethics* (Grand Rapids: Eerdmans, 1970), 238.

12. C. S. Lewis, *That Hideous Strength: A Modern Fairy-Tale for Grown-Ups* (London: John Lane the Bodley Head, 1945), 185.

13. "A Reply to Professor Haldane," in Walter Hooper, ed., *Of Other Worlds: Essays and Stories by C. S. Lewis* (New York: Harcourt Brace Jovanovich, 1966), 74–85. Lewis wrote that the "good" scientist in *That Hideous Strength* (the chemist William Hingest) "leaves [Belbury] because he finds he was wrong in his original belief that 'it had something to do with science.' To make it clearer yet, my principal character [the sociologist Mark Studdock], the man almost irresistibly attracted by [Belbury] is described as one whose 'education had been neither scientific nor classical, merely "Modern." The severities both of abstraction and high human tradition had passed him by . . . He was . . . a glib examinee in subjects that require no exact knowledge'" (78).

14. C. S. Lewis, *The Screwtape Letters* (London: Geoffrey Bles, 1942; repr., San Francisco: HarperOne, 2001), 4. Page references are to the HarperOne edition.

powers of an omnicompetent state and an irresistible scientific technique: we shall at last get a race of conditioners who really can cut out all posterity in what shape they please."[15] And in his 1949 essay, "The Humanitarian Theory of Punishment," he decried the emerging tendency to treat criminals as badly conditioned organisms to be rehabilitated, rather than as responsible agents serving sentences that fit their crimes. By reducing these persons to mere mechanisms, Lewis wrote, we are being anything but humanitarian. Moreover, if crimes are viewed not in terms of the misuse of free choice, but as some kind of "social sickness," then the idea of limited punishment evaporates, for it is entirely up to the "doctors" to decide when "the patient" is well. Here too Lewis leaves us in little doubt about the power he attributes to behavioral technology:

> To undergo all those assaults on my personality which modern psychotherapy knows how to deliver; to be taken without consent from my home and friends; to lose my liberty; to be remade after some pattern of "normality" hatched in a Viennese laboratory to which I never professed allegiance; to know that this process will never end until either my captors have succeeded or I grow wise enough to cheat them with apparent success—who cares whether this is called punishment or not? That it includes most of the elements for which any punishment is feared . . . is obvious. Only enormous ill-desert could justify it; but ill-desert is the very conception which the Humanitarian theory has thrown overboard.[16]

Why was the Lewis of the 1940s so in awe of techniques that, at that point in time, had been tested mostly on dogs, rats, and pigeons in quite restricted laboratory conditions? Part of it has to do with the confident rhetoric of imminent breakthrough that characterized some social scientists of that time—most famously B. F. Skinner, who, just as Lewis was writing his dystopian novel *That Hideous Strength*, was writing his behaviorist utopia, *Walden Two*.[17] In Skinner's fictitious community, children are programmed through

15. C. S. Lewis, *The Abolition of Man* (Oxford: Oxford University Press, 1943), 43.

16. C. S. Lewis, "The Humanitarian Theory of Punishment," *20th Century: An Australian Quarterly* 3, no. 3 (1949): 5–12, reprinted in Hooper, ed., *God in the Dock*, 287–300. This quotation betrays Lewis's limited knowledge of psychology. The techniques of behavioral conditioning were "hatched" not in Vienna (where Freud developed psychoanalysis as a clinical endeavor), but in Leningrad by Pavlov, and later at Harvard by B. F. Skinner, both of whom were adamantly opposed to Freud's "Viennese" mentalism.

17. B. F. Skinner, *Walden Two* (New York: MacMillan, 1948). There is an oral tradition in psychology that Skinner's antihero in *Walden Two*—the philosopher Augustine Castle, a straw-man character who attempts to defend the reality of human freedom and dignity among the happily-conditioned inhabitants of Walden Two—was patterned after C. S. Lewis. I have not been able to trace the origins of this claim, but it is certainly plausible, since Skinner's *Walden Two* appeared just a year after Lewis was the subject of a cover story in America's *Time* magazine.

the judicious use of positive reinforcement to grow up without the negative emotions of selfishness, envy, and hostility. They are, readers are told, no more free from their genetic and environmental constraints than apple trees are "free" to produce or not produce apples. But because rewards rather than coercive means are used to shape them, the inhabitants of Walden Two have the happy illusion of being free, in a way that is quite compatible with their actually determined lives.

Over half a century later, it is easy to point out that Skinner never went beyond this fictional blueprint to set up anything even remotely like Walden Two. And his followers who have tried to do so have produced communities that are only a pale shadow of Skinner's ideal in terms of size, self-sufficiency, and behavioral control.[18] Still, Lewis was not being entirely paranoid when he worried about the dystopian possibilities of behavioral technology. A. N. Wilson observed about *The Abolition of Man* that

> it was written at a period when, abroad, Hitler and Stalin were defying all previously understood notions of decency—indeed, inventing value or non-value systems of their own—while at home Lewis was finding himself, at the Socratic Club and elsewhere, with philosophers like A. J. Ayer who absolutely denied the possibility of attaching meaning to sentences which were not either verifiable through sense perception or verifiable as a priori truths . . . Murder, dishonesty, theft, unkindness, disregard of the old, cruelty to children, ruthless "justice" untempered by mercy: that these should be considered abhorrent, Lewis gently explains, is no longer taken for granted . . . Where does that leave us? Lewis predicts that it will leave us in the hands of unscrupulous operators who do not believe in humanity itself. The abolition of man will have occurred because there will [no longer be] reason to regard man . . . as a moral being.[19]

But if it is possible to have both scrupulous and unscrupulous natural scientists, why would Lewis not more clearly affirm the same ambiguity about the social sciences? And yet he did not. Moreover, in a 1946 essay he combined his distaste for social science with his public ambivalence (at that time) about women's rational capacities. While conceding that "the emancipation of women . . . probably has many good results" he worried that the greater

18. See, for example, Kathleen Kinkade, *A Walden Two Experiment: The First Five Years of Twin Oaks Commmunity* (New York: Wm. Morrow, 1973); and *Is It Utopia Yet? An Insider's View of Twin Oaks Community In Its Twenty-Sixth Year* (Louisa, VA: Twin Oaks, 1994).

19. A. N. Wilson, *C. S. Lewis: A Biography* (London: Norton, 1990), 198–99. The reality of the Socratic Club's ongoing struggle with philosophers like A. J. Ayer was echoed by Lewis when he wrote that the "Logical Positivist menace" was making Christian apologetics very challenging, and that at the Socratic Club "the enemy often wipe the floor with us." C. S. Lewis to Dom Bede Griffiths, April 22, 1954, in Walter Hooper, ed., *The Collected Letters of C. S. Lewis*, vol. 3, *1950–1963* (San Francisco: HarperSanFranciso: 2007), 462.

mingling of the sexes at Oxford "reduces the amount of serious argument about ideas."

> The only serious questions now discussed are those which seem to have a "practical" importance (i.e., the psychological and sociological problems), for these satisfy the intense practicality and concreteness of the female. That is, no doubt, her proper contribution to the common wisdom of the race. But the proper glory of the masculine mind, its disinterested concern with truth for truth's own sake, with the cosmic and the metaphysical, is being impaired . . . We are being further isolated: forced down to the immediate and the quotidian.[20]

In these writings, Lewis clearly viewed the social sciences as less intellectually rigorous than the humanities or the natural sciences.[21] Indeed, for him they were only dubiously intellectual at all, being overly focused on practical concerns that appeal to women, whose interests and aptitudes he regarded as less suited to abstract thought. Men, however, were ideally made for sterner stuff, unlike the Mark Studdocks whose education is "neither scientific nor classical, merely 'Modern.'"[22] As I noted earlier, by the time he wrote *The Discarded Image* in the early 1960s, Lewis was more of a critical realist. He had become less insistent that reason and observation, together with an appropriate regard for past authority, could lead either science *or* humanities scholars to timeless truths with little distortion, provided they were willing to work hard and not be swayed by emotion. But in his writings of the 1940s and '50s, he was less conciliatory: he regarded facts, axiomatic intuition, reason, and past authority as the combined paths for the discernment of truth. And he saw social scientists as being too cavalier in their regard for these epistemological paths, and particularly the last: that of past authority.[23]

20. C. S. Lewis, "Modern Man and His Categories of Thought," in Walter Hooper, ed., *Present Concerns* (San Diego: Harvest, 1987), 61–66 (quotation from pp. 62–63). This was originally a memo solicited from Lewis in 1946 by Bishop Stephen Neil for the Study Department of the World Council of Churches.

21. There is a certain irony to Lewis's attitude, in that when English literature was first accepted at Oxford as an area of study, just around the time when Lewis matriculated, it too was considered intellectually "soft" and "unrigorous"—unlike the study of "Mods" (classics) or "Greats" (philosophy).

22. Lewis, *That Hideous Strength*, 185.

23. "I am a rationalist," Lewis wrote in the 1930s. "For me, reason is the natural organ of truth; but imagination is the organ of meaning." "Bluspels and Flalensferes: A Semantic Nightmare," in C. S. Lewis, *Rehabilitations and Other Essays* (London: Oxford University Press, 1939), 265. And in his wartime address "Why I am Not a Pacifist," Lewis presented a formulaic approach to resolving ethical disputes: "Every moral judgment involves facts, intuition, and reasoning, and, if we are wise enough to be humble, some regard for authority as well . . . Thus, if I find that the facts on which I am working are clear and little disputed, that the basic intuition is unmistakably an intuition, that the reasoning which connects the intuition with the particular judgment is strong, and that I am in agreement or (at worst) not in disagreement with authority, then I can trust my moral judgment with reasonable confidence. And if, in addition,

So although Lewis's views about gender changed considerably between the 1940s and 1960s, there is less evidence that his dualistic view of the right ways to study humans underwent a similar shift. For Lewis, the territory of the natural sciences was the physical; the territory of the humanities—literature, philosophy, theology, and the arts—explores timeless rational and moral truths that are accessible, at least in large measure, to well-trained (especially male) minds. Social scientists, in claiming epistemological ground between these two, were seen as trivializing their human subjects at best, and undermining their freedom and dignity at worst. The latter, Lewis believed, was because the social sciences by their very nature are more concerned with questions of what people *should* do, and therefore their practitioners will be more tempted than people in other disciplines to manipulate human behavior in accord with their own interests. To Lewis, "while the unarguable intuitions on which we all depend are liable to be corrupted by passion when we are considering truth and falsehood, they are *much more liable, they are almost certain* to be corrupted when we are considering good and evil":

> For then we are concerned with some action to be here and now done or not done by ourselves. And we should not be considering that action at all unless we had some wish either to do or not to do it, so that in this sphere we are bribed from the very beginning.[24]

Lewis did have more use for some social theories than for others. There is, for example, another kind of sociology given passing mention in *That Hideous Strength*, in contrast to Mark Studdock's enchantment with large institutions and quantitative generalizations. It is represented by Studdock's former colleague and rival, Arthur Denniston, who (to the puzzlement of his academic peers) has joined the small and decidedly unmodern community of Christians at St. Anne's-on-the-Hill. "A brilliant man at one time," comments one Belbury insider, "but he seems to have gone quite off the rails since then with all his distributivism. They tell me he's likely to end up in a monastery."[25]

Distributivism was a societal vision—a kind of "third way" between capitalism and socialism—promoted in the early twentieth century by British Catholic thinkers such as Hillaire Belloc and G. K. Chesterton.[26] Reflecting the Catholic social teaching begun by Pope Leo XIII in the late nineteenth century, its adherents worried that under the forces of modernity people would

---

I find little reason to suppose that any passion has secretly swayed my mind, this confidence is confirmed" (p. 39).

24. Lewis, "The Weight of Glory," 36 (emphasis added).

25. Lewis, *That Hideous Strength*, 5.

26. See, for example, Hillaire Belloc, *The Servile State* (1912; repr., Indianapolis: Liberty Classics, 1977); G. K. Chesterton, *The Outline of Sanity* (1926; repr., Norfolk, VA: I.H.S., 2001). *Distibutivism* is alternatively referred to as *distributism* or even *distributionism*.

become alienated laborers in an impersonal factory system, or alternately, passive (even if well-fed) clients of a bureaucratic state.[27] In their view, the ideal state would consist of local groups of economically independent families, some a bit richer than others perhaps, but all possessing various means (e.g., tools, land, skills) to achieve self-sufficiency, without having to work for the companies in which capital and the means of production were fast becoming concentrated. Its best-known recent exponent has probably been the British industrial expert, E. F. Schumacher, who, as an adult convert to Catholicism, adapted some of its distributivist teachings.[28]

Lewis and Freudian Psychoanalysis

Lewis was clearly attracted to the distributivist social vision, with its emphasis on local economic cooperatives—reminiscent of the medieval craft guilds—and family self-sufficiency. It is reflected in the way his little community of Christians (St. Anne's-on-the-Hill) operates in *That Hideous Strength*. It was embodied in the early twentieth century "Arts and Crafts" movement of which his poet-friend Ruth Pitter was a part, making hand-decorated house furnishings. He alludes to it in *Mere Christianity*, when he describes the ideally Christian society as one that would be economically egalitarian, but still authority-ranked by age, class, and gender.[29] But Lewis's passing references to this nonmainstream social movement are of less significance than his engagement with a more influential twentieth-century social-psychological theory—namely, psychoanalysis.

27. Pope Leo XIII, *Rerum Novarum* (1891), reprinted in David J. O'Brien and Thomas A. Shannon, *Catholic Social Thought: The Documentary Heritage* (Maryknoll, NY: Orbis, 1992), no. 9.

28. E. F. Schumacher, *Small Is Beautiful: Economics As If People Mattered* (New York: Harper and Row, 1973).

29. In *Mere Christianity* Lewis wrote: "The New Testament, without going into detail, gives us a pretty clear hint of what a fully Christian society would be like . . . It tells us there are to be no passengers or parasites: if a man does not work, he does not eat. Everyone is to work with his own hands, and what is more, everyone's work is to produce something good . . . To that extent a Christian society would be what we would now call Leftist. On the other hand, it is always insisting on obedience—obedience (and marks of outward respect) from all of us to properly-appointed magistrates, from children to parents, and (I am afraid this is going to be unpopular) from wives to husbands . . . If there were such a society, and you or I visited it, I think we should come away with a curious impression. We should feel that its economic life was very socialist and, in that sense 'advanced,' but that its family life and code of manners were rather old-fashioned—perhaps even ceremonious and aristocratic. Each of us would like some of it, but I am afraid very few of us would like the whole thing. That is just what you would expect if Christianity is the total plan for the human machine" (C. S. Lewis, *Mere Christianity* [London: Collins, 1952], 76). It's clear that Lewis himself *would* be one of the few who liked "the whole thing."

Because it took the mind seriously and originated in clinical practice rather than the laboratory, psychoanalysis seemed less of a threat to Lewis than many other trends in social science. In his 1942 essay "Psycho-Analysis and Literary Criticism," he interacted with some of the standard works of Freud and Jung, giving a mixed review of the former and an enthusiastic endorsement of the latter.[30] Freud, of course, was one of those "conflict theorists of the mind" who held that we are not as respectable and rational as we consciously believe, and that our darker motives—particularly those associated with sex and aggression—express themselves in disguised form by way of dreams, slips of the tongue, and even our artistic endeavors. So, for example, a Renaissance artist who painted nothing but Madonnas holding babies might harbor unconscious Oedipal fantasies about his mother, which he sublimated in a socially acceptable art form. And the poet who writes about heroes slaying dragons may be equally suspected of wanting, unconsciously, to be just such a hero himself, rewarded at the end of his endeavors with sexual access to the "princess" he wants to marry.

Interestingly, Lewis did not deny that such self-serving motives are at work in poets, writers, and other artists. He simply denied that they could explain all art—particularly works by people who are highly trained and talented in their fields. It is certainly the case, he conceded, that as both children and adults, people (himself included) imagine tales in which they are the hero, wed the beautiful princess, and so on. But they also imagine—and are attracted to—stories about quite *different* people, and sometimes even mythical beings, that are pursuing more mysterious and transcendent ends. Both sorts of daydreams, Lewis wrote, "may become the source of literature." But:

> A man who is really hungry does not dream of honey-dew and elfin bread, but of steak and kidney pudding: a man really lustful does not dream of Titania or Helen, but of real, prosaic flesh and blood. Other things being equal, a story in which the hero meets Titania and is entertained with fairy food is less likely to be a [Freudian] fantasy than "a nice love story" of which the scene is London, the dialogue idiomatic, and the episodes probable.[31]

Moreover, the more experienced the artist, the more likely it is that the first kind of imagining will be eclipsed by the second. "I do not suppose I am in disagreement with psycho-analysis," Lewis wrote, "if I say that, even where a work of art originated in a self-regarding reverie, it becomes art by ceasing to be what it was . . . The very root from which the dream grew is severed

---

30. "Psycho-Analysis and Literary Criticism," reprinted in C. S. Lewis, *Selected Literary Essays*, edited by Walter Hooper (Cambridge: Cambridge University Press, 1969), 286–300.
    31. Ibid., 289.

and the dream is planted in a new soil; it is killed as [wish-fulfilling] fantasy before it is raised as art."[32]

And, Lewis added, it is no good saying that poetic images of red roses and secret gardens are "nothing but" disguised references to seductive virgins or beautiful princesses whom the writer (or reader) wants to possess. This is so because, however much writers and readers of literature are interested in sex—or drink, or power—they rarely cease to want these things embellished by something else. They want not just female flesh, but a beautifully clad, inspiring woman; not just a war, but a *just* war; not mere drink, but a drink to someone, or to something, deserving of honor:

> Let us grant that the body was, in fact, concealed behind the garden; yet since the removal of the garden lowers the value of the [literary] experience, it follows that the body gained some of its potency by association with the garden . . . We really want both. Poetry is not a substitute for sexual satisfaction, nor sexual satisfaction for poetry. But if so, poetical pleasure is not sexual pleasure *simply* in disguise. It is, at worst, sexual pleasure *plus* something else, and we really want the something else for its own sake . . . As far as this I think the Freudians are forced to go, and it is enough to save literature. In order to explain the symbols which they themselves insist upon we must admit that humanity is interested in many other things besides sex, and that admission is the thin edge of the wedge . . . Even if it could be shown that latent erotic interest was as 90 [per cent] and the interest in gardens as 10, that 10 would still be the subject of literary criticism. For clearly the 10 is what distinguishes one poem from another.[33]

Lewis thus concluded that Freud was right in what he affirmed, but wrong in what he denied: literature and other forms of art include but also go beyond the use of symbols and myths as stand-ins for our fleshly instincts. Even if our images of roses and secret gardens often point downward, as disguised symbols of the flesh, they can also point upward to transcendent truths that are both aesthetic and moral.[34] In their latter forms, Lewis suggested, they are one of the ways that God subtly "gets through" to human beings.

He made the same point in a slightly different way in *Mere Christianity*. There Lewis distinguished between psychoanalysis as merely a clinical technique for dealing with neurotic symptoms, and psychoanalysis as a totalizing worldview that reduces all symbols of the transcendent to disguised versions of our desires for sex, aggression, and bodily comfort. The first he accepted

32. Ibid., 290. This is adapted from 1 Cor. 15: 42–44, where Paul writes: "So it is with the resurrection of the dead. What is sown is perishable; what is raised is imperishable. It is sown in dishonor, it is raised in glory. It is sown in weakness, it is raised in power. It is sown a physical body, it is raised a spiritual body."

33. Lewis, "Psycho-analysis," 295, 296.

34. For a further treatment of this theme, see Lewis's essay "Transposition" in Walter Hooper, ed., *The Weight of Glory and Other Addresses* (San Francisco: Harper, 1980), 25–46.

as a potentially helpful tool; the second, as we have already seen, he rejected. So, for example, if a psychoanalyst helps me to understand and overcome an irrational fear of water, that is all well and good, and something to be grateful for. But now, as well as being freed to swim in the ocean, I am also free to decide whether or not to save—at the risk of my own life—a stranger's child I may one day see drowning nearby.[35] And that choice is something that the psychoanalyst can neither explain nor evaluate, Lewis wrote. It is a choice made before God, and one that God will eventually judge—not in the abstract, but on the basis of whatever advantages and burdens each person has carried through life:

> Most of a man's psychological make-up is probably due to his body: when his body dies, all that will fall off him, and the real central man, the thing that chose, that made the best or worst out of this material, will stand naked. All sorts of nice things which we thought our own, but which were really due to good digestion, will fall off some of us: all sorts of nasty things which were due to complexes or bad health will fall off others. We shall see then, for the first time, everyone as he really was. There will be surprises.[36]

Mind the Gap!

In his analysis of Freud, Lewis displays a rare example of just what Elizabeth Anscombe argued for: he accepts the validity of multiple perspectives on human behavior (rational, emotional, physical, spiritual) as long as none is allowed to swallow up or write off the others. He was thus right to credit Freud for what he affirmed—namely, that self-serving passions affect dreams and imagination—while faulting him for what he denied: that our symbolic life includes more than disguised self-interest, even when it emerges from the latter.[37] But the opposite must now be said of Lewis himself: while astutely criticizing Freud for what he denied, he lapsed back into his theologically problematic affirmation of Platonic mind/body dualism. To understand why this is troublesome, it might be helpful to mention that as I was writing this chapter I happened to be in London. While there, I took "the tube" (subway) to the Victoria and Albert Museum, which richly documents the social and artistic currents present in England during Lewis's lifespan. These include the Arts and Crafts Movement, and the pre-Raphaelite artists (also much admired

35. This is my example, but it parallels Lewis's somewhat awkward illustration from the World War II era in which he wrote *Mere Christianity*.

36. Lewis, *Mere Christianity*, 82.

37. A good introduction to the way more differentiated forms of knowledge emerge from simpler, sensory ways of dealing with the world can be found in Michael Polanyi, *The Study of Man* (Chicago: University of Chicago Press, 1958).

by Lewis) who tried to recapture a simpler, preclassical style of painting, often representing medieval themes such as romantic love and knightly battles.

If you know the London tube system, you will recall the famous loudspeaker warning, as you exit from your train, to "Mind the gap!" between the car and the platform. The gap is only a couple of inches wide, but that is enough for the absent minded to risk getting a shoe stuck in it—hence the persistent warning. It is, moreover, a good image for what is problematic in Lewis's answer to Freud. Like many Christians of his time (and, alas, our own) Lewis ends up portraying a "God of the gap"—and hence, by extension, a Platonic or Cartesian "person of the gap." Thus for Lewis, artistic symbolism may be 90 percent "fleshly," but there is still a 10 percent "gap" into which what some people call "the things of God" can still be fitted. Similarly, "most of man's psychological make-up is . . . due to his body," but there is a kernel of pure spirit that remains "when his body dies, and the real central man, the thing that chose . . . will stand naked."[38]

The problem with "God of the gaps" thinking—the plural indicates that such "gaps" have been postulated by well-meaning Christians in many disciplines—is that the gaps keep getting smaller and smaller. In terms of our tube metaphor, the train of our "fleshly" self keeps arriving at the station in progressively bigger models, threatening to swallow up completely the platform guarding our residual "spiritual" core. The result, as we saw from Lewis's analysis of Freud—and his fear of behaviorism—is that the space we seem able to reserve for God's free action (and that of the human "soul") gets more and more constricted. This problem confronts Christian dualists whether they are dealing with the findings of biology, psychology, economics, or any of the natural or social sciences.

With Lewis, as we have seen, another feature of this nature/grace (or secular/sacred) dualism was that he put most societal institutions—such as law, government, and commerce—on the secular, or "fleshly," side of the gap. He saw them as at best incidental to "real" Christian life and, at worst, as products of the fall. At the start of World War II, Lewis expressed this dichotomy to one of his former students in almost Manichean terms: "But what state of affairs in this world can we view with satisfaction? . . . In fact, one comes to realize, what one had always admitted theoretically, that there is nothing here that will do us good: the sooner we are safely out of this world the better."[39] In what

38. Lewis, *Mere Christianity*, 82.

39. C. S. Lewis to Dom Bede Griffiths, OSB, May 8, 1939, Walter Hooper, ed., *The Collected Letters of C. S. Lewis*, vol. 2, *1931–1949* (San Francisco: HarperSanFrancisco, 2004), 258. In *Mere Christianity* Lewis asserted that "next to Christianity, dualism is the manliest and most sensible creed on the market" (44). And two years before his death he could still write: "I have always come as near to dualism as Christianity allows—and the New Testament allows one to go v[ery] near. The devil is the (*usurping*) Lord of this age." C. S. Lewis to Griffiths, December 20, 1961, Hooper, ed., *Collected Letters*, vol. 3, 1303.

theologian N. T. Wright calls "a moving but deeply misleading passage" in *Mere Christianity*, Lewis extended this dualism even to the physical world: he referred to it as "that anesthetic fog which we call 'nature' or 'the real world' [which will] fade away."[40] And even in the last chapter of the last book he wrote, Lewis's "speculations" about the doctrine of the resurrection of the body are still heavily tinged with Platonic (and Berkeleyesque) idealism. "What the soul cries out for," he wrote in *Letters to Malcolm*, "is the resurrection of the senses. Even in this life matter would be nothing to us if it were not a source of sensations . . . Matter enters our experience only by becoming sensation . . . That is, by becoming soul . . . At present we tend to think of the soul as somehow in the body. But the glorified body of the resurrection as I conceive it—the sensuous life raised from its death—will be inside the soul."[41]

In his better moments, Lewis knew better. He knew that the material world, created by God, is "good . . . very good," as the account in Genesis 1 repeatedly affirms. In *Mere Christianity* he writes that the sacraments of bread and wine are important because they affirm a material world that God made and likes. Yet, as Wright points out, when Lewis discusses Jesus in *Mere Christianity*, he never once mentions Christ's resurrection. And he consistently refers to heaven "in ways that go far too far towards Plato."

> [Lewis] tells us that if we aim at heaven, we'll get earth thrown in, and this is not only true, but appealing; but he never indicates how this works out, never engages with the New Testament's picture of the new heavens and new earth which ultimately make sense of the whole thing . . . Along with [his] astonishing omission of Easter [is] the complete absence of anything to do with Jesus' announcement of God's kingdom. This is less surprising, though still regrettable, because, to be frank, the Western church in the middle of the twentieth century didn't understand what the kingdom of God was all about . . . I think the fruits of the omission show up elsewhere, where Lewis has little or no concern for a social or cultural ethic, still less a political or ecological one.[42]

40. N. T. Wright, "Simply Lewis: Reflections on a Master Apologist After 60 Years," *Touchstone: A Journal of Mere Christianity* 20, no. 2 (March 2007), 28–33. The reference to *Mere Christianity* is from p. 180.

41. C. S. Lewis, *Letters to Malcolm, Chiefly on Prayer* (London: Geoffrey Bles, 1964), 121, 123. Lewis quickly pulls his punches by adding these words: "Guesses, of course, only guesses. If they are not true, something better will be" (124). See also Roger Lancelyn Green and Walter Hooper, *C. S. Lewis: A Biography* (London: Collins, 1974), 234–35.

42. Wright, "Simply Lewis," 29 and 32. In this paper Wright also notes that twentieth-century misunderstanding of Jesus's teaching about the kingdom was in part due to the church's "relentless de-Judaizing of the whole story . . . What Lewis totally failed to see—as have, of course, many other scholars in the field—was that Judaism already had a strong incarnational principle, namely the Temple, and that the language used of Shekinah, Torah, Wisdom, Word and Spirit in the Old Testament [the language the early Christians drew on] was a language designed, long before Jesus' day, to explain how the one true God could be both transcendent over the world *and* living and active within it, particularly within Israel" (31). See also N. T.

Lewis was just one of many twentieth-century Christians who embraced a nature/grace dualism, only to find that the second part—what they thought of as the "supernatural" spheres of worship, thinking, and virtuous personal living—kept getting pushed into a smaller and smaller space. At the same time, the supposedly natural or "secular" spheres represented by biology, economics, sociology, psychology, and politics kept expanding their reach, even as they continued to be seen as largely irrelevant to "spiritual" life, or perhaps even harmful to it. Aside from the supposed threat of the "secular" swallowing up more and more of the "sacred," what's wrong with this picture? At least two things.

The Long Reach of Lewis's Dualism

The first is that the picture itself is misleading. It does not adequately reflect the biblical narrative of creation, fall, redemption, and especially the final promise of "a new heaven *and* a new earth" where by God's light "the nations will walk."[43] In that four-part cosmic drama, Christians (indeed all humans, whether they know it or not) now live, as it were, with one foot in act 3 and the other in the first part of act 4. That is to say, they live in a space-time arena that is permeated *both* by the power of Jesus' resurrection "making all things new"[44] and the reality that this renewal will not be complete until God brings down the curtain on human history. In this ambiguous era, even though they have been dealt a mortal blow, the demonic forces the apostle Paul referred to as "principalities and powers"—and which Lewis also took very seriously— still try to corrupt both individuals and the social structures given by God as the scaffolding for human life.

The outcome of that battle is portrayed in vivid apocalyptic language in the book of Revelation. But theologians have found more condensed metaphors to express the tension within which, in the meantime, the world as a whole must operate. N. T. Wright speaks of the overlap between the heavenly "already" and the earthly "not yet" in terms of tectonic plates that rub against each other, causing unpredictable earthquakes that shake things up, sometimes for worse, but eventually for the better.[45] Closer to Lewis's time, Oscar Cullman spoke in terms of living "between D-Day and V-Day": that is, between the time when the decisive turning point in a war has been reached—after which mop-up operations occur side by side with the rebuilding of civil society—and

---

Wright, *Simply Christian: Why Christianity Makes Sense* (San Francisco: HarperSanFrancisco, 2006), especially chaps. 6–7 and 14–16.

43. Rev. 21:1, 24.
44. See Rev. 21:5.
45. Wright, *Simply Christian*, 161.

the time when full peace has been restored.[46] In the 1960s, Francis Schaeffer wrote of the Christian mandate to set up "pilot plants." By this he meant "stake-outs" or experiments in all areas of life that, by the power of Christ's spirit, substantially embody God's kingdom in terms of justice, beauty, proper worship, and right relationships.[47]

Lewis, in *Mere Christianity*, does get this picture partly right, using (as Oscar Cullman did) words that dramatically invoke the battlefield metaphor:

> Christianity agrees . . . that this world is at war. But it does not think this is a war between independent powers. It thinks it is a civil war, a rebellion, and that we are living in a part of the universe occupied by the rebel. Enemy-occupied territory—that is what this world is. Christianity is the story of how the rightful king has landed, you might say landed in disguise, and is calling us all to take part in a great campaign of sabotage. When you go to church you are really listening to the secret wireless from our friends. That is why the enemy is so anxious to prevent us from going.[48]

This imagery certainly captures the "not yet" quality of our time in cosmic history, while rightly asserting the ultimate victory of God over the principalities and powers with which humans must contend. But it gives those powers too much credit. If we really lived completely in "enemy-occupied territory," then we could never in good conscience sing "This *is* my Father's world." And it really would be the case that, apart from going to church to "listen to the secret wireless," we would have to see our task in the world mainly as "a great campaign of sabotage." Except as ways to make a living, tend to the wounded, and/or get rest and recreation between battles, everything else—from doing science to engaging in politics to writing literary criticism—would be of less importance, indeed would be ultimately ephemeral, compared to our "real" life in the church.

Let me be clear that I do not want to underrate the importance of the church's preaching of the Word and dispensing of the sacraments—for which no other institution can really substitute. And Lewis could never be accused, in this passage or any other, of underrating the church's unique mission. The problem, again, is his tendency to go "too far toward Plato"—to relegate the rest of our bodily and societal life to an incidental, if not inferior, status and confine "the things of God" largely to worship, apologetics, and evangelism. Lewis, though a scholar and lover of literature, maintained that even the best literary creations are of less importance than the salvation of a single soul. If

---

46. Oscar Cullman, *The Christology of the New Testament* (Philadelphia: Westminster, 1959).

47. Francis Schaeffer, *The God Who Is There* (Grand Rapids: Eerdmans, 1968). See also Wright, *Simply Christian*, chaps. 1–4.

48. Lewis, *Mere Christianity*, 36.

you are a nature/grace dualist, this is at least consistent, and in one sense it is true even if you are not. But it does not help equip the saints for the work of building up God's kingdom, as opposed to merely struggling against the forces of unbelief. It reflects an incomplete understanding of redemption, because it underrates the importance and continuity of God's work *in creation*. Indeed, the Latin root of the word *salvation* is *salus*, which means "health"—not a disembodied, otherworldly life.

This would be less of a problem if Lewis were not so widely read and invoked as the person who got "mere" Christianity exactly right. But one has only to go online to find literally hundreds of people quoting and commending his dualistic leanings using the very passages I have been challenging, as well as many others. And even well-trained Christian academics have fallen into the trap of embracing Lewis's Cartesian view of knowledge. Some simply accept his view that the most valid ways of studying reality are to be found in the "pure" sciences (which "disinterestedly" study the physical) or "pure" humanities (which "disinterestedly" study the spirit). Some have even embraced Lewis's notion that social scientists are questionable interlopers who by definition harbor power interests less likely to be seen among those in other disciplines.[49]

How are we to deal with this habit of dividing the sacred from the secular, and thus the "right" from the "wrong" ways to study human nature? To begin with, we need to affirm that there *is* a division in human life—one reflecting the tension between our allegiance to God and the temptations of those rebel powers of which Lewis wrote. But that division does not go *between* certain activities—with "spiritual" ones on one side and "worldly" ones on the other. It goes right through the middle of all of them. Thus, we can "do church"—or family life, or physics, or art, or politics (to name just a few)—in obedience to God or in partial or complete thrall to demonic powers, or idols, of various sorts. And no sphere of life is less exempt from such temptation than any other. We only have to recall the reach of sexual abuse in the church—or the church's co-optation by Hitler during the Nazi era—to know that there is no guarantee that its "cleansing and invigorating inequalities" (as Lewis idealized them in the 1940s) will always be a more healthy alternative to the supposedly second-best, fall-based democracy of our "secular" life.[50]

However, Lewis was right about one thing: such idols are not a separate, independent category of being. They are subtle distortions of the good structures of creation, and thus very hard to recognize. Recall theologian Lewis Smedes's trenchant definition of an idol: "Just slice one piece of creation off

49. See, for example, Henry F. Schaeffer III, *Science and Christianity: Conflict or Coherence?* (Watkinsville, GA: Apollos Trust, 2003), especially chap. 7; and also Paul L. Holmer, *C. S. Lewis: The Shape of His Life and Thought* (New York: Harper and Row, 1976).

50. C. S. Lewis, "Membership," reprinted in *The Weight of Glory and Other Addresses*, 38.

from the whole, and expect miracles from it."[51] Thus science can easily slide into scientism; love may be eclipsed by lust; the pursuit of just government can degenerate into the abuse of power; the church that is meant to be a "hospital for sinners" may become a supposed "hotel for saints." The list could go on and on. The point is that no set of human activities is more or less "spiritual" than another. All are built into creation, and all are part of the human mandate to develop that creation as God's stewards. All are fallen, and all are equally capable of redemption—or regression. Moreover, the current act of the biblical drama, as N. T. Wright points out, "isn't just about our own private pilgrimage. It's about becoming agents of God's new world—workers for justice, explorers of spirituality, makers and menders of relationships, creators of beauty . . . [The Bible is] a book designed to be read by those who are living the present in light of God's future—the future that has arrived in Jesus and now demands to be implemented."[52]

To do justice to this nondualistic view of life and scholarship, we need what Bishop Lesslie Newbigin calls "a declericalized theology."[53] We need to reaffirm, with Abraham Kuyper, that "there is not one square inch of creation about which Jesus Christ does not say, '*That's mine!*'"[54] Newbigin explains it as follows:

> I am thinking here . . . of the doctrine [called "sphere sovereignty"] that God has given—as part of the order of creation—a measure of autonomy to each of the major areas of human life, including such areas as art, science, politics, ethics and faith. This means that the human community that is responsible for the development of each of these spheres is responsible directly to God, and not to the community of faith (the church), which has no direct authority over them . . . Each sphere in society has a God-given task and competence which are limited by the sphere's own intrinsic nature . . . This seems to me an important line of thinking that avoids both the post-Enlightenment idea of the total autonomy of these spheres, and the medieval idea that all these spheres should be under the authority of the church . . . For such a declericalized theology, the church will be servant, not mistress.[55]

Again, it needs to be said that in his better moments Lewis had a better-developed creation theology. He knew, for example, that the human urge to

51. Lewis Smedes, *Sex for Christians* (Grand Rapids: Eerdmans, 1976), 26.

52. Wright, *Simply Christian*, 189. See also Al Wolters and Michael W. Goheen, *Creation Regained: Biblical Basics for a Reformational Worldview*, 2nd. ed. (Grand Rapids: Eerdmans, 2005).

53. Lesslie Newbigin, *Foolishness to the Greeks: The Gospel and Western Culture* (Grand Rapids: Eerdmans, 1986), 141.

54. Abraham Kuyper, "Sphere Sovereignty," Inaugural Address at the Free University of Amsterdam, October 20, 1990. Reprinted in James D. Brett, ed., *Abraham Kuyper: A Centennial Reader* (Grand Rapids: Eerdmans, 1998, 461–90 (quotation from p. 488).

55. Newbigin, *Foolishness to the Greeks*, 143.

pursue truth and beauty was not just part of an "anesthetic fog [that will] fade away." Thus, in a sermon to students still studying at Oxford during World War II, he pointed out that

> plausible reasons have never been lacking for putting off all merely cultural activities until some imminent danger has been averted or some crying injustice set right. But humanity long ago chose to neglect those plausible reasons. They wanted knowledge and beauty now, and would not wait for the suitable moment that never comes . . . The insects have chosen a different line: they have sought first the material welfare and security of the hive, and presumably they have their reward. Men [sic] are different. They propound mathematical theorems in beleaguered cities, conduct metaphysical arguments in condemned cells, make jokes on scaffolds, discuss the last new poem while advancing on the walls of Quebec, and comb their hair at Thermopylae. This is not panache [i.e., ornamentation or posturing]: it is our nature.[56]

Here again, Lewis gets it half right. He affirms that the pursuit of knowledge and beauty is built into human nature, so it will not (and should not) be overwhelmed by seemingly more urgent concerns—even in wartime. Yet even here, he is tempted back into dualism: the pursuit of knowledge and beauty is such a lofty part of the human spirit that it may even trump the need to rectify "crying injustice." But the Bible as a whole does not allow us to choose between these. From Genesis to the Prophets, through the Gospels to the book of Revelation, the message is that redemption is meant to apply both to individuals and to social structures; both to the realm of beliefs and ideas and to our life together—in church and marriage, to be sure (as Christian dualists have long recognized) but also in the marketplace, the schools, the political forum, the law courts, and every other sphere of life. This is not panache: it is a vital part of what it means to be living "between D-day and V-Day." It means not underestimating the residual forces of evil, let alone our own finitude, yet working to restructure all activities of life in accordance with the vision of God's kingdom where (as the psalmist put it) justice and peace will embrace.[57] Or, in another of N. T. Wright's metaphors, "we are already to be penciling the sketches for the masterpiece that God will one day call us to help him paint."[58]

In a rare passage in *Mere Christianity*, Lewis did move briefly beyond his Platonic reflex to dichotomize "spiritual" from "secular" activities. He wrote that

56. C. S. Lewis, "Learning in Wartime," reprinted in Walter Hooper, ed., *Fern-Seed and Elephants and Other Essays on Christianity by C. S. Lewis* (London: Collins, 1975), 26–38 (quotation from p. 28).

57. See Ps. 85:8–12.

58. Wright, *Simply Christian*, 206.

[when people say] the Church ought to give us the lead, they ought to mean that some Christians—those who have the right talents—should be economists and statesmen . . . and that their whole efforts in politics and economics should be directed to putting . . . [the Golden Rule] into action . . . [And] the application of Christian principles to, say, trade unionism or education must come from Christian trade unionists and Christian schoolmasters, just as Christian literature comes from Christian novelists and dramatists and not from the bench of Bishops getting together and trying to write plays and novels in their spare time.[59]

This is a good summary of what Newbigin meant by "declericalized" theology—and in it, note how Lewis now assumes that economics (one of those social sciences that often applies numbers to people) is a valid Christian calling. But this insight is not developed further, and in the bulk of Lewis's writings it is overwhelmed by the dualistic mind-set that he inherited from his classical and philosophical (and indeed, his churchly) training.

C. S. Lewis and Jungian Psychology

This brings us to the second major problem with Lewis's dualism. Because he routinely dismissed the methods of the social sciences, Lewis for much of his life felt free to make assertions about "what men are like" and "what women are like" without ever having to defend them empirically. We have already seen several examples of this in his earlier writings: men have a more disinterested sense of justice than women; women are more concerned with practical issues than with abstract truths; neither women nor men want women in positions of authority; women's "fierce maternal instinct" is such that, when it is working right "children will be fruit enough" for them; Christlike husbands must work to elevate weak and ignorant wives. Lewis, to be sure, was not the only scholar on either side of the Atlantic to embrace such assumptions.[60] But the fact that he wove them so often into his portrait of "mere" Christianity means that their influence has been felt long after most of his readers have learned, for example, to contextualize and question standard Edwardian notions of class, ethnicity, and British imperial privilege.

As I noted in an earlier chapter, Lewis is in some ways to be commended for treating gender as an important topic in an era when many scholars considered it to be completely trivial. But when he tosses off such generalizations, he (ironically) falls into the same habit he accused social scientists of adopting: that of shifting women and men about "as if they were mere geometric figures," each with the same shape.[61] (It also shows that one does not have

59. Lewis, *Mere Christianity*, 75.

60. See, for example, Elizabeth Scarborough and Laurel Furomoto, *Untold Lives: The First Generation of American Women Psychologists* (New York: Columbia University Press, 1984).

61. Lewis, "Priestesses in the Church?" 238.

to be a social scientist in order to use ideas in a polemical and manipulative way.) Again, this would be less troublesome if Lewis were not regarded by so many as the penultimate authority on Christian living. And it would also be less problematic if Lewis had not been so enchanted by another psychoanalytic figure whose views, in large part, just happened to coincide with his own. That figure was Freud's early disciple and later rival, the Swiss-German psychologist Carl Gustav Jung.

In his 1942 essay on psychoanalysis, Lewis devoted only about half as much attention to Jung as he did to Freud—but this is because he had almost nothing to criticize in Jung's theory, which he described as "a much more civil and humane interpretation of myth and imagery."[62] Jung, who was born almost a quarter of a century before Lewis, was the son of an impoverished Swiss Reformed pastor who married a woman of a somewhat higher class. In some ways Jung's early life was the reverse of Lewis's, whose intellectually gifted mother died when he was only nine. Jung's mother was a more constant, but also a more disturbing, presence: she was mentally ill during his early years, and throughout her life (behind an outwardly-respectable lifestyle) she was fascinated by the occult and in the habit of attending séances about which her husband knew nothing. Lewis lost his childish Christian faith in his early years at boarding school; Jung spent his school years living at home, increasingly attracted by his mother's apparently free-floating spiritualism and repelled by the rigidity of his father's rural Calvinism.[63]

Spiritualism, as we know from Lewis's own accounts, was a source of fascination even to well-educated people at the turn of the twentieth century, despite (or perhaps in reaction to) the growing influence of naturalism and logical positivism. Lewis himself was tempted by it as a child, as an Oxford student, and even after his wife's death.[64] But for Jung it was at the core of his psychology, and the reason for his break with Freud in 1910, after working with him for six years to win psychoanalysis a place of respect as an academic theory

62. Lewis, "Psycho-Analysis," 296.
63. An excellent account of Jung's life and intellectual development can be found in Dierdre Bair, *Jung: A Biography* (New York: Little Brown, 2004).
64. In *Surprised by Joy*, Lewis notes that a caretaker at his first boarding school introduced him to spiritualism. He mentions that as an Oxford undergraduate, he met "Magicians, Spiritualists and the like," and that though tempted by their activities, he knew by then that "joy" did not lie in that direction (143–44). Yet as late as 1961, mourning the death of his wife in *A Grief Observed*, he writes of longing for assurance of her continued existence. But he concludes: "At any rate, I must keep clear of the spiritualists. I promised [Joy] I would. She knew something of those circles" (C. S. Lewis, *A Grief Observed* [London: Faber and Faber, 1961], 11). The seriousness with which some Edwardian-era academics took spiritualism is reflected in William James's 1902 book, *The Varieties of Religious Experience* (New York: Simon and Schuster, 1997), which has never gone out of print. A detailed account of James and other spiritualists of that era can be found in Deborah Blum, *Ghost Hunters: William James and the Search for Scientific Proof of Life After Death* (New York: Penguin, 2006).

and psychotherapeutic technique.[65] Jung challenged Freud's reductionistic account of the unconscious, theorizing (as Lewis did) that at its deeper levels, it was a repository of much more than just sexual and aggressive symbolism. Rather, it included meaningful "archetypes" or historically recurring mythic symbols, acquired by the human race over time and passed on by some mysterious process that was at least as much spiritual as it was cultural.[66] Some of the archetypes Jung included in what he called the "collective unconscious" were: the Hero, the Great Mother, the Lover, the Wise Old Man, the Eternal Boy (think here of Peter Pan), the Self (i.e., each person's center of individual integrity), the Animus and Anima (or masculine and feminine ideals), and the Shadow (i.e., each person's darker, more destructive side).

Much of Jung's clinical work (including dream analysis) was focused on getting clients to strive for what he thought was a developmentally appropriate balance among these archetypes. And at first glance, his system appears to be a helpful tool for counseling psychologists, or even today's Christian spiritual directors, not a few of whom embrace Jung's teachings.[67] Who could argue against the wisdom of learning to balance the "Hero" with the "Wise Old Man" in your personality if you are a man, or the "Lover" with the "Great Mother" if you are a woman? Given his love of myth, and his conviction that it could sometimes be a prolegomenon to the gospel, it is not surprising that Lewis was attracted to Jungian psychology. But there are problems with Jung's theory and its application that should have given Lewis pause.

In the first place, the number and range of mythical archetypes is almost limitless. Thus, if a client does not respond as a therapist thinks he should to dream images of Wise Old Men or Peter Pan figures, it can always be blamed on interference by another archetype, such as the Shadow. Another way of putting this is to say (in philosopher Karl Popper's terms) that Jung's theory is "unfalsifiable": no empirical evidence can stand against it, since the therapist

65. By his own account, Jung chose psychiatry as his medical specialty in part because it might allow him to pursue his primary interests—namely, spiritualism and religiosity. His Zurich University doctoral thesis, on "The Psychology and So-Called Pathology of Occult Phenomena," drew on the work of William James, Theodore Flournoy, and other well-known students of spiritualism of that era. See Bair, *Jung*, chap. 4, and also Francis X. Charet, *Spiritualism and the Foundations of C. G. Jung's Psychology* (Albany, NY: State University of New York Press, 1993).

66. See C. J. Jung and Violet S. De Laszlo, *The Basic Writings of C. J. Jung* (New York: Modern Library, 1997), especially part 1.

67. In addition to the bestselling books of John and Staci Eldredge (cited in chapter 3), see, for example, Stu Webber, *Tender Warrior: Every Man's Purpose, Every Woman's Dream, Every Child's Hope* (Sisters, OR: Multnomah, 1993); Leanne Payne, *Crisis in Masculinity* (Grand Rapids: Baker Books, 1995); James Arraj, *Jungian and Catholic?* (Chiloquin, OR: Inner Growth Books, 1991); Marvin J. Spiegelman, *Catholicism and Jungian Psychology* (Tempe, AZ: New Falcon, 1995).

can always invoke some kind of "auxiliary hypothesis" (e.g., another archetype) to explain any client's behavior that doesn't accord with the theory.[68]

Lewis was quite alert to this "heads-I-win, tails-you-lose" problem in Freud's theory. He noted that when someone protests that his love of literary images is more than just a cover for lust, the Freudian analyst can always assume that defense mechanisms are at work. He "may reply that such a reaction of resistance is just what he expected to find and confirms his suspicions . . . [or] that our conscious taste rejects his interpretation because of our inhibitions."[69] But in his discussion of Jung, Lewis sets aside all skepticism. "Thanks to my training [as a literary scholar]," he wrote, "I can suspend my judgment about the scientific value of Jung's [theory] . . . I perceive at once that even if it turns out to be bad science it is excellent poetry."[70]

What did Lewis mean by this? First of all, simply that his historical and literary tastes resonated with Jung's invocation of ancient myth and legend. "My unreflective reaction to all this," he wrote, "can only be expressed in some such words as 'Isn't this grand?'"

> Well, I know where I am now . . . I am with Collingwood discovering behind the Arthurian legend some far-off echo of real happenings in the thick darkness of British history . . . with Wordsworth, sinking deep and ascending into regions "to which the heaven of heavens is but a veil" . . . with my own past self, hoping, as a child, for that forgotten, that undiscovered room. I am with the British Israelites and Baconians and searchers for Atlantis, with Renaissance magicians and seekers for the sources of the Nile. In a word, I am enjoying myself immensely.[71]

Lewis did admit, in this article written for his academic peers, that just because a theory arouses powerful emotions about what is "dim, remote, long buried, and mysterious" doesn't make it valid. And yet, he continued, humans *do* meditate on these primordial images, both the pleasant and the scary ones, and on "one particular primordial image, which itself needs explanation as much as any of the others."[72] Here Lewis seems to be referring back to that complex of locked-room, lost-Atlantis, secret-garden metaphors that meant so much to him personally, and that are a recurring feature of imaginative literature throughout the ages. Could it be, he hinted, that there is a Being who is the source of these Edenic pictures, and who wants to take us to an even better Garden than any that we could have imagined? "I can only say," he wrote, "that the mystery of primordial images is deeper, their origin more

68. Karl Popper, *The Logic of Scientific Discovery* (New York: Harper, 1959).
69. Lewis, "Psycho-Analysis," 293.
70. Ibid., 297.
71. Ibid., 298.
72. Ibid., 299, 300.

remote, their cave more hid, their fountain less accessible than those suspect that have yet dug deepest, sounded with the longest cord, or journeyed farthest in the wilderness." The real destination buried in those images was not apparent to Jung and most of his followers. But (Lewis concludes) "Why should I not be allowed to write in this vein as well as everyone else?"[73]

Gender Archetypes and Gender Roles

Again, at first glance, this kind of exercise seems at worst harmless, and at best an inspired way of getting people (as it did Lewis) to consider the claims of God on their life. But despite its "spiritual" overtones, Jung's theory is arguably just as confining as Freud's. This is because, to the extent that the archetypes are seen as ideals to which people should aspire, one's nonconformity to them can be treated as either pathological or perverse. When Jung postulated the masculine Animus, and its feminine counterpart the Anima, he was engaging in yet another version of nature/grace dualism. He was suggesting—as Lewis did for much of his life—that the "eternal forms" of masculinity and femininity were on a higher plane than shortsighted whining about the confines of gender roles, and that "healthy" people should set aside the latter and embrace the former.

We have seen how Lewis, in *That Hideous Strength*, traces just such a transformation in Jane Studdock, who, after becoming a Christian, learns to submit to her hapless husband, set aside her academic ambitions, and "have children instead."[74] The point is emphatically *not* that, for women, the intellectual life is preferable to nurturing children, or vice versa. It is that Lewis, in his uncritical embrace of archetypal thinking, tries to force readers into choosing between the two. There is kind of a victor's justice at work in this process, since it is obviously the articulate and famous—whether they are neo-Pagan psychologists like Jung or well-meaning Christian apologists like Lewis—who get to assert what the lofty, "spiritual" (and thus behavioral) contents of the archetypes are. And Lewis's embrace of these archetypes clearly predated his reading of Jung.

For example, when writing in 1933 to his friend Arthur Greeves about George MacDonald's fantasy novel *Lillith* (the character refers to a Jewish legend about a lover of the primal Adam who was later displaced by Eve), Lewis confidently described her as "the real ideal somehow spoiled: she is not primarily a sexual symbol, but includes the characteristic *female* abuse of sex, which is love of power, as the characteristic male abuse is sensuality."[75]

73. Ibid., 300.
74. Lewis, *That Hideous Strength*, 380.
75. C. S. Lewis to Arthur Greeves, September 1, 1933, Walter Hooper, ed., *The Collected Letters of C. S. Lewis*, vol. 1, *1905–1931* (San Francisco: HarperSanFrancisco, 2004), 119 (emphasis original).

And almost a decade later, when he was working on *Perelandra*, he wrote the following to his friend and colleague Sister Penelope:

> I've got Ransom to Venus and through his first conversation with the "Eve" of that world: a difficult chapter. I hadn't realized, till I came to write it, all this *Ave-Eva* business. I may have embarked on the impossible. This woman has got to combine characteristics which the Fall has put poles apart—she's got to be in some ways like a Pagan goddess and in other ways like the Blessed Virgin. But if one can even get a fraction of it into words it is worth doing.[76]

Worth doing for whom, the reader may well wonder. And when we recall that Lewis, with his contempt for social science, regarded serious empirical testing of these stereotypes as either intellectually vacuous or potentially de-humanizing, we are left with the impression that these archetypal traits are simply God-ordained. Either men and women will embrace them, or their very souls will be at risk. There is no third way.

Am I perhaps being too hard on both Jung and Lewis? Jung did, after all, postulate that men had a subterranean Anima, or feminine archetype, that they should learn to listen to, just as women had an Animus, or masculine one. There is, he insisted, a man in every woman and a woman in every man. And by the early 1950s, Lewis had clearly added this Jungian nuance to his thinking. We can see it in another of his letters to Sister Penelope, in which he responds to her speculation that the primal Adam may have been a hermaph-rodite before the creation of Eve from one of his ribs:

> I don't quite feel we sh[ould] gain anything by the doctrine that Adam was a hermaphrodite. As for the (rudimentary) presence in each sex of organs proper to the other, does that not occur in other mammals as well as in humans? Surely pseudo-organs of lactation are externally visible in the male dog? If so there w[ould] be no *more* ground for making men (I mean, humans) hermaphroditic than any other mammal . . . No doubt these rudimentary organs have a spiritual significance: there ought spiritually to be a man in every woman and a woman in every man. And how horrid the ones who haven't got it are: I can't bear a "man's man" or a "woman's woman".[77]

This statement does represent a shift from Lewis's more gender-dichotomous thinking of the 1930s and 1940s, and it anticipates his more complete rejec-

76. C. S. Lewis to Sister Penelope, CSMV, November 19, 1941, Hooper, ed., *Collected Letters*, vol. 2, 496. "Ave-Eva" is a palindrome (a phrase that spells the same way forward and backward) that Lewis used to express his conviction that ideal femininity combines traits attributed to the Virgin Mary (as in "Ave Maria" or "Hail Mary") with those of the primal, earthy "Eva," or Eve.

77. C. S. Lewis to Sister Penelope, CSMV, January 10, 1952, Hooper, ed., *Collected Letters*, vol. 3, 157–58.

tion of gender archetypes in the 1960s, as revealed in *A Grief Observed*. But his 1950s statement is still problematic, because it continues to assume that masculinity and femininity are eternal, "spiritual" essences. The difference is that we are now required to get the balance between the two just right.[78] Moreover—though Lewis himself seems to have been less inconsistent on this point—it is worth noting that Jung and his followers have been in general more inclined to help men develop their Anima, or feminine side, than to encourage women to pursue any so-called masculine aspirations.[79]

In sum, Lewis gives us a fairly nuanced critique of Freudian psychoanalysis, but fails to exercise a similar analytic distance in his treatment of Jung's theory of archetypes. When we add to this his general hostility to the social sciences and any methods for empirically testing these archetypes, we are left only with Lewis's shifting speculations about what really *is* the "spiritual" essence of masculinity and femininity, and his assumption that they are somehow an essential part of "mere" Christianity. Clearly it is time to join Elizabeth Anscombe in affirming the legitimacy of multiple perspectives on human behavior and to find out what social scientists have learned about gender differences and similarities. That is the subject of the next chapter.

78. Psychologists have pointed out that, on the practical level, this move toward a more androgynous view of persons simply increases the demands made on both sexes: under it, women must now be (for example) nurturant, professionally successful, and athletically accomplished in almost equal measure, all the time. So too (in its most consistent rendering) must men. See, for example, Hilary M. Lips, *Sex and Gender: An Introduction*, 5th ed. (New York: McGraw Hill, 2005), chap. 1.

79. Thus, although Jung mentored both men and women intellectually, he usually encouraged men to become independent psychoanalysts with their own clientele, whereas his women acolytes were often persuaded to study archeology, cultural anthropology, or classics in order to become Jung's research assistants as he developed his theory of the archetypes (Dierdre Bair, personal communication, June 2004). More recently, American feminists took issue with a similar inconsistency that they saw in Robert Bly's neo-Jungian bestseller, *Iron John: A Book about Men* (Reading, MA: Addison-Wesley, 1990). See, for example, Kay Leigh Hagan, ed., *Women Respond to the Men's Movement* (San Francisco: HarperSanFrancisco, 1992).

7

Men Are from Earth, Women Are from Earth

The Psychology of Gender Since C. S. Lewis

We have seen that for much of his life, C. S. Lewis supported both an essentialist and a hierarchical view of gender. He did so on grounds that disallowed any appeal to empirical social science, though he happily entertained certain ideas from psychoanalysis, particularly the archetypal concepts of Carl Gustav Jung. We also saw that today's supporters of gender hierarchy and essentialism often cite Lewis's writings to support their position. But some appeal to the findings of social science as well. They have set aside Lewis's dualistic notion that human bodies can be studied by means of natural science, but minds should be studied only through the methods of the humanities—philosophy, literature, theology, and so on. And more than a few believe the social sciences *do* confirm that there are large, stable differences between the sexes—for example, that men are much more aggressive, justice-oriented, and mathematical than women, or that women are much more verbal, care-oriented, and empathetic than men. As we have seen, C. S. Lewis accepted many of these gender stereotypes until later in his life. The purpose of this chapter is to see just how well they stand up to empirical scrutiny.

Complementarity Anxiety: A Fear Shared by Both Sides

For present-day Christians, this discussion is complicated by a further nuance. In the American evangelical context, the debate between gender hierarchicalists and egalitarians is most clearly seen in the two parachurch organizations I described earlier: the Council on Biblical Manhood and Womanhood (CBMW) and Christians for Biblical Equality (CBE). Each group has a loyal following, a detailed website, and a multiauthored handbook—an interdisciplinary volume challenging the other side's position and defending its own as being both "more biblical" and "more scientific."[1] But despite their differences, these two groups share a concern to defend the concept of "gender complementarity"—roughly, the notion that "men and women are different." This gets expressed in various ways, most naively by some who talk as if men and women have completely distinct sets of psychological traits. We could call this (after the bestselling book of the same title) the "Men are from Mars, Women are from Venus" point of view.[2]

More common is the recognition that gender differences are "general" or average in nature, rather than absolute dichotomies. The easiest way to understand this is to consider the physical trait of height. We know it is not the case that all men are of one height, while all women are of a different (shorter) height. In each group there is a range of heights that fits a normal distribution, or "bell curve"—with a minority of very tall and very short people at the extremes, and a greater number of people in between. (See figure 1 below.) Moreover, the "bell curves" for men's and women's heights overlap greatly, so that there is even a percentage of women who are taller than the average male, and a percentage of men who are shorter than the average female. (See figure 2, below, for just such a set of overlapping bell curves.) Many gender complementarians have read enough social science to realize that the same is true of psychological traits, such as aggression or verbal ability: there is no absolute distinction between the sexes. But as long as there is an *average* difference between men and women in these qualities, this is still somehow regarded as "gender complementarity." We might call this the "*Most* men are from Mars, and *most* women are from Venus" point of view.

In either of these versions, the idea of gender complementarity is used to defend both gender hierarchy and gender equality. For gender hierarchicalists, stereotypical gender differences combine with a patriarchal reading of certain biblical texts to support different church and family roles for women

---

1. The CMBW handbook is John Piper and Wayne Grudem, eds., *Recovering Biblical Manhood and Womanhood: A Response to Evangelical Feminism* (Wheaton: Crossway, 1991). The CBE counter-challenge can be found in Ronald W. Pierce, Rebecca M. Groothuis, and Gordon D. Fee, eds., *Discovering Biblical Equality: Complementarity without Hierarchy* (Downers Grove, IL: InterVarsity, 2004). Among Catholics, an analogous volume defending gender essentialism and gender hierarchy is Stephen B. Clark, *Man and Woman in Christ: An Examination of the Roles of Man and Woman in Light of Scripture and the Social Sciences* (Ann Arbor, MI: Servant Books, 1980).

2. John Gray, *Men Are from Mars, Women Are from Venus* (New York: HarperCollins, 1992).

Figure 1

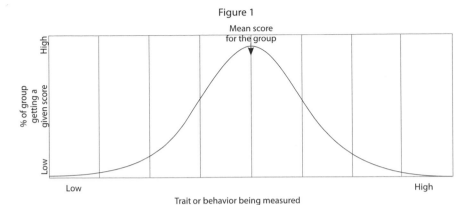

A normal ("bell curve") distribution
It is divided into eight "standard deviations" in order to
measure the "spread" or "variability"'of scores

Figure 2

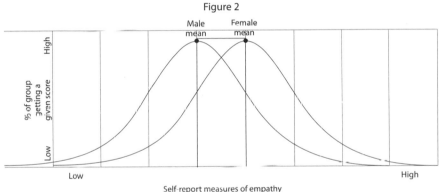

Two overlapping distributions (male and female)
scores showing an effect size (d) of 1.00

Notice that the average difference *between* the two groups is much
smaller than the spread (or variability) of scores *within* each group

and men, and to affirm male headship in both spheres. In addition, gender complementarity is invoked to challenge the idea of androgyny—that is, the notion that healthy people will exhibit stereotypical traits of both sexes. This is because (notwithstanding the later C. S. Lewis's support of it) androgyny is regarded as the beginning of a slippery slope toward the endorsement of homosexuality. Thus, the editors of *Recovering Biblical Manhood and Womanhood* have written:

> We are concerned not merely with the behavioral roles of men and women, but also with the underlying nature of manhood and womanhood themselves. Biblical truth and clarity in this matter are important, because error and confusion

over sexual identity leads to . . . parenting practices that do not train boys to be masculine or girls to be feminine [and to] homosexual tendencies and increasing attempts to justify homosexual alliances.[3]

To egalitarians, by contrast, gender complementarity means that women and men have different but equally beneficial strengths, and different but equally troublesome weaknesses. Therefore, many of them argue, it is both biblical and practical for women and men to share church and home leadership roles more or less equally. For example, William Webb has written in *Discovering Biblical Equality* that

> the egalitarian claim that status differences between men and women are a cultural construct, and not inherent in the sexual distinction, hardly constitutes a move towards a wholesale rejection of male-female complementarity . . . God's design includes not only undisputed differences in sexual and reproductive function . . . but also the general psychological differences that can be discerned in studies comparing groups of men and groups of women. One might well argue that the best way to celebrate these general differences is the inclusion of women in leadership positions, since women can bring a focus that complements that of men. In an integrative sense egalitarians are stronger advocates of complementarity than hierarchical complementarians![4]

Moreover, by affirming gender complementarity, even while denying its link to male headship in church and family, egalitarians hope to defend themselves against accusations of moving toward what is perceived as an unbiblical acceptance of homosexuality.

In the rest of this chapter I will try to show that people on both sides of this debate have misread the psychological literature, in a misguided attempt to essentialize certain gender differences and read them back into Scripture. At the end of the chapter, I will suggest that we need to think of "gender" more as a *verb* than a *noun*—that is, that "gendering" is something we are responsibly and flexibly called to *do* more than to *be*. This is a position that I believe is more in keeping with the biblical drama of creation, fall, redemption, and future hope, with C. S. Lewis's better impulses, and with the psychological literature on gender that has accumulated since his time.

A Brief Sermon on Method

If many complementarians on both sides of the male headship debate have misunderstood empirical findings in the psychology of gender, there must be reasons why this has happened. And indeed there are. For one thing, good

3. Piper and Grudem, *Recovering Biblical Manhood and Womanhood*, 26.
4. Pierce et al., *Discovering Biblical Equality*, 402n1.

social science journalism is still more the exception rather than the rule, and important qualifiers often get lost in translation. Moreover, such qualifiers are sometimes deliberately ignored for rhetorical or ideological reasons. So we need to begin with some clarification about how research in the psychology of gender is done. In particular, three things need to be understood:

1. Research in neither the biological nor the social sciences can resolve whether nature or nurture contributes more to gender-related psychological traits and behaviors in humans. And even if it could, neither natural nor social scientists would be able to say whether there are gender differences that should be encouraged or rejected. As Lewis himself knew full well, in a fallen world we cannot move from "what is" to "what ought to be" on the basis of scientific findings alone.

2. There are very few consistent sex differences in psychological traits and behaviors. Those that do exist are always *average*—not absolute—differences, and for almost all of them, the small, average difference between the sexes is exceeded by the amount of variability on that trait within members of each sex. In other words, most of the "bell curves" for women and men, showing the distribution of a given psychological trait or behavior, overlap almost completely. As time passes, some overlap even more. It is misguided at best—and deceptive at worst—to make pronouncements about "gender essentials" when much more variability exists *within* than *between* the sexes, and when even the remaining differences are unstable.

3. To adapt one of Freud's most famous dictums, we cannot assume that anatomy is destiny until we have controlled for opportunity. Thus, even when cross-cultural studies find consistent, gender-linked behavioral differences, we cannot say that these confirm the existence of *essential* gender differences unless we have controlled for differing opportunities available to women and men in all the cultures that have been studied. We should note that, despite being born at the height of the British Empire—with its romanticizing of the "White Man's Burden"—and despite having a brother who served in the Far East, C. S. Lewis was remarkably indifferent to what was happening in other cultures—especially non-Western ones. So this is an omission that we need to correct.

Let's now examine these three points in more detail.

1. Research in neither the biological nor the social sciences can resolve the nature/nurture controversy regarding gendered psychological traits and behaviors in humans.

The crucial terms here are the words *human* and *psychological*. We should not be surprised, given our creational overlap with other living beings, that much can be learned about the structure, function, and healing of our bodies from animal research. But without doubt the most unique biological feature of human beings is the plasticity of our brains. The legacy of a large cerebral cortex puts us on a much looser behavioral leash than other animals. As a result, more than any other species, humans are designed for continuous adaptation—for passing on what we have learned culturally, not just what we have been programmed to do genetically. We are, as it were, hardwired for behavioral flexibility.[5] Indeed, how could humans carry out the cultural mandate to subdue the earth (Gen. 1:28) as God's accountable regents if this were not so? And at the other end of the biblical drama, how could we "bring the glory and the honor of the nations"—suitably cleansed—before God (Rev. 21:26) if people had no more behavioral flexibility than even their closest primate neighbors? And in between, what would be the point of reading and taking to heart Jesus' parable of the talents (Matt. 25:14–30)?

But haven't the social sciences shown us that men and women have clearly different talents—at least on average—and that these are rooted in nature? Well, let us consider what we have to do to be able to conclude that biological sex clearly causes even a small, average psychological difference in human males and females. First, we would have to be able to manipulate sex like an independent, experimental variable. That is to say, we would have to be able to randomly assign people to be born with an XX or an XY pair of chromosomes apart from all the other genetic baggage they come with (in the same way that we randomly assign people to "real drug" or "placebo" conditions in medical trials, in order to cancel out the other individual differences they bring to the experiment). Clearly we cannot do this—nor, ethically, would we want to, even if we could. Babies come to us as genetic "package deals," and they get half of the package from each parent, with sex chromosomes only a small part of their inheritance.

But perhaps we could take advantage of that marvelous natural experiment known as identical twins, who have shared the same uterus, share the same genes, and have been shown to stay pretty similar on many psychological measures, even when raised in different environments. Surely it says something about the power of biology when identical twins share a greater vulnerability to, say, alcohol addiction or schizophrenia than fraternal twins or ordinary siblings, who have fewer genes in common. Yes, it does—though not as much as many people think.[6] However, this methodology can never tell us about

5. See, for example, Mary Stewart Van Leeuwen, "Of Hoggamus and Hogwash: Evolutionary Psychology and Gender Relations," *Journal of Psychology and Theology* 30, no. 2 (2002): 101–11; and *My Brother's Keeper: What the Social Sciences Do (and Don't) Tell Us about Masculinity* (Downers Grove, IL: InterVarsity, 2002), chap. 7.

6. For example, even among identical twins raised together, if one twin develops schizophrenia, the chances of the other twin developing it are a little less than one in two. This risk, while definitely higher than among unrelated individuals, is hardly in the same category as

the origins of gendered behavioral or personality differences, simply because identical twins are always of the same sex.

Well, then (descending to the level of science fiction) perhaps we could randomly assign a mixed-sex group of infants to be raised as members of the other sex after they're born. Then we could see to what degree they remain stubbornly "masculine" or "feminine" despite being raised as the other sex. But aside from the fact that this comes close to the sort of "science" that was done in Nazi Germany, but is repudiated (at least so far) in our own society, it wouldn't even begin to approximate a double-blind experiment—of the sort we use to test the effectiveness of new medicines, for example—because the cat would be out of the bag as soon as the babies' caretakers began changing their diapers. From then on, we would be completely unable to separate "essential" gender differences from those caused by the expectations—and training—of the caretakers. Finally, as noted earlier, even if we could find a sure-fire method to ascertain that boys (for example) are hardwired to be violent, or girls are hardwired to be catty gossips, this would still tell us nothing about the desirability of either trait.

We can, of course, come closer to disentangling nature from nurture in experiments with animals. It is the case, for example, that if pregnant mother rats are injected at a critical stage with testosterone, their female offspring may exhibit activity and mating patterns more typical of male rats. But though humans share many biological traits with other mammals, they also have many differences, the most important of which has been mentioned already: subhuman animal behavior is much more strongly controlled by genetic and hormonal patterns. In humans, hormones don't really "rage"; it would be more accurate to say that they merely "insinuate," because our highly developed brains make it possible for us to respond to biological urges in a greater range of ways. Even when studying only physical diseases and their cure, and not complex behaviors, no good scientist would dream of generalizing from animal research to humans without making careful qualifiers and (where ethically feasible) testing humans directly.

The upshot of all this is that with humans, it is almost impossible to disentangle biological sex from the other genetic and environmental forces in which it is always embedded. This means we cannot meet two essential conditions for inferring causality: the manipulation of one factor (sex) and the control of other factors (both biological and environmental). Thus, all data on sex differences, no matter what research method is used, are correlational data. This means that though we can sometimes use sex to *predict* whether people are likely to differ (for example, in aggression) we cannot assume that sex has *caused* those differences. As every introductory social science student learns, you cannot draw conclusions about causality from merely correlational data.

---

the 100 percent likelihood that identical twins will share the same eye color or blood type. For human psychological or behavioral traits, predispositional vulnerability is greatly magnified (or reduced) by environmental forces.

"In that sense," writes one psychologist of gender, "it is more accurate to speak of 'sex-related' differences than of sex [caused] differences."[7] So when we read about a study that describes an observed sex difference of such-and-such a magnitude, that's all it is: a description of results obtained in a particular place and time with a particular sample of persons, but almost always unable to disentangle causality. It is a *description*—not an *explanation*—about the origins of the observed sex differences. Any conclusions drawn about male and female "essences"—biological or metaphysical—are purely speculative.

2. On almost all behavioral and psychological measures that have been developed, the distributions ("bell curves") for women and men overlap almost completely.

Ah yes, you may reply, but look how large and consistent those sex differences are—in nurturance, verbal skills, spatial abilities, and so on. Surely this strongly suggests (even if it can't absolutely *prove*) that women and men have innately different talents—"beneficial differences," in the language of complementarians on both sides of the debate. Doesn't everybody know that men are from Mars and women are from Venus—at least on average? But just how large and consistent *are* such differences, after a century of measuring them in domains such as aggression, verbal skills, moral judgment, and so on? In other words, just how much do (or don't) those "bell curves" overlap for women and men? Because there is so much confusion on these matters (among people of every political and religious stripe) some more comments on social science methodology are in order.

First, there is what is known among social scientists as the "file drawer effect." Since the time psychology journals began publishing over a century ago, there has actually been a bias against accepting studies comparing males and females that find no statistically significant differences. In this kind of research, it appears that *no* news is *bad* news for your career, because studies finding no sex differences are likely to remain unpublished (thus ending up in the author's file drawer). You can perhaps see what this means. Even if we did a literature review of *many* studies on any of the usual gender-stereotype suspects—aggression, empathy, moral reasoning, etc.—done over *many* years, the results would be distorted toward finding more, rather than fewer, sex differences, just because of the publishing bias I have just described.[8]

Second, there is a lot of popular misunderstanding surrounding the term "statistically significant." A *statistically* significant research result is not nec-

7. Hilary M. Lips, *Sex and Gender: An Introduction*, 5th ed. (New York: McGraw Hill, 2005), 109.

8. There now exist both print and online media aimed at reducing the "file drawer" effect, including *The Journal of Articles in Support of the Null Hypothesis* (www.jasnh.com) and the *Index of Null Effects and Replication Failures* (www.jasnh.com/m9.htm).

essarily a *practically* significant one. In statistical tests of significance, if an obtained, average difference between two groups (e.g., women and men doing a math test, people taking an experimental drug versus a placebo, etc.) could have occurred fewer than five times out of a hundred "by chance" then it is said to be a "significant" difference. And with a large enough sample of people, and a small enough variability among scores, even a tiny average difference between two groups—i.e., groups whose bell-curve scores overlap almost completely—may be "significant" in this strictly statistical sense. On the other hand, because of the file drawer effect, a much larger difference that "just misses" being statistically significant will not likely see publication, even though its potential *practical* significance may be greater.[9] I will return shortly to the question of just how big or small such "average" psychological sex differences actually are. But before doing so, let me sketch the third and final point in my "sermon on method."

3. *We cannot assume that anatomy is destiny until we have controlled for opportunity.*

Many scholars are honest enough to acknowledge the methodological difficulties I have just described. But some go on to claim that if a certain gender difference holds up cross-culturally—that is, across many different cultural environments—we can more safely conclude that it is "natural" and "fixed." One oft quoted study of this sort was a thirty-seven-nation survey of mate-selection preferences, completed in the 1990s by Texas psychologist David Buss.[10] This study found a (statistically) significant tendency for men in all these nations to rank "youth and beauty" higher than women, and for women to rank "wealth and power" higher than men, in potential mates. Buss, appealing to theories from evolutionary psychology, suggested his findings meant that men everywhere are genetically predisposed, for purely reproductive reasons, to look for youth and beauty in prospective wives, because the more fertile the wife, the more copies of her husband's genes she can pass on. But a woman, on this account, is genetically more predisposed to want ambition and wealth in a husband, so that her children will be well cared for and survive long enough to get copies of her genes into the next generation.[11]

---

9. Thus the file drawer effect can work either way: it can mask large differences that just fail to attain statistical significance, as well as differences that are neither statistically nor practically significant. Most journals in the psychological sciences only publish about 5 percent of the studies that fail to meet traditional levels of statistical significance, the rest ending up in the "file drawers" of their researchers.

10. David Buss, *The Evolution of Desire* (New York: Basic Books, 1994).

11. Evolutionary psychologists use the term "sexual selection" (originally coined by Charles Darwin) for this theory about the differing—and supposedly competing—"reproductive strategies" of males and females.

Methods for Teasing Apart Nature and Nurture

However, Buss's study (and others like it) makes no attempt to control for the differing *opportunities* that face women and men in the cultures surveyed. That powerful, older men marry gorgeous younger women, more than vice versa, is certainly the case in many cultures. But as science journalist Natalie Angier has wryly observed, "If some women continue to worry that they need a man's money because the playing field remains about as level as Mars—or Venus if you prefer—then we can't conclude anything about innate preferences."[12] We are back to the problem described earlier: we have not disentangled nature from nurture, the effects of biology from the effects of differing cultural opportunities, on women's or men's behavior.

More recently, two social psychologists, Alice Eagly and Wendy Wood, did try to control for varying opportunities by sex.[13] They took the countries of Buss's study and rank-ordered them according to two indices of gender equality recently devised by the United Nations Development Program. One is the Gender-Related Development Index (GDI), which rates nations on the degree to which their female citizens do as well as males in life span, education, and basic income. (All three of these gender asymmetries are present, to varying degrees, in all nations.) The other is the Gender Empowerment Measure (GEM), which rates nations on the degree to which women, in comparison to men, have entered the public arena as local and national politicians, and as technicians, professionals, and managers.[14]

Using these measures, Eagly and Wood found that as gender equality in Buss's thirty-seven-nation list increased, the tendency for *either* sex to choose mates according to (so-called) evolutionary criteria decreased. So it seems that sex differences in mate-selection criteria may be less the result of evolved biological strategies than of the historically-constructed sexual division of labor, which requires women to depend on men's material wealth and men to depend on women's domestic and childrearing skills. As this wall of separation breaks down—a process nicely traced by the two UN measures—both sexes begin to look for more generically human (and might we add, biblical?) qualities in potential mates—criteria such as kindness, dependability, and a pleasant personality.[15]

12. Natalie Angier, *Women: An Intimate Geography* (Boston: Houghton Mifflin, 1999), 331.

13. Alice H. Eagly and Wendy Wood, "The Origins of Sex Differences in Human Behavior: Evolved Dispositions Versus Social Roles," *American Psychologist* 54, no. 6 (1999): 184–230.

14. For further explanation of the development and use of these measures, see *Human Development Report of the United Nations Development Program* (New York: Oxford University Press, 1995).

15. Even in Buss's original study, when asked what qualities are most important in a mate, *both* sexes, on average, ranked love, dependability, emotional stability, and a pleasing personality as the highest four. Only in the fifth rankings did the sex differences predicted by Buss's

The study I have just described comes about as close as any to teasing apart the influences of nature and nurture on gendered human behavior on a worldwide basis. In doing so, you might note that it gives a poke in the eye not just to idealist-leaning gender essentialists, but to naturalists who prefer to appeal to evolutionary biology instead. In addition, longitudinal studies—those that do repeated measures on the same group of people over many years—can also help us get a little closer to disentangling the effects of nature from those of nurture. However, such studies are uncommon because they are so complex, expensive, and time-consuming to conduct.

One of the most important longitudinal studies in the psychology of gender began in 1922, when Stanford psychologist Lewis Terman began studying over one thousand gifted American children—all with IQ scores of over 140. In this study intelligence test scores were already controlled for, because participants of both sexes were unusually bright. At regular intervals—indeed, until the original participants were past retirement age—they were reinterviewed and retested. Throughout the study Terman (and some of his successors at Stanford) continued to believe both in innate gender differences and in the innate stability of intelligence test scores. But they also knew that "the rat is always right." And here is what they found.

A high childhood IQ score was a better predictor of adult public achievement and adult IQ scores for the males in the study than for the females. Almost all the males went on to pursue professions in law, medicine, science, engineering, or various university-based disciplines, and over the years their intelligence test scores remained largely stable. But more than two-thirds of the girls—even those with IQs over 170—became homemakers or office workers in adulthood, and over the years their scores tended to decrease. By contrast, occupation—not gender—accounted best for test score stability over the participants' lifespan. Those (fewer) women and (more) men who continued to use their intelligence and education in professional careers were much more likely to display stability of test scores from childhood through adulthood. Culture was thus a better predictor than gender of adult test score stability. It seems that the old adage about physical skills—"Use it or lose it"—applies to mental skills as well.

My point is not that high-powered careers are "better" than pink- or blue-collar jobs—or homemaking—for either sex. Nor am I implying that human "intelligence" is completely captured by standardized tests like the ones used in Terman's study. These do a good job of assessing logical, mathematical, and verbal skills, but were not designed to tap (for example) social, mechanical, or artistic abilities. Nor is my point that once you stop using certain mental skills, you can never recover them. Most of the Terman study measures were collected before universities began welcoming back older women students, many of

evolutionary hypothesis emerge. And, as Eagly and Wood showed, those (already low-ranking) differences were ranked even lower as gender equality increased.

whom have outperformed their younger classmates. Most of the measures also predated the era when some parents began homeschooling their children—often having to keep up with them in subjects from precalculus to English literature. Older dogs can certainly learn new tricks—or recover old ones!

My point is simply this: if a large group of boys and girls begin with equally-high test scores in childhood, but gradually diverge in adulthood in a way better accounted for by the kind of work they do than by their sex, then we have come about as close as we can to separating the effects of nature from nurture. For it would take a lot of intellectual gymnastics to show that "innate" intelligence and "innate" gender traits so interact that they produce IQ stability in men—and women—who enter and stay in the professions, but not in women who specialize in domestic care or office jobs. Whatever their childhood potential, human brains are uniquely responsive to environmental opportunities and constraints. That, as we have already seen, is largely what makes humans so different from other animals.

The Advent of Meta-Analysis

It is worth remembering that without even much respect for the social sciences, C. S. Lewis eventually came to a similar conclusion, just around the time Terman's subjects were reaching middle age. "In most societies at most periods," he wrote in *The Four Loves*,

> friendships will be between men and men or between women and women . . . Where men are educated and woman not . . . or where they do totally different work, they will usually have nothing to be friends about. But we can easily see that it is this lack, rather than anything in their natures, which excludes Friendship: for where they can be companions they can also become Friends. Hence in a profession (like my own) where men and women work side by side, or in the mission field, or among authors and artists, such Friendship is common . . . In one respect our own society is unfortunate . . . The necessary common ground, the matrix, exists between the sexes in some groups but not in others. It is notably lacking in many residential suburbs.[16]

And this brings us back to our earlier question: just how large—and how stable—are psychological differences between the sexes, not just in the abilities represented by standardized intelligence tests, but in traits such as conformity, aggression, moral decision making, and other presumed gender stereotypes?

I have already noted some reasons why statistical tests of significance are problematic as ways of capturing either the *size* or the *practical* significance of gender differences. (Indeed, they are problematic when used exclusively in any

16. C. S. Lewis, *The Four Loves* (London: Collins, 1963), 68–69.

type of research.)[17] As a result of such criticisms, a technique known as meta-analysis was developed in the 1970s for use in all areas of science, including research on gender. As its name implies, this refers to a "super-analysis": one that can combine the results of many (from several dozen to several hundred) studies on sex differences in a given domain—for example, studies measuring aggression, verbal ability, empathy, or some other stereotypically gendered trait. Meta-analysis differs from earlier ways of reviewing the literature. Previously, authors gave equal weight to all studies examined, did a tally of how many did or did not show statistically significant sex differences, and then came to an "eyeball" or intuitive judgment as to whether reliable sex differences exist in a given domain.[18] Instead, meta-analysis converts the findings of a large sample of studies into a common metric known as the *effect size* across those studies.

This is done not just by "averaging all the average sex differences," but also by taking account of the *size* of each study's sample, and the range, or *variability*, of the scores found in each.[19] Meta-analysis thus allows us to ask, across many studies of sex differences of a certain trait or behavior, just how large that difference (known as "d") appears to be. Pictorially, it is a way of expressing how far apart the tops of the two gender-related bell curves are—the tops representing the place where the male and female average (or "mean") scores are located.[20] In other words, across many studies of a particular behavior or trait, meta-analysis allows us to ask just how much the male and female bell curves overlap.[21] If you look back at figures 1 and 2, you will note that such bell curves, or "normal distributions" are (by convention) divided vertically into eighths. Each one-eighth-wide strip is called a "standard deviation from

17. For an accessible discussion of these issues, see Christopher Shea, "Psychologists Debate Accuracy of 'Significance Test,'" *The Chronicle of Higher Education*, August 16, 1996, 12, 17.

18. An example of the use of this earlier method would be Eleanor E. Maccoby and Carol N. Jacklin, *The Psychology of Sex Differences* (Stanford, CA: Stanford University Press, 1974). As well as predating the use of meta-analysis, the Maccoby and Jacklin review concentrated almost entirely on studies involving preadolescent (and especially preschool) children, as those were the most available measures at the time.

19. Pictorially, the "variability" of scores refers to how "fat" or "skinny" the bell curves are for the groups in any study. It is important to take account of because, other things being equal, the skinnier the bell curves, the less likely it is that an average difference between the groups in the study is just due to chance.

20. Thus meta-analysts, unlike those using standard tests of significance, do *not* simply ask, "Did the average difference between the groups—however large or small—manage to make the .05 cutoff for statistical significance?"

21. This is another way of asking whether the differences *between* the male and female scores are bigger or smaller than the amount of variability *within* each sex group, or, alternately, asking how much of the *variance* in the scores can be explained by the sex of the participants in the study. The best meta-analyses will include as many unpublished studies as possible (to reduce the file drawer effect), and also have clear methodological standards for which studies are included—e.g., only studies whose measures have demonstrated construct validity, only experiments in which participants are randomly assigned to conditions, etc.

the mean," and it is in just such standard deviation units that the effect sizes for gender or any other variable (called "*d*"—for "difference") are expressed. The example in these figures shows (pictorially) a meta-analysis of several dozen studies in which people rated their own degree of empathy—one of the traits on which women are stereotypically thought to exceed men. Because the tops of the bell curves are exactly one standard deviation apart, in the direction of women averaging higher empathy scores than men, we would say that, in this meta-analysis, a *d* of -1.00 was found. (If the bell curves of the men and women were reversed, with men's scores being higher, we would say, by convention, that a *d* of +1.00 was found.)

But here is the important thing to notice. As you can see from figure 2, even when an average effect size (or *d*) for gender is one full standard deviation, the range of scores *within* each sex is still much greater than the average difference *between* the sexes. There is even a sizable "triangle" representing the scores of males who *exceed* the female mean in empathy, and another for females' that are lower than the male mean. And, as I noted earlier, it makes no sense to appeal to gender essentials—whether of a "spiritual" or a biological kind— from research results where the range of scores *within* male or female groups is so much greater than the small, average difference *between* those groups. It would be like saying that women are "essentially" shorter than men, or that men are "essentially" taller than women.

Moreover, in the meta-analyses of gender differences that have been done since the 1970s, an effect size even as large as 1.00 is rare. Table 1, below, shows some representative results of meta-analyses that have been done in recent years, on many of the usual gender-stereotype suspects.[22] Two are for physical differences—height and throwing speed. These (not surprisingly) do yield larger effect sizes, though if pictured they would still show substantial overlap between women's and men's scores. But most of the effect sizes for psychological measures—for example, helping behavior, math and reading skills, verbal fluency, and adult aggression—range from 0.0 (no difference) to around .35 (about a third of a standard deviation).[23] Again, it is wishful thinking to draw essentialist conclusions about either sex when the distributions of their scores, on almost all stereotypical traits, overlap so completely and consistently.

22. For a compact and very understandable introduction to the meta-analytic literature as it applies to the psychology of gender, see Janet Shibley Hyde, "The Gender Similarities Hypothesis," *American Psychologist* 61, no. 5 (September 2005): 581–92, from which table 1 is adapted.

23. By convention, effect sizes (*d*s) of 0.0–.35 are considered small; those from .36–.65 are medium, and those above .65 are considered large. It is worth noting that, according to one review, 60 percent of the effect sizes found in the psychology of gender literature are in the "small" range, as compared to only 36 percent in all other combined areas of psychology where meta-analyses have been done. See Janet S. Hyde and Marcia C. Linn, *The Psychology of Gender: Advances through Meta-analysis* (Baltimore: Johns Hopkins University Press, 1986); and Janet S. Hyde and Elizabeth Ashby Plant, "Magnitude of Psychological Gender Differences: Another Side to the Story," *American Psychologist* 50, no. 3 (March 1995): 159–61.

Table 1

Some Effect Sizes ("average ds") from Various Meta-Analyses of Studies of Sex Differences

NOTE: Effect size criteria are as follows:
negligible=.20 or less; small=.21–.35; medium=.36–.65; large=.66 and above

Trait or Behavioral Measure	Effect Size (average *d*)	Which Sex Scores Higher?
Height (US & UK)	2.00	M
Throwing Velocity	2.18	M
Empathy		
a) Self-Reported	1.00	F
b) Behaviorally Observed	.05	F
Helping Behavior	.34	M
Spatial Rotation		
a) Children	.38	M
b) Adults	.54	M
Interpersonal Distance	.54	F
Desires Many Sex Partners	.87	M
Math Computation		
a) Children	.22	F
b) Adults	.00	Neither
Math Problem Solving	.32	M
Reading Skills		
a) 5–6 years of age	.31	F
b) 11–19 years of age	.02	F
Verbal Analogies	.16	M
Verbal Fluency		
a) Studies prior to 1973	.23	F
b) Studies after 1973	.11	F
Aggression		
a) Children	.58	M
b) Adults	.27	M
Rough-and-Tumble Play	.45	M
Moral Reasoning		
a) "Care" Orientation	.28	F
b) "Justice" Orientation	.19	M

Of particular interest are the meta-analyses of moral reasoning styles. Recall that C. S. Lewis discussed this supposed gender difference in *Mere Christianity*, saying that husbands should be the heads of families because in disputes with outsiders, they will almost always act more fairly than their wives, whose instinctual attachment to their own family members overshadows any concern for impartiality. However, over the past few decades several hundred studies have been done testing these very assumptions—namely, the extent to which men (more than women) solve moral problems using "justice" criteria, and the extent to which women (more than men) use relationship, or "care" criteria. As table 1 shows, when meta-analyses of these studies have been done, the effect sizes, though in the direction suggested by Lewis, are quite small: +.19 for the use of justice criteria; -.28 for the use of care. What this means is that, contrary to Lewis and the people who carelessly quote him on this matter, both sexes almost always use both criteria for solving moral problems, and use both almost equally.[24]

Meta-analysis produces other embarrassments, not just for rigid gender essentialists, but for those who think that even small average sex differences are pregnant with relational, ecclesiastical, and social policy implications. For example, as noted earlier, the meta-analytic d for women's versus men's empathy scores based on public self-report is around -1.00—that is, in the direction of women scoring more empathetic than men. This is already a modest difference, and one that (like all behavioral sex differences) shows a wider range of scores within each sex than the small average difference between the sexes. However, in a meta-analysis of studies using unobtrusive measures—i.e., when people do not know they are being measured for empathy—the effect size shrinks to almost nothing (-.05, as you can see in table 1). You don't have to be a rocket scientist to guess what this suggests: people can (and do) behave quite differently depending on how intense the external social pressures are to behave in a "gendered" fashion. A similar difference, by the way, is found in analyses of women's and men's stated interest in babies: when asked publicly, men are more apt (though not nearly as much as some people think) to say that they are not interested in babies. When asked privately, they express, on average, close to the same level of interest as women.[25]

Here is a final wrinkle, one that takes us back to the question of how stable psychological gender differences are. Meta-analyses involving very large numbers of studies are sometimes divided according to the age of the people

24. For example, N. T. Wright, whose thoughtful critique of Lewis's Platonism I cited in the last chapter, unfortunately states (with no accompanying argument) the following about Lewis's discussion of male headship in *Mere Christianity*: "His reflections on marriage, despite his bachelor disclaimers, are worth pondering deeply (especially his final comments about it being important for the man to be in charge of what he calls the couple's 'foreign policy'" [i.e., its relationships with people outside the family]). See Wright, "Simply Lewis: Reflections on a Master Apologist After 60 Years," *Touchstone: A Journal of Mere Christianity* 20, no. 2 (March 2007), 28–33.

25. Good textbook introductions to meta-analytic research can be found in Lips, *Sex and Gender*, chaps. 3 and 4; and Vicki S. Hegelson, *The Psychology of Gender* (Upper Saddle River, NJ: Prentice Hall, 2002), chap. 3.

taking part in the studies. Thus, in table 1, meta-analytic results for studies of aggression and "spatial rotation" (the kind of skill that helps you picture how something will look from a different angle) are divided between studies done with children, and those done with adults. In studies of aggression using children, the meta-analytic effect size is only +.58—about half a standard deviation's difference in favor of boys. This means—yet again—that the spread of both boys' and girls' scores is much greater than the small difference that separates the top of their respective bell curves. But when only adult studies are considered, the effect size shrinks by more than half—to +.27—and this in spite of the fact that "raging hormones" (such as testosterone) have been at work in men since puberty. This strongly suggests that, whatever the origin of the modest gender difference in childhood aggression, cultural agents work hard to reduce it even further. For spatial rotation scores, the instability is in the opposite direction: the effect size, while still small, favors males more in adulthood than in childhood. There are naturalistically inclined psychologists—often over-generalizing from animal models—who try to link this small increase to greater testosterone levels in adult males. But it would take a lot of mental gymnastics to explain why increased testosterone causes *higher* average spatial scores in adult men, when increased testosterone is also associated with *lower* levels of aggression. Cultural explanations for both shifts make more sense.

Meta-analyses can also be divided according to the particular era in which the studies were done. For example, a meta-analysis of studies on gender differences in verbal fluency done prior to 1973 (when gender-stereotypical roles were more strictly imposed on people of both sexes) found an overall, small effect size (*d*) of -.23—that is, in the direction of women scoring higher than men. But an analysis of studies conducted after 1973 (once the second wave of feminism had begun to loosen gender roles for both sexes) found an effect size of -.11—less than half the size of the earlier one. Sudden genetic mutations in men or women since 1973 are unlikely to have caused such a shift. Genes in humans just don't mutate and spread that fast. Nor is it likely that God's mind has changed since 1973 about the true nature of manhood and womanhood, with accompanying adjustments of our verbal skills—especially when the differences were so slight to begin with. Indeed, half a century ago, Dorothy L. Sayers wondered why women and men were called "opposite sexes" rather than "neighboring sexes."[26] Fifty years and many meta-analytic studies later, it seems that women and men are very close neighbors indeed. Sayers's sentiment was aptly updated for today's gender-anxious readers on a bumper sticker I caught sight of once. It read: "Men are from Earth; Women are from Earth—Get Used to It!"

26. Dorothy L. Sayers, "The Human-Not-Quite-Human," in *Unpopular Opinions: Twenty-One Essays* (London: Gollancz, 1946), 37.

Attempts to Evade These Findings

It is not necessarily the case that people who believe in gender archetypes deliberately set out to distort the findings I have just described. In addition to having their confusion fed by careless science journalists and other writers, there is a problem that social psychologists call the "availability heuristic." This is the common human tendency to generalize from the most dramatic examples of things or events that we have "available" to us, even if these are not representative. Thus, for example, table 1 notes that a meta-analysis of children's activity showed boys, on average, somewhat more likely than girls (by an effect size of $+.45$) to engage in "rough-and-tumble play." This means that in terms of sex, although the vast majority of children in a playground will be indistinguishable on this trait, the most extreme rough-and-tumbler is likely to be a boy, and the least extreme is likely to be a girl—just as the tallest student in a college classroom is most likely to be a male, and the shortest to be a female. But because of the availability heuristic, if you compare counts of children's behaviors collected by carefully-trained observers with casual estimates by their teachers, the latter will often confidently say that boys are almost always much more vigorous in their play than girls, despite the fact that sex is actually an extremely poor predictor of who will (or won't) engage in rough-and-tumble play. Teachers have selectively noticed the few extreme boys and girls—perhaps not surprisingly, since these may be seen as potential "problem" children—and generalized to all the others. The rest of us often do the same.

However, some convinced gender essentialists (along with careless science journalists and trendy Mars-Venus advice book writers) actively do try to evade these findings. The most common strategy is simply to ignore or distort them: to pretend that small, shifting *tendencies* are absolute gender *dichotomies*, or something close to it, and to assume that statistical significance is always the same as practical significance. Too many people yearn for simple black-and-white explanations of complex relations, including those involving men and women. As one of my students once cynically observed, "Tendencies don't sell books; dichotomies do."

Another strategy is to pathologize the findings I have just summarized: to claim that even if gender-related traits overlap, we must work to polarize them further, in order to approximate God's—or nature's, or society's—"optimal design" for men and women. This was the approach taken by philosopher Jean-Jacques Rousseau in his eighteenth century educational treatise *Emile*. Rousseau believed that "rational, active man" and "emotional, passive woman" were perfect comple-ments for each other. He conceded that men's and women's natural inclinations were not this rigidly dichotomous. But he added that if women and men were not trained to become "opposites" they would never be attracted to each other, get married, and have children.[27] Two centuries later, this kind of thinking was repackaged as sociological functionalism, whose adherents maintained that a strict division of labor by sex—whether or not there were corresponding natural (or spiritual) blueprints for it—was "functional" for the flourishing of society and so should be tampered with only very cautiously, if ever.[28]

There is a third strategy for rescuing gender archetypes, often seen in Christian advice–book writers who liberally quote C. S. Lewis's writings. Some gender essentialists have reluctantly conceded that neither the Bible nor the natural or social sciences can come definitively to their rescue. Consequently, they take refuge in Jungian archetypes and their precursors in various Pagan mythologies.[29] In a previous chapter, we saw examples of this in the best-selling books of John and Stasi Eldredge. A generation earlier, Elisabeth Elliot, in her 1982 book *Let Me Be a Woman*, warned Christian readers that Eve, in taking the initiative to eat the forbidden fruit, was trying to be like the ultimately-masculine God of the Bible. God was portrayed as a metaphysically gendered Being, and "taking initiative" was deemed to be a masculine, not a feminine, trait. Elliot also appealed to the ancient Chinese concepts of *yin* and *yang* to buttress her "Christian" argument for gender essentialism.[30] Her brother Thomas Howard, in a 1978 article titled "A Note from Antiquity on the Question of Women's Ordination," openly admitted that the Bible does *not* supply enough resources to justify talking about God or humans in terms of eternal gender archetypes. Undeterred by this, he invited his readers to consider the abundance of sexual imagery in Pagan myths and came to the conclusion that "a Christian would tend to attach some weight to this."[31] Really? Why?

Where Does All This Leave Us?

Perhaps the most cautious way of responding to the meta-analytic literature on gender comes from some behavioral biologists, who (arguing largely from animal research) suggest that both sexes are *capable* of the full range of human behaviors, but that the *thresholds* for various behaviors may vary by gender.[32]

27. Jean-Jacques Rousseau, *Emile*, trans. Allan Bloom (New York: Basic Books, 1979).

28. For example, Talcott Parsons and Robert F. Bales, *Family, Socialization and Interaction Process* (New York: Free Press, 1955). For a critical assessment of functionalism as it applies to gender, see Michael S. Kimmel, *The Gendered Society*, 2nd ed. (New York: Oxford University Press, 2004), especially chap. 3.

29. For a review of some of these, see Faith Martin, "Mystical Masculinity: The New Questions Facing Women," *Priscilla Papers* 12, no. 1 (Winter 1998): 6–12.

30. Elisabeth Elliot, *Let Me Be a Woman* (Wheaton: Tyndale, 1982).

31. Thomas Howard, "A Note from Antiquity on the Question of Women's Ordination," *The Churchman: A Journal of Anglican Theology* 92, no. 4 (1978): 323.

32. For example, Perry Treadwell, "Biologic Influences on Masculinity," in Harry Brod, ed., *The Making of Masculinities: The New Men's Studies* (Boston: Allen and Unwin,

This would mean, for example, that men and women are both capable of (even violent) aggression, but that men might yield to such impulses somewhat more readily than women; and that men are as capable of nurturing children as women but might not exhibit such behavior as quickly. This "differing thresholds" theory might help account for why meta-analyzed gender differences tend to be smaller for laboratory studies than for ones conducted in the real world. Laboratory settings are routinely shielded from a host of real-world social influences (including ones that elicit gender-stereotyped behavior), so they may allow "possible" behaviors to trump more or less "probable" ones, in both sexes. But in the end, this qualifier about thresholds doesn't help gender essentialists much, because even in the animal research on which it is based, the thresholds *themselves* are variable, and the resulting gender distributions overlap greatly, just as they do for actual behaviors. And, as I have noted, it is always risky to generalize from animals to humans, since human brains are structured for much more behavioral flexibility than those of even their closest primate neighbors.

Here is yet another wrinkle. Meta-analysis is used in many areas of biological and social science. For example, it is used in drug versus placebo studies, to help decide whether even a small effect size (in favor of a certain cancer drug, for example) might translate into quite a few lives saved. And this is indeed sometimes the case: seemingly small effect sizes can translate into important practical outcomes—especially if you are one of the patients who might benefit from the drug. But, warns meta-analysis specialist Janet Hyde, "In terms of costs of errors in scientific decision making, psychological gender differences are quite a different matter from curing cancer."[33] As long as patients are not harmed by a given cancer drug—even if only a small minority benefit from it—then it can be approved and marketed. Indeed, ethically, we probably *should* make it available, even if some people may mistakenly inflate its effectiveness. But the practical cost of inflating small gender differences, as writers using Mars-Venus rhetoric routinely do, can be considerable. For example, despite accumulated evidence to the contrary, many writers *still* assume that men are almost entirely justice-oriented in their interpersonal relations, and women are almost entirely care-oriented.[34] And as Janet Hyde notes,

> One consequence of this overinflated claim of gender difference is that it reifies the stereotype of women as caring and nurturant and men as lacking in nurturance. One cost to men is that they may believe that they cannot be nurturant,

1989), 259–85.

33. Hyde, "The Gender Similarities Hypothesis," 587.

34. This "received wisdom" is in large part the result of Harvard psychologist Carol Gilligan's book *In a Different Voice: Psychological Theory and Women's Development* (Cambridge, MA: Harvard University Press, 1982).

even in their role as father. For women, the cost in the workplace can be enormous. Women who violate the stereotype of being nurturant and nice can be penalized in hiring and evaluations.[35]

As another example, boys are still stereotypically seen as being better at math than girls, despite effect sizes (based on national samples of children's and adolescents' math scores) that are close to zero, or sometimes even favor girls slightly. One hazard of such stereotyping "is that mathematically talented girls may be overlooked by parents and teachers because these adults do not expect to find mathematical talent among girls . . . [In addition] research has shown repeatedly that parents' expectations for their children's mathematics success relate strongly to outcomes such as children's mathematics self-confidence and performance."[36] And even people who are trying to help women and girls sometimes—with help from the availability heuristic—get caught in the trap of perpetuating the very stereotypes they are trying to challenge. For example, it has been a common assumption in the past couple of decades that girls' self-esteem plummets during adolescence, while boys' does not.[37] But meta-analysis of the relevant studies shows a close-to-zero sex difference. "In short," writes Janet Hyde, "self-esteem is roughly as much of a problem for adolescent boys as it is for adolescent girls. But the popular media's focus on girls . . . [may lead] parents, teachers, and other professionals to overlook boys' self-esteem problems, so that boys do not receive the interventions they need."[38]

Hyde's last point is an important one. It reminds us that nothing revealed by meta-analytic research means we should ignore the minority of persons— of either sex—who may struggle with mathematics, or self-esteem, or verbal communication, or any of the (so-called) gender-stereotypical traits. If, for example, you are an emotionally communicative woman married to an emotionally withdrawn man (or vice-versa, for that matter) you may very well benefit from advice on how to understand each other's styles, or how to compromise on their use. In terms of the old proverb: if the shoe fits, wear it. But the operative word here is *if*. What meta-analysis tells us is that we should not try to force everyone into the same two shoes, one pink, and one blue (or one from Mars and one from Venus). We should not reflexively cast these differences in gendered terms. And we should avoid, or at least take with a *very* large grain of salt, the people who do—regardless of how many books they

35. Hyde, "The Gender Similarities Hypothesis," 590. Hyde goes on to quote meta-analytic studies showing fairly large effect sizes for prejudice against female (but not male) job applicants who show "agentic" (i.e., assertive) qualities.

36. Ibid.

37. This has been in part due to the popularity of clinical psychologist Mary Pipher's book, *Reviving Ophelia: Saving the Selves of Adolescent Girls* (New York: Ballentine, 1994).

38. Hyde, "The Gender Similarities Hypothesis," 590.

have sold. This is because gender, as we should now realize, is a very poor predictor of gender-stereotypical behavior.

The research I have reviewed in this chapter indicates that women and men, boys and girls, are overwhelmingly more alike than different. As with all scientific findings, this does not tell us whether that similarity is a "good" or a "bad" thing—a result of creation, our fallenness, or something in between. Yet if there is a cosmic "fit" between our own design and the tasks to which God calls us, it should—in the long run—show up empirically. That is what C. S. Lewis meant when he wrote that "experience . . . is such an honest thing. You may take any number of wrong turnings, but keep your eyes open and you will not be allowed to go very far before warning signs appear."[39] In other words, the careful investigation of human behavior should, over the long haul, not conflict with the overall trajectory of the biblical drama. In what way might the work summarized in this chapter point to such a convergence?

In biblical-theological terms, men and women are first and foremost human beings, made in the image of God and called to be God's regents on earth, subject to the limits of their finitude and the ambiguity of life "between D-Day and V-day." Decisions about who should do what (and the training and resources that flow from these) should therefore be made on the basis of individual gifts and not on the basis of gender—any more than we would automatically allocate tasks and resources on the basis of skin color, ethnicity, or class. If we return to the biblical account of humankind's creation, in Genesis 1:26–28, we should note that God is not portrayed as saying to the first woman, "Be fruitful and multiply," and to the first man "Subdue the earth." Both mandates are given to both members of the primal pair: "And God blessed them, and said to them, 'Be fruitful and multiply, and fill the earth and subdue it.'" This does not mean that men and women always and everywhere should do exactly the same things. But it strongly suggests that any attempt to dichotomize the cultural mandate too rigidly along gender lines is bound to run into trouble eventually—as it has in our own era—because it is creationally distorted and therefore unjust to both sexes.

And the question of justice is really what is at the heart of this matter. In America, wise Christians have often pointed out that God is not "for" Republicans, or "for" Democrats, but that God is for justice—and that, depending on the time and on the issue, one party or the other may better embody what that means. Likewise, God is not "for" androgyny or "for" gender complementarity. God is for just and loving relationships between men and women—and because of this, we may be called to "do gender" differently at different times and in different places. Loving and just relationships between men and women will obviously not look quite the same in a nomadic, herding society (such as we meet in the early books of the Bible) as they will in a nineteenth-century

---

39. C. S. Lewis, *Surprised by Joy* (London: Collins, 1955), 77.

family farming community, or in a twenty-first-century post-industrial city. That is why I suggested at the beginning of this chapter that we should think of gender more as an active verb than as a noun.

This may still sound too loose and relativistic to some readers. Does it not—as gender hierarchicalists and essentialists have warned—send us along a slippery slope toward an acceptance of free love and what Freud once called "polymorphously perverse" sexuality? But here again, experience does not allow us to take too many wrong turnings. Empirical social science and biblical wisdom have also begun to converge on other aspects of gender relations. Some of these convergences might have surprised and gratified C. S. Lewis, if he had lived long enough to learn about them. To these we will pay particular attention in the next two chapters.

::::::::::::::::::::::

8

"Nature Speaks Chiefly in Answer to Our Questions"

C. S. Lewis and Some Neglected Issues in the Psychology of Gender

During my days as a graduate student in the late 1960s, professors who had begun to appreciate the limits of scientific objectivity would recount what has come to be known as "The Drunk under the Lamp Post" parable. They asked students to picture a drunken man who has lost his car keys late one night and is groping for them in the illumination cast by a streetlight. A policeman on his beat comes by and asks if he can help. The drunk stumblingly explains that he lost his car keys half a block away, outside a tavern. "Then why are you looking for them here?" asks the policeman. "Because," the drunk replies woozily, "this is where the light is!"

The point of this parable, for students of both the natural and the social sciences, is that we can never shine the light of our scholarly attention on everything at once. Historical forces and funding opportunities—not to mention the politics of what C. S. Lewis famously called the "inner ring" of scholarly communities—push people to focus largely on what is "paradigmatically correct" in their disciplines at a given time. Now, unlike the dysfunctional searching of our drunkard, this kind of selective attention is not always counterproductive. Directing resources toward a limited number of problems often leads to significant discoveries: think, for example, of the progress in physics that followed Newton's assertion of the universal law of gravitation, or in genetics following the discovery of the structure of DNA.[1] Still, by looking only in the circle of what is currently illuminated, it is possible to ignore or downplay theories that were useful in the past—and that may again prove important when reigning explanations are challenged by better data. For example, the theory of a "steady-state" universe was eventually eclipsed by the big bang theory, but for a long time it faced resistance from scientists who saw it as suggesting that there really might be a God who had created the universe *ex nihilo*.

I have noted that as he grew older, C. S. Lewis became less of a pure realist in his view of science and more of a critical realist. He continued to respect the tools of reason as well as the voice of experience, but increasingly recognized that there can be no such thing as immaculate perception or flawless rationality. "In recent years," he wrote to a colleague the year before he died,

> I have become increasingly aware how far changes in man's model of the universe respond not (as we were taught) to the invasion of new phenomena but to a subjective demand for a new model.
>
> Not, to be sure, that evidence (in a sense *true* evidence) for the new model is not produced. But nature speaks chiefly in answer to our questions: and here, as in the law courts, the pattern suggested by the witness's answers is largely pre-determined by the shape of the examination.[2]

In previous chapters I focused on how Lewis's earlier answers to questions about gender were in many ways "pre-determined by the shape of the examination." His commitment to an essentialist theory of gender, drawn in no small part from his passion for classical, medieval, and Renaissance literature, prompted him to defend stereotypical gender roles and gender hierarchy in church and family, even as he preached gender equality in political and economic life, and largely practiced it in relations with his students and colleagues. Moreover, his commitment to Cartesian dualism made him question the worth of the emerging social sciences, on the grounds that apart from

1. See, for example, Thomas S. Kuhn, "The Function of Dogma in Scientific Research," in Alistair C. Crombie, ed., *Scientific Change* (New York: Basic Books, 1963), 9–15.

2. C. S. Lewis to Erich Heller, November 27, 1962, Walter Hooper, ed., *The Collected Letters of C. S. Lewis*, vol. 3, *1950–1963* (San Francisco: HarperSanFranciso: 2007), 1385. Lewis was responding to Heller's book *The Disinherited Mind* (London: Bowes & Bowes, 1959), and particularly to Heller's following observation: "One knows of course, how many scientific theories, for very long periods of time, stood the test of experience until they had to be discarded owing to man's decision, not merely to make other experiments, but *to have different experiences*" (p. 26; emphasis original). See Walter Hooper's editorial notes on Heller in *Collected Letters*, vol. 3, 1384–85.

their bodies, humans cannot be treated "like counters, or identical machines."[3] On the contrary, he believed, "You can only get to know them"—that is, by examining them in terms of their individually-storied lives, and in light of great religious, philosophical, poetic, and romantic literature.[4]

In the last chapter I showed how Lewis's intellectual skepticism about the social sciences (combined, paradoxically, with his fear of their practical power) has helped to perpetuate misconceptions about gender that are not supported by accumulated research. In this and the next chapter, I propose to do the opposite: to show that some of Lewis's writings about gender relations had a prophetic edge to them, in the sense that they have steadily accumulated empirical support, even though they are treated as "paradigmatically incorrect" by much of the secular academy. I will deal with two topics about which Lewis wrote formally or informally—namely, divorce and parenting. About these issues in particular, people are tempted to look only where the current light is shining, and as a result they risk drawing conclusions that are at best simplistic and at worst harmful. If, as Lewis wrote, "nature speaks chiefly in answer to our questions," then it is important to ask the right questions. On these two intrinsically gendered topics Lewis was perhaps less of a "dinosaur" and more of a prophet, posing thoughtful questions and suggesting prescient answers.[5] The rest of this chapter will examine Lewis's treatment of divorce, and in the following chapter I will consider his writings about parenting. In each case we will see that some of his ideas and practices are now slowly gathering support among social scientists and others.

"Something Like Cutting Up a Living Body": C. S. Lewis on Divorce

A few years ago, I happened upon a National Public Radio program that featured a discussion between two Southern Baptist ministers. Since Southern Baptists are not generally known to be friendly toward this "liberal" media

3. C. S. Lewis, "Membership," in *The Weight of Glory and Other Addresses* (Grand Rapids: Eerdmans, 1965), 37; "Priestesses in the Church?" reprinted in Walter Hooper, ed., *God in the Dock: Essays On Theology and Ethics* (Grand Rapids: Eerdmans, 1970), 238.

4. C. S. Lewis, *That Hideous Strength: A Modern Fairy-Tale for Grown-Ups* (London: John Lane the Bodley Head, 1945), 185. For a thoughtful defense of Lewis's Cartesianism see the book by the late Yale theologian and philosopher Paul Holmer, *C. S. Lewis: The Shape of His Faith and Thought* (New York: Harper and Row, 1976).

5. Some of what follows overlaps with my essay "Teaching Equal Regard to the Abandoned Generation: Case Studies from a Psychology of Gender Class," in John Witte Jr., M. Christian Green, and Amy Wheeler, eds., *The Equal-Regard Family and Its Friendly Critics: Don Browning and the Practical Theological Ethics of the Family* (Grand Rapids: Eerdmans, 2007), 173–201. Lewis most famously described himself as a "dinosaur" (or "Old Western man") in his 1955 inaugural address for the Cambridge chair in Medieval and Renaissance Literature. See "*De Descriptione Temporum*" in C. S. Lewis, *They Asked for a Paper* (London: Geoffrey Bles, 1962), 9–25.

outlet, I was curious to find out what had drawn them there. It turned out to be a survey finding with which I was already familiar—namely, the disjunction between the so-called biblical literalism of American Christian conservatives and their high rate of divorce. A nation-wide survey of religious attitudes and behaviors had found that 34 percent of "born again" adults (defined as having made an individual commitment to Jesus that is still personally important to them, and expecting to go to heaven as a result of this commitment) had experienced divorce—not statistically different from the 35 percent rate among respondents who rejected the born-again label. Morcover, close to 90 percent of those divorces had occurred after—not before—the respondents' conversion experience. Even worse for the image of conservative Christianity, the rate of marital stability was found to be significantly higher in the more secular states of the Northeast than in the "Bible Belt" states of the South.[6]

Now findings like these are in need of some qualifiers, if we are not to end up seeming to lie with statistics. For example, if the data are adjusted for respondents' socioeconomic class, level of education, and age of first marriage—all of which differ significantly between the Bible Belt and Northeastern states—it turns out that serious and faithful (as opposed to nominal) church involvement is one of the *best* (not worst) predictors of marital stability.[7] Nevertheless, given the claims so often made for the power of Christian conversion to armor people against godless social trends, the Baptist ministers were understandably a bit chastened. After all, it does not say much for the strength of biblical literalism among born-again Americans when over 50 percent of a representative sample *rejects* Jesus' saying that adultery is the only ground for divorce.[8]

Why, these two pastors wondered aloud, do conservative Christians hear so many sermons and interest-group messages castigating abortion and homosexual practice, but almost none decrying divorce, when the Bible itself has so much more to say about the importance of marriage than about the other two issues? The truth of the matter, one of them finally admitted, is that preachers routinely "cherry-pick" Scripture: they focus on the issues that they, their congregations, or wider church circles have decided will be the defining ones, regardless of what Scripture as a whole addresses. The Bible, like nature, is made "to speak chiefly in answer to our questions." When this becomes a habit, prophetic utterance becomes highly selective, if not totally muted. On a purely pragmatic level, one of the pastors added, it is hard to preach against divorce if some of the most influential members of your congregation are on their second or third marriages.

6. "Born-Again Adults Just as Likely to Divorce as Non-Christians," *The Barna Update*, September 8, 2004, www.barna.org.

7. See, for example, W. Bradford Wilcox, *Soft Patriarchs, New Men: How Christianity Shapes Fathers and Husbands* (Chicago: University of Chicago Press, 2004).

8. *The Barna Update*, September 10, 2004; Matt. 19:9.

Two decades before the advent of no-fault divorce in America, C. S. Lewis—
most famously in *Mere Christianity*, but also in the last essay he wrote for
publication in 1963[9]—decried the growing trend toward easier divorce in England. Ironically, as we will see later, he experienced its complications in his
own life when he decided to marry Joy Davidman, an American soon-to-be
divorcée who came to live in England with her two young sons in 1953. And
Davidman herself, who embraced Christianity after a secular Jewish upbringing and a young adulthood spent in the Communist Party, had expressed a
similarly rigorous Christian ethic about the permanence of marriage in her
popular work on the Ten Commandments, *Smoke on the Mountain*. "Our
Lord's command about marriage was as sharp and straight as a sword," she
wrote:

> Your wife is your wife for good, He said; you can't get rid of her, except for adul-
> tery (and only one Gospel permits even that exception) and a divorced woman
> is committing adultery if she remarries. Now this is a difficult doctrine, as the
> disciples were the first to point out, for it says nothing about what constitutes
> a marriage in the first place, nothing about marriages ended by the act of God,
> nothing about the woman's rights of action, and nothing about the status of
> the divorced man. All that is left to those who come after. Nevertheless, it is
> clear as far as it goes. We can only escape it by deciding arbitrarily to throw out
> that part of the Gospels as fake: or else by throwing out the divinity of Christ
> altogether so that we needn't obey his commands at all.[10]

Lewis, in *Mere Christianity*, was equally insistent on the importance of
lifelong marriage. "The Christian idea of marriage," he wrote, "is based on
Christ's word that a man and a wife are to be regarded as a single organism—
for that is what the word 'one flesh' would be in modern English."

> As a consequence, Christianity teaches that marriage is for life. There is, of
> course, a difference here between different churches: some do not admit divorce
> at all; some allow it reluctantly in very special cases . . . [But] churches all agree
> with one another about marriage a great deal more that any of them agrees with
> the outside world. I mean, they all regard divorce as something like cutting up a
> living body. Some of them think the operation so violent that it cannot be done
> at all; others admit it as a desperate remedy in extreme cases . . . What they all
> disagree with is the modern view that it is a simple readjustment of partners,
> to be made whenever people feel they are no longer in love with one another,
> or when either of them falls in love with someone else.[11]

9. C. S. Lewis, "We Have No 'Right to Happiness,'" reprinted in Hooper, ed., *God in the Dock*, 317–22.

10. Joy Davidman, *Smoke on the Mountain: The Ten Commandments in Terms of Today* (London: Hodder and Stoughton, 1955), 82. See also Lyle W. Dorsett, *And God Came In: The Extraordinary Story of Joy Davidman* (New York: MacMillan, 1983), chap. 3.

11. C. S. Lewis, *Mere Christianity* (London: Collins, 1952), 92–93.

At the same time, neither writer was legalistic or historically insensitive about divorce—even before it invaded their joint lives as a very personal dilemma. Davidman noted the apostle Paul's pronouncement that Christians married to unbelievers are not bound for life if the latter desert the marriage.[12] She also suggested there are marriages "which *God* puts asunder . . . cases of desertion and presumed death, cases of danger to body and soul, cases where children must be saved at all costs from a destructive parent."[13] And Lewis put it to his mid-twentieth-century British audience (many of whom availed themselves of whatever rites of passage they wanted in the Church of England, even if they rarely darkened its doors otherwise) that perhaps it was time to distinguish more clearly between Christian and non-Christian unions. "If people do not believe in permanent marriage," he wrote, "it is perhaps better that they should live together unmarried than that they should make vows they do not intend to keep. It is true that by living together without marriage they will be guilty (in Christian eyes) of fornication. But one fault is not mended by adding another: unchastity is not improved by adding perjury."[14]

Both Lewis and Davidman also appealed to natural law arguments for the presumptive permanence of marriage.[15] Davidman cited the protection of children and the vulnerability of wives, whose disruption by divorce can leave them economically, socially, and emotionally devastated. Lewis, likewise, wrote that the keeping of marital promises, even when romantic love has lost its initial glow, is socially important in order "to provide a home for the children [and] to protect the woman (who has probably sacrificed or damaged her own career by getting married) from being dropped whenever the man is tired of her."[16] But whether writing for audiences in America or Britain, both must have sensed they were shouting into the wind, since laws in both countries were becoming steadily more lenient and divorce rates were rising in the wake of each shift. In the nineteenth century, grounds for divorce were largely confined to adultery and cruelty; by the mid-twentieth century they had expanded to include desertion and were moving steadily toward mutual consent, after a period of separation, as the only requirement. Today, however, we have several decades of data on the consequences of divorce for both children and adults. Toward the end of the chapter I will summarize what

12. 1 Cor. 7:15.

13. Davidman, *Smoke on the Mountain*, 84 (emphasis original).

14. Lewis, *Mere Christianity*, 94. For a comprehensive historical, legal, and theological analysis of marriage, see John Witte Jr., *From Sacrament to Contract: Marriage, Religion and Law in the Western Tradition* (Louisville: Westminster John Knox, 1997).

15. Lewis appealed to the concept of natural law, or the *Tao* even more explicitly in *The Abolition of Man*, where he defined it as "the belief that certain attitudes are really true, and others really false, to the kind of thing the universe is and the kind of things we are" ([Oxford: Oxford University Press, 1943], 17).

16. Lewis, *Mere Christianity*, 95.

that research tells us. But first let us see how Lewis and Davidman handled their own "divorce dilemma," as Christian writers who defended the norm of lifelong marriage.

The Great Divorce Dilemma: The Marriage of C. S. Lewis and Joy Davidman

Social scientists, whose academic worth Lewis often questioned, have increasingly come to agree with his view of divorce. Increasingly, they (and the people they study) are concluding that divorce cannot be treated as "a simple readjustment of partners, to be made whenever people feel they are no longer in love, or when either of them falls in love with someone else." As Lewis put it, in terms of its effects on all the people involved, divorce is "more like having both your legs cut off than it is like dissolving a business partnership or even deserting a regiment."[17]

But "Lewis the writer" was also "Lewis the person," and little did he suspect, when he wrote about marriage and divorce in *Mere Christianity*, that he himself would fall in love with a divorced woman when he was in his mid-fifties. Having become famous for defending a Christian ethic of lifelong marriage, how did he cope with the discovery that he might want to make an exception for Joy Davidman? How did he deal with the possibility that marrying her would simply allow his critics to brand him a hypocrite?

When C. S. Lewis married Joy Davidman (first in a civil ceremony in 1956, then according to Anglican rites in 1957), church policy was quite strict regarding divorce. The Church of England denied remarriage to the guilty party of a divorce prompted by adultery, though its Bishops differed as to whether an innocent party, like Joy Davidman, could be remarried in the church. The Bishop of Oxford adamantly believed not, and Lewis, in his earlier life, apparently agreed with this stance.[18] Moreover, his civil marriage to Joy was prompted—or so Lewis wrote at the time—purely by kindness: her visa to stay in England had been denied renewal (perhaps because of her previous links to the American Communist Party), and only by marrying a UK citizen could she and her sons remain there. Lewis wrote to his Belfast friend Arthur Greeves, a few months before the event, that it would be a "marriage" purely in the legal sense, since "the 'reality' w[oul]d be, from my point of view adultery and therefore mustn't happen. (An easy resolution when one doesn't in the least want it!)"[19]

17. Ibid., 93.
18. See, for example, Lewis's letter to Mrs. Locksley, May 13, 1952, Hooper, ed., *Collected Letters*, vol. 3, 188–89.
19. C. S. Lewis to Arthur Greeves, October 30, 1955, Hooper, ed., *Collected Letters*, vol. 3, 669.

Other people in Lewis's circle saw it differently. His friend and erstwhile student, George Sayer, recalls Lewis telling him prior to the civil marriage that he loved Joy, and couldn't abide the thought of her having to return with her children to the situation she had fled in America. (Among other things, her former husband was a physically abusive alcoholic, in addition to being a chronic philanderer.) Lewis had also told Douglas Gresham, Joy's younger son, that he would do everything he could to prevent the two boys from returning to America and facing a possible custody claim from their father.[20] But how would other people—both Christian friends and secular critics—react if the famous champion of lifelong marriage were known to have married a divorced woman? Joy Davidman's biographer, Lyle Dorsett, succinctly summarizes Lewis's dilemma:

> The prospect of giving up these loved ones forced Lewis to move quickly. On April 23, 1956, he and Joy were married in a civil ceremony at the Registry Office in Oxford . . . But Lewis was still reluctant to take on his critics and bring Joy into his life as a wife. Rather than seek permission from the Church of England for a proper religious marriage, he pretended that this civil ceremony was nothing but a convenience—a way to keep Joy in England for her sake and the boys' benefit, rather than for his happiness as well . . . [Only] a handful of others knew of the civil wedding. Jack was obviously not proud of this arrangement, and he did all he could to keep it a secret. Joy respected Lewis's feelings on this, never mentioning it in her letters to America until the status of the relationship changed several months later [after Joy was found to have cancer].[21]

By this time, Lewis had assumed his professorial chair at Cambridge, commuting back and forth from Oxford, where he still lived with his brother. When in Oxford he began to spend more and more time with Joy in her home at Headington, which was within walking distance of The Kilns. This led casual observers to wonder what was going on, and those closer to Lewis to conclude that his civil marriage to Joy was much more than an act of pity. Eventually, to protect Joy's reputation, Lewis made plans to move her and the boys into The Kilns. He also sought permission to marry in a church ceremony, pointing out that since Bill Gresham had already been divorced before he married Joy, their union was never valid in the eyes of the church, so there was no reason to withhold the sacrament from her now.

The Bishop of Oxford was not impressed with this argument, and refused the petition. But before Lewis could decide how to resolve his dilemma, tragedy intervened with the abrupt discovery that Joy had advanced cancer of the femur and a further malignancy in her breast. Doctors concluded that she had very

20. Lyle W. Dorsett, *A Love Observed: Joy Davidman's Life and Marriage to C. S. Lewis* (Wheaton: Harold Shaw, 1998), 121.
   21. Ibid., 122.

little time to live, and while she remained in hospital for a series of operations, Lewis moved Joy's sons into The Kilns, where they could be cared for between terms at Dane Court, their boarding school in Surrey. He also posted a terse announcement of his marriage in the London *Times*.

It was at this point that Lewis contacted a former student, Peter Bide, who was an Anglican priest in another diocese. Bide was known for having delivered some effective healing prayers, and Lewis initially asked him to come to Oxford to pray over Joy. But in short order he also inquired if Bide would be willing to marry them according to Anglican rites. "Joy desperately wanted to solemnize her marriage before God," Bide recalled, "and to claim the grace of the sacrament before she died. It did not seem to me in the circumstances possible to refuse her the outward and visible sign of grace which she so ardently desired, and which might lead to a peaceful end to a fairly desperate situation."[22] The marriage service, with Holy Communion, took place on March 21, 1957, at Joy's bedside in an Oxford Hospital, with Warren Lewis and one of the nurses as witnesses.[23]

Reprieve and Release

A few days later, Joy Davidman Lewis was taken by ambulance to The Kilns, which had been quickly adjusted to accommodate a dying invalid. Though not in much pain, she was very weak and also emotionally burdened by the way her own helplessness "drain[ed] [Jack's] energy and fill[ed] The Kilns with nurses, a sickbed, and two normally noisy boys that she could not corral."[24] Lewis himself put his shoulder to the wheel without complaint and also appealed to his long list of correspondents for prayers on behalf of his household. He was particularly frank with his closest women colleagues. "Joy is at home, doomed, and totally bed ridden," he wrote to his poetry mentor, Ruth Pitter. "We have two nurses and much of my day is spent on the duties of a hospital orderly. But she is, thank God, without pain and wonderfully cheerful: at times even happy. I know we have your prayers."[25] And in a letter to Dorothy L. Sayers, responding to her latest book on Dante, he added, "you will gather that my feelings had changed. They say that a rival often turns a friend into a lover.

22. Peter Bide to Lyle Dorsett, September 17, 1981, as quoted in Dorsett, *A Love Observed*, 126.

23. Peter Bide subsequently had his knuckles rapped by the Bishop of Oxford for failing to ask his permission to do the ceremony and was then sent back to his own Bishop to be formally disciplined. The Bishop of Chichester, George Bell, was mystified by Bide's action in marrying a couple who were "married already," but in the end simply said, "Anyway, you won't do it again, will you Peter?" Bide reports that he was able to give the Bishop that assurance. See Hooper, ed., *Collected Letters*, vol. 3, 1651.

24. Dorsett, *A Love Observed*, 127.

25. C. S. Lewis to Ruth Pitter, April 15, 1957, Hooper, ed., *Collected Letters*, vol. 3, 847.

Thanatos [i.e., death], certainly (they say) approaching but at an uncertain speed, is a most efficient rival for this purpose. We soon learn to love what we know we must lose. I hope you give us your blessing; I know you'll give us your prayers."[26]

Due to the popularity of *Shadowlands*, the 1993 film about Joy Davidman and C. S. Lewis, many people know that Joy did, in fact, experience a remarkable remission of her cancer, a remission that was to last for over two years. By July of 1957, Lewis was able to write to an American correspondent that his wife was in "apparently perfect health, no pain, eating & sleeping like a child, spirits usually excellent, able to beat me always at Scrabble and sometimes in argument. She runs the whole household from her bed . . . We are crazily in love."[27] By September, he could write to his former student, Dom Bede Griffith, that his wife's condition had improved "wonderfully . . . Tho' she is still a cripple, her *general* health has never been better, and she says she has never been happier."[28] By November, when it was confirmed that her cancer-damaged femur was actually healing, he wrote to another American friend that "the improvement in [Joy's] condition is . . . miraculous; not only is there no pain, but she is *walking*. She can now get around the ground floor of the house alone, with of course, a stick and a special shoe for the leg which is permanently shortened . . . When I see her state now, and contrast it with that in which she was six months ago, I realize what deep cause for gratitude we both have."[29]

By December, Joy was ready to resume writing herself, and what with his own work, and his brother's popular volumes on French history, Lewis joked that he might "put up a plate on the door reading Lewis, Lewis and Lewis Inc., Book Factory."[30] By March of 1958, the live-in nurses were dismissed, and Joy was able to climb stairs, go out for car rides, and supervise the much-needed renovation of The Kilns.[31] At the end of May, Joy herself wrote to one of Jack's friends that she'd even "got a fence around the woods and all the trespassers chased away; I shoot a starting-pistol at them and they run like anything!"[32] That same summer, the couple flew to Ireland for a holiday, and

26. C. S. Lewis to Dorothy L. Sayers, June 25, 1957, ibid., 861–62. Lewis had previously written to Sayers, just after his civil marriage was announced, that "[Joy] is in hospital (cancer) and not likely to live; but if she gets over this go she must be given a home here. You will not think that anything wrong is going to happen. Certain problems do not arise between a dying woman and an elderly [sic] man. What I am mainly acquiring is two nice stepsons" (Lewis to Sayers, December 24, 1956, ibid., 819).

27. C. S. Lewis to Mrs. Johnson, July 9, 1957, ibid., 866–67.

28. C. S. Lewis to Dom Bede Griffiths, OSB, September 24, 1957, ibid., 884.

29. C. S. Lewis to Vera Gebbert, November 12, 1957, ibid., 894.

30. C. S. Lewis to Vera Gebbert, December 16, 1957, ibid., 908.

31. The Lewis brothers' down-at-the-heel bachelor household was famous around Oxford, and was often described by their acquaintances as a "midden," or dung-heap.

32. Joy Davidman Lewis to Roger Lancelyn Green, May 23, 1958, ibid., 948.

by autumn Lewis reported that his wife "walks up the wooded hill behind our house and shoots—or more strictly shoots *at*—pigeons, picks peas and beans, and heaven knows what."[33] By the spring of 1959, both she and her husband were digging in the garden.[34]

Sadly, Lewis was to write for additional prayers by the fall of that year. Joy's cancer returned with a vengeance, this time with more pain and less hope of a reprieve. Yet they determined to take one more trip by air—this time to Greece with Roger and June Green. "I sometimes think I'm mad to be taking Joy to Greece in her present condition," Lewis wrote an American friend in early 1960. "But her heart is set on it. They give the condemned man what he likes for his last breakfast, I am told." In any event, the trip was "a wonderful success," with Joy "perform[ing] prodigies, climbing to the top of the Acropolis . . . com[ing] back exhausted and full of aches. But I w[oul]d not have denied her it."[35] Within a month, a recurrence of her breast cancer led to a mastectomy on one side, making her "an Amazon," as she cheerfully put it.[36] Less than two months later, after a last brief burst of strength, she died in Oxford's Radcliffe Infirmary, shortly after receiving Absolution, and asking Jack to cremate rather than bury her: "Don't buy me a posh coffin," she pleaded. "Posh coffins are all rot."[37]

Pastoral Realities and Theological Convictions

To read Lewis's letters from this period in his life is, in a sense, to see a man learning to adjust his theological convictions to the messier business of actual life. He had done his best to stay within the confines of church policy, but when his wife by civil marriage was apparently dying, he did not hesitate to take advantage of its ambiguity in order to make her his wife by Christian marriage. With Joy's physical reprieve, Lewis's life seemed to take on a more balanced quality. He continued to produce scholarly and popular works (including—with her help—*The Four Loves* and *Reflections on the Psalms*[38]), but by all accounts became a less intellectually combative and more emotionally accessible person. Commenting himself on the way that theory and practice had merged in his marriage, he wrote to one friend—using the terms he explored in *The Four Loves*—that "it is nice to have arrived at all this by something which

33. C. S. Lewis to Jessie M. Watt, August 28, 1958, ibid., 966.

34. Through the months that Joy had been improving, Lewis himself experienced a lot of back pain, first thought to be the result of a slipped disc, then of osteoporosis.

35. C. S. Lewis to Mary Willis Shelburne, March 26, 1960, and April 19, 1960, Hooper, ed., *Collected Letters*, vol. 3, 1141, 1147.

36. According to legend, female Amazon warriors removed one breast the better to aim their bows. See Lewis's letter to Chad Walsh, May 23, 1960, ibid., 1153.

37. Ibid., editor's notes, 1169.

38. C. S. Lewis, *Reflections on the Psalms* (London: Geoffrey Bles, 1958).

began in Agape [charity], proceeded to Philia [friendship], then became Pity, and only after that, Eros. As if the highest of these, Agape, had successfully undergone the sweet humiliation of an incarnation."[39]

Nor did his colleagues and critics pounce on him for hypocrisy when they learned of his marriage to a divorced woman. There were, of course, the predictable jokes about C. S. Lewis being "Surprised by Joy," but for the most part, people seemed pleased that he could, as he himself put it, experience "in my sixties the happiness that passed me in my twenties."[40] But three years after his wife's death, in the last essay he wrote for publication—titled "We Have No 'Right to Happiness'"—Lewis returned to the topic of divorce. This time—perhaps because he wrote it for a mass-market American magazine—he avoided theological language and stuck to natural-law kinds of arguments.[41]

He began by describing two marital breakups that had occurred in his own neighborhood: "Mr. A. had deserted Mrs. A. and got his divorce in order to marry Mrs. B., who had likewise got her divorce in order to marry Mr. A." The deserted parties, it seems, had ceased to make their spouses "happy": Mrs. A. had lost her looks by bearing children and nursing her husband to health through a long illness; Mr. B. had been badly injured during World War II and had lost his job. But, Lewis added, with studied irony:

> You mustn't, by the way, imagine that A. was the sort of man who nonchalantly threw a wife away like the peel of an orange he'd sucked dry. Her suicide was a terrible shock to him. We all knew this, for he told us so himself. "But what could I do?" he said. "A man has a right to happiness. I had to take my one chance when it came."[42]

Lewis's point was that Mr. A. spoke as if happiness—more specifically, sexual happiness—was a natural right, something built into what it means to be human, like the right to life, or to food and shelter. Lewis affirmed the existence of natural law (which he elsewhere called the *Tao*)[43] and said that it was "basic to all civilization. Without it, the actual laws of the state . . . cannot be criticized because there is no norm against which they should be judged."[44] But, he added, when the writers of the American Declaration of

39. C. S. Lewis to Dom Bede Griffiths, OSB, September 24, 1957, Hooper, ed., *Collected Letters*, vol. 3, 884.

40. Comment to Nevill Coghill in the summer of 1958, as quoted in Roger Lancelyn Green and Walter Hooper, *C. S. Lewis: A Biography* (London: Collins, 1974), 270. One notable exception was J. R. R. Tolkien who, as a devout Catholic, was perturbed by Joy's divorced status, and perhaps by the fact that he learned of the marriage only second-hand.

41. Lewis's essay "We Have No 'Right to Happiness'" was originally published in the US in *The Saturday Evening Post*, December 21, 1963, 10, 12.

42. Lewis, "We Have No 'Right to Happiness,'" in Hooper, ed., *God in the Dock*, 317.

43. C. S. Lewis, *The Abolition of Man* (Oxford: Oxford University Press, 1943).

44. Lewis, "We Have no Right to 'Happiness,'" 318.

Independence included "the pursuit of happiness" as a human right, "they did not mean that a man was entitled to pursue happiness by any and every means—including, say, murder, rape, robbery, treason and fraud. No society could be built on such a basis. They meant 'to pursue happiness by all lawful means'; that is, by all means which the Law of Nature eternally sanctions and which the laws of the nation shall [reflect]."[45]

They did of course mean to extend the "lawful right" to pursue happiness to a greater range of people—that is, "to 'man' and not just men of some particular caste, class, status or religion."[46] But they did not mean to enshrine either a right to every kind of happiness, or any means to achieve whatever lawful happiness a person might want to pursue. And even people who talk glibly of a "right to happiness" *per se* do not really mean what they say, for they are almost always talking only about sexual happiness. Thus, for example, one defender of Mr. A's "right to happiness," a young woman Lewis calls Clare,

> was rather leftist in her politics, and would have been scandalized if anyone had defended the actions of a ruthless man-eating tycoon on the ground that his happiness consisted in making money, and he was pursuing his happiness. [Clare] was also a rabid teetotaler; I never heard her excuse an alcoholic because he was happy when he was drunk. A good many of Clare's friends . . . often felt—I've heard them say so—that their own happiness could be perceptibly increased by boxing her ears. I very much doubt if this would have brought her theory of happiness into play.[47]

Nowadays, Lewis wrote, though we agree that no other impulse in our nature (such as greed or gluttony) should be given free rein, "every unkindness and breach of faith seems to be condoned provided that the object aimed at is 'four bare legs in a bed' . . . It is like having a morality in which stealing fruit is considered wrong—unless you are stealing nectarines." And to criticize such a stance, he added, is not necessarily to be hostile toward sex: "If I object to boys who steal my nectarines, must I be supposed to disapprove of nectarines in general? Or even of boys in general?" The point, Lewis wrote, is that Mr. A's pursuit of his "right" to (sexual) happiness was "an offense against honesty . . . and offense against good faith (to solemn promises), against gratitude (toward one to whom he was deeply indebted) and against common humanity."[48] For Lewis, it was such virtues—not subjective happiness *per se*—that were truly part of "natural law."

We do not know if Lewis was thinking of Bill Gresham, Joy Davidman's first husband, when he wrote this essay three years after her death. It is cer-

45. Ibid., 318–19.
46. Ibid., 319.
47. Ibid.
48. Ibid., 320.

tainly the case that even while married to Joy, Gresham pursued a series of extramarital sexual affairs, insisting that "a guy has to recharge his battery every so often."[49] And he did sound a lot like Lewis's "Mr. A." when he wrote to Joy in England of his determination to get divorced and marry her cousin. Over against Joy's Christian conviction that they should stay together and try to mend the marriage, Gresham argued that "people cannot fall in love by will power and they certainly cannot fall back in love by it . . . Affection and intellectual comraderie [sic] are not a marriage . . . People who set out to 'make a go of the marriage' for the sake of the children are setting up a situation of affinity enforcers and reality deniers."[50]

But there is growing evidence to suggest that it is really the Bill Greshams who are the "reality deniers." As we will see shortly, there is a positive correlation between the quality of marriage and couples' support for the norm of lifelong marriage. By itself, this correlation is ambiguous, because we don't know the direction of causality: it could be that people who are fortunate enough to have good marriages are happy to endorse lifelong togetherness (why would they not, under the circumstances?). But a longitudinal study from 1980 to 2000 suggests that the causal influence is, in fact, largely from changed attitudes to changed marital quality. As the authors of the study put it:

> Individuals who strongly support the norm of lifelong marriage tend to experience increases in martial happiness and decreases in marital conflict over time. In contrast, individuals who are accepting of divorce tend to experience declines in marital happiness and increases in marital conflict. Presumably, people who believe strongly in lifelong marriage are motivated to work on marital problems and find ways to resolve them.[51]

Learning from Experience: Social Scientists Look at Divorce

When Lewis and Davidman wrote in the mid-1950s, American statisticians were already predicting that soon one in three marriages would end in divorce.[52] By the end of the 1970s, most states in America had adopted no-fault divorce laws, many of which waived even the requirement of mutual consent. This meant that either party in a marriage could end it at will—sometimes without even a mandatory waiting period. In effect, getting out of a marriage was becoming easier than getting out of a car loan agreement.[53]

49. As quoted in Dorsett, *A Love Observed*, 74.
50. Ibid., 90, 91.
51. Paul R. Amato, Alan Booth, David R. Johnson, and Stacy J. Rogers, *Alone Together: How Marriage in America Is Changing* (Cambridge, MA: Harvard University Press, 2007), 257.
52. Davidman, *Smoke on the Mountain*, 79.
53. A small number of American states still require waiting periods prior to divorce, ranging from a couple of months to a year and a half. UK divorce law is stricter, requiring a two-year

All this was accompanied by a series of popular assumptions which, had he lived to hear them, might have made Lewis rethink his skepticism about social science and plead for some hard data. The most popular of these was the presumption that as long as parents were happy, children would be happy. Conversely, if spouses "didn't get along," then the children would clearly be happier if their parents divorced. And since divorce was supposed to make both parents happier, it seemed like a win-win situation. After minor adjustments by everyone, parents would learn from their mistakes and form better second marriages, and children would acquire new stepparents, and perhaps stepsiblings, to add to the family they already had. In 1953, when William Gresham—Joy Davidman's American husband—wanted to leave her for another woman (Joy's own cousin, as it turned out), he suggested this "optimum solution" in a letter sent to her while she was visiting England: Joy should marry "some really swell guy," and then when he and her cousin got married, the reconstituted families could live near each other, "so that the Gresham kids could have Mommy and Daddy on hand."[54]

By the turn of the third millennium, the divorce rate (as a percentage of marriages) had reached almost 46 percent in America and 43 percent in the UK, with other countries in the industrialized world reflecting more or less similar trends. But as decades of data accumulated on the correlates of marital breakup, a growing number of social scientists—of all political and religious stripes—began to question the soothing nostrums about divorce that had become part of the cultural landscape. They were aware that research on the effects of divorce has many of the same methodological complications as research on gender differences. For example, we cannot randomly assign children to grow up in intact or broken homes, any more than we can randomly assign them to be one sex or another. So it is hard to make definitive pronouncements about what causes what: the data are correlational rather than experimental. But as I noted in the previous chapter, by doing meta-analytic and longitudinal studies, and by being careful to control for relevant social factors (in divorce research this includes things like education, wealth, ethnicity, and religiosity) we can come to a closer understanding of causes and effects. And what researchers began to find is that, as C. S. Lewis put it half a century ago, divorce is "more like having both your legs cut off than it is like dissolving a business partnership."[55]

Let's begin with what meta-analyses of divorce studies reveal. In the early 1990s, two American sociologists pooled data from almost a hundred studies on the correlates of divorce for pre-adult children, examining measures of academic achievement, mental health, relations to parents, and social and

---

separation of the parties even for a divorce based on mutual consent, and a five-year separation for a unilateral divorce.

54. Quoted in Dorsett, *A Love Observed*, 91.

55. Lewis, *Mere Christianity*, 93.

sexual behavior.[56] They also did a separate meta-analysis of studies of adult children of divorce, using similar measures and some additional ones—of the adults' marital quality, occupational success, and physical and mental health, for example.[57] As it turns out, compared to children from intact families, children of divorce, on average, face greater risks at every age. At younger ages they are significantly more likely to drop out of school, engage in early and risky sexual activity, have strained relationships with peers and parents, get into trouble with the law, and need mental health intervention. As adults, they are on average less successful in their careers, less physically and mentally healthy, less self-confident, and more likely themselves to get divorced than children of intact families.

Other research has shown that such negative effects occur even in adult children who have gone through so-called "good" divorces—that is, ones in which both parents maintain contact and shared responsibility for their children (the "optimum solution" proposed to Joy Davidman by her adulterous husband in the 1950s).[58] Elizabeth Marquardt's 2005 national study of fifteen hundred young adults, half from "good" divorces and half from intact families, found that the children of such divorces often recalled feeling like exiles from the parental homes between which they had to commute. They remembered having to treat these homes as conflicting spaces with competing expectations. They recalled feeling pressure to take sides and keep secrets in parental conflicts. They often felt they had to assume the role of parent or therapist toward one or the other of their own parents in the emotional upheaval following the divorce, and admitted to being ambivalent about risking marital commitment as a result of such experiences. Some felt that, despite promises to the contrary, one or both of their parents had let them down—for example, by making commitments for visits or school events that they did not keep, or by putting their post-divorce desire to pursue new sexual relationships above the needs of their children. Although most of these young adults were functioning well publicly—indeed, often *over*-functioning—clearly they did not remain emotionally unscathed.[59]

Could this be just another case of lying with statistics? Those who support a broader diversity of family forms often say so—for example, that the poorer outcomes for children of divorce are caused mainly by the economic stress that often accompanies divorce and single parenthood, and could be largely overcome

56. Paul R. Amato and Bruce Keith, "Parental Divorce and the Well-Being of Children: A Meta-Analysis," *Psychological Bulletin* 100 (1991): 26–46.

57. Paul R. Amato and Bruce Keith, "Parental Divorce and Adult Well-Being: A Meta-Analysis," *Journal of Marriage and Family* 53 (1993): 43–58. The combined number of respondents in the two Amato and Keith meta-analyses was approximately 93,000 people.

58. See, for example, Constance Ahrons, *The Good Divorce: Keeping Your Family Together When Your Marriage Comes Apart* (New York: HarperCollins, 1994).

59. Elizabeth Marquardt, *Between Two Worlds: The Inner Lives of Children of Divorce* (New York: Crown, 2005).

by putting a better social safety net in place.[60] But even when family income is controlled for, the difference in outcomes between children of divorce and those from intact families, while somewhat smaller, is still statistically significant. Stepfamily formation, for example, almost always results in a rise in household income (compared to single-parent homes)—yet it does not, on average, lessen any of the problems for children of divorce that have been described.[61]

Other critics point to sampling as a possible artifact. Divorce studies do not usually compare conflict-ridden families that have undergone divorce with families who have stayed together *despite* their conflicts. Thus, some argued, children in conflict-ridden but intact families would show the same range and size of problems as children of divorce, demonstrating that damage was not caused by divorce *per se*, but by the miserable homes children lived in *prior* to divorce. However, this argument was challenged by the results of a large longitudinal social survey in the UK—one that involved the families of almost every child born during the first week of March 1958. At regular intervals over the next thirty-three years, interviews about family life were conducted with the children's mothers, fathers, teachers, and (eventually) with the children themselves, of whom over two-thirds were still in the study at age thirty-three. As the study continued, some parents divorced while others did not. This allowed the researchers to examine, through time, the conflict similarities and differences between the two groups.

Interestingly, this study found only half the difference in problems suffered by children of divorce could be accounted for by predivorce levels of conflict in the home. This strongly suggests that there is something about the divorce experience itself that produces many of the problems.[62] It is true that children of high conflict marriages (ones characterized by chronic physical and/or verbal abuse) generally do fare better if their parents divorce. However, in both Britain and America high-conflict marriages precede only about a third of all divorces. The rest are mainly the result of a desire by one or both parties to revert to their own individual economic, professional, and romantic agendas.[63]

60. For example, Stephanie Coontz, *The Way We Never Were: American Families and the Nostalgia Trap* (New York: Basic Books, 1992); Judith Stacey, *In the Name of the Family: Rethinking Family Values in a Postmodern Age* (Boston: Beacon, 1996).

61. Andrew Cherlin, *Marriage, Divorce, Remarriage*, rev. ed. (Cambridge, MA: Harvard University Press, 1992).

62. Andrew Cherlin, "Longitudinal Studies of Effects of Divorce on Children in Great Britain and the United States," *Science* 252 (1991): 1386–89. It turns out that spouses wanting out of low-conflict marriages share a number of characteristics: they are more likely than the population at large to be risk-takers, to have a favorable view of divorce, to be somewhat socially isolated (with little religious or extended family involvement), to have another potential partner in mind or in fact, and *not* to have experienced divorce themselves as children (thus having little conception of how disorienting it is likely to be for their own children).

63. See Sara McLanahan and Gary Sandefur, *Growing Up with a Single Parent* (Cambridge, MA: Harvard University Press, 1994); Alan Booth and Judy Dunn, eds., *Stepfamilies: Who Bene-*

One group of sociologists summarized this mind-set as follows:

Spouses [too often] operate as autonomous individuals who contract to stay together as long as their needs for personal growth and self-fulfillment are met . . . If people's psychological rewards from the relationship are less than expected, individuals will dissolve their unions relatively quickly to seek out more promising opportunities with new partners. Serial marriage, however, is unlikely to meet children's deep-seated needs for stability and long-term emotional bonds with parents.[64]

These comments come from a study, both longitudinal and cross-sectional, that took place in America between 1980 and 2000. The cross-sectional portion involved identical surveys of two random national samples twenty years apart, each of about two thousand married persons. The longitudinal portion involved repeated interviews of parents and children from the original 1980 sample over almost twenty years.[65] And its strongest finding was this: on every measure of well-being (school performance, social skills, relations with parents, etc.) low conflict divorce has devastating effects on kids. Contrary to the conventional wisdom that only if adults are happy will their kids be happy, children seem to be largely unaware of subterranean malaise between their parents. They take for granted the stability and routine of their home life (however much they may complain about it at times) and this enables them to get on with developmentally appropriate tasks in their own lives. When this stability is shattered, the consequences can be serious, leading the authors of these studies (even though some were *themselves* divorced parents of children) to conclude that if couples are not in a high-conflict marriage, they should "try to stick it out until the kids are grown."[66]

And "sticking it out" may be more than just the lesser of two evils in terms of children's health. Another finding of the American longitudinal study was

---

fits? Who Does Not? (Hillsdale, NJ: Lawrence Erlbaum, 1994); Paul R. Amato and Alan Booth, *A Generation at Risk* (Cambridge, MA: Harvard University Press, 1997).

64. Amato et al., *Alone Together*, 262.

65. Paul R. Amato and Stacy J. Rogers, "A Longitudinal Study of Marital Problems and Subsequent Divorce," *Journal of Marriage and the Family* 59 (1997): 612–24.

66. As quoted in Marie Brown, "Happy Marriages," *Penn State Research Online* 23, no. 1 (January 2002), http://www.rps.psu.edu/0201/happy.html. It is noteworthy, for example, that only about 10 percent of undergraduates in America's top fifty universities are from divorced families, compared to about a third in universities overall. Since about 1990, educated Americans of both sexes and all ethnicities have become increasingly likely to marry *before* having children, and to *stay* married, which is then associated with increasing benefits—educational and emotional—for their children, compared to those who do not come from stable marriages. See Dean Lillard and Jennifer Gerner, "Getting to the Ivy League: How Family Composition Matters," *Journal of Higher Education* 70, no. 6 (November–December 1999): 706–30; and Kay S. Hymowitz, *Marriage and Caste in America: Separate and Unequal Families in a Post-Marital Age* (Chicago: Ivan R. Dee, 2006).

that divorced people *themselves* were on average no happier in later marriages than in their first. Indeed, second (and subsequent) marriages are even more likely to break up than first ones. Other studies show that couples who report being unhappily married at one point, yet stay together, usually experience relationship improvement after five years. In this sense, staying married is rather like finishing a university degree, or training for a marathon: there are times when neither is a bed of roses, but in most cases "sticking it out"— whether or not you have religious reasons for doing so—pays off, both for parents and children.[67]

But having read my "sermon on method" in the previous chapter, readers will recall that statistical significance is not the same as practical significance. So it is fair to ask just *how large* the effect sizes are when comparing outcomes for children of divorce with children of intact families. Meta-analytic studies of divorce involving younger children have examined a variety of measures of wellbeing (e.g., levels of aggression, anxiety, academic achievement, self-esteem, relations with peers and parents), and on all of these the children of divorce do statistically worse. But the effect sizes are small—the median is about .14: a mere seventh of a standard deviation's separation between the two groups.[68] Meta-analytic studies of adult children also show that the risks associated with divorce are modest in terms of effect sizes (ranging from .10 to .30)—but that they last longer than most people like to believe. These risks include depression, low life satisfaction and marital quality, marriage breakdown, less formal education, and lower income.[69]

Still, as in studies of gender differences, the distributions of scores (children of divorce vs. those from intact families) overlap greatly. Moreover, the range of scores *within* each group is much larger than the small average difference *between* the two groups. This, in one sense, is good news: it means that while divorce does increase the *risk* of negative outcomes for both younger and older children, it is far from being an automatic sentence of doom. In the overlapping parts of the distributions, children of divorce and those from intact families are quite similar. Thus it seems fair to wonder whether we should even dwell on the differences, any more than we should emphasize the small differences between women and men on behavioral and psychological tests, since emphasizing small differences over greater similarities can lead to pessimistic overgeneralizations about life outcomes for the children involved.

There is, however, an important distinction between the two types of studies. As we saw in the last chapter, overemphasizing the small differences between females and males can lead people to apply confining stereotypes to members

67. Linda J. Waite and Maggie Gallagher, *The Case for Marriage: Why Married People Are Happier, Healthier, and Better Off Financially* (New York: Doubleday, 2000).
   68. Amato and Keith, "Parental Divorce and the Well-Being of Children."
   69. Amato and Keith, "Parental Divorce and Adult Well-Being."

of both sexes, thus reducing the scope of their activities and accomplishments. If people ignore the large overlap of men's and women's scores, it is easy to conclude that men cannot "really" be nurturers, or women cannot "really" be leaders. However, meta-analytic studies showing the advantages of growing up in an intact family are more comparable to medical studies of therapeutic drug effectiveness, in that even a modest effect size can translate into a lot of lives saved or improved. To make a more specific medical comparison: the decrease in emotional and social risk that comes from growing up in an intact family is roughly comparable to the decrease in physical risk (e.g., for getting lung cancer) that comes from growing up in a nonsmoking family.

And here we see how not just nature, but social policy, responds "chiefly in answer to our questions." Almost all Western states have concluded that smoking produces public health problems that seriously deplete tax revenues. Thus, though they have not banned the sale of tobacco outright, they have progressively restricted its advertising, as well as the range of places where smoking is allowed. As a result, in the past forty years in America alone, adult smoking rates have been halved—from about 40 percent to 20 percent.[70] This is an astonishing societal turnaround, as anyone knows who lived through the decades when smoking was promoted as a normal (and glamorous) activity. Today, smoking is known to be the biggest cause of preventable disease and death in modern society, and law and social policy—as well as cultural attitudes and behavior—have shifted accordingly. Even among smokers there are few who continue to defend the practice as harmless, let alone glamorous. By contrast, in spite of comparable risk levels, it is still common for people to think that high rates of divorce, like death and taxes, are simply inevitable: that we cannot put this particular genie back in the bottle, and that anyway, it's not a big deal for most people, socially or psychologically.[71]

As a self-confessed chain-smoker, C. S. Lewis might not have appreciated this comparison—let alone the development of a "nanny state" that curtailed people's right to smoke in public places.[72] But there are challenges to the cur-

70. US Centers for Disease Control and Prevention, 2007.

71. In addition to the social and psychological costs already summarized, divorce—like smoking—is a considerable drain on the public purse, costing American taxpayers (by conservative estimates) some $112 billion per year (or an average of about $300 of each individual's state and federal tax bill). Public costs associated with divorce include expenditures associated with court appearances, collection of child support payments, mental health, criminal justice and antipoverty programs, and lost taxes from adults who, because of economic impoverishment caused by divorce, pay fewer taxes themselves. Similar costs have been noted in the UK and other industrialized nations. See Benjamin Scarfidi, Principal Investigator, "The Taxpayer Costs of Divorce and Unwed Childbearing" (New York: Institute for American Values, 2008), http://center.americanvalues.org.

72. Lewis and his brother both began smoking in early adolescence. They were so dependent on the habit that by 1940 Lewis, writing to Warren about his grudging admiration for a colleague who managed to give up smoking for Lent, added: "You know, you and I could no

rent culture of divorce that he might have welcomed. One example is the rise in America of what is called the Community Marriage Policy (CMP) movement. First developed by evangelical journalist Michael McManus, it calls for all church ministers in a given area to agree that they will only perform marriages for couples that have undergone a several-month preparation period, using research-based programs that include extensive premarital inventories,[73] communication and conflict resolution skills training, and mentoring by older married couples. Almost two hundred fifty US communities have implemented CMPs, and a 2004 study which matched CMP and non-CMP counties in the US found that divorce rates declined twice as quickly in the former as in the latter: about 18 percent compared to 9 percent over a period of seven years.[74] Regardless of their level of religious observance or their attitude toward marital permanence, most Americans still prefer to get married in a religious setting, so CMPs are a powerful contributor to marital stability: people cannot use churches as quick "marriage mills" in CMP communities, since all churches in that community have agreed to use the same rigorous standards of preparation.

Lewis would also have been glad to hear that the divorce rate has been slowly declining in the UK and America since shortly after he last wrote about it. In fact, the study that interviewed separate American samples in 1980 and 2000 found two trends that were contrary to popular wisdom. The first was that people's

---

more do that than we could fly to the moon." C. S. Lewis to Warren Lewis, February 11, 1940, Walter Hooper, ed., *The Collected Letters of C. S. Lewis*, vol. 2, *1931–1949* (San Francisco: HarperSanFrancisco, 2004), 346. To an American correspondent (inquiring about his views on alcohol and tobacco) he wrote in the 1950s: "Smoking is much harder to justify. I'd like to give it up, but I'd find this v[ery] hard, i.e., I *can* abstain, but I can't concentrate on anything else while abstaining—not-smoking is a whole time job." C. S. Lewis to Mrs. Johnson, March 13, 1956, Hooper, ed., *Collected Letter*, vol. 3, 719 (emphasis original). Lewis's biographer and former student, George Sayer, recalls visiting Lewis a few months before his death, when he was semi-convalescent and advised by his medical caretakers not to smoke: "He was wearing pyjamas and a dressing gown. He walked forward, clutched me, and said, 'Thank God, a friend. You see a dying man. For God's sake, and as you value our friendship, go and get me some cigarettes. And, don't on any account, let them see you bring them in.' I did as he asked, intending to let him have only one cigarette out of the pack. He smoked it greedily, inhaling deeply." George Sayer, *Jack: C. S. Lewis and His Times* (San Francisco: Harper and Row, 1988), 247–48.

73. These inventories, done separately by members of the couple, cover attitudes to marital challenges such as children, sex, in-laws, finances, religion, gender roles, and conflict and communication styles. The goal is to find out in which of these areas couples are in substantial agreement, and which are likely to cause relationship problems. The predictive power of such scales is good, and the very process of filling them out leads about 10 percent of couples to postpone or cancel their wedding plans. Details of such programs can be found at www.smart marriages.com.

74. Paul J. Birch, Stan E. Weed, and Joseph A. Olsen, "Assessing the Impact of Community Marriage Policies on County Divorce Rates," *Family Relations* 53, no. 5 (2004): 495–503. See also Michael McManus, *Marriage Savers: Helping Your Friends and Family to Stay Married* (Grand Rapids: Zondervan, 1993).

views on the permanence of marriage—regardless of gender, class, ethnicity, or religiosity—had become stronger during the twenty-year interval, yielding an effect size (.24) almost as great as the one that separates nonsmokers from smokers in terms of reduced physical risks.[75] The second finding was that, by the second wave of research in 2000—and again regardless of gender, class, or ethnicity—higher percentages of people were attending religious services regularly and rating religion as a more important influence in their daily life.[76]

Both of these trends, if they continue, bode well for the restabilization of marriage and for its quality, since marital satisfaction is positively correlated both with serious religious commitment and with commitment to the norm of marital permanence. The authors of the study comment that "rising support for the norm of lifelong marriage suggests that people may be growing weary of a culture in which nearly half of all marriages end in divorce."[77] One is reminded of Lewis's observation that "experience is such an honest thing. You may take any number of wrong turnings, but keep your eyes open and you will not be allowed to go very far before warning signs appear . . . The universe rings true whenever you fairly test it."[78] Though Lewis was originally speaking of individual experience, his observation also applies at the aggregate level: cultures cannot flout norms built into creation without eventually beginning to see the lack of wisdom in doing so.

C. S. Lewis would probably not have been surprised by any of the research findings I have just summarized. His aversion to divorce was never just a case of adherence to an isolated divine command about lifelong marriage. He regarded marriage as a crucible for testing and refining an entire web of basic Christian—indeed, essentially human—virtues. "We know," he wrote in his last essay,

> that [our erotic passions] sometimes last—and sometimes don't. And when they do last, this is not because they promised at the outset to do so. When two people achieve lasting happiness, this is not solely because they are great lovers but because they are also—I must put it crudely—good people; controlled, loyal, fair-minded, mutually adaptable people.[79]

75. Amato et al., *Alone Together*, chap. 6. Specifically, the 2000 sample was *more* likely than the 1980 sample to agree with items such as "Marriage is for life, even if the couple is unhappy," "If one spouse becomes mentally or physically disabled, the other spouse should stay, regardless of his or her own happiness," and "Couples are able to get divorced too easily these days." The 2000 sample was *less* likely than the 1980 sample to agree with items such as "The personal happiness of an individual is more important than putting up with a bad marriage," and "In marriages where people fight a lot, children are better off if the parents divorce or separate."

76. Ibid., chap. 7. The effect sizes were modest, but positive in each case: .13 and .10.

77. Ibid., 202.

78. C. S. Lewis, *Surprised by Joy: The Shape of My Early Life* (London: Collins, 1955), 177.

79. Lewis, "We Have No 'Right to Happiness,'" in Hooper, ed., *God in the Dock*, 321.

His use of the generic word "people" is also noteworthy. Whereas in *The Four Loves* he wrote of marital sacrifice in asymmetrical terms—something that might demand a "crucifixion" on the part of husbands for the sake of their weaker wives—after four years of marriage, he described the virtues necessary to its success as generically human, not gendered, qualities. How Lewis himself responded to this challenge as a husband and a stepfather, and how many of his instincts and convictions have also been supported by social science research, is the theme of the following chapter.

9

"True to the Kind of Things We Are"

C. S. Lewis and Family Life

At the age of forty-five, in the Durham University lectures that would become *The Abolition of Man*, C. S. Lewis confessed that he did "not enjoy the society of small children." But, he continued, "because I speak from within the *Tao*, I recognize this as a defect in myself—just as a man may have to recognize that he is tone-deaf or color-blind."[1] Within what age range he intended to include "small" children is not clear, but we do know what he meant by the *Tao*. It was the Chinese term Lewis used as shorthand for a conviction shared by ancient Greek, Stoic, Monotheistic, and Oriental thinkers alike:

> It is the doctrine of objective value, the belief that certain attitudes are really true, and others really false, to the kind of thing the universe is and the kind of things we are. Those who know the *Tao* can hold that to call children delightful or old men venerable is not simply to record a psychological fact about our own parental or filial emotions at the moment, but to recognize a quality that *demands* a certain response from us whether we make it or not.[2]

1. C. S. Lewis, *The Abolition of Man* (Oxford: Oxford University Press, 1943), 17.
2. Ibid.

Lewis is here expressing his conviction that "lawfulness" does not just pertain to the physical world. Certain virtues (like delighting in children and revering elders) are demanded of us just because of "the kind of things we are" as creatures made by God. And while we may not all have equal success in living up to these virtues, we need to recognize that they are the kinds of standards we should aspire to and grieve when we fail to reach them. To be sure, Lewis also affirmed that persons image God in their capacity for rationality and creativity. As a result of this paradox (we are creatures, but creatures made to be God's agents) humans are called to practice freedom within form, live life within law, and follow love within limits. As stated repeatedly in *The Abolition of Man*, Lewis did not believe that all statements of value are reducible to subjective feelings or that it doesn't matter what we believe, so long as we are sincere.

In the face of growing moral relativism, Lewis defended the virtues and moral forms he held to be immutable. The younger Lewis, as we have seen, argued on behalf of enduring gender forms, or archetypes, to which women and men were called to conform themselves. "Suppose," Jane Studdock in *That Hideous Strength* wondered, just after her conversion, "Suppose one were a *thing* after all . . . designed by Someone Else and valued for qualities quite different from what one had regarded as one's true self? Supposing all those people . . . who had found her sweet and fresh when she also wanted them to find her interesting and important, had all along been simply right and perceived the sort of thing she was?"[3] But the older Lewis concluded that femininity and masculinity were not such immutable forms after all. "It is arrogance in us [men] to call frankness, fairness, and chivalry 'masculine' when we see them in a woman," he wrote in *A Grief Observed*. "It is arrogance in them [women] to describe a man's sensitiveness or tact or tenderness as 'feminine.' But also what poor, warped fragments of humanity most mere men and mere woman must be to make the implications of that arrogance possible. Marriage heals this . . . By a paradox, this carnival of sexuality leads us out beyond our sexes."[4]

This was not the only paradox in Lewis's life. Another (of which he was perhaps less aware) is this: although Lewis did not marry until his late fifties, this did not stop him from making quite public pronouncements on the nature of marriage. But he publicly said and wrote very little about childrearing, on the grounds that he had no children of his own.[5] Yet his private correspon-

---

3. C. S. Lewis, *That Hideous Strength: A Modern Fairy-Tale for Grown-Ups* (London: John Lane the Bodley Head, 1945), 318 (emphasis original).

4. C. S. Lewis, *A Grief Observed* (London: Faber and Faber, 1961), 40–41.

5. Thus, for example, Canon Harold Arthur Blair, one of Lewis's hosts when he gave talks on Christianity to the Royal Air Force during World War II, recalls that "we had a delightful four days of him . . . with the R. A. F. officers and men, but had a rather bad time with the girls' school: the school-marms got at him in a school-marmish way with questions about bringing

dence—not to mention his *Chronicles of Narnia* and the stream of letters from and to children that they prompted—betray a steadily growing interest in children and childrearing, made stronger by the fact that he was four times a godparent, shared his household with a number of young women evacuees during World War II, and acquired two young stepsons upon his marriage to Joy Davidman. His informal writings show that, in all these relationships, Lewis had good intuitions about childrearing, in contrast to his earlier and better-publicized views on gender archetypes. Positively, he was able to recall and reproduce the best features of his own childhood when he wrote for and interacted with children. Negatively, he was something of a wounded healer: concerning childhood challenges such as schooling, or the loss of a parent, he had a sense of what he wanted to avoid seeing repeated, especially in the lives of his stepsons. And as we shall see, he regularly ignored his own publicly proclaimed theories about gender in his actual interactions with children.

All of this was underscored by Lewis's assumption that children share the dignity of being made in God's image, and are called by God to develop their gifts and moral sensibilities in age-appropriate ways. And in his *Narnia* chronicles, they share with adults—in ways reflecting the peculiar challenges of childhood—the usual temptations of pride, envy, greed, sloth, gluttony, anger, and lust.[6] In this chapter—again with an eye to some relevant social science theory and research—I will look at Lewis's informally recorded views about childrearing, beginning with his role as a godparent and ending with his step-parenting experiences with David and Douglas Gresham.

"A Bachelor Who Has Seldom Even Talked to Children"

Within two years of his conversion to Christianity, and some fifteen years before he began writing children's stories, C. S. Lewis was asked to be godfather to Laurence Harwood, the third child of his friends Daphne and Cecil Harwood. In a 1933 letter to the child's mother, Lewis described this as a "novel honour," and recalled the christening service fondly: "How is my godson? I hope his laughing all through the service does not mean that he is going to grow up an *esprit fort* [strong spirit]: but as soon as he is old enough, I shall try to collaborate with you in preventing this."[7] If this suggests that the younger Lewis

---

up children, which he would not answer as he had none of his own." See Walter Hooper, ed., *The Collected Letters of C. S. Lewis*, vol. 2, *1931–1949* (San Francisco: HarperSanFrancisco, 2004), 666, note 72.

6. This is Dante's classic list of the Seven Deadly Sins, though in young children the sin of lust is less explicitly sexual.

7. C. S. Lewis to Daphne Harwood, December 28, 1933, Walter Hooper, ed., *The Collected Letters of C. S. Lewis*, vol. 3, *1950–1963* (San Francisco: HarperSanFranciso: 2007), 130. Lewis's other godchildren were Lucy Barfield, the adopted daughter of Owen Barfield, his friend and colleague from his student days at Oxford (b. 1935); Sarah Neylan, the daughter of his former

had authoritarian leanings regarding childrearing, that suspicion is allayed in a subsequent letter about his godson, to whom he sent a book token, or gift card, for his seventh Christmas. In response to his mother's query as to how they should spend it, Lewis replied that "as a bachelor who has seldom even talked to children I should be very foolish if I gave any advice as to books for Lawrence [sic]; if I felt qualified to choose books I should send books—not tokens."[8]

But as the public C. S. Lewis began integrating "Christianity, reason and romanticism"[9] for adult readers, the private Lewis was gradually applying some of his ideas to children. His love of fairy tales and myths may have led him to see in them more than he should have as prolegomena to the Christian gospel, but he correctly perceived their value to children's development. As early as 1935, in a letter to his Belfast friend Arthur Greeves, he voiced concern about a five-year-old relative of Janie Moore, who was visiting The Kilns with his mother:

> [Janie] reads him the Peter Rabbit books every evening, and it is a lovely sight . . . Would you believe it, that child had never been read to or told a story by his mother in his life? Not that he is neglected. He has a [full time] nurse . . . a hundred patent foods, is spoiled, and far too expensively dressed: but his poor imagination has been left without any natural food at all . . . not a fairy tale nor a nursery rhyme.[10]

A year later, Lewis wrote to his friend Owen Barfield about *The Silver Trumpet*, a children's book Barfield had written some years earlier.[11] In that letter, he joined his colleague J. R. R. Tolkien in expressing the belief that sanitized fairy tales—those that edit out the tragic and scary parts—neither fool children (who, being small and vulnerable, know that the world is complex and unpredictable) nor engage their imaginations in developmentally helpful ways:

> My Dear Barfield: I lent *The Silver Trumpet* to Tolkien and hear that it is the greatest success among his children that they have ever known. His own fairy-

---

student Mary Shelly Neylan (b. 1939); and Richard Blake, son of Janie Moore's daughter, Maureen Moore Blake (b. 1945).

8. C. S. Lewis to Daphne Harwood, January 6, 1939, ibid., 238.

9. Part of the subtitle to Lewis's (1933) allegorical autobiography *Pilgrim's Regress*.

10. C. S. Lewis to Arthur Greeves, December 7, 1935, Hooper, ed., *Collected Letters*, vol. 2, 171. In the same letter Lewis notes about the boy, Michael, that "[my brother] gets on with him much better than I do. That is, I theoretically hold that one ought to like children, but am shy with them in practice: he theoretically dislikes them, but is actually the best of friends" (171).

11. Owen Barfield, *The Silver Trumpet* (London: Faber and Faber, 1925). This is a fairy tale after the style of Hans Christian Andersen, featuring a grail-like search for a lost silver trumpet representing the triumph of good over evil.

tales, which are excellent, have now no market: and [*The Silver Trumpet*'s] first
reading—children are so practical!—led to a universal wail "You're not going
to give it back to Mr. Lewis, are you?"

All the things which the wiseacres on child psychology in our circle said when
you wrote it turn out to be nonsense. "They liked the sad parts" said Tolkien,
"because they were sad and the puzzling parts because they were puzzling, as
children always do." The youngest boy liked [the princess's scheming sister]
Gamboy because "she was clever and the bad characters in books usually aren't"
. . . In fine, you have scored a direct hit.[12]

When Lewis made these observations, child psychology—a relatively new
field at the time—was something of a battleground between the competing
schools of psychoanalysis and Pavlovian-style behaviorism. While the former
put much emphasis on children's emotional attachment to parents (particularly
mothers), the latter stressed the need to condition children from an early age for
independence and self-sufficiency.[13] Later psychologists would admit that this
was a false dichotomy, and that children need ongoing, secure attachments to
their caretakers at the same time as they journey toward greater independence.
What Lewis (and Tolkien) intuited was that children need something else too:
a safe, symbolic space in which they can examine the conflicting emotions
inside them and the ambiguity of the world around them.

Fairy tales, like Lewis's later *Chronicles of Narnia*, generally end "happily ever after"—but not without treachery, failure, injuries, and evil spells
beforehand. But it is not just that fairy tales and traditional nursery rhymes
(which can also be quite vicious) let children deal with the reality of evil and
tragedy, as well as their own conflicting emotions, in safe imaginary doses—
though that is true.[14] It is that the best fairy tales participate in what Tolkien

12. C. S. Lewis to Owen Barfield, June 28, 1936, Hooper, ed., *Collected Letters*, vol. 2, 198.
Tolkien's four children ranged from seven to nineteen years of age at this time, and it may be that
only the younger two are being referred to here. Lewis's reference to Tolkien's "own fairy-tales"
probably includes *The Silmarillion*, which Tolkien began in the 1920s, and *The Hobbit*, which he
began writing for his children around 1930. It would be almost another quarter-century before
his fantasy tales began to acquire world-wide acclaim.

13. A clear and accessible history of this era in child psychology can be found in Deborah
Blum, *Love at Goon Park: Harry Harlow and the Science of Affection* (New York: Perseus,
2002).

14. Lewis and Tolkien were not alone in their concern to keep imaginative literature in the
lives of children. Their colleagues Owen Barfield and Cecil Harwood had a lifelong involvement with Anthoposophy, a movement founded by Rudolf Steiner (1861–1925) as an attempt to
overcome what was seen as a false dichotomy between scientific and "spiritual" truth. It is this
movement that is the basis for the worldwide dispersion of Waldorf/Steiner schools, which put
equal stress on scientific and imaginative modes of education. For more on Lewis's interaction
with anthroposophist friends see the entries on Owen Barfield and Cecil Harwood in Walter
Hooper, ed., *The Collected Letters of C. S. Lewis*, vol. 1, *1905–1931* (San Francisco: HarperSan-
Francisco, 2004), 979–82, 998–1000; and the material on The "Great War" Letters in Hooper,
ed., *Collected Letters*, vol. 3, 1596–1646, which include Lewis's written debate with Barfield

called "sub-creation": a recasting of the ultimate cosmic drama of creation, fall, redemption, and future hope in an imagined other world, such as Lewis's Narnia, or Tolkien's Middle Earth. As such, Lewis believed, fairy tales foster not only children's emotional and imaginative development, but their moral and religious sensibilities as well. In an era that tended strongly toward either behaviorist or psychoanalytic reductionism, Tolkien, Lewis, and their allies (including the Barfields, the Harwoods, and later members of the Inklings) worked hard to preserve this "third way" of reaching children—and adults who were once children. The enduring success of *The Lord of the Rings* and the *Chronicles of Narnia* suggests that they were not wrong.

Authoritative, Not Authoritarian

By 1942, Lewis had become a godfather twice more, to Owen Barfield's daughter Lucy (to whom he later dedicated *The Lion, the Witch, and the Wardrobe*) and to Sarah Neylan, the child of his former student, Mary Shelley Neylan.[15] "Congratulations on the birth of your daughter," he wrote to Mary Neylan a few months after she gave birth. "It makes the production of mere books seem rather silly, for at the very best they can never say or do any more than you put into them."[16] As we saw in an earlier chapter, most of Lewis's subsequent correspondence with Mary Neylan was centered on helping her to understand Christianity after she became a serious seeker.[17] But he obviously enjoyed letting his whimsical side come out in his letters to godchildren, which often sound like warm-up exercises for the children's stories he would eventually write.

To the six-year-old Sarah Neylan he wrote a letter in 1944, thanking her "for sending me the pictures of the Fairy King and Queen at tea (or is it breakfast?) in their palace, and all of the cats (what a lot of cats they have! And a separate table for them. How sensible!)." He also told her he was "getting to be quite good friends with an old Rabbit who lives in the Wood at Magdelen

---

about Anthroposophy in the late 1920s. After his conversion to Christianity in 1931, Lewis had more sympathy for his friends' anthroposophical leanings, though he insisted they still fell short of Christian orthodoxy. For a somewhat different analysis of the developmental importance of fairy tales (based on psychoanalytic theory) see Bruno Bettelheim, *The Uses of Enchantment: The Meaning and Importance of Fairy Tales* (New York: Random House, 1975).

15. Lewis's fourth godchild was Richard Francis Blake (b. 1945), the first child of Maureen Moore Blake and her husband Leonard Blake.

16. C. S. Lewis to Mary Neylan, March 21, 1939, Hooper, ed., *Collected Letters*, vol. 2, 254.

17. Mary Neylan asked Lewis to be her child's godfather after she professed faith in 1941. Lewis readily agreed, but still added "Whether I can be of any use to her (prayers apart) until she is grown up is v[ery] doubtful—I'm not much good with children." C. S. Lewis to Mary Neylan, April 1942, ibid., 517.

[College]. I pick leaves off the trees for him because he can't reach up to the branches . . . I wrote this about it:

> A funny old man had a habit
> Of giving a leaf to a rabbit
>   At first it was shy
>   But then by and by,
> It got rude and would stand up and grab it."[18]

However, Lewis had too much respect for the doctrine of sin to fall into the trap of romanticizing childhood. In the winter of 1939, he had a long conversation in his rooms at Oxford with Mary Neylan, at her request, which touched on her concerns as a new mother about parenting. (Janie Moore's recorded comment to Lewis about this meeting was: "That fool of a woman wanted you, of all people, to tell her how to bring up a baby."[19]) "You remember [Mrs. Neylan]," he wrote to Warren Lewis, away in France at the start of World War II:

> She teaches at Dartington Hall, co-educational, no punishments, and no obedience expected unless the *reason* for the order can be made clear to the child. She now has a child of her own and finds it all won't work, and what with that the general stress of things is just beginning to throw out a tentative feeler in the direction of Christianity.[20]

Lewis was clearly skeptical about the kind of "progressive" education practiced at Neylan's school (even though Janie Moore's daughter Maureen later considered applying to teach there, and Lewis arranged through Mary Neylan for her to visit Dartington). Some have even suggested that it was the model for Experiment House, the questionable school attended by Jill Pole and Eustace Scrubb in *The Silver Chair*, though as Alan Jacobs notes in *The Narnian*, rather too much has been made of this comparison.[21]

Yet here again Lewis was ironically prescient. The successors to the "wiseacres in child psychology" that he deplored in the 1930s had, by the 1960s, collected enough data to affirm that the optimal parenting style for the development of children's social *and* intellectual competence—regardless of the child's sex—combines emotional warmth, age-appropriate reasoning, and consistently enforced expectations. This has come to be known as "authoritative" parenting, and it is the style most apt to help children be self-confident and persistent in mastering intellectual and other challenges, while developing

---

18. C. S. Lewis to Sarah Neylan, July 16, 1944, ibid., 618–19.
19. C. S. Lewis to Warren Lewis, December 31, 1939, ibid., 315.
20. Ibid., 314 (emphasis original).
21. Alan Jacobs, *The Narnian: The Life and Imagination of C. S. Lewis* (San Francisco: HarperSanFrancisco: 2005), 259.

good social skills and expressing emotions in appropriate ways.[22] "Authorita-tive" parents and teachers are not "authoritarian"—valuing obedience as an end in itself, favoring forceful or even punitive measures to curb children's willfulness, or rejecting reason and compromise in favor of automatic adult authority.[23] Rather, they are secure about maintaining the standards they hold for their children, but model caring concern as well as confident, self-controlled behavior. They praise children for trying to meet expectations, and make judi-cious use of disapproval and punishment—both of which tend to work best when they come from adults who have also been warm and caring.

By contrast, "permissive" parents and teachers, of the sort Lewis decried at Dartington Hall, make few demands on children. Rather than seeing themselves as agents responsible for shaping children's attitudes and behaviors, they prefer to act as resources for children to use or not as they see fit. They let children regulate their own activities as much as possible, discourage deference to ex-ternal authority, and believe in using reason rather than punishment. In some cases, this style of childrearing can be so uninvolved that it verges on neglect. Permissively reared children, though superficially sociable, can be rebellious and defiant if their desires are not met. They tend to lack perseverance, even in the face of age-appropriate tasks, and are more easily drawn to delinquent activities than authoritatively reared children.

Pencil-Boxes and a "Rose Macaulay" Child

Lewis was clearly a fan of authoritative childrearing, though he would have little chance to practice it in a sustained way until Joy Davidman's sons came into his life in his mid-fifties. But from autumn of 1939 till fall of 1943, young

22. The most thorough longitudinal studies of parenting styles and their outcomes have been conducted under the leadership of University of California psychologist Diana Baumrind (b. 1927) who, intriguingly, moved in the same Jewish-Communist circles as Joy Davidman (b. 1915) as a young woman in New York City, and may well have crossed paths with the latter as a member of the American Communist Party in the mid-1940s. Baumrind remained a neo-Marxist through-out her life, but was also influenced as a young woman by the Catholic Worker movement. See in particular her monograph on "Current Patterns of Parental Authority," *Developmental Psychology Mongraphs* 4 (1971): 1–103; and her volume on *Child Maltreatment and Optimal Caregiving* (New York: Garland, 1995). For a discussion of the cross-cultural implications of this research, see Çiğdem Kağitçibaşi, *Family and Human Development Across Cultures: A View From the Other Side* (Mahwah NJ: Lawrence Erlbaum, 1996). See also Hedrike Vande Kempe, "Diana Blumberg Baumrind (1927–)" in *The Feminist Psychologist*, Newsletter of the Society for the Psychology of Women (Division 35 of the American Psychological Association), 24, no. 3 (Summer 1997): 8–9.

23. Children raised by authoritarian parents tend to do well in school, and not to engage in antisocial activities (such as vandalism or taking drugs). However, they also tend to be anxious and withdrawn, and to react poorly to frustration, either withdrawing in the face of challenges or becoming hostile.

girls—usually three at a time—were an off-and-on presence at The Kilns as evacuees from areas in danger of German bombing.[24] In late 1940, Lewis wrote to his colleague Sister Penelope that "my brother is not only safe from France, but, better still, back on the retired list and living at home: so what with that and a house full of really delightful refugee children (I am a bachelor and never appreciated children till the war brought them to me) I have very much to be thankful for."[25] In early 1942, he took pride in sending Dorothy L. Sayers some French prose—"not by me but by one of our evacuees—delightful creatures. I'd never lived with children before—oh that world of pencil-boxes! O *bel età dell-oro!*"[26]

What is intriguing is that, in his recorded relationships with these (mostly unnamed) girl children, Lewis again shows himself to be a better man than his theories. The first volume of his space trilogy, *Out of the Silent Planet*, had been published in 1938, and soon after refugee children arrived at The Kilns, he began to draft *Perelandra*, with its polemical defense of masculine and feminine archetypes. It was in late 1941 that he told Sister Penelope he had "got Ransom to Venus and through his first conversation with the 'Eve' of that world: a difficult chapter . . . This woman has got to combine characteristics that the Fall has put poles apart—she's got to be in some ways like a Pagan goddess and in other ways like the Blessed Virgin. But if one can get even a fraction of it into words it is worth doing."[27] Yet in his recorded dealings with the girls who moved in and out of The Kilns during the war, he was anything but a strict promoter of feminine archetypes.

The first children arrived in September of 1939, to a household on an eight-acre spread that included dogs, cats, chickens, and a pond with a pair of swans. Lewis wrote to his brother that the children seemed "nice, unaffected creatures and all most flatteringly delighted with their new surroundings. They're fond of animals which is a good thing (for them as well as for us)."[28] A week later, Oxford had an early-morning air raid warning, and the children were herded to an underground shelter. "I must say they all behaved well, and though v[ery] hungry and thirsty before the all-clear went, we quite enjoyed the most perfect late summer morning I have ever seen":

> Another thing which w[oul]d amuse you is the daily [swim] . . . which is in two shifts because they have not enough bathing suits to go around, and each

24. All the evacuees accepted by Janie Moore were girls, though the precise reason for this is unclear. She may have felt they would be easier to manage than boys and/or that that they could help with indoor tasks. See Hooper, ed., *Collected Letters*, vol. 2, 270, note 101.

25. C. S. Lewis to Sister Penelope, CSVM, October 24, 1940, ibid., 451.

26. Italian: "Oh that happy golden age!" C. S. Lewis to Dorothy L. Sayers, April 1942, ibid., 515.

27. C. S. Lewis to Sister Penelope, CSMV, November 19, 1941, ibid., 496.

28. C. S. Lewis to Warren Lewis, September 2, 1939, ibid., 270.

shift interminable because of the insatiable appetite of children . . . We had me
bawling "Time to come out" and a head disappearing and then emerging ten
yards further away to say "What?" and then twenty yards further away still to
say "I can't hear what you say."[29]

Due to his brother's military call-up, and Janie Moore's resentment of his
attendance at "blood-feasts" (her term for Holy Communion), it was Jack
Lewis who took the girls to church, apparently quite happily. "But Lord!" he
wrote to his brother, "what a thing youth is. Last Sunday when I came from
church—the children had been but gone out after the sermon—they met me
on the avenue, jumping with joy, to tell me 'War has been declared'—and one
added 'Perhaps there'll be [another] air raid *tonight*!!'"[30]

These girls were clearly not shrinking violets, and it is obvious that Lewis
reveled in their high spirits. But, he wrote to his brother, "the nicest . . . is a
Rose Macaulay child—pure boy in everything but anatomy, [and] a reader of
[boys' stories]. Quite a new phenomenon to me."[31] With his reference to a "Rose
Macaulay child," Lewis had in mind one of his own peers. Rose Macaulay
(1881–1958) was a Somerville College graduate and a novelist, several of whose
books Lewis had read. The daughter of a distinguished family of scholars, she
grew up an unapologetic tomboy and dreamed of joining the Royal Navy. As
it turned out, she spent World War I in activities just as challenging, first as a
nurse then as a civil servant in the war office's propaganda department. After
the war she added journalism and literary criticism to her accomplishments.
The girl who was her namesake might have become Lewis's favorite, had
she not been taken home within three weeks of her arrival "by a peripatetic
lip-sticked mother who has changed her mind."[32] The other children, though
"nice" sometimes seemed to Lewis to be "poor modern creatures," unable to
dream up their own amusements. "The Rose Macaulay one was different," he
noted, "and usually 'missing' in the wood or on the pond."[33]

An Adolescent Admirer

The young woman who stayed longest at The Kilns was a shy but bright
teenager named June (also called Jill) Flewett, the daughter of a classics master at St. Paul's school in the London suburb of Hammersmith. Raised as a
Roman Catholic, she attended a convent school that was relocated to Oxford
when wartime bombing began in 1939. Twelve-year-old Jill was billeted in the

29. C. S. Lewis to Warren Lewis, September 10, 1939, ibid., 273.
30. Ibid.
31. Ibid.
32. C. S. Lewis to Warren Lewis, September 18, 1939, ibid., 276.
33. Ibid., 277.

Oxford home of three maiden sisters, where she remained through the spring of 1942. When they were unable to keep her after that, she looked for other housing, and was interviewed and accepted by Janie Moore, who had been billeting Sacred Heart Convent pupils since 1940. But before she could take up residence in the fall, her school returned to London and she continued her secondary education there, finishing in 1943 at the age of sixteen. Aiming for a career in the theater, she planned to audition for a place in the Royal Academy of Dramatic Art (R.A.D.A.).

Meanwhile Mrs. Moore, though famous for her prickly relations with the women staff of The Kilns, had somehow taken a shine to young Jill Flewett (and vice-versa) despite the difference in their ages and the brevity of their acquaintanceship. Knowing that she liked animals and country life, Janie Moore invited Jill to The Kilns for a two-week visit in the summer of 1943, just before her R.A.D.A. audition. As it turned out, she ended up staying almost two years.

Jill Flewett was clearly beyond the "pencil-box" stage. Moreover, given the exigencies of wartime and Janie Moore's declining health (at seventy-three, she had varicose veins and had to stay off her feet as much as possible), help was needed on the domestic front. The Kilns' gardener, a lugubrious Cotswold native by the name of Fred Paxford, had taken a job in a nearby munitions factory, and so could spare only a few hours a week to work at home. It was equally hard to get indoor domestic help, and complicated by the fact that Janie Moore's daughter Maureen had recently married and moved away from Oxford. In addition, Sacred Heart, which had supplied recent boarders to The Kilns, had moved back to London. Under Paxford's tutelage, Jill—like Britain's "Land Girls" of World War II—took charge of two dozen chickens, three rabbits, and a huge vegetable garden, as well as some indoor tasks.[34] She postponed going to R.A.D.A., and as a result had to reaudition before finally joining its program in January of 1945.

Apart from a fondness for animals and country living, what would have drawn a young woman to make such a sacrifice? Here, it seems, is where life began to imitate art. Before coming to The Kilns, Jill Flewett had no idea who lived there besides Mrs. Moore. But as a devout Catholic girl she had read and been impressed by some of C. S. Lewis's fiction and apologetic writings. When she arrived at The Kilns, she discovered that its other two residents were a

34. The Women's Land Army (WLA) was a British civilian organization that, during both World Wars, recruited women to take the place of male agricultural workers who had been drafted for military service. Though the idea was initially resisted by the male farmers in whose homes they were to be billeted, there were over a quarter of a million Land Girls (as they were called) working by 1917. With farming more mechanized by the start of World War II, fewer manual farm laborers were needed, but the Land Army still numbered about eighty thousand, and was even assigned a Royal Patron to give it added patriotic luster. The WLA continued through much of the postwar food-rationing period, disbanding only in 1950.

pair of stout middle-aged men, one of which was referred to as Mrs. Moore's "son." Some time later, she learned not only that "Jack" was a fictive son, but also that he was C. S. Lewis! "Here was this man," she wrote many years later, "whom I'd been chatting away to quite freely and I suddenly realized that he was somebody who could see into my inner soul . . . Of course I fell madly in love with him. It was a tremendous crush, and I would have lain down and he could have walked all over me for the next two years. Every smile, every kind word was like daylight, like the summer."[35]

There is no evidence that Lewis took unfair advantage of this hero-worship—or even knew the extent of its force in young Jill's life. But he was later to experience a coincidence neither of them would have predicted. While she was in residence at The Kilns, Lewis published his essay on "Psychoanalysis and Literary Criticism," with its critique of Freudian reductionism. Eight years later, in 1950, Jill Flewett married a grandson of Sigmund Freud—who (more coincidence) had gone to Dartington Hall as a child![36] In the meantime, Lewis's first recorded interaction with her was an intellectual one. Jill's father was a classics teacher who had coedited a book of Latin poetry, a copy of which was sent to Lewis when Jill went back to London in September of 1943 to do her R.A.D.A. audition. He wrote to thank her and discussed at length some points about scanning Latin poetry. He added that at The Kilns "we all try to hope you'll pass your audition, but we don't always succeed," and went on to report on the foibles of the household pets, affirming that she was sorely missed by everyone there, four-footed and otherwise.[37]

In the event, Jill passed her audition, but chose to delay her admission to R.A.D.A. in order to return to The Kilns, supposedly just till the spring of 1944. "We are happy here at the moment," Lewis wrote to Sister Penelope that winter, "because a perfectly saintly girl is staying and helping Jane till May."[38] But when May came around, Jill was loathe to leave. "I suppose I felt

35. As quoted in Hooper, ed., *Collected Letters*, vol. 2, 1034.

36. Clement Freud, a writer, met June Flewett (who later took the stage name Jill Raymond) in 1950 through mutual theater connections. He was born in Berlin in 1924, but came to England as a refugee from the Nazis with his grandfather and other family members in 1933. (Sigmund Freud had famously remarked as he left Germany that, in an earlier era, the Nazis "would have burned me; now they are content to burn my books.") Clement and June/Jill married in London in September of 1950, with Warren Lewis in attendance, Jack being unable to come. Lewis's later letters, and his brother's diaries, show that both of them were on friendly terms with the couple for many years thereafter. Clement Freud was ambivalent about his grandfather's fame and once remarked that he was not sure he'd met anyone whose life had been improved by psychotherapy. In 1973, he entered parliament as MP for the Isle of Ely. He was knighted in 1987, his wife thereby becoming Lady (Jill) Freud, and he became Rector of St. Andrews University in 2003. Jill Freud was modestly successful as a young stage and screen actress, and has been more so as the director of a summer theater company in Southwold since the 1980s.

37. C. S. Lewis to Jill Flewett, September 13, 1943, Hooper, ed., *Collected Letters*, vol. 2, 589–90.

38. C. S. Lewis to Sister Penelope, CSMV, February 19, 1944, ibid., 603.

they couldn't manage without me," she wrote almost half a century later.
"Also, I knew that the burden would fall on Jack as he was already under
strain with the demands of his work at Magdalen, the [radio] broadcasts and
his own writing, while looking after [Janie Moore] as much as he could."[39]
Yet despite the obvious advantage of her presence for his own work, in September of 1944 Lewis wrote to Jill's mother (with whom he had a cordial
relationship, in part because of the off-ration eggs Janie Moore was able to
send the Flewetts during the war) urging her to invoke parental authority to
bring Jill (or June, as she was often called at The Kilns) home and begin her
studies at R.A.D.A.:

> Every argument which my mind brings against this conclusion I regard as a
> temptation—a keen temptation, because when June goes the only bright spot
> in our [domestic] prospect goes with her. But putting ourselves out of it, I think
> she ought to go. From the point of view of her career she is wasting her time by
> staying: she is not getting chances of making friends and I think she is working
> too hard. I have told her that this is my view; and since, in talking to June it is
> no use to appeal to selfish motives . . . I told her she had a duty to you and her
> father in the matter. June's own view is simply and definitely that she will not
> leave here of her own free will: only if she is made to! The decision obviously
> rests with you and Mr. Flewett.[40]

Aside from confirming Lewis's support of authoritative parenting (and
surrogate parenting) his letter shows that this young woman was greatly appreciated at The Kilns. Indeed, it has been suggested that Jill Flewett was
Lewis's model for the character of young Lucy when he later began writing
the *Chronicles of Narnia*. But in the end, she did leave to redo her R.A.D.A.
audition in January of 1945, and Janie Moore avowed that she didn't "know
how she could have come through this time at all without June."[41] (In addition to her varicose veins, she had suffered a minor stroke in 1944.) Warren
Lewis wrote in his diary the day before she left that "our dear, delightful June
Flewett leaves us tomorrow . . . She is not yet eighteen, but I have met no one
of any age further advanced in the Christian way of life . . . from a personal
selfish point of view I shall feel the loss of June very keenly: for in addition to
her other virtues, she is a clever girl, and with her gone, it means that when
J[ack] is away, there is no one to talk to in the house."[42] Likewise, Jack Lewis
wrote to Jill/June's mother:

39. Jill Freud to Walter Hooper, January 27, 2003, Hooper, ed., *Collected Letters*, vol. 2,
622.
40. C. S. Lewis to Winifred Flewett, September 5, 1944, ibid., 623.
41. Ibid., 624.
42. Warren H. Lewis, *Brothers and Friends: The Diaries of Major Warren Hamilton Lewis*,
edited by Clyde S. Kilby and Marjorie L. Meads (San Francisco: Harper & Row, 1982), 180–81.

I have never really met anything like her unselfishness and patience and kindness and shall feel deeply in her debt as long as I live . . .Tell June that the Hens were asking for her first thing this morning: that Warnie is even more depressed than usual: and that the cats, under this shared calamity, sank their common differences and slept, mutually embracing, in the same box . . . We shall all be on tenterhooks till we hear the result of her exam.[43]

After passing her second audition, Jill settled in at R.A.D.A., with her tuition and living expenses paid for by Lewis. This was not a novel action on his part: since 1941 he had been putting two-thirds of his royalties into a tax-free charitable trust, from which he provided money to various people—including students—who were in need of it. His support of Jill Flewett reflected his recognition of her ability and gratitude for her work at The Kilns during the domestic shortages of the war. Moreover, the fact that she got along well with Mrs. Moore had given the Lewis brothers an almost two-year sabbatical from the "senseless wranglings, lyings, back-bitings, follies and scares" that Jack Lewis later described as Janie Moore's usual style of relating to female staff at The Kilns.[44]

Jill Flewett confirmed Lewis's judgment of her by completing the R.A.D.A. program with a double distinction, and it seems that members of the Lewis household saw her perform even as a student.[45] After finishing, she went on to a stage and movie (and eventually television) career. The Lewis brothers followed her progress with enthusiasm, seeing her in stage productions and even in a movie when it came to Oxford. Jack Lewis, the self-styled intellectual and cultural "dinosaur," made no attempt to steer Jill Flewett away from either modern drama or the celluloid medium.[46] And, as with Mary Neylan, there is not the slightest indication that he thought she should choose between motherhood and her career, which she continued through the raising of four children.[47]

Warren Lewis stated more than once in his diaries that he considered Janie Moore to be an intellectual Philistine with whom he could not have a rational conversation.

43. C. S. Lewis to Winifred Flewett, January 4, 1945, Hooper, ed., *Collected Letters*, vol. 2, 636, 637.

44. C. S. Lewis to Mary Van Deusen, April 18, 1951, Hooper, ed., *Collected Letters*, vol. 3, 108.

45. See Lewis's letter to Jill Flewett of September 10, 1946, Hooper, ed., *Collected letters*, vol. 2, 739.

46. See, for example, Lewis's letter to June Flewett of September 23, 1947, ibid., 805. Lewis had, in fact, seen the Walt Disney first full-length cartoon film, *Snow White and the Seven Dwarfs*, in 1937, and while he grumbled about some if its "vulgar" artistic effects, he also affirmed that "all the terrifying bits were good, and the animals really most moving: and the use of shadows (of dwarfs and vultures) was real genius. What might not have come of it if this man [i.e., Walt Disney] had been educated—or even brought up in a decent society?" Lewis to A.K. Hamilton Jenkin, January 11, 1939, ibid., 242.

47. Lewis's letters to Jill Flewett in this period mainly speak of his welcoming "a Freud descent on The Kilns," indicating that he enjoyed several visits from her and her family (cf. C. S. Lewis to Jill Freud, March 18, 1961, Hooper, ed., *Collected Letters*, vol. 3, 1229).

Moving Closer to Parenthood

A contemporary novelist from another culture has aptly noted that "children aren't coloring books. You don't get to fill them in with your favorite colors."[48] If Lewis's accounts and those of others are accurate, in his mentorship of both girls and boys—godchildren, casual guests, or wartime evacuees—he never tried to "fill them in with favorite colors." While endorsing authoritative parenting, as well as children's intellectual, imaginative, and moral formation, he consistently treated them as individuals, rather than as masculine or feminine caricatures. Even as he was defending gender archetypes and gender hierarchy in *Perelandra* and *That Hideous Strength*, Lewis was drawn to youngsters who behaved otherwise, like the "Rose Macaulay child" who came to The Kilns in the early days of the war, and the hardworking, country-loving Jill Flewett who lived there toward its end.

How are we to make sense of this discrepancy? Dorothy L. Sayers attributed Lewis's "shocking nonsense about women and marriage" not to his "bad theology," but to the fact that he was "a rather frightened bachelor."[49] I suggested in previous chapters that his belief about myths as prolegomena to the gospel led Lewis to borrow too much from them in his account of "mere" Christianity, including their ideas about gender archetypes. And, as we have seen, he was not alone in these beliefs. Social scientists, whose number-crunching habits Lewis frequently disparaged, continued for many decades to assert some kind of deep "essence" of masculinity and femininity, even when they admitted that this dichotomy was not borne out empirically: they simply assumed that they needed to develop better, or more subtle, measures to get at the "real thing."[50]

It is also possible that, like many others of his time, Lewis, on some level, had a yearning for "normalcy" after the social, political, and economic upheavals of two world wars. One historian of psychology has noted that "invoking certainty [about gender norms] can appear to arrest the flux of an uncertain reality."[51] And it is certainly the case that in both Britain and America, the decades following World War II were characterized by a sharp return to the doctrine of separate spheres for women and men. The irony is that, in the midst of this societal about-face, Lewis married a feisty, intellectually accomplished woman who refused to fit within such coloring-book outlines. Joy Davidman's post-conversion writings—built now on a biblical rather than a Marx-

---

48. Khaled Hosseini, *The Kite Runner* (New York: Riverhead Books, 2003), 21.

49. Barbara Reynolds, ed., *The Letters of Dorothy L. Sayers*, vol. 3, *1944–1950* (Cambridge: The Dorothy L. Sayers Society & Carole Green, 1998), 375.

50. For a historical overview of social scientists' attempts to measure "masculinity" and "femininity" from the late nineteenth century until after the second wave of feminism, see Jill G. Morawski, "The Measurement of Masculinity and Femininity: Engendering Categorical Realities," *Journal of Personality* 53 (June 1985): 196–223.

51. Ibid., 206.

ist foundation—even anticipated some of the concerns of the second wave of feminism that was to burst forth shortly after she died.[52] And the record of Lewis's relationship with her sons suggests that he treated them first and foremost as individuals as well.

Lewis's first personal encounter with Joy Davidman had occurred in the latter half of 1952, when she came on her own to England, in part to finish her book on the Ten Commandments, which she dedicated to Lewis on its publication. Lewis, who had corresponded with Joy (as he did with many of his fans), read the manuscript of *Smoke on the Mountain* during her visit, and later wrote a glowing foreword to its British edition. In fact, Joy was a guest at The Kilns in December of 1952 when she received the fateful letter from Bill Gresham, stating that he had fallen in love with her cousin and wanted a divorce. Joy confided its contents to Lewis, and later recorded that "he strongly advised me to divorce Bill."[53] Ten months later, the divorce now in process, she returned to England with her sons David, nine and a half years old, and Douglas, just turned eight. Very opposite in temperament and interests, the two boys reacted quite differently to this upheaval in their lives. Douglas saw it as something of an adventure, but David more as a traumatic exile from America and from his formerly intact family. Furthermore, though the product of a secular Jewish family on his mother's side (and nominal Episcopalianism on his father's), he had also been unsettled by his mother's embrace of Christianity, seeing it as a betrayal—rather than a completion—of her Jewish roots.

In November of 1953, Joy settled in London, in a neighborhood that was something of a writers' colony. With somewhat irregular financial support from Bill Gresham, she sent her sons as boarders to Dane Court School in nearby Surrey, determined that they would get the best English schooling she could afford. She continued to work on her own fiction and nonfiction projects, as well as doing some freelance articles and editing, including some for each of the Lewis brothers. But making ends meet was a struggle, despite some added help from her parents back in New York. Not surprisingly, given his record of helping other young people with educational expenses—including Jill Flewett

---

52. See especially Joy Davidman, *Smoke on the Mountain: The Ten Commandments in Terms of Today* (London: Hodder and Stoughton, 1955), chap. 7.

53. Joy Davidman to Chad and Eva Walsh, December 3, 1956, as quoted in Lyle W. Dorsett, *A Love Observed: Joy Davidman's Life and Marriage to C. S. Lewis* (Wheaton: Harold Shaw, 1998), 91. There is indirect evidence, however, that Lewis was more ambivalent, knowing the belief that he and Davidman shared on the ethic of lifelong marriage. In a 1953 letter to an American correspondent whose husband was dying, he noted that she was learning, in the process, to be more loving than loved, and added: "God knows, many wives have had to learn it by a path harder than bereavement: having to love unfaithful, drunken, or childish husbands. And have succeeded too: as God succeeds in loving us." C. S. Lewis to Elinor Sandeman, December 22, 1953, in Hooper, ed., *Collected Letters*, vol. 3, 393. But Lewis was also aware that Joy Davidman had long tried to maintain her marriage to an "unfaithful, drunken [and] childish husband," and that her "success" was moot when Bill Gresham decided unilaterally to divorce her.

and some of his own godchildren—Lewis began to contribute to David and Douglas Gresham's schooling shortly after their arrival in England. That he began this in the spring of 1954, just after he had met the boys around Christmas of 1953, is no doubt significant.

It is not clear why Joy Davidman and her sons got invited to The Kilns for that early winter visit, and after it was over Joy admitted to her estranged husband that she "shouldn't dream of visiting Jack too often—we're much too exhausting an experience for that quiet bachelor household."[54] But even without the mediation of Janie Moore (who had died in 1951) the Lewis brothers took the visit in stride and seemed increasingly to enjoy the youngsters. "We have had an American lady staying in the house with her two sons aged 9½ and 8," Jack Lewis wrote to Ruth Pitter at the time:

> I now know what we celibates are shielded from. I will never laugh at parents again. Not that the boys weren't a delight: but a delight like surf-bathing which leaves one breathless and aching. The energy, the *tempo* is what kills. I have now perceived (what I always suspected from memories of our childhood) that the way to a child's heart is simple: treat them with seriousness & ordinary civility they ask no more. What they can't stand (quite rightly) is the common adult assumption that everything they say should be twisted into a kind of [condescending] jocularity.[55]

Children had not been housed at The Kilns since the end of World War II, but in the meantime Lewis had begun to write the *Chronicles of Narnia*, in which this attitude to children is simply assumed. By the end of the visit, he had lent the typescript of *The Horse and His Boy* to the Gresham children (who had read previous volumes in the series) and promised to dedicate it to them when it was published.[56] He and his brother also taught David how to play chess, enthused over Douglas's wood-chopping skills, and took the boys and their mother on a four-mile hike, as well as a climb to the top of Magdalen tower. "[The children] said as soon as they got back to the ground, 'Let's do it again!'" Lewis wrote to an American pen friend. "Without being the least

54. Joy Davidman to William L. Gresham, December 22, 1953, as quoted in Dorsett, *A Love Observed*, 95.

55. C. S. Lewis to Ruth Pitter, December 21, 1953, Hooper, ed., *Collected Letters*, vol. 3, 390. One is reminded here of Lewis's comment to Dorothy L. Sayers about a year later, to the effect that he had only "dimly perceived that the old-fashioned way of talking to young women . . . was v[ery] like an adult way of talking to young boys . . . It explains not only why some young women grew up vapid but also why other grew up (if we may coin the word) *viricidal*" (August 5, 1955, ibid., 639).

56. *The Horse and His Boy* was the fifth of the *Narnia* chronicles to be published. Previous volumes had been dedicated to the children of Lewis's English colleagues, including one of his godchildren. The sixth volume was dedicated to a large family of American children (the Kilmers) who, with their parents, were regular correspondents with Lewis. The final volume, *The Last Battle*, for some unknown reason contains no dedication.

priggish, they struck us as being amazingly adult by our standards and one could talk to them as one would to 'grown-ups'—though the next minute they would be wrestling like puppies on the sitting room floor."[57] And to another (married) correspondent he wrote: "Whew! Lovely creatures—couldn't meet nicer children—but the pace! I realize I have never appreciated you married people enough and never dreamed of the calm wh[ich] descends on the house when the little cyclones have gone to bed and all the grown-ups fling themselves into chairs and the silence of exhaustion."[58]

About a year and a half later, Lewis found a semi-detached house suitable for Joy and her sons in Headington, within walking distance of The Kilns. He encouraged them to move there from London and undertook to pay the rent. "Precisely what kind of relationship Jack and Joy had at this time is debatable," writes Joy's biographer Lyle Dorsett:

> A number of Lewis's friends were, and still are, confident that Joy forced herself on Lewis, hounded him continually, and in essence became a nuisance. The only reason he befriended her, some say, was pity for her and the boys . . . Joy could not, however, have baited the strong-willed Lewis into walking to her house every day for a visit. Brother Warnie noted in his diary that once Joy moved to Headington "she and J[ack] began to see each other every day. It was now obvious what was going to happen . . . [Jack was] in her house every day, often stopping until eleven at night."[59]

Nor is it likely that Lewis the scholar—who had assumed his new chair at Cambridge in January of 1955—would have spent so much time and energy on Joy's sons, once they moved to Oxford, had he not become quite attached to them. Moreover, he understood their differences in temperament and talent and responded accordingly. David, the moody intellectual, loved to haunt Oxford's famous Blackwell's bookshop; Lewis not only took him there, but paid his book bills. He tutored David in Latin, and when he wanted to begin Greek, bought him a grammar and a dictionary. Douglas, the outdoorsman, got a soccer ball when he yearned for one. Both children swam in the quarry pond at The Kilns, and eventually Lewis bought them a horse and stabled it behind the house. By the time he undertook his "marriage of convenience" to their mother, Lyle Dorsett concludes, "Lewis was not only in love with Joy Davidman, but loved David and Douglas as well."

> Jack paid for the boys' schooling, clothing and gifts . . . He felt protective of them; he felt responsible for their education and upbringing. Indeed, he was

57. C. S. Lewis to Vera Gebbert, December 23, 1953, Hooper, ed., *Collected Letters*, vol. 3, 394.

58. C. S. Lewis to Nell Berners-Price, December 26, 1953, ibid., 395.

59. Dorsett, *A Love Observed*, 112, 113.

beginning to feel like their father. He most certainly empathized with them regarding their school experience. Neither David nor Douglas liked Dane Court, and Jack's heart ached for them because he could recall the misery he felt as a student at Malvern.[60]

A Wounded Healer

In all this, Lewis was careful not to interfere in the boys' (albeit long-distance) relationship with their father back in America. His first known correspondence with Bill Gresham is a letter thanking the latter for a sympathetic note sent to Lewis when he learned, late in 1956, that his former wife had cancer. "The boys are of course with me," Lewis wrote, "and I'm learning a lot."

> They're a nice pair and easy to get on with—if only they got on better with one another, but of course they are v[ery] different types and have no tastes or interests in common. According to school reports both have brains (David more) and are both disinclined to work. (Who isn't)? . . . I'd write more and better [but] the Christmas period with all domestic help away for its holidays, the boys to look after, Warnie ill upstairs and a daily visit to poor Joy, and dog & cat & geese & hens, and eternal, merciless letter-writing, have left me tired—almost like front-line tiredness.[61]

Lewis's reference to his brother's "illness" requires some explanation. Warren Lewis was a binge drinker—a fact that his brother referred to only indirectly in most of his letters. ("Warnie's illness," or "My brother has had one of his turns," is how he might put it to those in the know.) Indeed, Major Lewis had been pressured to retire from the military at the young age of thirty-seven due to his unpredictable relationship with alcohol, and he returned only briefly to active duty at the start of World War II. So despite his later success as a popular historian of the seventeenth century—and his assistance to Jack as his secretary/typist—Warnie was something of a loose cannon because of his alcoholism. Indeed, in a moment of rare candor, Lewis once asked his friend George Sayer if he should "show his teeth" to his brother regarding his drinking. "There is nothing I should dislike more, but it might work," he added. "The knowledge that he causes vast expense and upsets the entire household influences him not at all."[62]

60. Ibid., 122, 121.
61. C. S. Lewis to William Gresham, December 30, 1956, Hooper, ed., *Collected Letters*, vol. 3, 820–21.
62. George Sayer, *Jack: C. S. Lewis and His Times* (San Francisco: Harper and Row, 1988), 201. In spite of this, the Lewis brothers were clearly devoted to one another: Jill (Flewett) Freud recalled that the only time she ever heard Jack Lewis raise his voice to Janie Moore was when she once said something critical of his brother. This may go some way toward explaining why Lewis was so circumspect about his brother's problem, quietly sheltering him at The Kilns and

Lewis's experience of his brother's alcoholism—as well as memories of the trauma caused by his own mother's death from cancer—may help explain why his next correspondence with Bill Gresham, in the spring of 1957, had such a different tone. Gresham had written to say that, in the event of Joy's death, the boys were to return to America to live with him—and being their biological father, he may have had the legal leverage to make that happen. Joy, still languishing in the hospital after operations on her leg and breast, was devastated by this proposal, but far too ill to challenge it herself. So on the same day, Jack Lewis wrote two separate letters to Bill Gresham: one at Joy's request, and the other to express his own feelings. On Joy's behalf, he wrote,

> You have tortured one who is already on the rack; heaped extra weights on one who is being pressed to death. There is nothing she dreads so much as a return of the boys to your charge . . . Their return to the U.S.A. when their education is finished is of course quite a different matter. Now, bitterly against their will, coming on top of the most appalling tragedy that can happen to childhood (I went through it and know), tearing them away from all that has already become familiar and shattering all sense of security that remains to them, it would be disastrous. If you realized the cruelty of what you were proposing to do, I am sure you would not do it.[63]

On his own behalf, Lewis acknowledged to Gresham that he could not "judge between your account and Joy's account of your married life." But, he added, that was not what mattered now. "What you and I have to think of is the happiness of the boys."

> I don't remember that Joy ever doubted your *intention* to support them: she doubted, and doubts, your *power* to do so . . . The boys remember you as a man who fired rifles thro' ceilings to relieve his temper, broke up chairs, wept in public, and broke a bottle over Douglas's head. David knew, and resented,

---

at Magdalen College, and gently nudging him into Oxford's Acland nursing home when he needed more help to dry out. In the years after the war, Warren Lewis became more evasive, often escaping to Ireland for longer and longer binges, and ending up in nursing home care there. This caused added stress to his brother in the years of Janie Moore's decline, and later during Joy Davidman's. Indeed, Warren Lewis did not even attend his own brother's funeral in 1963 because he was in a drunken stupor that day. George Sayer reports that from about 1949 on, Jack "spoke freely to me and to other friends about Warren's alcoholism. . . . He was devoted to his brother and deeply worried about his future. Yet, except through prayer, he was powerless to help" (Sayer, *Jack*, 201). Jack did try, without success, to get Warnie to join (the then-novel) Alcoholics Anonymous movement. And in her few years at The Kilns, Joy Davidman—drawing on the experience of her first marriage to the hard-drinking Bill Gresham—helped Warren Lewis to curtail his drinking binges, which renewed in force after her death and during his brother's decline. Warnie viewed Joy Davidman with great affection and dedicated to her one of his history books that she helped edit.

63. C. S. Lewis to William Gresham, April 6, 1957, Hooper, ed., *Collected Letters*, vol. 3, 844–45.

the fact that you were living with your present wife while still married to his mother . . .

Whose happiness w[oul]d you foster by forcing them back to you now? Not your own. The most patient man on earth w[oul]dn't be happy with two resentful boys who regard themselves as prisoners in his house. Not your [present] wife! You bring her two extra mouths to feed, both mouths belonging to boys who do not like her. And certainly not the boys!

Wait, Bill, *wait*. Not now. A bone that breaks in a second takes long to heal. The relation between you and your sons has been broken. Give it time to mend. Forcible surgery (without anaesthetics) such as you are proposing is not the way.[64]

Lewis, in these letters, made a point of assuring Gresham that his two sons had "never heard a word against you from me." Even so, he added, "Douglas burst into tears on hearing your plans," and while "you may suspect that a letter you will get from David was 'inspired' by Joy and me, [i]n reality it was expurgated, i.e. the letter he meant to send was much stronger, and Joy made him tone it down."[65] Then—departing from his usual embrace of Christian self-sacrifice—Lewis showed his teeth to the boys' father:

If you do not relent, I shall of course be obliged to place every legal obstacle in your way. Joy has, legally, a case. Her (documented) desire for naturalization . . . and the boys' horror of going back, will be strong points. What is certain is that a good deal of your money and mine will go into the lawyers' hands. You have a chance to soothe, instead of aggravating, the miseries of a woman you once loved. You have a chance of recovering at some future date, instead of alienating forever, the love and respect of your children. For God's sake take it and yield to the deep wishes of everyone concerned except yourself.[66]

Parenting without a Partner

In the end, Bill Gresham yielded to everyone else's wishes. A protracted legal battle was avoided, and his sons stayed in England. Joy Davidman entered her

---

64. C. S. Lewis to William Gresham, April 6, 1957, ibid., 843–44 (emphasis original). Douglas Gresham's recorded memories of his father's alcoholic rages were even more dramatic, and he credited his love of the outdoors partly to his fear of being in the house with his father during his early life in upstate New York: "When Dad drank . . . he would roar around the house, uncontrollable and at times dangerously violent. Once he broke a bottle over my head; he smashed to matchwood a good guitar when he repeatedly failed to master a difficult run. I can remember porch chairs being reduced to small pieces against the pillars of the front of the house. For me, the house became slowly but inevitably a place of tension . . . [but] anywhere on the farm, in the woods, or down at the creek was safe" (Douglas Gresham, *Lenten Lands* [New York: MacMillan, 1988], 5–6).

65. C. S. Lewis to William Gresham, April 6, 1957, Hooper, ed., *Collected Letters*, vol. 3, 845.

66. Ibid.

remarkable two-year recovery period, during which Lewis's letters are sprinkled with occasional comments on the boys' development. "The younger stepson is an outdoor, cheerful boy," Lewis wrote to an American acquaintance the summer of 1957. "Everyone's friend, just the right amount of mischief, and certain to fall on his feet anywhere."

> The elder is our problem child . . . lots of brains, but inclined to use them in every subject except his school work (tries to teach himself Hebrew and neglects his Latin!), a bad mixer, can be spiteful and feels his mother's situation (poor little devil—I was thro' all that at about his age) dreadfully. He'll either be a great scholar or a total waster.[67]

Blunt as this assessment may sound, Lewis was sensitive to the dreams and struggles of his problem teenager. (He was later to write to his American friend Chad Walsh that "adolescence is a pretty horrid thing whatever the sex, age or nationality of the patients!"[68]) Unhappy at Dane Court, David was allowed to come back to Oxford and become a day student at Magdalen College School in the fall of 1957. Passionate about his Jewish heritage, he got private lessons in Hebrew from a colleague of Lewis's who worked at Oxford University Press. Later, he was able to transfer to a Jewish prep school near London when another of Lewis's colleagues recommended the move.[69] He eventually passed O- and A-level exams in Hebrew, adding Yiddish to his language studies along the way. Meanwhile, his brother Douglas—underachieving and equally unhappy at Dane Court—was transferred to a small school in Wales in the spring of 1960, where he did so much better that he became head prefect there.

By the end of 1959, Joy's cancer had returned, but it seemed to be spreading only slowly, so plans were made for her former husband to make a trip to England to see his sons the following summer. But in the meantime, the cancer became more aggressive, and Joy abruptly reentered hospital about two months before Bill Gresham's scheduled arrival. Lewis then had to inform him that his ex-wife died on July 13, 1960. "This need involve no change in your plans," he added, "but I thought you should arrive knowing it."[70] The visit did take place, with the result that Gresham, seeing his sons doing well in Lewis's care, was once again willing to have them remain in England.[71]

67. C. S. Lewis to Mrs. Johnson, July 5, 1957, ibid., 867.
68. C. S. Lewis to Chad Walsh, October 1961, ibid., 1289.
69. See Lewis's letter to Cecil Roth, March 20, 1962, ibid., 1325.
70. C. S. Lewis to William Gresham, July 15, 1960, ibid., 1170.
71. In September 1962 Bill Gresham, going blind and suffering from cancer, checked himself into a low-cost hotel in New York City and died from an overdose of sleeping pills. Informed of his suicide by Gresham's third wife, Lewis was the one who broke the news to his stepsons. David Gresham later went to New York to study Judaism between 1963 and 1966 (still supported financially by Lewis), but his return to the US does not seem to have been motivated by any desire to reconnect with his father's family.

Throughout the period of his grief over Joy's death, as Lewis jotted down the thoughts that would be published as *A Grief Observed*, both boys were in residence at The Kilns.[72] Although he declared in that volume that it was almost impossible to talk to them about their mother,[73] Lewis's letters from that time show him taking great comfort especially from Douglas Gresham's presence. Less than six weeks after Joy's death, he wrote to a former student, thanking her for her enthusiastic reception of his novel *Till We Have Faces*. And, alluding to the fact that the *Narnia* series was now complete, he added: "My small stepson entirely agrees with your children about the present wicked misdirection of my talents, and asks 'When are you going to stop writing all that bilge and write interesting books again?'"[74]

The same week, he wrote to his friend Arthur Greeves about Joy's death, adding that "W[arnie] is away on his Irish holiday and has, as usual, drunk himself into hospital. Douglas—the younger boy—is, as always, an absolute brick, and a very bright spot in my life."[75] Less than two weeks later, Douglas was reported to be reading the manuscript of a new children's book by Lewis's friend Roger Lancelyn Green.[76] "My youngest stepson is the greatest comfort to me," he wrote to an American pen friend around the same time.[77] Though an indifferent student, Douglas (and his stepfather) were determined that he would pass his O-level exams in order to go on to agricultural college, so he was later sent to a small, intensive prep school in Surrey. He eventually did do a year at agricultural college, then got practical experience on a farm in Somerset, where he met his wife, an Australian nurse who was a niece of the farm's owner.[78]

72. By September of 1960, both boys were day students at Magdalen College School.

73. "I cannot talk to the children about her," Lewis wrote in *A Grief Observed*. "The moment I try, there appears on their faces neither grief, nor love, nor fear, nor pity, but the most fatal of all non-conductors, embarrassment. They look as if I were committing an indecency. They are longing for me to stop. I felt just the same after my own mother's death when my father mentioned her. I can't blame them. It's the way boys are . . . Or are the boys right? What would [Joy] herself think of this terrible little notebook to which I come back and back? Are these jottings morbid? . . . But what am I to do? I must have a drug, and reading isn't a strong enough drug now. By writing it all down . . . I believe I get a little outside it. That's how I'd defend it to [Joy]. But ten to one she'd see a hole in the defence" (11–12). Douglas Gresham later wrote about this time that he "could not talk to Jack about Mother, for I knew that if I did, he would weep and so also would I, and although I now feel that this might have been good for both of us, then it would have been anathema for me to cry openly, for as an English schoolboy I found it difficult to show my emotions" (*Lenten Lands*, 133–34).

74. C. S. Lewis to Anne Scott, August 26, 1960, Hooper, ed., *Collected Letters*, vol. 3, 1181.

75. C. S. Lewis to Arthur Greeves, August 30, 1960, ibid., 1181–82.

76. See his letter to Roger Lancelyn Green, September 9, 1960, ibid., 1182.

77. C. S. Lewis to Mary Willis Shelburne, September 24, 1960, ibid., 1188.

78. Douglas Gresham and Meredith Conan-Davies married in 1967 and spent the next twenty-five years in Australia, having five children. They returned to live in Ireland in 1990.

Nor did Lewis lose touch with the young people who had been part of his life before his marriage. To his goddaughter Sarah Neylan, he sent a gift and a "hundred thousand congratulations" on the occasion of her marriage in November of 1960, though he added: "I couldn't come to the wedding, my dear. I haven't the pluck. Any wedding, for the reason you know, would turn me inside out now."[79] To Jill (Flewett) Freud and her husband, he wrote a Christmas note that same year, congratulating them on their respective successes in journalism and television. Jill, who had apparently added TV commercials to her acting jobs, elicited the wry comment that "Warnie and I are such old fogies now that neither of us is clear as to what a 'commercial' is; are you one of the people who interrupts the programme to explain that all sensible house-wives use FOAM, DAZ or whatnot?"[80] With his godson Laurence Harwood—now working for England's National Trust—Lewis had an extended correspondence in 1962, when Harwood helped him look for a farm where Douglas Gresham could gain some agricultural experience. "Thanks very much for all your pains," Lewis wrote to Harwood early in 1963. "You're more like a godfather (fairy type) than a godson."[81] Lewis's mentoring relationships with children, begun in the 1930s, were starting to come full circle.

Gliding Up to the Gate

Less than three years before his own death, Lewis wrote to an older American friend (who had just joined the somewhat troubled household of her daughter and son-in-law): "Probably the safe rule will be 'When in doubt what to do or say, do or say nothing.' I feel this very much with my stepsons. I so easily *meddle* and *gas*: when all the time what will really influence them, for good or for ill, is not anything I do or say but what I *am*. And this unfortunately one can't know and can't much alter, though God can."[82]

Lewis was sixty-two at the time, and his health was in decline: he had prostate trouble that upset the functioning of his kidneys, while the resulting kidney trouble (and doctors' concerns about his heart) precluded an operation that could correct his prostate. "I live on a no-protein diet, wear a catheter, sleep in a chair, and have to stay on the ground floor," he wrote to Roger Lancelyn Green in the fall of 1961. "But you needn't pity me too much. I am in no pain and I quite enjoy the hours of uninterrupted reading which I now get."[83] With intermittent help (between binges) from his brother, he kept

79. C. S. Lewis to Sarah Neylan, November 21, 1960, ibid., 1210.
80. C. S. Lewis to Jill Freud, December 22, 1960, ibid., 1218.
81. C. S. Lewis to Laurence Harwood, January 26, 1963, ibid., 1408.
82. C. S. Lewis to Mary Willis Shelburne, February 24, 1961, ibid., 1242–43 (emphasis original).
83. C. S. Lewis to Roger Lancelyn Green, September 6, 1961, ibid., 1282.

up his voluminous correspondence, and was able to edit some earlier essays for publication that winter. The now-teenage Douglas added energy to the household when he was home from school, indifferent to even the worst of weather as he skated on the pond with friends, wearing skates that had been Jack's during his own youth in Ireland.

Lewis's health improved somewhat, and he was able to resume his weekly commute to Cambridge in April of 1962. But within a year his heart problems had worsened, and in the summer of 1963 he experienced a heart attack and went into a coma during a routine visit to Oxford's Acland Nursing Home. An Anglican priest was brought in to give him the rite of extreme unction— only to be surprised an hour later when Lewis abruptly came out of his coma and asked for some tea. Though he was only sometimes lucid in the weeks of recovery that followed, a stream of friends and colleagues came to see him in Acland. These included his stepsons, and an erstwhile housemate: Janie Moore's daughter Maureen, now a music teacher at Lewis's own former school, Malvern. In another example of life imitating art, Maureen Moore Blake had only a few months earlier learned that, via her long-estranged father's side of the family, she had inherited a baronetcy and a small estate in Scotland, thus becoming Dame Maureen Dunbar of Hempriggs. Though Lewis had only heard of this secondhand, he recognized Maureen immediately, and addressed her as "Lady Dunbar of Hempriggs." When she commented that she was amazed he even remembered this, Lewis replied: "On the contrary. How could *I* forget a fairy tale?"[84]

Though able to return to The Kilns with the presence of a full-time nurse, Lewis was, as he put it, "officially an extinct volcano," and in August of 1963 he resigned his chair and fellowship at Cambridge.[85] Douglas Gresham, now almost eighteen, helped clear out his rooms and bookshelves at Magdalene College, and Lewis settled into a reasonably comfortable, if fragile, existence at home in Oxford. "Tho' I am by no means unhappy," he wrote to his friend Arthur Greeves, "I can't help feeling it was rather a pity I did revive in July. I mean, having been glided so painlessly up to the Gate it seems hard to have it shut in one's face and know that the whole process must some day be gone through again . . . But God knows best."[86] Peacefully living with Warnie and their domestic helpers at The Kilns, C. S. Lewis finally glided up to the Gate on November 22, 1963.

84. Biographical Appendix to Hooper, ed., *Collected Letters*, vol. 1, 987. It was during this same crisis that Lewis—deserted by the hard-drinking Warnie, who had gone to Ireland on one of his recurring binges—met and engaged as his secretary the young American scholar Walter Hooper, who was later to become Lewis's literary executor. See Hooper, ed., *Collected Letters*, vol. 3, 1441–46, for details of this transition.

85. C. S. Lewis to Roger Lancelyn Green, August 11, 1963, Hooper, ed., *Collected Letters*, vol. 3, 1449.

86. C. S. Lewis to Arthur Greeves, September 11, 1963, ibid., 1456.

"Lewis's relationship to Joy brought him out of hiding," writes Joy David-man's biographer Lyle Dorsett. It is certainly the case that marriage made him more emotionally accessible to people, including his own stepsons.[87] But as we have seen in this chapter, he was by no means completely hidden be-forehand, nor was he (as he put it in mid-life) "tone-deaf" when it came to children. Lewis was both thoughtful and whimsical in his relationships with his four godchildren. Though he was an appropriately authoritative steppar-ent, remembrance of his own childhood wounds helped him to treat Douglas and David Gresham with wisdom and sensitivity. And in his relationships with girls especially—as with his relationships to adult women—Lewis was again a better man than his theories.

87. Dorsett, *A Love Observed*, 146.

10

"Suppressed by Jack"

The Two Sides of C. S. Lewis

In 1954, about a decade before his death, C. S. Lewis was appointed to the newly minted chair of Medieval and Renaissance English Literature at Cambridge University. In his inaugural lecture he expressed approval of the fact that his mandate was medieval *and* Renaissance literature, since he did not agree with historians who saw a sharp break between these two so-called eras.[1] Too many, he said, had identified "medieval" with the death of learning that supposedly began with the fall of the Roman Empire, and "Renaissance" with the recovery of classical languages, art forms, and a spirit of unfettered inquiry. But, Lewis reminded his audience, even in the so-called Dark Ages, Latin continued as the language of law and scholarship. Aristotle's texts were recovered, studied, and applied, and new styles were developed in art, architecture, and poetry. "Change is never complete, and change never ceases," Lewis remarked. "And nothing is quite new; it was always somehow anticipated and prepared for."[2]

Nevertheless, he continued, scholars—including literary historians—still need to divide history in terms of somewhat distinct eras or periods, and "the

1. C. S. Lewis, "*De Descriptione Temporum*" ("On Defining the Eras"), in *They Asked for a Paper* (London: Geoffrey Bles, 1962), 9–25.
2. Ibid., 11.

241

best one can hope is to choose those that falsify the least."[3] And for Lewis, the most significant divide in Western history was not between the Classical epoch and the Dark Ages, nor between medieval and Renaissance eras. Nor was it between all of these and the seventeenth century beginnings of modern science, marked by acceptance of the Copernican revolution, Decartes's sharp distinction between mechanical bodies and immaterial minds, and (in England) the founding of the Royal Society of gentleman scientists. For even in the seventeenth century, Lewis pointed out, the "scientific" frame of mind had not yet become widespread:

> Science was not the business of [ordinary] man because man had not yet become the business of science. It dealt chiefly with the inanimate, and it threw off a few technological byproducts. [But] when Watt makes his [steam] engine, when Darwin starts monkeying with the ancestry of Man, and Freud with his soul, and the economists with all that is his, then the lion will have got out of his cage. Its liberated presence in our midst will become one of the most important factors in everyone's daily life. But not yet, not in the seventeenth century.[4]

The really important change, said Lewis, was the one "which divides the present from, say, the age of Jane Austen and [Sir Walter] Scott"—authors who began writing around the beginning of the nineteenth century.[5] Between Jane Austen and us, he continued, came the birth of machines, which altered humans' relationship to nature and, in addition, encouraged people to think that whatever was "newer" must automatically be "better." Further tectonic shifts took place in politics, art, and religion. Thus, government became increasingly preoccupied with rhetoric, political charisma, and so-called progress, rather that simply keeping the peace. Artistic realism in literature and painting gave way to deliberately cultivated ambiguity. And, Lewis said, though there were certainly religious skeptics in Jane Austen's day, "some kind and degree of religious practice were the norm; now, though I would gladly believe that both the kind and degree have improved, they are the exception."[6]

Lewis explained that he was simply describing—not judging—this historical shift. This was a wise qualifier to make, because as a Christian he knew full well that, given the human condition, *no* era can be romanticized as an Edenic, pre-fall time. "Newer" is indeed not automatically "better"—but then, neither is "older." Yet despite his qualifier, Lewis was clearly playing the curmudgeon in his Cambridge lecture. For example, it is difficult to believe that he is merely "describing" the rise of the social sciences when his sole reference to them is a dismissive phrase about Freud's "monkeying . . . with [man's] soul and

3. Ibid.
4. Ibid., 16–17.
5. Ibid., 17.
6. Ibid., 20.

the economists with all that is his." And it is hard not to suspect that he was playing to the male student audience at Cambridge when he scoffed at the suggestion that Britain was "lapsing" back into Paganism. "The post-Christian is cut off from the Christian past and therefore doubly from the Pagan past," he asserted. "A post-Christian man is not a Pagan; you might as well think that a married woman recovers her virginity by divorce."[7] Since Lewis was on record as having a high view of premarital chastity and marital permanence for *both* sexes, why single out women in such a gratuitous and sexualized way? Such remarks may account for the fact that Joy Davidman—who was there to hear it—later wrote that the lecture was a "great success . . . but I think, for once, he was sacrificing accuracy in the interests of a good show."[8]

Lewis described himself to the assembled students as a premachine person, one who belonged "far more to the Old Western Order than to yours." Indeed, he said, he was like a Neanderthal or a dinosaur that had suddenly and inexplicably appeared behind a podium at Cambridge:

> You don't want to be lectured on Neanderthal man by a Neanderthaler, still less on dinosaurs by a Dinosaur. And yet . . . if a live dinosaur dragged its slow length into the laboratory, would we not all look back as we fled? . . . I would give a great deal to hear an ancient Athenian, even a stupid one, talking about Greek tragedy. He would know in his bones so much that we seek in vain.[9]

He explained that he stood before his audience "somewhat as that Athenian might stand. I read as a native texts that you must read as foreigners. It is my settled conviction that in order to read Old Western Literature aright, you must suspend most of the responses and unlearn most of the habits you have acquired in reading modern literature." And, he concluded, "Speaking not only for myself, but for all other Old Western men whom you may meet, I would say . . . use your specimens while you can. There are not going to be many more dinosaurs."[10]

Defiant Dinosaur or Closet Caterpillar?

In retrospect, it is hard to know how much Lewis was genuinely concerned about the demise of Old Western values, and to what extent (as Joy Davidman suspected) he was "putting on a good show." On the one hand, those who take the Bible seriously would agree that to grasp an ancient text in all

7. Ibid.

8. Joy Davidman to William L. Gresham, November 30, 1954, as quoted in Lyle W. Dorsett, *A Love Observed: Joy Davidman's Life and Marriage to C. S. Lewis* (Wheaton: Harold Shaw, 1998), 115.

9. Lewis, "*De Descriptione Temporum*," 24.

10. Ibid., 25.

its complexity, readers must set aside many of their modern reading habits and try to understand the historical context, literary forms, and even some of the original languages used by its writers. (My husband the Old Testament scholar tells his students that reading the Hebrew Scriptures in translation is like looking at a black and white television program: you can get the basic message, but you miss the rich details that are present in the original language.) And while the Edwardian-born Lewis was surely exaggerating when he claimed to "read as a native texts that you must read as foreigners," he certainly did have a superb knowledge of the medieval and Renaissance world, one that had previously drawn students to his lectures at Oxford and was later to captivate readers of *The Discarded Image*.

In the epilogue to that posthumously-published volume he admitted that the medieval worldview—now a "discarded image" with its hierarchical chain of being, its fascination with astrology, and its attribution of varying degrees of "soul" to all living things—"delights me as I believe it delighted our ancestors. Few constructions of the imagination seem to me to have combined splendour, sobriety and coherence in the same degree."[11] That its astronomical and biological assumptions were "not true" according to the canons of modern science mattered little to Lewis.[12] By the end of his life he was enough of a post-positivist to affirm that *all* scientific theories, including contemporary ones, are at best approximations to reality. Each is "like a stencil. It determines how much of [the] total truth will appear and what pattern it will suggest."[13] And, like the medieval "discarded image," each is based on (often unacknowledged) metaphysical commitments, not just on empirical data. Any new model, Lewis wrote, "will not be set up without evidence, but the evidence will turn up when the inner need for it becomes sufficiently great . . . Nature gives most of her evidence in answer to the questions we ask her."[14]

So Lewis for most of his life felt quite free to explore the questions posed by the medieval model and to commend many of its answers in his novels, his literary studies, and even in his Christian apologetics. If scientists aren't required to have total certainty before they explore the implications of a model, why should literature scholars? Thus Lewis wrote as if class and gender were divinely fixed anthropological essences and social categories. He scorned capitalism and modern machine technology—even while using trains, motorcycles, cars, and (late in life) planes—and dreamed of a return to independent, local guilds of artists and craftsmen. He wrote that life on earth was a school for the development of personal virtue, to prepare us for our "true" home in heaven, so that concerns about social justice, or even personal success, were

---

11. C. S. Lewis, *The Discarded Image: An Introduction to Medieval and Renaissance Literature* (Cambridge: Cambridge University Press, 1964), 216.

12. Ibid., 216.

13. Ibid., 223.

14. Ibid., 222–23.

of secondary importance. While he modeled a robust Christian intellectualism and effectively challenged the assumptions of metaphysical naturalism, he spoke about earth and heaven (as N. T. Wright put it) "in ways that go far too far towards Plato."[15]

On the other hand, as we saw in earlier chapters, Lewis was always less conservative in his private than in his public life about issues concerning both gender and class. He voted early in his career to impose a quota on women students at Oxford, yet continued to mentor pupils of both sexes in an even-handed and conscientious way. He wrote about women's inferior rational and moral capacities in the wartime broadcast talks that would become *Mere Christianity*, even as he was relying on the women of Somerville College to form the backbone of the Socratic Club. He asserted in 1946 that the quality of intellectual discussion declined when women were included,[16] but ten years later claimed credit for promoting occasions at Oxford where men and women could meet as intellectual equals.[17] During World War II, when he wrote his space trilogy, he treated belief in gender archetypes almost as a confessional issue, even while writing admiringly in letters about young women billeted at The Kilns who defied feminine stereotypes.

Lewis was equally ambiguous with regard to class. In the mid-1940s he publicly proclaimed his belief that God did not create an egalitarian world, and that "if we had not fallen . . . patriarchal monarchy would be the sole lawful form of government."[18] At the same time, he told Britons to "rejoice that we have contrived to reach much legal democracy," and added that "we still need more of the economic [kind]."[19] In 1944, he publicly scoffed at the suggestion that education should be equalized for all classes, stating that doing so would simply lower academic standards for everyone.[20] Yet as early as 1928, he had confided in a letter to his father that his best pupils at Magdalen came not from the most elite boarding schools, but from second-tier ones, or were "wafted up on county scholarships from [state] secondary schools."[21]

In the 1940s Lewis publicly railed against "the intrusion of bureaucracy" into British life. He wrote that as "the State grows more like a hive or an ant-

15. N. T. Wright, "Simply Lewis: Reflections on a Master Apologist After 60 Years," in *Touchstone: A Journal of Mere Christianity*, vol. 20, no. 2 (Mach 2007): 28–33.

16. C. S. Lewis, "Modern Man and His Categories of Thought," in *Present Concerns*, ed. Walter Hooper (San Diego: Harvest, 1986).

17. C. S. Lewis, "Interim Report," in ibid.

18. C. S. Lewis, "Membership," reprinted in *The Weight of Glory and Other Addresses* (Grand Rapids: Eerdmans, 1965), 36.

19. C. S. Lewis, "Equality," reprinted in *Present Concerns*, 17–20.

20. See his 1944 essay, "Democratic Education," reprinted in *Present Concerns*, 32–36.

21. C. S. Lewis to his father, Albert Lewis, November 3, 1928, Walter Hooper, ed., *The Collected Letters of C. S. Lewis*, vol. 1, *1905–1931* (San Francisco: HarperSanFrancisco, 2004), 779.

hill," it reduces people to "homogenous units,"[22] and as late as 1958 he warned Britons that they were becoming "willing slaves of the welfare state."[23] Yet in 1963 (when his own health was failing) he wrote two letters to an American friend who was struggling to pay her medical bills, in which he admitted that Britain's National Health Service, while not perfect, was "better than leaving people to sink or swim on their own resources."[24] Hearing of his American friend's troubles, he wrote, "makes me unsay everything I ever said against our English welfare state."[25] In 1931 he publicly stated that scholarly elites should not have to worry about "the preservation and propagation of life," but be supported in their academic pursuits by the less intellectually gifted.[26] Yet only a year later, he admitted in a letter to a friend that his defense of the Aristotelian ideal of scholarly leisure had been a cover for his own "besetting sin [of] laziness," and that the Greeks' contempt for labor and their tolerance of slavery were simply wrong.[27]

Which was the real C. S. Lewis? Was it the public, self-proclaimed "dinosaur" of his Cambridge inaugural lecture—a man suspicious of the modern age, and by implication any leveling of class and gender relations that came with it? Or was it the more private Lewis—the one who wrote in letters, and in his (initially secret) memoir A Grief Observed as if challenging gender and class stereotypes was not always a capitulation to secular modernity, but might sometimes lead to a better approximation of God's intentions than what had gone before? My conclusion is that C. S. Lewis was some of both—though increasingly the latter as he aged. While he was clearly enchanted by the "discarded image" of the medieval world, and wanted to immerse his readers in its coherent beauty, he also knew as a Christian that good and evil are complexly intertwined in every era and in every human institution. Consequently, none is beyond criticism: though "newer" is not automatically "better," neither is "older."

In his less Platonic moments, Lewis also knew that this world does matter to God as more than just a training ground in personal virtue before we go "further up and further in" to heaven.[28] Christians are called to be light and salt in a broken world: they are to erect signposts pointing to "a new

22. Lewis, "Equality," 20; "Priestesses in the Church?" reprinted in Walter Hooper, ed., God in the Dock: Essays On Theology and Ethics (Grand Rapids: Eerdmans, 1970), 238.

23. C. S. Lewis, "Is Progress Possible? Willing Slaves of the Welfare State," in God in the Dock, 311–16.

24. C. S. Lewis to Mary Willis Shelburne, July 7, 1959, Walter Hooper, ed., The Collected Letters of C. S. Lewis, vol. 3, 1950–1963 (San Francisco: HarperSanFrancisco, 2007), 1064.

25. C. S. Lewis to Mary Willis Shelburne, June 10, 1963, ibid., 1429.

26. C. S. Lewis, "Our English Syllabus," in Rehabilitations and Other Essays (London: Oxford University Press, 1939), 81–82.

27. C. S. Lewis to Dom Bede Griffiths, July 16, 1940, Walter Hooper, ed., The Collected Letters of C. S. Lewis, vol. 2, 1931–1949 (San Francisco: HarperSanFrancisco, 2004), 639.

28. C. S. Lewis, The Last Battle (London: The Bodley Head, 1956), 203.

heavens and a new earth, in which righteousness dwells."[29] Or, to change the metaphor, Christians are to be less like dinosaurs than like caterpillars. Living in an intermediate state between their larval past and their butterfly future, they carry the past with them (both appreciatively and critically) as they work toward a better life ahead. Moreover, they strive to bring God's kingdom righteousness to earth—not just fit themselves better for heaven— while knowing that complete healing will come only when "the author walks onto the stage and the play is over"[30]—or, more accurately, when a new and better play begins. Lewis may have been temperamentally more of a dinosaur, but he was a closet caterpillar as well: more closeted in his earlier years, but progressively less so in later life.

Penetrating the Smoke Screen

As we have seen, Lewis's classical, philosophical, and literary interests—in addition to his Edwardian upbringing—inclined him, for much of his life, toward a hierarchical and essentialist view of class and gender. He admitted in 1943 that "mankind is so fallen that no man can be trusted with unchecked powers," and thus that "legal and economic equality are absolutely necessary remedies for the fall, and [as] protections against cruelty."[31] Yet he denied that "the old authority in kings, priests, husbands or fathers, and the old obedience in subjects, laymen, wives, and sons was in itself degrading or an evil thing." Instead, he thought the "old authority" was "intrinsically as good and beautiful as the nakedness of Adam and Eve."[32] So he looked for some kind of compromise between his reflexive social conservatism and his Christian acknowledgment of human depravity. He urged his readers to preserve on the voluntary level (especially in church and home) the hierarchy and ceremony that they had steadily abandoned in public life, because "the man [sic] who cannot conceive a joyful and loyal obedience on the one hand, nor an unembarrassed and noble acceptance of that obedience on the other . . . is a prosaic barbarian."[33] In such passages, Lewis certainly seems to be presenting himself as a defiant dinosaur: a member of a species possibly bound for extinction, but determined to defend the glory of the past as much as possible within the confines of his Christian understanding.

Yet, a decade later, he did *not* use his Cambridge inaugural to romanticize gender or class hierarchy, as he had done in so many of his previous writings. He certainly wanted the listening students not to become thoughtless presen-

---

29. 2 Pet. 3:13 (NASB).
30. C. S. Lewis, *Mere Christianity* (London: Collins, 1952), 63.
31. Lewis, "Equality," 17, 18.
32. Ibid., 18.
33. Ibid.

tists, who assume that history has little to teach them. And he wanted them to develop the intellectual and imaginative skills needed to enter as fully as possible into the mind-set of an earlier era. But he did not defend that era's gender and class relations as immutable or ideal—let alone biblical—neither in his Cambridge inaugural, nor in his final books, including *A Grief Observed*, *Letters to Malcolm*, and *The Discarded Image*. In the latter two volumes, as in his Cambridge inaugural, he was simply silent about such matters, and in *A Grief Observed*, as we saw in an earlier chapter, he actually repudiated his previously published views on gender hierarchy and gender archetypes.

How are we to account for this dichotomy? Why, for so much of his life, did the public C. S. Lewis treat gender archetypes, as well as gender and class hierarchy, almost as litmus tests for Christian orthodoxy, while the private Lewis just as often wrote and behaved as if they were nothing of the kind? And why did it take so long for the private Lewis to show a more public face? There are several possibilities, each of which may contribute something to the answer.

In the first place, Lewis was a complex and even secretive person, and was recognized as such by both himself and his friends.[34] We have seen how he kept his civil marriage to Joy Davidman concealed from all but a few people for almost a year, and how he understated his brother's descent into alcoholism for even longer. In midlife, at his brother's suggestion, he reassembled his previous letters with a view to preserving them in "The Lewis Papers"—except for those that referred to his early sexual attitudes and experiences. Those that he had written to Arthur Greeves he asked the latter to edit or destroy, and all the letters he had sent to Janie Moore were burned by the latter in the mid-1940s, after she had suffered a small stroke and feared she might be close to death.[35] When he wrote *Surprised by Joy* (subtitled *The Shape of My Early Life*) he included not even a passing mention of Janie Moore, the woman with whom he had shared a household for more than two decades, and with whom he had spent countless hours as an Oxford undergraduate. According to one of his fellow Inklings (R. E. "Humphrey" Havard) so much was omitted or glossed over in Lewis's autobiography that an additional volume should be written, and titled *Suppressed by Jack*.[36]

More recently Michael Ward, who for several years was curator at The Kilns, has persuasively argued that, without ever telling anyone, Lewis used the seven planets of medieval cosmology as an imaginative grid for the seven *Narnia* chronicles. In accounting for such apparent secrecy, Ward notes that Lewis

34. See Michael Ward, *Planet Narnia: The Seven Heavens in the Imagination of C. S. Lewis* (New York: Oxford University Press, 2008), especially chap. 1.

35. This event was later recalled by Jill Flewett, who was living at The Kilns at the time. See Hooper, ed., *Collected Letters*, vol. 2, 1034.

36. George Sayer, *Jack: C. S. Lewis and His Times* (San Francisco: Harper and Row, 1988), 198.

valued privacy and saw no need to decompartmentalize the various segments of his life. Oxford friends, for instance, may never have heard mention of his Belfast friends. His [monetary] benefactions were hidden from nearly all his intimates and the gifts themselves were almost always made anonymously. He kept his own identity camouflaged in certain publications, using four different [pen names] in the course of his career . . . He lent *Dymer* [his early poetic work] to a friend without revealing that he himself was the author and he kept up the façade as "N. W. Clerk" in [some of his] private correspondence.[37]

Another significant aspect of Lewis's secrecy is that he almost never brought public attention to any revisions in his own thinking, particularly about social issues such as class and gender. Even his repudiation of gender archetypes in *A Grief Observed* was originally done under a pen name, and (as he privately admitted) with "small stylistic disguisements all the way along."[38] As we have seen in previous chapters, Lewis preferred to test any changes of opinion in private correspondence with friends and colleagues. When he had solidified a change in his own mind, rather than waving a public flag about it, he simply dropped from future published writings any reference to the opinion he once held—whether it had been about modern poets, the welfare state, or right relations between classes and sexes. The significance of this for his fellow Christians should be clear. If, as Lewis himself consistently preached, it is inappropriate to use Scripture as a trove of timeless, disconnected proof-texts (there is an old evangelical saying to the effect that "a text without a context becomes a pretext") it is even less appropriate to treat C. S. Lewis's own writings in this way. Taking his private and public writings together, Lewis turns out to be very much a moving target.

"I Don't Believe It! It's Pastiche!"

A second possibility is that the younger Lewis was at least partly engaging in pastiche when he defended gender archetypes and gender hierarchy. Pastiche is a form of writing that intentionally mimics the style (and often the content) of other writers, sometimes as a flattering tribute, but just as often as satire or ridicule. When it borrows from a variety of sources, pastiche can result in a hodge-podge of style and content—which delights some readers, but leaves others frustrated by its inconsistencies. For example, J. R. R. Tolkien (who had spent eleven years creating an elaborate and coherent picture of his mythical

37. Ward, *Planet Narnia*, 7. See also Lewis's letter to Arthur Greeves of May 13, 1955, where he says about the (just-published) *Surprised by Joy*, "My doctor friend [i.e., Havard] says that the [book] leaves out too much and he is going to supplement it by a book called Suppressed By Jack!" (Hooper, ed., *Collected Letters*, vol. 3, 750).

38. C. S. Lewis to Laurence Whistler, March 4, 1962, Hooper, ed., *Collected Letters*, vol. 3, 1320.

Middle Earth in *Lord of the Rings*) was offended by the plot inconsistencies and loose ends that he perceived on hearing Lewis read aloud the first chapters of *The Lion, the Witch and the Wardrobe*. "It really won't do, you know," he was heard to say to another Inkling. "Moreover," adds Inklings biographer Humphrey Carpenter, "the story borrowed so indiscriminately from other mythologies and narratives (fauns, nymphs, Father Christmas, talking animals, anything that seemed useful for the plot) that for Tolkien the suspension of disbelief, the entering into a secondary world, was simply impossible . . . and he turned his back on it."[39]

Whether there is as much hodge-podge in the *Narnia* chronicles as Tolkien thought is a conclusion that Michael Ward has now challenged in his book, *Planet Narnia*. But it is certainly the case that Lewis enjoyed writing the kind of pastiche that mocks the sacred cows of others, sometimes while mimicking their style. For example, when he saw belief in progressive evolution growing among intellectuals (some of whom even envisaged evolutionism as a new religion, complete with its own liturgy and hymns) Lewis wrote an "Evolutionary Hymn," set to the tune "Savior, Like a Shepherd Lead Us":

> Lead us, Evolution, Lead us
> Up the future's endless stair.
> Chop us, change us, prod us, weed us,
> For stagnation is despair.
> Groping, guessing, yet progressing,
> Lead us nobody knows where.[40]

A few years earlier, Lewis had written an open letter to one of his intellectual sparring partners, the literary critic E. M. Tillyard who (unlike Lewis) argued that literature was primarily a window into the psyche of its author.[41] He ended the letter with such a nineteenth century flow of rhetorical flourishes and pseudo-flattery that Owen Barfield, who read the letter in Lewis's presence, recalled that he "slapped the book down and shouted: 'I don't believe it! It's *pastiche*!'"[42] Apparently Lewis had no rejoinder to Barfield's implied accusation—namely, that he was not completely serious about his intellectual battle with Tillyard, but was simply striking a pose—perhaps playing devil's advocate over against the literary establishment in order to enjoy the public

39. Humphrey Carpenter, *The Inklings* (New York: Ballentine, 1981), 223, 234.

40. Lewis first sent this six-verse poem to Dorothy Sayers (who also liked writing satirical doggerel) in a letter dated March 4, 1954 (Hooper, ed., *Collected Letters*, vol. 3, 434–37). It was later revised for publication, and can be found in C. S. Lewis, *Poems* (San Diego: Harcourt Harvest, 1992), 55–56.

41. Lewis had coauthored *The Personal Heresy: A Controversy* with Tillyard (Oxford: 1939), in which they took opposite sides on the question as to whether writing is indeed a window into its author's psyche.

42. As quoted in Carpenter, *The Inklings*, 61.

flap that ensued. "It left me the impression," Barfield recalled, "not of 'I say this,' but of 'This is the sort of thing a man might say.'"[43] The question must then be asked: if Lewis the literary critic was sometimes posturing for the sake of effect—like throwing a cat into a clutch of pigeons—was the younger Lewis sometimes adopting a similar pose when he promoted gender archetypes and gender hierarchy?

For example, in 1942 Lewis became an enthusiastic reader of the fantasy novels of Eric R. Eddison, with whom he then started a pastiche-style correspondence in mock Tudor English. In the first of his letters he explained that he was introduced to Eddison's novels by one of his women students: "som poore seely [i.e., pitiable] wench that seeketh a B.Litt. or a D.Phil., when God knows [she had] better bestowed her time maykinge sport for some goodman in his bed and bearing children for the stablishment of this reaulme or els to be at her beads in a religious house."[44] This sounds very much like an anticipation of the stance he took in the Space Trilogy, to the effect that women should get married and have children, or if single, lead a celibate life under male authority.

Lewis also challenged Eddison's portrayal in one of his novels of a goddess-like creator. According to philosophers such as Plato and Plotinus, Lewis reminded Eddison, God "must nedes be by us [conceived] as masculine."[45] When Eddison replied that he saw no harm in imagining a goddess "not Maker indeed, but . . . Conceiver and Bestower, of all Worldes,"[46] Lewis shot back that he was "now in a fair waye to esteeme you a verie stinkynge hereticke in philosophie . . . when it is a thing openlie manifeste to all but disards [i.e., blockheads] and verie goosecaps that feminitie is to itself an imperfection, being placed by Pythagoreans in the sinister column with matter and mortalitie." Men—unless blinded by love—are quite happy to do without the company of women, he added. But any woman "will escape from her sisters and seeke to the conversation of men, as seyking by instincte of Nature so to receive the perfection she lacketh . . . *Materia appetit formam ut virum femina*" ["Matter seeks out its form, as a woman seeks out a man."][47]

It's hard to believe that Lewis is being completely serious here. For one thing, if he really regarded the masculinity of God and the inferiority of women as confessional issues, why did he appeal only to the classical and neo-classical philosophers—with their sub-Christian contempt for "matter and mortalitie"—in his letters to Eddison? Recall too that this is the person

43. Ibid.

44. C. S. Lewis to E. R. Eddison, November 16, 1942, Hooper, ed., *Collected Letters*, vol. 2, 535.

45. C. S. Lewis to E. R. Eddison, December 19, 1942, ibid., 541.

46. E. R. Eddison to C. S. Lewis, January 10, 1943, as quoted in ibid., 542.

47. C. S. Lewis to E. R. Eddison, December 29, 1943, ibid., 543. The Latin quotation comes from Aristotle's *Physics*, chap. 1, section 9a.

who had tutored Mary Neylan a decade earlier and continued to mentor her career as a scholar-teacher for years afterward, even dedicating his volume on George MacDonald to her. Since Neylan had gone down from Oxford with a fourth class B.Litt. degree, surely (if Lewis *was* serious in his letters to Eddison) she would qualify as "a seely wench . . . [who had] better bestowed her time makynge sport for some goodman in his bed." Yet when such attitudes (albeit less strongly expressed) found their way into his published writings, people took them at face value. And Lewis may well have sat back and enjoyed the resulting flap, just as he may have enjoyed exaggerating his differences with E. M. Tillyard, or setting a puzzle for future readers by covertly pegging each of his *Narnia* chronicles to one of the seven planets of medieval cosmology.

However, if this *was* part of Lewis's rhetorical strategy, it was bound to backfire on him occasionally. Thus, in 1948, he expressed surprise that *Time* magazine, in its cover story about Lewis, had called him a misogynist. "Who said I disliked women?" he expostulated to one of his American correspondents. "I never liked or disliked any *generalization*."[48] But what on earth did he expect? That readers would recognize in his literary appropriation of "the discarded image" some of the same make-believe that he had served up to Eddison in his mock-Tudor letters? If so, it was a naïve assumption on his part—especially about Americans, who have always tended toward greater literalism than their English counterparts, when reading the Bible or anything else.

An Anxious Edwardian Bachelor

Lewis's ambiguity about women may be due in part to his secretiveness, and in part to his penchant for pastiche. But these probably do not tell the whole story. His historical location—between the close of the Victorian age and the birth of the welfare state—gave him plenty of reason to be skeptical about any vision of "progress," whether social, economic, or technological. As a young man, he was wounded in a badly conducted war that was supposed to end all wars, only to see another world war begin two decades later, bringing years of air raids, food shortages, and professional and personal dislocation. "What makes it worse," he wrote to his friend Arthur Greeves in 1939, "is the ghostly feeling that it has all happened before—that one fell asleep during the last war and had a delightful dream and has now waked up again."[49] And at the end of World War II, he wrote to another friend that "the early loss of my mother, great unhappiness at school, and the shadow of the last war and presently the

48. C. S. Lewis to Margaret Fuller, April 8, 1948, Hooper, ed., *Collected Letters*, vol. 2, 849 (emphasis original).

49. C. S. Lewis to Arthur Greeves, September 15, 1939, Hooper, ed., *Collected Letters*, vol. 2, 274.

experience of it [have] given me a very pessimistic view of existence."[50] The food rationing begun during World War II did not end until almost a decade after its end, its effects on the Lewis household only partly cushioned by the fact that they raised their own vegetables, rabbits, and chickens, and by the many post-war food packages sent to Lewis by his American fans.

Nor should we downplay the value of Lewis's intellectual skepticism about "progress" in politics and science. Fascism and communism were two of the ways in which tyranny had disguised itself as progress during Lewis's lifetime, and he feared the same thing happening in more subtle ways at home, particularly through the wedding of science to an increasingly bureaucratic state. Modern scientists are methodological determinists: whatever their personal convictions may be about the existence of rationality and free will, as professionals they approach the natural and social world as if everything in them is governed by strict, impersonal laws. Lewis recognized that when such deterministic models are indiscriminately applied to humans, they can weaken belief in rationality and morality. For if humans are really just larger rats, or slower computers, then they cannot be held morally responsible for their actions, nor can they be assumed to be rational in their political deliberations. As one Lewis scholar has summarized it,

> Under the old order, politics involved serious reflection about justice and the common good. But the more man thinks he is determined by non-rational causes, the less important serious reflection becomes. Under the new order, all that matters is achieving the end result, and the only question is not "What is just?" but "What works?" . . . As long as man was regarded as accountable for his actions, there were certain limits beyond which the state was not supposed to tread . . . [But] if people act because of environmental and biological necessities, the government no longer need deal with them as free moral agents. Under the new system, preemption replaces punishment as the preferred method of social control. Instead of punishing you for making the wrong choice, the state simply eliminates your choice.[51]

I have already stated my reasons for believing that Lewis was too Cartesian in his belief that social scientists are illicit trespassers into territory belonging rightly to philosophers, theologians, and humanities scholars. But that does not mean that his concern for the potential abuses of the social (as well as natural) sciences was unwarranted. He had already seen enough to doubt that these disciplines could lead people to a new golden age. To this day, social scientists (and the institutions that support them) must work to make sure that

50. C. S. Lewis to Dom Bede Griffiths, OSB, December 20, 1946, Hooper, ed., *Collected Letters*, vol. 2, 747.

51. John G. West Jr., "Finding the Permanent in the Political: C. S. Lewis as a Political Thinker," http://www.discovery.org/a/457.

their methodological determinism does not deteriorate into a metaphysical determinism that leads to complete moral and epistemological relativism, and hence to the conclusion—as Lewis warned—that only might makes right.

So there were plenty of historical reasons for Lewis to be skeptical about change and for his caution to generalize—at least in his more public writings—to skepticism about changes in class and gender relations. But I do not think we yet have the whole story, because his public conservatism about gender archetypes and gender hierarchy also had some internal inconsistencies. We should recall that Lewis came of age at a time when (especially male) homosexuals were even more stigmatized than women. Indeed, consensual homosexual acts were not decriminalized in England until four years after Lewis's death. Yet even in his otherwise unhappy school days, Lewis did not think that sex between young men (though he claimed not to have been tempted by it himself) was the worst thing about public school life. As we saw in an earlier chapter, he viewed such relationships—however flawed—as one of the few arenas in which the routinely vicious competition among schoolboys was temporarily softened.

In addition, from young adulthood on Lewis knew that one of his closest friends, Arthur Greeves, was homosexual, and thus would never play cosmic "Sky-Father" to any "Earth-Mother," as his description of Eros in *The Four Loves* idealized.[52] And while he did not condone active homosexuality, in none of his writings did Lewis show a degree of homophobia that came close to matching what A. N. Wilson has called his "spells of clubroom misogyny."[53] On the contrary, seven years before the British decriminalization of homosexuality, Lewis wrote to a colleague that "to make [homosexuality] criminal cures nothing and only creates a blackmailer's paradise. Anyway, what business is it of the State?" Only a small hint of resentment surfaces in his next comment: "One is fighting on two fronts: a) *For* the persecuted Homo[sexual], against snoopers and busybodies [and] b) For ordinary people *against* the freemansonry of the highbrow Homos who dominate so much of the world of [literary] criticism and won't be v[ery] nice to you unless you are in their set."[54]

Once again we need to ask: why the difference as regards women? It was only a decade before his own death—two years after Janie Moore had died, and just a few months after first meeting Joy Davidman in England—that Lewis wrote frankly (to an acquaintance whose husband had just died) about some events that also help explain his ambivalence toward women:

> I first met this "cold blast on the naked heath" at about 9, when my Mother died, and there has never been any sense of security or snugness since. That is,

52. C. S. Lewis, *The Four Loves* (London: Collins, 1963), 95.
53. A. N. Wilson, *C. S. Lewis: A Biography* (London: Norton, 1990), 292.
54. C. S. Lewis to Delmar Banner, May 27, 1960, Hooper, ed., *Collected Letters*, vol. 3, 1154 (emphasis original).

I've not quite succeeded in growing up on that point: there is still too much of "Mammy's little lost boy" about me. Your position is of course v[ery] different, because dependence on a husband is more legitimate than dependence (after a certain age) on one's Mother, and also because, at your age, tho' [a husband's death] will feel just as bad, it is not so likely to go down into the unconscious and cause a *trauma*.[55]

All his biographers agree that the handling of nine-year-old Jack Lewis's grief was badly bungled by his father, however unintentionally. He was shipped off to a poorly-run boarding school within weeks of his mother's death, partly because Albert Lewis was himself too devastated by grief to cope with his sons, and partly because he wanted them to be taught by men in order to be toughened up—preferably in England, where they would also cease to talk like bog-trotting Irish and learn to be gentlemen. Mercifully, Jack joined his brother two years later at a much better school. Its teachers were again all male, but he was also able to form an emotional bond with the school's kindly matron. Unfortunately, a few months later she was dismissed when the headmaster (a good scholar, but a poor judge of his pupils' emotional needs) decided that her relationship with young Jack Lewis was inappropriately close. Much later, his friend and fellow poet Ruth Pitter speculated that "losing his mother (cruel loss at age [nine] and horribly emphasized by the circumstances) must have seemed like a black betrayal. If [Jack] was mistrustful of women, it was not hatred, but a burnt child's dread of fire."[56]

A young boy loses his mother and has his relationship with a surrogate cut short. He is otherwise immersed in all-male settings (at school, at home, and later as an Oxford undergraduate) and so has almost no contact with female peers. When another mother-surrogate appears, he latches on to her as the most important part of his life next to his scholarship. He forms a household with her when he becomes an Oxford don—an eminently safe arrangement, but one so charged with ambivalence that after her death his brother writes: "And so ends the mysterious self imposed slavery in which J[ack] has lived for at least thirty years."[57] During those years, almost none of his ongoing relationships with females are peer relations. He rarely interacts with Oxford female colleagues outside of faculty meetings. He tutors women students, supervises the Oxford woman chaplain who runs the Socratic Club, and corresponds with intelligent but "safe" women—married (like Dorothy Sayers, or his former pupil Mary Neylan, or the wives of his friends), far away (like his American fans), or vowed to celibacy (like Sister Penelope).

55. C. S. Lewis to Phyllis Elinor Sandeman, December 31, 1953, ibid., 398.
56. As quoted in Don W. King, "The Anatomy of a Friendship: The Correspondence of Ruth Pitter and C. S. Lewis, 1946–1962," *Mythlore* 91 (Summer 2003): 13.
57. As quoted in Wilson, *C. S. Lewis*, 224.

Only in 1946, when he is close to fifty, does he begin a tentative, more than letter-writing friendship with Ruth Pitter, the gifted poet whom, by his own admission, he might have married had Joy Davidman not appeared on the scene. For reasons related to his own past, it was not just with regard to general feelings of security that C. S. Lewis had "not quite succeeded in growing up." Making the transition from a surrogate mother like Janie Moore to a potential marriage partner was a developmental task for which he was less prepared than many people. He was for much of his life, as Dorothy Sayers put it, "a rather frightened bachelor."[58] And when he did marry, he chose not Ruth Pitter (who was his own age) but a woman seven years younger than his former pupil Mary Neylan, and a full seventeen years younger than himself.

A Final Assessment

C. S. Lewis began his academic career as a strict rationalist who claimed that good literature was completely independent of its writer's personality. By the end of his life, he had become a critical realist who wrote that "no model is a catalogue of ultimate realities, and none is a mere fantasy. Each is a serious attempt to get in all the known phenomena . . . but also, no less surely, each reflects the prevalent psychology of an age."[59] On the personal level, the older Lewis was also ready to admit that the events surrounding his mother's death had impeded aspects of his own psychological development. And though he never expressly said it, those events may have made it difficult, until much later in life, for him to write about women in ways that were not highly romanticized at one extreme, or bordering on contempt at the other.

None of this would have mattered if Lewis had taken the path of least resistance and, like many of his male contemporaries, simply written as if women did not exist. But his immersion in the medieval "discarded image," combined with his concern for the practical side of Christian life, did not allow him to take this path. So for much of his life Lewis the essayist wrote about marriage and divorce, about women's roles in the church, and about classical forms of love as if he were looking in a rear-view mirror. Lewis the novelist wrote a space trilogy in which masculine and feminine archetypes are in a fixed, platonic hierarchy created and blessed by God. Moreover, his hostility toward the emerging social sciences prevented him from publicly acknowledging the degree to which gender and class relations are socially constructed and in many ways unjust. His private correspondence and his actual behavior toward women reveal a different and much less traditional Lewis. But not until the *Narnia* chronicles and after, as he published *Till We Have Faces*, *The Discarded Image*, and *A Grief Observed*, do the private and public Lewis begin to converge.

58. Reynolds, ed., *Letters of Dorothy L. Sayers*, vol. 3, 375.
59. Lewis, *Discarded Image*, 222.

Moreover, the disjunction between the public and private Lewis would have little significance if he had not, by so many Christians, been turned into a species of plaster saint whose every published pronouncement has been accorded almost canonical status.[60] Lewis himself did not have a docetic view of the Bible—that is, one that ignores the human side of its composition and treats its inspiration almost as a matter of divine dictation by God. So in spite of his early polemic against "the personal heresy," it is unlikely that he would have wanted others to treat his own writings in a similar, decontextualized way. His most responsible biographers have, of course, not done this. Yet as recently as 2001 his own stepson, Douglas Gresham, urged readers of Lewis's works to set aside their "subjective interests" in him as a human being and recognize "the power of the Holy Spirit of God behind Jack's work, governing it, channeling it, guiding him all the time."[61] This, frankly, is too great a burden to place on any Christian writer—let alone his readers, who are implicitly being told that they cannot dispute any of the writer's pronouncements without offending the Holy Spirit.

It is frequently said that C. S. Lewis is at his best when—as a rationalist—he presents philosophical concepts in a clear way that assists readers in their own spiritual formation, and when—as a romantic novelist—he creates enchanted worlds which, by the very quality of their enchantment, point readers to the One who is the source, sustainer, and redeemer of all things. I do not dispute either of these judgments, particularly with regard to the later Lewis. For by the time he wrote the *Narnia* chronicles and *Till We Have Faces*, Lewis seems to have realized that enchantment does not require strict gender archetypes as a way to draw readers toward God. But I would go a step further. Lewis should also be recognized for those rare moments in his writing when he tries to express what a world might look like in which the sacred is *not* artificially divided from the secular—a world in which Christian responsibility is dispersed horizontally in terms of appropriate talents, rather than vertically downward through a hierarchy based on class, gender, or religious status.

In an earlier chapter, I noted the one passage in *Mere Christianity* where Lewis moves beyond his Platonic habit of dichotomizing "spiritual" from "secular" activities and arranging them hierarchically. Here his view is remarkably horizontal:

> [When people say] the Church ought to give us the lead, they ought to mean that some Christians—those who have the right talents—should be economists and statesmen . . . and that their whole efforts in politics and economics should

---

60. At the turn of the millennium, there were approximately two hundred individual fan clubs, reading groups, and C. S. Lewis societies around the world.

61. As quoted in John Ryan Duncan, *The Magic Never Ends: The Life and Work of C. S. Lewis* (Nashville: Thomas Nelson, 2001), 3. Gresham makes a similar statement in a video version of *The Magic Never Ends* (Duncan and Crouse Entertainment Group, 2002).

be directed to putting [the Golden Rule] into action . . . [And] the application
of Christian principles to say, trade unionism or education must come from
Christian trade unionists and Christian schoolmasters, just as Christian literature comes from Christian novelists and dramatists and not from the bench of
Bishops getting together and trying to write plays in their spare time.[62]

In another chapter I noted that Lewis had a similar insight as early as
1940, when he wrote to his former pupil, Mary Shelley Neylan, about what
he perceived to be the limits of male headship:

I take it to be chiefly about man *as* man and woman *as* woman, and therefore
about husbands and wives, since it is only in marriage that they meet *as* epitomes
of their sex. Notice that in I Cor XI just after the bit about the man being the
Head, St. Paul goes on to add the baffling reservation (v. 11) that the sexes "in
the Lord" don't have any separate existence. I have no idea what this means,
but I take it must imply that the existence of a man or woman is not exhausted
by the fact of being male or female, but that they exist in many other modes.
I mean, you may be a citizen, a musician, a teacher etc. as well as a woman,
and you needn't transfer to all these personalities everything that is about you
[as a] wife.[63]

One might argue, as Dorothy L. Sayers did, that Lewis was mistaken to
essentialize gender hierarchy even in marriage. But what is more important to
notice is his recognition—later to be given passing mention in *Mere Christianity*—that the "modes" (or spheres, or activities) of life have been so arranged
by God that each has its own autonomy. Thus, Lewis recognized, it is the task
of Christian novelists (not their Bishops) to apply their Christian worldview in
the writing of novels. It is the responsibility of Christian teachers, musicians,
politicians, and economists to do likewise in their respective spheres. And as
Bishop Lesslie Newbigin affirmed half a century later, "For such a declericalized theology, the church will be servant, not mistress."[64]

As Lewis was coming to recognize, those spheres are defined by the nature
of their *activities*—writing, teaching, composing, etc.—not by the sex or
class of the people who partake of them. This does not mean that everyone
will be on a level playing field everywhere: as Lewis explained to Mary Neylan, one's authority in one sphere (e.g., as a teacher) does not automatically
generalize to all other spheres. (For example, as a parent, I have a defined
authority over my sixteen-year-old son in terms of his domestic behavior, his
education, etc. But if he happens to be the lifeguard at the local pool, *he* has

62. Lewis, *Mere Christianity*, 75.
63. C. S. Lewis to Mary Shelley Neylan, April 18, 1940, Hooper, ed., *Collected Letters*,
vol. 2, 395.
64. Lesslie Newbigin, *Foolishness to the Greeks: The Gospel and Western Culture* (Grand
Rapids: Eerdmans, 1986), 143.

a defined authority over *me* when I am in that setting!) What it *does* mean is that authority is much more horizontally dispersed than was envisaged in the era of Lewis's "discarded image." Granted, people can be hardworking and devout (or slothful and careless) Christians under either a vertical or a horizontal way of organizing society. But, as Lewis was beginning to realize, the great vertical "chain of being" represented by the discarded image is not chiseled in stone.

Thus, for people (of whom I am one) who have profited in their Christian formation from the arguments of Lewis the rationalist, or from the enchantments of Lewis the romantic novelist, a further challenge awaits. We need to incorporate into our worldview, and our activities, the less-frequently cited insights of the C. S. Lewis who gradually set aside his views on class and gender that could starkly oppose male to female, and finally stated "a preference for *people*."[65]

65. C. S. Lewis to Dorothy L. Sayers, August 5, 1955, Hooper, ed., *Collected Letters*, vol. 3, 639 (emphasis original).

Index